CICERO'S PHILOSOPHY OF HISTORY

Cicero's Philosophy of History

MATTHEW FOX

OXFORD
UNIVERSITY PRESS

This book has been printed digitally and produced in a standard specification in order to ensure its continuing availability

OXFORD
UNIVERSITY PRESS

Great Clarendon Street, Oxford OX2 6DP
Oxford University Press is a department of the University of Oxford.
It furthers the University's objective of excellence in research, scholarship,
and education by publishing worldwide in

Oxford New York

Auckland Cape Town Dar es Salaam Hong Kong Karachi
Kuala Lumpur Madrid Melbourne Mexico City Nairobi
New Delhi Shanghai Taipei Toronto
With offices in
Argentina Austria Brazil Chile Czech Republic France Greece
Guatemala Hungary Italy Japan South Korea Poland Portugal
Singapore Switzerland Thailand Turkey Ukraine Vietnam

Oxford is a registered trade mark of Oxford University Press
in the UK and in certain other countries

Published in the United States
by Oxford University Press Inc., New York

ISBN 978-0-19-921192-0

For Miriam, Isaac, and Simeon

Preface

The first seed for this book was an undergraduate encounter with Cicero's *Orator*. I was convinced that Cicero's presentation of the grand style was so manifestly excessive in its enthusiasm that readers did not have to look far to perceive an ironic quality which would undermine any aspirations Cicero might have had to be identified as the ideal orator. Cicero struck me then (in the mid-1980s, when I still expected that the more radical aspects of poststructuralism might have a lasting impact on the way classical authors were read) as intent on providing us with the material for his own deconstruction (paradox intended). Twenty years later I found myself castigated for suggesting that an ironic undercutting of the idealized Rome in *De re publica* was the result not of a generalized deconstructive impulse (to which I had failed to appeal), but could be connected to Cicero's original intentions.[1] The problem of authorial intention, therefore, has dogged my work on Cicero's prose treatises since I first encountered them, even though I have never myself been convinced that any theory or body of evidence could show me how to disentangle conclusively Cicero's intentions from my own responses to his writings. We all make our own Ciceros, but while, say, those working on Ovid are used to this idea, those working on Cicero are less so, and there are, after all, all those letters and speeches which provide so much more 'historical' material to corroborate the reading of Cicero. I am interested in Cicero's intentions, as I am also interested in the intellectual context in which he articulated his ideas, and also in the possibility that, whatever his, or any other writer's or speaker's intentions, that person does not have the ability to control the range of interpretations to which their expressions are subject.[2] However, my argument will go beyond this rather weak position: I shall present as strong a case as I can for the idea that, because

---

[1] Oliensis (2002).

[2] Among the enormous literature on this topic I have found Burke (1995), pp. xv–xxiv, and Attridge (2004), 95–111, concise and illuminating.

produced in a tradition of philosophical scepticism, Cicero's dialogues actually foster a manner of thinking that avoids presenting concrete resolutions to philosophical questions, and thus represent a particularly open-ended kind of writing. Cicero's philosophy, in effect, invites readers to draw their own conclusions, and, unlike in his speeches, seems not to be particularly concerned what those conclusions are. This philosophy does not depend upon a dogmatic form of authorial control, not even concerning the image of the author which readers forge for themselves.

In the readings that follow, of a small selection of Cicero's theoretical works, I will be suggesting that ambiguity and multiple interpretation are useful tools for achieving a better understanding of the details of Cicero's arguments. Plurality in reading may be the result of Cicero's own ambitions for his philosophy, or it may be the more general result of the fact that Cicero's texts, like all others, cannot determine the interpretations placed upon them.

Readers will, I think, find that I have not been complacent: I argue carefully for the potential for open-ended interpretations both in terms of the philosophical traditions in which Cicero was schooled and in terms of the misleading emphases in the scholarship which have prevented those traditions from being properly applied to a close reading of his works. It is important to try to understand the processes of intellectual conditioning which make Cicero what he is today, and which, in my case, have led to an interest in irony, dialogism, the dynamics of reception, and a non-authoritarian potential in Cicero's works that I seek to locate not just within myself but also in the context in which Cicero worked and in the processes whereby Cicero's thought have been transmitted.

If I thereby seem to suggest that I have found a way of approaching Cicero that is less historically arbitrary than the concepts, say, of performance or self-fashioning, I should not be taken to suggest that I have discovered a better route to Cicero's original intentions, about which I remain, until his reincarnation, entirely undecided, notwithstanding traces of the convenient rhetoric of intentionality which may sporadically appear in my writing. I also think it is worth speculating, from time to time, on what impression Cicero's works may have had upon their earliest readers.

I ought to clarify my view of the purpose of translations of Latin passages in a book such as this: it is emphatically not to provide a readable, naturalized English version of the Latin text. In a published translation, of course, naturalness and readability are essential, even if there is a loss of the precise connotations of the Latin, or even if this results in the translator having to adopt a style that he or she feels conveys the essence of the original. My translations may sometimes read rather awkwardly: I am trying to give the reader with no or little Latin as literal a translation as possible, so that the manner of Cicero's argument and presentation can be grasped, even if that grasp does not make Cicero look like someone who thought and wrote in English.

It is clear—and the wonderful translations of Cicero's letters by Shackleton Bailey are the best example—that decisions about what kind of style Cicero would have written in, had he written in English, have had an enormous role in perpetuating the image of him as a man unflappably pleased with his own achievements and, more importantly, as a conservative thinker. The dominance of a particular tradition of North American scholarship in the Loeb Classical Library, that edition's virtual monopoly on the translation of most of the texts examined here, and the peculiar history of the term *Republican* on that continent, have together, I suspect, had a profound effect upon scholarly interpretation of Cicero and his place in the American cultural and academic scene.

These are matters well beyond the scope of this book, although I hope to examine the translation of Cicero in a future study. In this context, it seems preferable to present Cicero where necessary in awkward, non-naturalized English, not to attempt to make the process of translation invisible, or to strive for a modern Ciceronianism in English style, since that Ciceronianism itself is problematic, to say the least. On a similar note, I have preferred, except in footnotes and references within individual chapters on particular works where lack of abbreviation would be obtrusive, not to abbreviate the titles of Cicero's works, or to make all titles follow a consistent system of nomenclature. My aim here has been clarity and ease of reading, so that readers dipping into this book will not need to adjust themselves to a convention, or have their reading disrupted by too much *Rep.*, *Fin.*, *Off.*, or *Nat.* In Chapter 10 I have given some samples of

John Toland's Latin, but have in other cases just presented a translation, on the assumption that only to a degree is his idiosyncratic Latin style going to be of interest.

Readers of a more rigorous philosophical bent may feel at times that I am skirting over serious philosophical problems; the gravest of likely criticisms will be that I have not engaged with any profundity with the question of the exact form of Academic philosophy that Cicero espoused. In this area, the scholarship is heavily dominated by the reading of Cicero as a source for the work of his Hellenistic predecessors. This has led to a strange approach to Cicero, in which the dynamics of his own texts are there, out of focus in the background, while sharper focus and proximity are reserved for the tensions between the different philosophical doctrines that he draws upon. I have read a fair amount of this literature, and refer readers to it in footnotes. However, I have made a deliberate decision to start by reading Cicero's texts themselves, to explore their forms of presentation, and not to approach them with the assumption that a patchwork of received doctrines will determine the quality of that presentation.

In other words, I have tried to find a way of combining an interest in Cicero's philosophical context with an approach which responds to his rhetoric. I have also, it will be evident, avoided those works of Cicero's where the portrayal of particular philosophical doctrines was of great prominence, as these are, by and large, ones in which historical representation plays a negligible role. That said, I am sure that more historical readings of those works are possible. I regard it as now established that Cicero's Academic interest was a constant feature of his career as a theorist, from *De inventione* down to *Topica*, and feel that it is worth attempting an exploration of a selection of his works on this basis. Scholars have been disputing for many years Cicero's exact relationship to the different philosophical schools, and their labours have not made his works any more accessible. I hope that the readings presented below will demonstrate that a more literary approach to Cicero can reveal a lot about the central issues of his philosophy, and that this can form an easier bridge to the ideological dilemmas of the late Republic than questions about the distinction between the third and fourth Academy, or the preservation of Peripatetic dogma. Of course, I cannot prove that my approach is closer to the one which inspired Cicero to write his philosophy; nor am I in any doubt as to how fruitful Cicero's works have been for historians of Greek philosophy.

I acknowledge the assistance of the Art and Humanities Research Council, which granted me a semester's research leave in 2003–4, and would like to express my thanks to the panel for the Research Leave Scheme for their faith in a project that turned out rather differently from the one originally planned. Thanks too to the School of Historical Studies at the University of Birmingham for the study leave to which that grant was attached, and also for awarding me £1,500 for teaching-relief in 2005–6 which facilitated the completion of the book.

It is a pleasure to thank those who accommodated and looked after me while I visited various libraries: Hero Chalmers and Steve Waters, Frederik Delattre, Ben Fox and Sonia Lambert, Helena Newsom and Brian Todd, Daniel and Anne Strauss, Helen Schlesinger and Richard Addis. I am fortunate in my closest colleagues at Birmingham: Diana Spencer, Elena Theodorakopoulos, and especially Niall Livingstone, with whom I have worked more closely on areas related to this book. All three have expressed unfailing interest in and support for my work, and have, in conversations too many to recall, given selflessly of their insight and experience.

In its wisdom, the University of Birmingham has decided to cease offering degree programmes that presuppose knowledge of Latin at entry. In 2005–6 I was fortunate to teach the last two cohorts of traditional Classicists in a special option on Cicero's philosophy in Latin, and my understanding of many of the passages of Cicero referred to in this book benefited from their scrutiny. Dominic Berry was kind enough to answer an unexpected enquiry about prose rhythm; Diana Robin responded promptly to lessen my ignorance of Filelfo. The audience to a paper at the 2004 Cicero Awayday in St Andrews was both encouraging and usefully critical. John Henderson and Peter Wiseman were very generous in reading a hefty quantity of entirely unsolicited draft material and giving encouragement and many useful criticisms. The anonymous readers at the Press were helpful and stimulating, and have saved me from numerous errors; thanks too to Hilary O'Shea and Jenny Wagstaffe at the Press. I am aware that imperfections remain; they are, of course, due to limits on my own reserves of time, perspective, knowledge, and diligence. I hope, however, that such failings as readers may encounter do not detract from the value of a different perspective on a neglected dimension of Cicero's writing.

While working on this book, I have been engaged in an ongoing dialogue with a procession of deceased teachers, mentors, and friends: Graham Tingay, Tom Stinton, Elizabeth Rawson, Dominic Montserrat, Michael Comber, Ian Lowery. My internal images of them, and recollection of their voices, have enabled me to imagine (in a way that is doubtless only a distant approximation) some aspects of Cicero's own dialogues with the dead; I continue to learn from my own memory of both the wisdom and eccentricity of these remarkable people who helped me enormously, both after and before their deaths, in the pursuit of better understanding and more sophisticated reading. But I dedicate this book to my children.

Contents

1

Introduction

The title of this book, *Cicero's Philosophy of History*, was chosen because it is both suggestive and slightly provocative: it suggests a topic which at first sight cannot exist: of course, there was no such thing as 'philosophy of history' in the ancient world, and Cicero did not write it. But I hope the suggestion that, in some form, Cicero represents an engagement with history that is profoundly philosophical will attract a variety of readers to explore in Cicero's writing a constellation of ideas that has not so far been tackled directly in existing scholarship. The title is a provocation because it challenges orthodox notions of how topics for scholarly studies are chosen: I am not engaged in recovering a lost body of Cicero's philosophy (that which deals with history); still less is it possible to give a comprehensive account of this category of Cicero's thought, to establish what Cicero's philosophy of history 'really was'; as if his philosophical works, ostensibly discussions of the most significant topics of the Greek philosophical schools, concealed a secret doctrine, a kind of philosophy not actually named either by Cicero or by the Greek writers on whom he drew: his philosophy of history. Nor am I going to claim, in a less implausible manner, that within Cicero's works on different aspects of theology and ethics, a coherent set of theories can be found, concerning historical causation, the structure of historical time, or teleology. Such an investigation might be possible, but it would involve an approach to Cicero's writings which is different from the one I adopt, and that approach would require considerable distortion of the manner in which Cicero presents his philosophy; a distortion which I am aiming to avoid by looking for a way of reading Cicero's dialogues that respects, as much as that is possible, the spirit in which they were composed.

It is the exploration of those writings, and in particular of their interest as pieces of literature, that lies at the centre of this book. Although they are writings in which, it can be argued, Cicero placed his highest stylistic and compositional ambitions, the prose treatises discussed here are barely visible within the canon of Roman literature as it is currently conceived, and are read, if at all, for the light they shed on rhetorical theory and the history of philosophy. One purpose of this book is to provide a means of approaching these works which unlocks their literary potential: and the key is historical representation. In the texts I examine, the representation of the past, and the manipulation of historical material, are central to the way in which Cicero works with his main theoretical subject. By focusing on the varied functions which history takes on, I shall be working to add substance to a number of different arguments: that Cicero's representation of the past is complex, ironic, and sometimes deliberately ambiguous; that his theoretical writings repay close reading, and that over and above the exploration of philosophical or theoretical ideas, they need to be examined for their imaginative effect; that the terms 'philosophy' and 'history' should be used with an awareness of the danger of anachronistic associations, and that the thinking which Cicero can instil in his readers is not always amenable to these categories; that these texts in general belong to a type of writing to which today's readers have little immediate connection, and that there are powerful trends in the reception of Cicero which obscure, rather than illuminate, central features of his philosophy.

Cicero's philosophy is always dialogic, in that it is composed in the form of dialogues which employ a range of different techniques to represent sometimes incompatible philosophical viewpoints via the voices of speaking characters: these characters occupy a strange position half-way between fact and fiction. In this sense, Cicero's dialogues are recognizable to readers of Plato, since Cicero's philosophical training took place within the school (the Academy) that prided itself on preserving the Platonic (or Socratic) tradition of philosophical dialogue. But Cicero's exploration of the historical potential of the dialogue form was more carefully targeted and elaborate than Plato's, and his exploration of the historical dimensions of the dialogue form, at least in some of his works, is surprisingly complex. The material for this book comes from the interplay between this dialogic form of philosophy and the Academic tendency of Cicero to represent more than one philosophical view, and to leave the resolution of opposing views to the reader. I shall argue that on the basis of this interplay, Cicero produces a sophisticated vision of the uses of history at Rome, one that is deliberately non-dogmatic in its approach to historical fact, but which appreciates the enormous power of historical representation.

In order to give a full account of what is in effect a 'philosophy of history' in the modern sense of that phrase, or a least, a philosophy of historical representation, I shall be occupied mainly with analysing a selection of Cicero's theoretical writings in which historical material is particularly important to the main arguments of the work and in which, therefore, it receives a fair degree of attention. However, the approach to reading Cicero in this manner is not one which has much tradition behind it; indeed, the whole tradition of Academic philosophy as Cicero understood it is so far from being mainstream even in some scholarship on Cicero, that the most obvious of Cicero's appeals to the Academic method have not been used to provide guidance as to how we might read these works so as to elucidate wider questions about the role of philosophy at Rome, Cicero's engagement with it, or the literary value of his theoretical writings.[1] The clearest example is the persistent tendency for readers of *De divinatione* or *De natura deorum* to ask what Cicero himself 'really thought' about prediction or the nature of the gods, or of *De re publica* to reconstruct Cicero's view of the best form of constitution. Such a question represents an approach to his writings that Cicero makes clear is inappropriate and unhelpful, and although those who work on this philosophy are for the most part aware of the significance of the Academic approach, those whose interest in Cicero is less technical, or who read Cicero because of a more general interest in the literature or history of the republic, have not had much access to it.

To provide more detail, *De natura deorum* is a useful example. Cicero spends three books outlining the three main approaches to theology represented by the dominant philosophical schools (Epicurean, Stoic, Academic). He prefaces the dialogue by explaining

---

[1] Lévy (1992) is the most important exception, a work which has had barely any impact on English-speaking scholars, and which is hard to obtain.

the context for the enquiry: a general outline of the main question (what *are* the gods?), followed by an explanation of his own interest in and approach to philosophy. This is just one of many similar prefaces in which Cicero relates the great outpouring of philosophical works to his political exclusion under Caesar's dictatorship, but it contains a particularly useful statement of the full ramifications of Cicero's adherence to the Academic approach.

qui autem requirunt quid quaque de re ipsi sentiamus, curiosius id faciunt quam necesse est; non enim tam auctoritatis in disputando quam rationis momenta quaerenda sunt.   (*De natura deorum* 1. 5. 10)

Those who want to know what I myself think on any particular question are being more curious than is necessary; for it is not the weight of authority so much as that of reason that should be looked for in an argument.

Cicero is pointedly directing his readers away from any enquiry into the particular views that he himself holds. For them to be thinking along these lines displays a kind of curiosity about Cicero's own person which is almost unseemly.

However, at the very end of the same work, during which, as usual, the various philosophical positions have been argued out between different characters, we find the following conclusion. The object of Velleius' criticism is Balbus, the proponent of Stoic views:

'quippe' inquit Velleius 'qui etiam somnia putet ad nos mitti ab Iove, quae ipsa tamen tam levia non sunt quam est Stoicorum de natura deorum oratio.' haec cum esset dicta, ita discessimus ut Vellcio Cottae disputatio verior, mihi Balbi ad veritatis similitudinem videretur esse propensior. (*De natura deorum* 3. 40. 95)

'Absolutely', said Velleius, '[Balbus] even thinks that dreams are sent to us by Jupiter, dreams which themselves are not so insubstantial as the arguments of the Stoics about the nature of the gods.' All that said, we departed, such that to Velleius the argument of Cotta seemed truer, but to me, that of Balbus seemed to bear a greater resemblance to truth.

Ostensibly there is a contradiction between these two passages. At the end of the work, Cicero seems to tell us quite openly that he is giving greater endorsement to the arguments of Balbus, who has represented the Stoic position. Indeed, he has just made Cotta, who has presented the Academic critique of Stoicism, point out that he has followed that argument only in the hope of having it defeated by the Stoic one. He is, therefore, using this intrusion of the authorial voice to lend his authority to a particular set of arguments—the opposite of what he claims to do in the preface. There are several viable solutions to this contradiction: the prologue was quite possibly written separately from the dialogue, so perhaps we should not expect the suspension of judgement expressed in the prologue to correspond exactly to what happens at the end of the work; Cicero wants to endorse the Stoic view by granting it a degree of his own authority, but only after giving the other views their due; Cicero has said at the start not that he will not endorse an argument, but rather that he will allow the arguments to speak for themselves, so the fact that he grants the Stoic argument some qualified endorsement does not contradict his earlier statement. On the other hand, he does leave his readers with Velleius' powerfully dismissive vision of the triviality of Stoic theology hanging in their minds; those arguments which Cicero may wish to endorse have no more solidity than dreams. But solutions along these lines miss the essential point: that we should not be trying to make our interpretation of this work immune to the possibilities of internal contradiction. I would interpret the end of the work as a challenge to the reader: to be aware of the constructed nature of the dialogue, to keep an open mind about drawing any conclusion from the words of individual speakers, and even to allow for the possibility that the final polarity (between Velleius and Cicero, the 'me' of the final sentence) cannot be taken at face value, since these two characters do not have anything like the same status within the dialogue: Velleius is a character, albeit with a historical correspondent. Cicero is both of these, but also, of course, the authorial 'I'. The standard formula, familiar from Plato, of the characters leaving the location of their discussion, is a signal to the readers to keep thinking, and to refrain from arriving at a premature synthesis.

The suggestiveness of moments such as this one does not need to be restrained by the quest for a clear statement of 'what Cicero thought'; and we misinterpret Cicero's style of philosophy if we regard the partial endorsement of Stoicism here as an unproblematic statement of Cicero's view. But the impetus to foreclose on such potential moments of contradiction by trying to find out what Cicero did think is enormous. This is a general point about how to approach philosophical doctrine. When dealing with history, which Cicero treats not as a matter of doctrine, but as an aid to dramatic representation and as anecdotal support for philosophical argument, the difficulty of arriving at *one* view of what Cicero thinks is even more problematic. The understanding of Cicero's philosophical encounter with history depends upon resisting the impetus to find Cicero's views, since, essentially, history in Cicero is hardly ever amenable to the kind of certainty which such a quest for an authoritative view demands. Rather, it is consistently treated with an open-ended kind of scepticism which denies certainty, and which emerges from the manner in which Cicero puts history to work in his dialogues, rather than from direct argument.

The opening and closing of *De natura deorum* demand, however, some kind of engagement with the idea of Cicero's own authority, as the first passage itself makes clear: Cicero directs his readers to avoid looking in his philosophy for an authoritative statement of his views. This authority has generally been seen by scholars as one which Cicero, in his literary output generally, is rather excessively keen to promote; indeed, recent studies of some of the works I include here depict Cicero as driven by the need to imprint his own, somewhat aberrant, view of Roman history on posterity, in order to make his own career look like the culmination of that history.[2] However, one of the principal claims of this book is that if we examine Cicero's historical representations, we can, by virtue of accepting a less dogmatic form of reading, gain access to a more complex vision of how he uses his philosophy not to enforce his own authority, but rather to explore its boundaries, and sometimes to go beyond them. In line with his professed adherence to the Academy, Cicero used historical representations as a way of promoting interpretations which do not rely upon his authority to contain them. They depend, rather, upon the authority of history, and that is an authority that is for Cicero rather unreliable. The methodological problem is whether an approach of a broadly literary kind which resists authoritarian readings can be demarcated from a reading which attributes the non-authoritarian impulse directly to Cicero. How far in practice would a deconstructive reading of Cicero, appealing to the

---

[2] Dugan (2005); Krostenko (2001); both these studies are also clear about the problematic nature of this enterprise.

open-endedness of all writing, differ from one which could directly trace to Cicero's brand of Academic scepticism an invitation to read his texts as non-authoritarian? This question is, I believe, impossible to answer in purely theoretical terms, so I can only make my own position, and the strategy of this book, clear.

It is beyond dispute that there has been a powerful trend to regard Cicero's main effort in his writings as directed towards a textual embodiment or performance of his own authority. This trend is not new; indeed, it can be related to the demise of the Academic approach to philosophy which Cicero himself laments; to Plutarch's portrait of Cicero as obsessed with his own reputation, and using his speeches to promulgate it; to Quintilian's belief that, in *De oratore*, Cicero was simply using Crassus as a mouthpiece for his own views on rhetoric.[3] We may wish to resist this trend by responding to the general claim that all texts are capable of multiple readings. There has not, however, been much sign of such forms of deconstruction being applied to Cicero. Rather, the most interesting scholarship from recent decades has succeeded in demonstrating with considerable subtlety the difficulties which Cicero encountered as a political orator, and how his innovations in rhetorical technique worked to overcome those difficulties. Through his speeches, he produced a picture of rhetorical accomplishment, and simultaneously projected an audience for that accomplishment, that constituted a literary culture within which his own achievements would appear to be the pinnacle.[4] The confidence of Cicero's oratory militates against any limitation upon his authority, and it is tempting to see in his rhetorical treatises the theoretical exploration of the authority which successful rhetoric undoubtedly did grant Cicero in the political arena.[5]

There are other reasons why readers have not looked for expressions of a questioning of authority in Cicero's works. His place in the Roman historical record is too prominent. Our unparalleled knowledge of his

---

[3] Plutarch, *Cic.* 24. 2; *Comp. Dem. Cic.* 2. 3; Quintilian, *Inst.* 10. 3. 1. See Dugan (2005), 86–9.

[4] Important milestones are May (1988); Vasaly (1993); Narducci (1997); Steel (2001).

[5] Krostenko (2001), 154–232. Dugan (2005) presents Cicero as undertaking a systematic 'self-fashioning', in theory at least, implying the improbability of a deliberately non-authoritarian self. His own work with the texts does not foreclose on the question as consistently as his explicit arguments. Steel (2005) touches briefly on the problematic quality of the match between theory and practice.

daily movements, rhetorical techniques, and political relationships make him an unlikely target for formalist, poststructuralist, or even (in old-fashioned terms) literary reading. There is, however, no intrinsic reason why the knowledge of Cicero that is available should act as a limitation on the kinds of readings to which his writings are amenable: although we know something about the composition of some of his works, that does not mean that Cicero tells us how to read them, and even if it did, we would be under no obligation to read them as he dictates. So part of my strategy is to accept that, like other texts, Cicero's theoretical writings can legitimately bear plural or ambiguous interpretation.

However, there are two further aspects, which are linked to each other: the possibility of a deliberately anti-authoritarian quality to Academic philosophy, and an understanding of why scholars have felt the need to look to Cicero as a source of authority, rather than its opposite. An important part of this book is its emphasis upon the manner in which traditions of interpreting Cicero have restrained the perceived potential especially of his theoretical writings. My interest in the reception of Cicero is not in the study of the effect of Cicero's writings on later authors, but rather, of trends in reading which have produced a particular image of Cicero. The image has certainly altered over the centuries, but it has never lost the authority which derived from Cicero's supremacy in Latin style and the unparalleled clarity of his vision of Roman values. This reception also reveals the neglect of the scepticism of Cicero's Academic training, and its clear insistence (as in the opening of *De natura deorum*) that philosophy consists in making a range of ideas available, rather than insisting on the supremacy of one particular doctrine. The difficulty of responding to this sceptical way of approaching Cicero has led to a widespread neglect of what were in fact the works which he regarded as the most important part of his literary legacy, which are largely read today only by specialists. It is essential to uncover the history of this neglect, to try to account for it in charting the changing hermeneutics of Cicero's philosophy, which have obscured the essentially open-ended, non-dogmatic approach to philosophy which characterizes Cicero's take on the Academy. Only by understanding the traditions of reading which have supplanted those which could respond more directly to the Academic method, can we begin to understand the potential of these works. That potential, I shall argue, rests in the fact that Cicero provides us, in his flexible and multifaceted historical thinking, with an encounter with the ideological dilemmas of the late Republic which surpasses any of its possible rivals in its passion, complexity, and critical sophistication.

The vision of Cicero himself as a flexible, creative, and non-dogmatic writer will perhaps surprise some readers: even in specialist scholarship, the dominant image of Cicero is of an author striving at every turn to coerce readers by the full force of his rhetoric, not of one who deliberately resists drawing conclusions or allowing competing visions to exist side by side. In order to allow this other Cicero to emerge from the texts, it is therefore necessary to understand the traditions in Cicero interpretation which have occluded a more complex relationship between text and reader, and have allowed the notion of Cicero as a dogmatist to hold sway: Cicero as rigidly attached to a particular ideological position which he is determined to foist upon his readers, whether within the scope of an individual speech or in his demarcation of the role of the statesman or orator.[6] Reception, therefore, is a topic that I shall frequently refer to; but reception meaning the examination of intellectual currents which have distorted Cicero, and made him into a writer much more monolithic than his imaginative workings with Roman ideology actually justify. My general sense that we need to be open to multiple possibilities in Cicero's writings intersects, therefore, with a specific interest in regaining access to the philosophical currents which worked against authority in philosophical writings, and which, I shall claim, can be observed in the manner in which Cicero presents his thinking as historical. So this book aims to shift ways of thinking about a number of different aspects of Cicero's writings and his historical context, and argues that, if we do readjust our understanding of how history and philosophy relate in Cicero, we will arrive at a

---

[6] Batstone (1994), on Cicero's first Catilinarian (a text obviously much less amenable to a flexible vision of authority than any philosophical one), makes the following acute observation: 'I believe that Cicero needed flexible authority supported by a range of symbolic associations more than he needed to establish the legitimacy of a particular symbolic system' (p. 218 n. 17). Batstone is arguing against too rigid a view of the processes by which authority is projected in the speech, one that is crucial to the creation of a consular persona, bucking the trend of recent scholarship on the speeches to highlight the success and coherence of Cicero's appeals to authority.

better account not only of his thought, but also of the philosophy and history of the late Republic and, beyond that, of our own involvement in the production of a particular vision of Cicero's authority.

The main material of this book will be those works where it seems to me that Cicero makes historical representation into a particularly central part of the method of the work in question. Such an approach does require justification, since there is a danger here of circular argument. The danger is this: because I am interested in historiography, I have chosen to discuss those works where historical representation is particularly prominent; this will in turn be proof of the sophistication of Cicero's understanding of the past. And because, although not in fact narrative histories or historical monographs of the kind that clearly had their own distinct generic identity long before Cicero was writing, they are nevertheless the first complete pieces of historical writing to survive from Rome, there is a further danger that I will be overestimating the importance of Cicero's way of using history, and will be making false assumptions about the relationship between history in philosophical dialogue and the more mainstream historical work of Cicero's contemporaries and their successors.

Such dangers are important, but they rest on a number of assumptions about method, and about the possible scope of an investigation into a set of texts, which, although they may be widespread, are by no means indispensable; it may indeed be better to dispense with them. The main assumption regards the kind of evidence, and the sort of testing to which that evidence is amenable, which is possible when reading an author such as Cicero. Because Cicero wrote a lot of philosophical books in a short space of time, there is a temptation to think that any aspect of technique that can be found in one dialogue will need to be tested, in the manner of a scientifically controlled experiment, against the techniques used in other dialogues. This would be a reasonably strong argument if we were dealing with a scientific project, but we are not; if on some occasions Cicero's treatment of history is more inert, at other times more energetic, this is not in itself a reason to ignore the ramifications of his more energetic treatments. Cicero may have embarked, in the final years of his life, on the production of a comprehensive philosophical curriculum in Latin, but that did not bring with it any obligation for him to be methodologically consistent. More problematic is the fact that at no point, either in the late works or in those which belong to an earlier phase (*De oratore*, *De re publica*), did Cicero make history itself into the subject of his philosophy.

However, Cicero makes it clear in a large number of places that what he is undertaking is the provision of a Roman form of a type of writing (philosophical prose) that has hitherto been found only in Greek.[7] There is clear evidence, which will emerge in the following chapters, that in naturalizing philosophy for a Roman readership, one of the forms of writing that Cicero could easily fall back on was history. History provided a solid anchorage against which Cicero could inflect philosophy with a sense of Roman culture. But it is clear from the letters which describe the composition of various works, as well as from programmatic statements (usually in the prefaces), that Cicero never thought that this process of naturalization could be totally effective. In other words, he was always aware that there would be an unnatural quality to presenting Romans talking like Greeks, or adopting a form of writing made famous by Plato (or his near contemporary, Heraclides of Pontus), in which instead of Socrates and similar figures, Roman statesmen and thinkers appeared. It is the experimental quality of Cicero's writing, the awareness of the pitfalls of Romanizing philosophy by integrating it into a representation of Rome's past, that provides the best support for the approach adopted in this book. That approach, therefore, is one that relies not upon the verification of one form of Cicero's method against others, nor upon discovering a comprehensive approach to history which he consistently implemented. It depends, rather, upon the exploration of Cicero's different ways of representing the past, exploring the details of those representations, and drawing out the ambiguities and contradictions within them. In this sense, my approach can conveniently be described as 'literary', in that it uses close reading to explore the consequences of the tensions over history and philosophy that are intrinsic to Cicero's project. The tensions can be directly linked to Cicero's programmatic statements, but they achieve a much fuller

---

[7] *De off.* 1. 3; *Tusc. disp.* 1. 3. 5–6; and in particular detail, *De fin.* 1. 2. 4–1. 4. 12.

realization when observed working within the representations of the philosophical works themselves.

For these reasons, I have focused on those works in which Cicero makes history work particularly hard, almost as a further character in his philosophical dialogues (*De re publica, De oratore, De divinatione*); or that singular work where he is directly concerned with history itself, albeit in the form of a genealogy of Roman oratory: *Brutus*. Read together, these works provide substantial material which will, I hope, facilitate future studies on dialogues where historical concerns are less prominent, but which would nevertheless repay analysis of a similar kind; *De natura deorum* or *Academica* would be obvious candidates; so too would *De legibus*, only the opening of which is discussed. History, in these dialogues, both in terms of the fictional casting and in terms of the integration of rather more technical philosophical material than is present in the works discussed below, plays a less prominent role, but for that very reason, the technicalities of the material take on a prominence which I have felt to be beyond my competence in the present study: to place the exact historical situation of the laws discussed in *De legibus*, for example, would require an exceptional knowledge of Roman law.[8] What I have sacrificed, however, in terms of coverage of a large number of works, I hope will be compensated by the detail of the readings, and also the wider exploration of the significance of Cicero's work with history. In particular, it is important to locate Cicero's exploration of historical representation within the historiography of the late Republic, and to think about what Cicero's approach can tell us about the problems of writing history. This is a question which has usually been addressed by thinking about Cicero's use of sources and knowledge of the past, rather than in terms of the creative dynamics of historical representation.[9] But I hope that by putting together readings of this particular selection of dialogues, I can present a persuasive case not just for the sophistication of Cicero's own historical thinking, but for its relationship to

---

[8] Girardet (1983) covers some of the ground; see too Powell (2001), which maps out the field in a way that corresponds more to current approaches, but doesn't explore it in detail.

[9] Fleck (1993).

that of his contemporaries and earliest readers. Beyond that, I shall
be pursuing the argument that once Cicero's philosophy of history
is named and understood, it requires us to think again about the
traditional picture of Cicero, and about his relationship to central
concerns about ideology and identity in the late Republic.

I will now devote some attention to the general aims of this book, and
my sense of its potential audience. The two greatest difficulties in
writing about Cicero are, on the one hand, the enormous size of his
own written output, and, on the other, the correspondingly gargantuan edifice which scholars have, over several centuries, generated on
the basis of it. These two difficulties deter many from working
on Cicero; in the UK, there are comparatively few who do so. And
Cicero, likewise, is poorly represented in the curricula of British
universities, his presence usually limited to study of the best-known
speeches. The deterrent effect, however, has had the unfortunate
result of giving much of the scholarship on Cicero a rather hermetic
character: Cicero scholars write for other Cicero scholars, and they
do so primarily in languages other than English. So while, for
example, one of my principal theses, that Cicero's dialogues are
self-conscious, knowing pieces of writing, where little can be taken
at face value, is self-evident to anyone familiar with the work of Alain
Michel, there are many (even working on Cicero) in the anglophone
world who seem entirely unfamiliar with his contribution.[10]
A fortiori, this thesis will strike as surprising those who, though
they may be professional literary scholars, have only a distant,
undergraduate acquaintance with a few of Cicero's speeches. Where
even the world of Cicero scholarship is fragmented, it is difficult to
write so as to appeal to a universal audience, and hard to find the
right balance between more technical questions and more general
ones. I feel in general that, given the character of much of the
scholarship and the neglect of Cicero by those who do not work
directly on him, it is a more urgent task to lay out the neglected

---

[10] Michel (1960, 1965). Michel is not referred to in e.g. Powell and North (2001),
Krostenko (2001), and Dugan (2005). Desmouliez (1982) is a good example of the
influence of his approach, as ultimately is the monumental Lévy (1992).

dynamics of Cicero's encounter with history to a wider audience, and to explore the further ramifications for other kinds of literature.

It is an important part of my argument that if we can understand what Cicero does with history in his dialogues, we will understand better the environment in which others thinking through history at Rome were operating; a better understanding of Cicero's work on history will obviously be of use to those interested in historiography. Less obviously, but more importantly, it will be valuable for anyone looking for detailed evidence of the cultural significance, and imaginative potential of Rome's past at a time when, in the shift from Republic to Principate, the relevance of past to present took on an importance which it is hard to overestimate. This book stakes a claim for the sophistication of Cicero's work on history, in particular the sophistication of its irony. Cicero is routinely thought of as providing the most important evidence about the late Republic in many areas, but not, as yet, in his ironic treatment of Roman history. This recognition will perhaps have greater resonance for those working in other areas of Latin literature and history than for those working on Cicero himself, for whom the sophistication of their hero will be nothing new. It is possible, even desirable, on this basis, to write a book specifically aimed at non-specialists, those with a passing interest in Cicero, and a more intense interest in the literature, identity, and ideology of the period. My presentation of Cicero will allow an easier comparison with those other dramatizers of the late Republic: Lucretius, or even Catullus, or Sallust. Cicero too, I shall argue, can yield up to literary analysis an imaginative reaction to the instabilities of the late Republic. I hope, of course, that Cicero specialists will also find something useful in the studies that follow. In particular, the mode of reading that I have followed is not that which is usually found in discussions of Cicero's dialogues. I have tended to avoid getting entangled in scholarly controversy in most areas which might be regarded as requiring specialist expertise: text, historical or philosophical source, prosopography or political context. Of course, this is partly a matter of personal disposition and experience, but perhaps I can make a virtue of that disposition: it is my belief that a focus on technicalities has not done Cicero's reputation any favours, and the complaints of John Toland (see Chapter 10) that Cicero has given rise to too much scholarly pedantry are ones that, three centuries later, produce a glow of sympathy within me.

What is needed, it seems to me, to rectify the current marginalization of Cicero is an encounter with him which focuses firmly on the experience of reading Cicero today; and, in particular, on reading those works in which he had most clearly focused his ambitions to transcend his own mortality. At two different points, first under the triumvirate, and later under Caesar's dictatorship, when it was clear to him that his achievements as an orator and a statesman had not guaranteed him a position of influence of Rome, let alone one of durable value, he turned with vigour to the production of a literary legacy, with the aim of preserving what he saw as his most valuable qualities. Instead of something which directly reflected his sense of an *auctoritas* (authority) lost within the Roman political system, however, what he chose to leave behind was a guide to philosophy: a series of meditations particularly on ethics and on the role that philosophy has to play in ordinary life.[11] By far the most important feature of this legacy, however, is that the desire for a posthumous literary *auctoritas* that would outweigh the disappointments of his career did not lead Cicero to produce doctrinaire or dogmatic philosophical teachings. His literary legacy may have been a compensation for his lack of historical significance after the Republic had slid into dictatorship; but he did not cling, in this great philosophical outpouring, to the notion of authority. Rather, his political disempowerment seems to have encouraged him in his belief that the best way to do philosophy involved precisely the opposite of authority.[12] Plutarch tells us that Cicero's major character failing was an obsession with his own reputation.[13] By the end of his life, Cicero seems to have embraced the opportunities offered by a non-authoritarian idea of reputation. This will strike many readers as a perverse interpretation; detailed arguments explaining it will be found in the following chapters.

---

[11] Henderson (2006) captures the drama of the later period particularly well; see too Fuchs (1959).

[12] For Strasburger (1990) and Lévy (1992) Cicero's philosophical scepticism is an expression of resistance to Caesar.

[13] See above, n. 3; Allen (1954).

A large part of this book concerns the question of how best to read these works; I will be discussing the hermeneutics of Cicero's dialogues: establishing a way of reading them which is both close to the assumptions with which they were composed and also amenable to a dynamic reading in which the richness of the individual texts becomes clear. This endeavour, however, comes at a point in the evolution of Classical criticism where the old distinction between literary and non-literary texts is becoming obsolete. I hesitate, therefore, to designate my approach to Cicero's philosophy as one that is overtly literary: in so far as I want to provide a framework in which these texts can be explored through a careful examination of individual sentences, and in which Cicero's chosen form of expression is interrogated in detail, I depend upon a form of close reading which owes its origins to a concern with textual detail, and an interest in recognizing the potential for texts to produce more than one interpretation. These studies will in this sense be literary in character; but at the same time, I want to look beyond the polarity between literary and non-literary, or historical approaches. I will indeed be looking to Cicero's own evaluation of his literary endeavours for the roots of a trend to treat his works as textbooks rather than as works of literature; Cicero was clearly uneasy about the limits of literary activity and, more seriously, about the problem of literary or rhetorical style in the presentation and effectiveness both of himself and of Roman statesmen in general. His ambivalence about literature, however, has not been integrated into the interpretative strategies adopted when reading these works: Cicero's dialogues as works of literature but, at the same time, as works of literature that interrogate the category of literature itself. The notion of literary criticism as predominantly interested in the formal properties of a work or with details of expression is out of place in this context; nevertheless, rhetoric and style were central to Cicero's practice as an orator, and play a vital role in his theoretical writings too; so I aim to combine an awareness of details of expression with an exploration of the aim and context of Cicero's rhetorical strategies. The context involves unravelling Cicero's own ambivalence about the potential of literature at Rome, as well as the manner in which he carried on his philosophical project.

Although scholars have now by and large moved away from treating Cicero's philosophy as derivative, Cicero's dependence upon Greek models has had a more persistent effect upon the kinds of readings that are thought appropriate to these works. They are still taken as guides to Greek philosophical thought, and Cicero's contribution is generally seen as the adaptation, however far-reaching, of a discourse that began in Greece, for a Roman audience. What scholars have generally yet to do, however, is perceive how problematic this process of adaptation was for Cicero himself, in particular since he was, by virtue of his own philosophical education, extremely disinclined to the production of textbooks of philosophy. Because the reputation of philosophy at Rome was largely established by two philosophical schools which were dogmatic in their traditions, the Stoic and Epicurean, there was most likely an expectation among Cicero's readers that philosophical writing would be dogmatic in its approach: that it would demand a particular lifestyle of its devotees in the way that both those other popular philosophical schools did. Apart from his last great work, *De officiis*, which, paradoxically, was also by far the most influential from the Renaissance until the nineteenth century, Cicero deliberately avoided writing the kind of philosophy that relied upon the authority of its author (and even in that work, it is possible to interrogate the authority which the pedagogic father/son structure entails). So, while transmitting his own acquaintance with Greek philosophy, Cicero needed to defeat the expectations of his readers, and establish philosophy in Rome in the form that recalled the aporetic traditions of the Academy, going back to Plato and Socrates, rather than the more doctrinal and more heavily literary philosophy of Stoicism or Epicureanism. But although scholars have examined the way in which Roman themes and historical anecdotes are carefully formed to communicate the different philosophical issues, what has not been clearly grasped is that this context demands a different kind of reading; in particular, because of the aporetic quality of the Academic tradition, the very literary aspects of the works, in particular the dynamics of the imaginative representation which Cicero undertakes in his philosophy, have a power to shape the understanding of philosophy itself that goes far beyond any conventional notion of the bounds of 'the literary'. Although Cicero's medium was the written dialogue, he was working on the assumption that writing was an inspirational medium rather than an instructional one; in his representation of Rome's history, that inspiration can be negative as well as positive, and the works I explore show exactly the ramifications of this Academic heritage when applied to history: and I mean history not in terms just of facts about the past, but the historical dimension of Roman identity, in which the character of the state and the destiny of the individual cohere.

There are two further aspects of the book which require introductory remarks: my focus on reception, and my understanding of ideology, and of the potential of my presentation of Cicero to challenge prevailing notions of his role in helping us to understand the ideological dilemmas of his time. These two aspects are in fact closely related; the picture of the ironic, non-authoritarian Cicero is one that contradicts prevailing currents in Cicero reception, in which, to generalize, any failure of Cicero to provide a stable notion of authority in his writings is, rather than a deliberate rhetorical strategy, an accidental result of the fact that he was, because of insecurity about his social position, or because of his failure to achieve any tangible result in the political arena, or both, also incapable of convincingly portraying a position of authority in his literary legacy. One way round this rather unhelpful polarization is to take the thoroughly modernist step of declaring that Cicero's own intentions are irrelevant to what he actually achieved in his writings, either because authorial intention represents an inaccessible arena, or because it presupposes a fallacious capacity on the part of authors to control readers' responses to their works. Cicero was a political failure, and failure characterizes too the inability of most of his philosophy to make up its mind on the central questions. The judgement of Cicero as a historical failure, however, can never be a simple matter of fact; it is rather the product of many centuries of reading and teaching Cicero's writings, and the production of a general sense, sometimes hard to define, of the character of Cicero as both a political personality and a writer. It is in order to unravel some of this complex material that I devote part of this book to questions of reception. Although I think it unrealistic to expect that we can bring our own understanding of Cicero's works conclusively into line with either his intentions or his effect upon his earliest readers, it is by no means impossible to raise our own awareness of the processes which influence the preconceptions with which we approach Cicero's writings. The more we can do that, the more immediately we can appreciate those moments where Cicero does tell us, with reasonable directness, what we should expect from his philosophy.

It is by looking at the reception of Cicero that we can also become aware of the issues at stake in positioning him as the principal ideologue of the late Republic, a position which, simply by virtue of the preservation of so much of his writing, and the highly rhetorical quality of much of his work, he is bound to occupy. In particular, by being aware of the different responses which Cicero's philosophy has awakened, it is possible to gain an insight into the manner in which he has become identified with notions of Romanness, and in particular notions of civic contribution in a Roman context. It is clear that Cicero was brilliant at evoking a durable and influential model of civic duty, and of expressing powerfully the idea of a political consensus formed around a shared set of values; *De officiis* is an explicit presentation in the form of a treatise of this aspect of his thinking: the reading of speeches and of this work as fundamental educational texts for many centuries had a powerful determining effect on the image of Cicero from the Renaissance on. However, what the exploration of Cicero's historical representations can show is that Cicero was unwilling to allow that sense of ideological coherence to remain unchallenged. In Chapter 10, I focus on what can be thought of as the end of the tradition of reading Cicero which allowed two aspects of his work to coexist comfortably: his ability to act as and to describe the idealized values of a republican, and his sceptical philosophical approach. It was, I shall argue, through the changing perceptions of the role of philosophy, and also of rhetoric, that began to occur in the Enlightenment, that the sceptical quality of Cicero's representations became a problem, and the more general picture emerged of Cicero as a would-be ideologue, whose political misfortunes only demonstrated how misguided his sense of the realities of the Republic were. If we can look with sufficient care at the conditions in which this understanding of Cicero took root, then we will be better placed to explore the most neglected aspect of Cicero's philosophy: its imaginative potential, the rich and sometimes bizarre nature of its presentation of Rome.

It was a struggle to make Rome look like a philosophically coherent society, and the signs of the struggle are apparent, if one can free oneself from the manner of reading that regards consistency as the highest goal, and instead allow the suggestive quality of Cicero's rhetoric more space. By examining traditions of reception, we can find a way of reading Cicero that grasps head-on the notion of imaginative representation, and makes the form of representation into the key area of analysis. Much of my supporting argument revolves around how Cicero himself locates (or more often, fails to locate) a picture of literary production through rhetoric into the identity of Rome, and his own identity within that city. This is a matter again of examining his historical representations not in terms of their argument, but in terms of the stories they tell, stories about Cicero himself and about other men to whom he may or may not be similar; a matter too of becoming more aware of the potential for conflicting or incompatible stories about Rome to exist side by side. In this conception of Cicero's play with an ironic form of historical writing, the greatest potential of this picture of Cicero becomes apparent: the philosophical works as show-pieces for the sophistication with which the past at Rome could be represented.

Chapters on history and memory (Chapter 6) and ironic history (Chapter 9) draw out the historiographical dimension, and help to define Cicero the historian: beyond questions of his sources of information, we should think about his sense of Rome's past, and what could be done with it within the context both of existing historical trends and of their subsequent development. In Chapter 6, notions of commemoration, and in particular the role of rhetoric in that process, are considered, so that Cicero's work with the past can be judged not just as the expression of his originality (which it undoubtedly was), but also as a manifestation of a characteristically Roman manner of dealing with history. In Chapter 9, I suggest that Cicero's way of allowing conflicting versions of history to exist side by side can conveniently be thought of as 'Ironic History', and that his practice can fruitfully be compared with that of Sallust and Tacitus, both of whom derive much of their impact from similar play with conflicting stories, and with ambiguous sources of historical authority. In the other chapters, I look in turn at a selection of the historically suggestive dialogues; first, Cicero's earliest fully-fledged philosophical writings: *De re publica*, which although not the earliest, is most helpful for setting the scene, then *De oratore* and *De legibus*, which act as illuminating supplements to *De re publica*, and which show something of the build-up to that work; thereafter, two works from the very end of Cicero's life, both rather on the fringes of his philosophical curriculum: *De divinatione* and *Brutus*. These works, one written before, one after Caesar's death, pick up on the historical dialectic explored in the earlier dialogues, but are much more personal, much more concerned with Cicero's own reputation, and with the danger of social and ideological fragmentation. In these later writings, the ambiguity with which Cicero approaches Rome's history takes on, unsurprisingly, a much more sinister, almost desperate character, and the struggle between optimistic and pessimistic visions of Rome is more sharply drawn.

So Cicero's philosophy of history requires a readjustment of our approach to Cicero. His writings do certainly produce a form of philosophy of history, but that philosophy does not revolve around positive doctrine. Cicero explores history as a discourse that can provide a foundation for social stability and continuity. But throughout his writings, he retains a scepticism about any such foundation, a scepticism which has several sources: his philosophical schooling; his rhetorical expertise, and sensitivity to the provisional quality of argument; a lack of credulity about processes of commemoration and representation typical of Roman political history. In order to allow this philosophy to emerge, it is necessary, therefore, to establish why it is that such a sceptical and even aporetic encounter with Rome's identity has been invisible in the dominant readings of Cicero; we need to investigate the roots of Cicero's disengagement from the ideological centre at Rome, while also tracing the tradition of reading that works in exactly the opposite direction: the vision of Cicero as somehow the typical Roman, a vision which is hard to square with the view of historical process that can be found in his writings. In the final chapter, I bring these currents together, in order to explore how far the multi-voiced Cicero could in fact fulfil his original purpose in providing useful guidance for the formation of citizens: not citizens whose highest aim was the grasp of an immutable truth, but citizens with the flexibility and self-awareness to remain open to a range of competing discourses.

2

Struggle, Compensation, and Argument in Cicero's Philosophy

Cicero's philosophical writing is at first sight deceptively straight-forward. It has an elegant and lucid manner, and, more important than a pure stylistic simplicity, it deliberately steers clear of intellectual obscurity. Both in the 50s and the 40s BCE, when Cicero's philosophical productivity really accelerated, his work had a pioneering aim: to introduce philosophy to a Latin readership. By its very nature, that aim imposed a particular flavour on the works which he produced: Cicero was mediating Greek philosophy for a Roman public, but in so doing persuading them that their prejudices against Greek philosophy, that it was abstract and removed from the problems which occupied them, were unfounded. It is possible, indeed, that even in the works of the 50s we can perceive a more pointed agenda: not just to bring philosophical discourse to Rome, but in the process to show that it could be done in a Roman manner, and that philosophy was not just the preserve of the Epicureans, with their high-minded disdain for public life, or of the Stoics, with their elaborate metaphysical system.

This was a project that only Cicero could have undertaken, since it was one in which his vision of philosophy was being represented. By deciding to establish philosophy in Latin, Cicero was expressing a personal vision of what philosophy was for, how it should best be written, and, most importantly, how it could be integrated into the social and intellectual world in which he lived.[1] The works themselves

---

[1] The clearest statement of this intention is the introduction to his *Academica*, where the characters debate the necessity for a Latin philosophy, *Acad*. 1. 2. 4–1. 3. 12. See too *Tusc. disp.* 1. 1. 1–4. 8; 2. 1. 1–3. 9; *De off.* 1. 1–5; 2. 2–3.

all have an ethical leaning, one which reflects the almost universal notion that the role of philosophy was to help the individual lead a better, more ordered life. The relative absence of technicality, and the emphasis upon working out philosophical issues by using the material from familiar anecdote, taken from both Roman and Greek traditions, make the works accessible. The various forms of dialogue adopted by Cicero to convey his philosophy mean that the reader is either being addressed by a friendly voice, coaxed gently through a series of arguments, or is a bystander at a similarly even-tempered and well-structured conversation, from the mouths of cultured and powerful figures, sometimes indeed Cicero and his own friends, sometimes similar figures from earlier periods in Rome's cultural development.

The elegance and facility of Cicero's philosophical works have made a few of them extremely important in the perpetuation of Cicero's literary reputation, as has the accessible vision of personal and political ethics which the dialogues generally represent (*De officiis* and *De natura deorum* were probably the most influential). This accessibility is deceptive, however, and has produced a vision of the naturalness and clarity of Cicero's philosophy which makes it hard to understand the complexity of the processes which underlie its inception. In this chapter, I will be exploring this complexity, drawing out the different strands in Cicero's thought which inspired his philosophical works, and laying down the basis for the main argument of the rest of this book: that, in spite of its potential to be interpreted as a confident expression of a philosopher at the height of his powers, Cicero's philosophical writing is a much more self-aware body of work, even self-doubting, in which philosophy is the tool of a revolutionary, rather than of a conservative country gentleman, and in which the difficulties of bringing philosophy to Rome are never far from sight. These difficulties, moreover, are more than simply a matter of the adaptability of philosophy to different cultures: they are a reflection of Cicero's own sense of personal and political fragmentation, and of the violent entropy of the final years of the Republic.

Although this chapter and the next are in some degree introductory to the detailed studies that come after, they are also the fruit of my reading of those texts. They present a view of Cicero's philosophical labours which is the result of those studies, and which is argued more strongly than an introduction that sets the scene in some more neutral manner for an encounter with those texts. There are good reasons, however, why I put this material first, rather than beginning with the works and then allowing these conclusions to emerge from them. In the preface I suggested, perhaps cavalierly, that we all make our own Cicero; this is true up to a point, but it is also a collective process. If I were simply to begin this book with *De re publica* and argue (as I already have in earlier publications) that it is a fundamentally ironic text in which Cicero uses the dialogue form in a manner that makes it difficult to find authoritative views of the *res publica* of the 50s, any reader predisposed to disagree would be in a good position to dismiss my reading as idiosyncratic or one-sided. As I moved to discuss more texts, there would be little encouragement to modify that view, and my deduction, following such readings, that a different method is needed to understand the complexity of Cicero's work with authority, would appear to be no more than rhetoric aimed at extracting a theory from something where the applicability of the arguments had yet to be proved. The point, therefore, of these introductory chapters is to shake up preconceptions about the character of Cicero's philosophical project, and to bring the idea that an anti-authoritarian approach was actually the norm, to the centre of the process of reading. I shall also show that the Academy represents not just a philosophical mind-set, but that it is profoundly connected with Cicero's own career, so that the work with conflicting or non-authoritarian material can be understood in relation to his political position and his ambitions for reform at Rome.

In this chapter, therefore, I shall examine what Cicero's own statements can show us about his philosophical position: I will focus on the sense that philosophy is an activity which Cicero perceives to be marginal to Rome, and relate that to Cicero's implementation of a non-dogmatic Academic methodology. In the next, I shall look at how the reception of Cicero has worked against recognition of the dynamic quality of his philosophy, looking precisely at those processes which make an appeal to non-authority seem like a misreading. I suggested above that Cicero's philosophy is surprising in its complexity, and that this is a complexity that is hidden beneath a deceptive lucidity. A closer study of Cicero reception shows, however, that it is engrained habits of reading that have compounded this complexity and made some of the basic assumptions about how to read philosophy seem difficult or artificial: what may look like an over-elaborate quality in my readings of individual texts will in fact resolve itself into a quite simple analysis, once the problems of approaching Cicero's philosophy are understood. The simple analysis is this: Cicero's philosophy explores the potential of authoritative positions, but it does not endorse them, and history plays a central role in that process. Developments in the understanding of both philosophy and rhetoric have made it hard to appreciate that the simultaneous presentation of conflicting kinds of representation could actually be the whole point of a philosophical work, and that readers could respond to such an approach without necessarily looking for one single authoritative position. They have made, in fact, what seems normal for Plato, seem impossible for Cicero. To move beyond this obvious absurdity, we need to understand what has happened to the hermeneutics of Cicero's dialogues, and the best way to do that is to think about reception as a force that shapes reading. The tradition of Cicero reception is still evolving; I shall outline what I regard as the most important influences for misunderstanding Cicero's Academic perspective, and thereby pave the way for readings of individual works, both from his earlier and his later career as a theorist, which demonstrate the tensions inherent in his approach to philosophy. Roman history provides a focal point for these tensions.

PHILOSOPHY, POLITICS, AND THE ACADEMY

One of the most important strands in the production of Cicero's philosophy is the notion that philosophy is in some senses a displacement activity for the real business of Roman public life. It is hard to know how far Cicero's contemporaries shared this view of philosophy, but what is clear is that the notion of displacement is central to Cicero's ambivalence about the success of his philosophical endeavours. In what follows, I shall be substantiating the following interpretation of Cicero's position, a position in which philosophical interests and the realities of Cicero's political career coalesce. In contrast to the very public Stoicism of Cato and Brutus, not to mention the Epicureanism which Cicero parodies in *In Pisonem*, but which was a doctrine to which his closest friend, Atticus, was deeply attached, Cicero was uncomfortable with these rather dogmatic philosophical schools. Instead, he professed himself a follower of the Academy, the school which Plato founded, and which, by the time Cicero encountered it, was characterized precisely by its deliberate abstinence from dogmatic teaching, an abstinence which is often described (with insufficient precision) as scepticism. Cicero's decision to mediate philosophy for a Roman readership cannot be divorced from his own philosophical preferences. It is only because Cicero did not subscribe to a particular set of doctrines that he was able to conceive of the notion of mediating Greek philosophy for Romans at all, since only within the Academic tradition was philosophical activity itself (rather than the achievement of a particular control over natural impulses and emotions) represented as the goal of a philosophical education.[2] Cicero's difficulty, therefore, was that, unlike Stoic or Epicurean philosophers, he did not regard it as the aim of philosophy to produce a particular type of behaviour in his readers. His message for Rome was more complex than the exhortations to control the emotions, have faith in the providential order of the universe, or aim for happiness; rather, it was an exhortation to 'do philosophy', and the adaptation of philosophy for Roman readers was also a justification for the relevance of this vision of philosophy to the Roman context.

The struggle between theory and practice lies at the root of all Cicero's philosophical writings, even his earliest ones. Cicero's whole philosophical project was coloured by his conviction that, even without being dogmatic, philosophy could make a difference to the way Rome functioned as a state and as a society. The problem was that, in contrast to the visible manifestations of philosophical behaviour in the Stoic tradition, the difference that philosophy would

---

[2] Neatly encapsulated by A. R. Dyck (2002), 320. It will be clear that I subscribe to the account of Cicero's scepticism described as the orthodoxy in Steinmetz (1989) and reaffirmed by Görler (1995), in which Cicero's adherence to the sceptical Academy remains consistent.

make to the state was rather hard to pin down; and the vacillation between different philosophical positions can be read as in some sense a parallel to Cicero's own apparent inconstancy in the political arena: he was pushed around by political circumstances, rather than being someone like Cato, whose political career was characterized by adherence to a fixed principle. So the constant emphasis in Cicero's philosophy is on the explanation of moments from Rome's past, the behaviour of prominent figures from history, the discussion of recent political events, or, centrally, of Cicero's own career, so as to emphasize their philosophical significance and provide a basis for the application of philosophical insight; philosophy does not, however, turn history into a series of doctrinal lessons; as we shall see in the reading of texts in the chapters that follow, it provides a flexible way of drawing potential instruction from history, but instruction that tends towards plurality rather than dogmatism. At the same time, one finds a continuous unease concerning the reputation of philosophy at Rome, and a defence of the value of philosophy as Cicero practises it, in contrast to the way in which Romans perceived Greek philosophers as behaving, detached from the public world and chatting idly in corners, as he puts it in the preface to his first major philosophical project, *De re publica*.[3]

Part of this anxiety about the public role of philosophy reflects Cicero's own insecurity about the relevance of his career as an intellectual to his political career: between *De re publica* and *De divinatione* Cicero's public position changed considerably, of course; the last philosophical works, written in the shadow of Caesar or in the wake of his assassination, dramatize, with varying degrees of urgency, the conflict between a sense of powerlessness and a need for some kind of political action which rests on philosophy. But even the earlier works, written after the return from exile, display an anxiety about the exact possibility of making philosophy relevant to Roman political life. The quality of Cicero's defensiveness about philosophy certainly varies, but it is a constant theme, and one that reflects the uniqueness of Cicero's position as a *novus homo*, and as a particularly over-educated one at that. This need to prove

---

[3] *Rep.* 1. 2. 2. See Blößner (2001).

the relevance of philosophy is not made easier by adherence to an Academic outlook, but it is precisely in this interplay between a deep commitment to philosophy and a certain scepticism about its exact practical ramifications that the unique character of Cicero's philosophical work rests. This ambivalence is in play even when the main material of the work is a summary of the insights of the Greek philosophical schools (prominently *De natura deorum, Tusculan Disputations, Academica, De finibus*); again, it is only as an Academic that Cicero could achieve the distance from philosophical doctrine necessary to provide a balanced summary of conflicting philosophical views. But at the same time, the philosophical insights run the risk of becoming purely academic, in the modern sense of the word, and the whole project foundering because of an undue interest in philosophical technicalities, and the forced or ambiguous quality of the connection between philosophy and Rome. By the end of this book, the context of this discussion will have broadened, and enough material will have been presented to allow an exploration of how tensions within Cicero's view of education (the ultimate goal of all his philosophical writing) relates to its modern counterparts.

A first step in that process is to examine some of the key themes in Cicero's own approach to the problems of relating philosophy to public life. I will then look at how Cicero's philosophy, as it was read from the Renaissance until the nineteenth century, moved from acting as a clear model for a philosophically engaged form of citizenship, to becoming marginal, as different notions of education and philosophy developed. Central, however, must remain the idea that there was something intrinsic to Cicero's approach to philosophy which determined both its influence and its eventual marginalization. The marginalization can be plausibly attributed to the disparity between Cicero's political position (eclipsed by figures more powerful and ruthless) and the attempt to impose his own view of Roman political institutions and civic identity through his philosophical works. The authority to which Cicero aspired in much of his writing seems undermined by the evident failure of his ambitions for the Republic to have any effect.

Rather than treating this failure as a concrete historical fact, however, we can look at the relationship between politics and philosophy in Cicero's career as the product of a reading of his works. If we realign our reading to pay greater attention to anti-authoritarian or defensive currents, and explore why those moments have generally been eclipsed by a general sense that Cicero's philosophy is an undertaking based upon self-confidence or even self-advertisement, we can achieve a richer understanding of how those works function: they dramatize a position that contained both intrinsic tensions (philosophy both as refuge from and salvation for the *res publica*) and external ones, based on Cicero's own changing and difficult political situation. Most readers, at this point in this book, will regard with surprise the claim that Cicero's philosophy provides by far the best evidence for the ideological struggles of the late Republic, but by the end of the next chapter, the basis for making such a claim will be clearer. In particular, the conservative manner in which Cicero's approach to politics is conventionally understood can be attributed in part to a misconception about the radical quality of his philosophical project, a misconception which can be traced in certain influential currents in the modern interpretation of ancient philosophy generally; but it is a misconception that results directly from Cicero's own insecurity about whether or not his enormous intellectual labour could result in any change in the fortunes of the collapsing Republic; that insecurity is reflected in the manner in which his philosophy was written.[4]

PHILOSOPHY AS REFUGE

Throughout his career, Cicero configured his philosophical writing as a refuge from the turbulent affairs of state in which he was caught up.[5]

---

[4] The presentation of Dugan (2005) contains many of the same elements as mine, but his emphasis is quite different. Dugan sees Cicero as motivated by his insecurity as a new man (*novus homo*, but also a more contemporary conception of those words) into the rewriting of Roman culture and history so as to occlude that sense of marginalization. I argue that Cicero leaves quite visible the difficulties of covering up that marginalization, and that his philosophical and theoretical self-awareness would discourage him from mistaking his own values for those of the Republic.

[5] A detailed summary of the evidence for this theme can be found in Leeman and Pinkster (1981), i. 17–21 (hereafter Leeman–Pinkster).

At the beginning of his correspondence with Atticus, when he was setting up his new villa at Tusculum in 67 BCE, his conception of literary activity as an antidote to political activity is clear to see, and can be read, given its prominence at the start of the correspondence, as a foundational theme in the establishment of Cicero's literary persona. Indeed, in almost all of the letters which come from the short first spate from the time before Cicero was consul, the setting up of the villa and its library are mentioned. One of Atticus' functions at this stage of their relationship was to supply bits of statuary removed from Greece as suitably inspiring décor for the parts of the villa given over to Cicero's intellectual pursuits, and, above all, a library.[6] Even at this stage in the correspondence, where discussion of the political scene at Rome is more restrained and brief than it becomes later on, there is a clear demarcation between the two realms of Cicero's life, the public and the private, and between the political and the intellectual world. In *Ad Atticum* 1. 4, for example, the letter divides neatly into two, the first half dealing with matters in Rome, the second with the question of statues and books. The letter ends revealingly:

libros tuos conserva et noli desperare eos <me> meos facere posse. quod si adsequor, supero Crassum divitiis atque omnium vicos et prata contemno.

(*Ad Atticum* 1. 4. 3)

Keep your books safe and don't despair that I can make them mine. If I achieve that, I will tower over Crassus in wealth, and look down on all men's estates and fields.

Riches, *divitiae*, are so defined that the conventional measure of wealth, possession of land, is contrasted with the possession of books, so that Cicero is marking himself out as repudiating the standard system of values applicable to the establishment of a country estate. Cicero establishes a distance between his own anti-materialist view of the value of a library and the usual discourse in which public success is expressed by material wealth.[7] The life of the mind

---

[6] *Ad Att.* 1. 1. 5; 1. 3. 2; 1. 4. 3; 1. 6. 2; 1. 7; 1. 8. 2; 1. 9. 2;1. 10. 3; 1. 11. 3. The topography of the villa is alluded to in Cicero's very latest philosophical works; see *Div.* 2. 8; *Tusc. disp.* 2. 9.

[7] As Shackleton Bailey (1965) points out *ad loc.*, this is probably the proverbially rich Crassus of the third century BCE rather than the triumvir.

is almost a counter-cultural activity.[8] Likewise in *Ad Atticum* 1. 11, the pleasure which Cicero derives from the thought of owning a library is contrasted with his *odium* towards the condition of public affairs:

tu velim quae nostrae Academiae parasti quam primum mittas. mire quam illius loci non modo usus sed etiam cogitatio delectat. libros vero tuos cave cuiquam tradas; nobis eas, quem ad modum scribis, conserva. summum me eorum studium tenet, sicut odium iam ceterarum rerum; quas tu incredibile est quam brevi tempore quanto deteriores offensurus sis quam reliquisti.

(Ad Atticum 1. 11. 3)

I wish you would send as soon as possible the things you have got ready for my Academy. It's amazing how much not just the use, but even the very thought of that place delights me. But be careful you don't give your books to just anyone: keep them safe for me as you wrote you would. I am gripped by a great passion for them, just as, now, by a hatred for all other business. You will not believe how much worse you will find things than you left them in how short a time.

The contrast here between pleasure (*studium, delectat*) and loathing (*odium*) is particularly powerful, given that Cicero is speaking of the mere thought of his library, let alone its use.[9] Furthermore, we can sense here the roots of an alienation from the public world, and a

---

[8] The contradiction, of course, between the anti-materialist and the lavish surroundings of the villa is a commonplace of the late Republic; the lavish gardens from which the historian Sallust railed against the materialism which led to Rome's decline, or the extraordinary country villa of Varro, with its fishing stream flowing through the dining hall while its owner propagated the worth of the pristine morality of the simple life of early Rome are the best-known examples. Edwards (1993), 152–60. See too *Ad Att.* 4. 10, where political marginalization is coupled with literary pleasures and disdain for an elaborate cuisine.

[9] cf. *Ad Att.* 1. 7, where *delectatio* is again emphasized, once more in relation to *otium*: *Omnem spem delectationis nostrae, quam cum in otium venerimus habere volumus, in tua humanitate positam habemus* ('I have placed on your kindness all hope of that enjoyment that I want to have when I get some leisure'), or *Ad Att.* 1. 5. 2, where *voluptas*, sensual pleasure, is used to describe the purchase of statues. The sad end of this story comes in *Ad Att.* 12. 46. 1, where Cicero complains to Atticus that the problem with devotion to *litterae* as a consolation for the death of his daughter is that they cause an excess of *humanitas*, leaving no room for the insensitivity which would make grief tolerable. That Cicero overcomes sufficiently the aversion caused by memories of Tullia at Tusculum not only to return there, but to set *Tusculan Disputations* there, is a clear indication of the ultimate success of his endeavour to turn his grief into philosophical productivity.

refuge in the life of the mind, that will develop into a much fuller form later on. The development of Cicero's self-image, as one whose true emotional commitment is to intellectual pursuits, given the failings of the current political system, is already established, even before his career had really suffered serious set-back.

In another letter (*Ad Att.* 1. 10. 4) Cicero describes the library as metaphorical fruit of thrifty farming, a *subsidium senectuti*, really an old-age pension: in other words, a form of sustenance drawn upon when the main occupations of adulthood, politics and the courts in this case, are no longer possible. The metaphor once again rests upon the dichotomy between material and intellectual nourishment. These may look like clichés, but they do so only because of the foundational role that Cicero plays in the development of an idea of *humanitas*. They establish Cicero in the literary record as one whose pursuit of philosophy has its roots in a withdrawal from public life, either voluntary, for the sake of pleasure, or compulsory, as, presumably, in old age. And this image is clearly not confined to the literary world, to the production of a purely literary persona, but also had a resonance for Cicero's colleagues in the Senate and the wider political sphere. During the first triumvirate Cicero writes to Lentulus, who in the establishment of the villa had probably provided the ships which enabled Atticus to transport sculptures from Greece to Italy,[10] that his consolation for exclusion from public life will come not just from his literary activity, but also from the fact that he already has an established position in the political community which will make this kind of refuge acceptable:

me quidem etiam illa res consolatur quod ego is sum cui vel maxime concedant omnes ut vel ea defendam quae Pompeius velit vel taceam vel etiam, id quod mihi maxime libet, ad nostra me studia referam litterarum; quod profecto faciam, si mihi per eiusdem amicitiam licebit.

(*Ad familiares* 1. 8. 3)

What consoles me is the fact that my character is such that for the most part people will leave me alone either to support whatever Pompey wishes, or to be silent, or even to devote myself to my enthusiasm for literature, my favourite alternative. I shall do this at once if my friendship for him will permit it.

---

[10] *Ad Att.* 1. 5. 2, and see Shackleton Bailey (1965), *ad loc.*, and on 1. 8. 2.

Here the movement out of the political arena into literature is unambiguous. This is the most familiar structure within which philosophical activity was represented by Cicero, and it was the one to which he repeatedly returned during the years of Caesar's dictatorship, when his exclusion from public life through the closure of the courts and the silencing of the Senate was most complete, and when the compensation of philosophy became most urgent.[11] The description of three alternatives in the letter to Lentulus, however, is particularly prophetic: compliance, silence, or writing do not, however, represent any kind of logical progression. The first and second presuppose a continued participation in public life and a deadening of the political will. The resort to literature is different. It connotes liberation from constraint, an ability to extricate himself from an impossible situation, and possibly more: *litterae* provide an alternative method for Cicero to fulfil his ambitions; how that fulfilment relates to the more conventional one of political success is a question upon which, ultimately, all interpretations of Cicero's philosophy must rest.

By the time Cicero had completed most of his philosophical project, the escape into philosophy had, of course, become much more substantial, and the terms in which Cicero could combine his exclusion from politics with a productive literary endeavour were capable of more complex elaboration. Here is an extract from one of his most extensive statements of his philosophical ambitions, from the second preface to *De divinatione*, written after Caesar's assassination:

ac mihi quidem explicandae philosophiae causam adtulit casus gravis civitatis, cum in armis civilibus nec tueri meo more rem publicam nec nihil agere poteram nec, quid potius, quod quidem me dignum esset, agerem, reperiebam. dabunt igitur mihi veniam mei cives vel gratiam potius habebunt, quod, cum esset in unius potestate res publica, neque ego me abdidi neque

---

[11] Another exemplary case is *Ad fam.* 9. 2. 5, to Varro in April 46: *studia* were formerly entertainment, now they are a form of salvation. Here Cicero envisages a clear political purpose to writing works of political theory: *gnavare rem publicam et de moribus ac legibus quaerere* ('to become expert on the state to enquire into customs and laws'). There is a textual problem with the word *gnavare*: Hunt (1981), 219. On the letter, Rösch-Binde (1998), 137–41.

deserui neque afflixi neque ita gessi quasi homini aut temporibus iratus, neque porro ita aut adulatus aut admiratus fortunam sum alterius ut me meae paeniteret.   (*De divinatione* 2. 2. 6)

Indeed, it was the grave state of society that gave me the reason for expounding philosophy. During the civil war I was not able to protect the republic in my usual manner, but nor could I take no action. But I found nothing to do that was worthy of me. My fellow citizens will forgive me, or rather, they will thank me, because, when the Republic was in the control of one man, I did not hide myself away nor desert my post, nor languish; nor did I behave like one enraged by the man or by the times. What is more, I did not get so caught up in admiration or praise for another man's fortune as to be ashamed of my own.

Cicero continues with a more specific discussion of how, under Caesar's tyranny, he had explicitly regarded philosophy as a substitute for politics: *in libris enim sententiam dicebamus, contionabamur, philosophiam nobis pro rei publicae procuratione substitutam putabamus* ('it was in my books that I pronounced my senatorial opinion, and gave my speeches at public meetings; for I thought that philosophy had taken the place of managing public affairs'). Here, just as in the letters, philosophy is still a compensatory activity, making up for the impossibility of taking part in the political process, but it is not construed as a form of withdrawal, or as a form of resignation to current political circumstances. Rather, it is a place where Cicero's voice can still be heard, and where his own independence from political circumstance can be restated. Philosophy has become active resistance to the collapse of the Republic, a realm in which Cicero's opinion can be expressed.[12] Not just the expression of despair at the state of the world, but a viable way of contributing, when conventional political involvement is impossible, to the improvement of that state. Earlier in the preface, Cicero has been discussing the various virtues of his philosophical project; as well as granting Latin thought independence from Greek, it would provide a resource for a renovation of the Republic, and to a wider audience than Cicero

---

[12] Cicero's apparent statement that his full political will lies within his philosophy has inspired historians to detect hidden polemic against Caesar in the philosophical works: Strasburger (1990); Wassmann (1996). From a different perspective, Lévy (1992), 633–4, for whom scepticism itself is a form of resistance.

had expected (*De div.* 2. 2. 4–5). Although philosophy originates, therefore, in the collapse of political institutions, it is a vehicle for the same voice of reform that Cicero would expect to use were those political institutions still intact. And here, Cicero is looking back: this summary from *De divinatione* presupposes at least to some degree that the situation has changed, and that full participation in the Republic may in fact return following the death of Caesar.

However, there is a striking disjunction between the political power that Cicero claims for philosophy at this point, and the kind of philosophy which he goes on to practise in this particular work. The discussion of the nature of divination is far removed from the vision of philosophy as a force for political reform that he conjures up in this preface. With regard to divination, I shall explore the details of the dialogue in detail in Chapter 8. What is important for my argument here is the power that Cicero grants to philosophy, even when it is acting as a substitute for political activity. It is almost as if Cicero envisages philosophy as a kind of resistance, where the political arena has been transformed into one where debate has risen to the level of a philosophical discussion. At the same time, there is a very optimistic vision of what philosophy is capable of, which is hard to square with Cicero's own relegation of philosophy to being a substitute for or refuge from real political engagement. There is an almost perverse polarization of different views of philosophy here: on the one hand, the salvation of the Republic, and on the other, the last resort of the one who has given up on the Republic. If we bring the two poles together, we are left with a vision of philosophy as having an intrinsically unstable relationship to politics. It is this instability, I shall argue, that can be observed in the ambivalent, at times contradictory, representation of Rome's history within the dialogues.

There is an evolution in the ways in which philosophy and politics intersect. Constant is the idealization of the life of the mind, the idea that literary work, later on, more explicitly, philosophy, is the truest expression of Cicero's intellect. This life is at first, however, a retreat and a refuge from a political career, and in the process becomes a substitute for it. This substitute then turns, at the point, after Caesar's death, when Cicero no longer feels so certain of the extinction of the Republic, into a programme for political reform. But there is no doubt that Cicero's ambitions for his philosophy appear far-fetched, and a cynical reading will see in his claims to be able to change the course of Rome through philosophy the plea of the disappointed and marginalized figure who never possessed the necessary political acumen to succeed in the cut-throat world of late Republican politics. Nevertheless, this appearance is the result of a misunderstanding of Cicero's philosophical ambitions, and of the character of his literary project. It is also, more profoundly, a misreading of the way in which literature and politics fitted together at Rome.

It is one of the aims of this book to try to shed some light upon this misreading. The central point is this: a key component in understanding Cicero's conception of politically active philosophy is the ambiguity of his position. Philosophy never stops being seen to some degree as a substitute for politics, and the life of the mind, in spite of its potential to produce political change, is always configured as a second-order activity in comparison with the real work of the state. Cicero's vision of philosophy's potential is shadowed by his sense of a distinction between philosophy and real life; and in the following chapters, I will be exploring how that notion of real life can be related to the historical record. Although sometimes Cicero seems to use history as a reliable testing-ground for the relevance of philosophical ideas to the actual institutions and political practices of Rome, there are other points where history is used in a more rhetorical manner, to provide material that will illustrate an argument, however unreliable the factual basis for that history may itself be. Very frequently, Cicero's evocation of the real life of Rome is historical; frequent too are those moments where it is doubtful how successful the integration of philosophy with history can be. It is possible to see, in this ambiguous treatment of history in philosophy, the consequences of a deeper ambiguity, concerning the relevance of philosophy to life, of which, of course, history is in some sense the repository. Although Cicero may aspire to show that philosophy provides the answer to the ills of the Republic, he also shows us that this aspiration can only with difficulty be grounded in historical reality. This double-edged quality has its roots in the early stages of Cicero's conception of himself as a philosopher, but there are other factors which I will now discuss. Beyond that, there is the evaluation of this double-edged quality, and how far readers of Cicero's philosophy can appreciate the non-authoritarian dimension of his writings.

GRIEF, PHILOSOPHY, AND SELF-COMMEMORATION

Political marginalization is one aspect of Cicero's devotion to philosophy; the other, frequently stated but less easy to integrate into a way of reading that philosophy, is the way in which grief drove Cicero to a remarkable rate of philosophical production.[13] Cicero's attempts to compensate, in his writings, for a sense of personal loss is amenable to different kinds of interpretation. These interpretations essentially differ in the degree to which they explore the notion of 'compensation'. The argument that I would like to pursue, but which will remain, in the absence of possible corroboration or negation, rather unformed, is that Cicero undertakes his philosophy in a spirit of despair.[14] In spite of his sense of mission, and his desire to bequeath a permanent philosophical

---

[13] Steinmetz (1990*b*), *passim*, and in outline pp. 141–2, lays out the works and historical circumstances with astonishing succinctness. Fuchs (1959) is still definitive; see too Henderson (2006). Particularly revealing letters include *Ad Att.* 12. 28; 12. 38*a*; 12. 40.

[14] At *Ad Att.* 12. 40. 2 Cicero defends his writing against apparent accusations that he has succumbed to grief (after Tullia's death) and let himself go: *legere isti laeti qui me reprehendunt tam multa non possunt quam ego scripsi. quam bene, nihil ad rem; sed genus scribendi id fuit quod nemo abiecto animo facere posset* ('those happy men who upbraid me cannot read as much as I have written; how well it is written is irrelevant, but it was a kind of writing that no one of abject spirit could do'). Cf. *Ad Att.* 12. 23. 2, where proof of Cicero's resistance is his question to Atticus about the philosophical embassy of 155 BCE. Perhaps we ought to distinguish between the despair at the death of Tullia and that caused by the political situation. Equally, this defensive statement of Cicero's confidence is not enough by itself to provide a basis for a confident reading. Interestingly, an almost identical expression of doubt about the quality of his writing (*nescio quam bene* ('I don't know how well')) occurs in the letter that gives detailed information about the composition of *Academica, Ad Att.* 13. 19, where it is followed by *sed ita accurate ut nihil posset supra* ('but so accurately that nothing more could be added') (13. 19. 3). The implication is that, whatever the literary merits of the work, it is so full an account of the Academy that no one could accuse Cicero of overlooking anything. The notion of literary merit, in these two letters, is secondary in Cicero's mind to the pedagogic function of his works, providing information about their philosophical topics.

legacy to Rome, this mission is predicated upon a sense that Roman institutions were unlikely to recover from the dictatorship of Caesar and the chaos consequent on his assassination. Only by regarding *De officiis* as more important than the other texts can one possibly think of Cicero's last works as functioning as some kind of rescue attempt, as a desire to capture and preserve the values of the Republic before they were lost. Certainly, the influence of *De officiis* was far greater than that of any of his other works, and doubtless that has had an effect upon the forms of interpretation available to those reading the other works. But although *De officiis* is more accessible, there is no reason to suppose that Cicero himself thought it more important. It is possible, indeed, that it was added as an afterthought, once the big questions of his philosophical curriculum had been tackled: a kind of popularizing synthesis with an unusually clear pedagogic function and practical focus.

The compensation that studies of theology, ideas of fate, or moral ends were supposed to offer is much less apparent than a treatise that tackles head-on the problem of public duty. An education based on these other texts (such as Cicero perceives at least as a possibility) can only with difficulty be thought of as one dedicated to the preservation of a set of values; Cicero cannot seriously have comforted himself for his sense of loss with the thought that his philosophical curriculum would produce a generation of new young men who were likely to save the Republic. The evident caution with which he depicts even the slight possibility of such a salvation in the second preface to *De divinatione*, the place where he surveys his philosophical production, is a clear statement of how qualified his ambitions were. Written, like *De officiis*, after Caesar's death, *De divinatione* presents a far more ambiguous picture of philosophy's potential than that more overtly didactic work:

quod enim munus rei publicae afferre maius meliusve possumus, quam si docemus atque erudimus iuventutem, his praesertim moribus atque temporibus, quibus ita prolapsa est, ut omnium opibus refrenanda atque coercenda sit? nec vero id effici posse confido, quod ne postulandum quidem est, ut omnes adulescentes se ad haec studia convertant. pauci utinam! quorum tamen in re publica late patere poterit industria. equidem ex eis etiam fructum capio laboris mei, qui iam aetate provecti in nostris

libris adquiescunt; quorum studio legendi meum scribendi studium vehementius in dies incitatur; quos quidem plures, quam rebar, esse cognovi.

(*De divinatione* 2. 2. 4–5)

For what greater and better service can I render to the state than to teach and
educate the youth, especially in the present time of moral decline where it (i.e.
the youth) has slipped so far that it needs the help of all men to restrain and direct
it. I don't, of course, believe that it can be done, nor indeed must it be expected,
that all young men would turn themselves to these studies. If only a few would!
Their hard work could nevertheless have a wide influence in the state. Nevertheless I gather the fruit of my labour from those who, advanced in years, find
respite in my books. Their enthusiasm for reading greatly heightens each day my
desire for writing. Indeed, I know there are more of them than I used to think.

The passage is, in fact, such an ambiguous statement of the success of
Cicero's project that it is tempting to read the last sentence as
ironically exaggerated: rather than the young men whom Cicero is
really hoping to reach, he has had to content himself with an audience of old men who, like him, have taken refuge from the state in
reading. Cicero's extraordinary literary productivity has been egged
on by men whose only goal is rest, the *quies* of *adquiescent*: hardly the
reforming strength that is the ostensible aim of the philosophical
project, and which will enable it to rescue the *res publica*. Indeed, the
notion of the retired gaining comfort from philosophy conjures up
precisely the disconnected Epicurean approach to philosophy within
the state which Cicero generally so powerfully rejects. *Studium vehementius in dies incitatur* ('with each day my enthusiasm is greatly
heightened') is particularly hyperbolic, since in the context of the
present passage we know that by now most of Cicero's planned
curriculum is already complete, and the image of him continuing
to write at the present rate in the desperate hope that, amongst the
many elderly readers, a few energetic young men may be lurking, is a
ludicrous one.[15] As I shall explore further in Chapter 8, exaggerated
ideological positions are an important part of *De divinatione* as a
whole, so this extreme moment is not at all out of place. This passage,
however, is a useful corrective to the strong desire to see the more

---

[15] He evokes a similar vision of literary failure as being when people write only for
people like themselves to read, at *Tusc. disp.* 1. 3. 6.

optimistic vision of a philosophical education presented in *De officiis* as somehow definitive.

The compensation of philosophy, then, is clearly of a less direct nature than the production of a vocational training for Roman statesmen. And it is here that questions need to be asked about the mismatch between Cicero's pain and the forms of expression which he chose to relieve it. This mismatch is in essence the contradiction between what is in effect an optimistic undertaking (the creation of a comprehensive philosophical curriculum which made accessible a wide range of Greek thought in Latin for the first time, the theme to which he immediately turns in the sentence following the passage cited above) and the relaxed, even verbose quality which characterizes most of his philosophical writing. One useful clue to how to think about this comes from a letter concerning the prefaces to his treatises. In August 44 Cicero wrote to Atticus describing his journey round Italy *en route* for Greece and charging him with various financial transactions (*Ad Att.* 16. 6). At the end he apologizes for sending him, as a preface to *De gloria*, the wrong prefatory material, and explains that he has a volume containing ready-made prefaces, and had simply distributed, without realizing it, one that he had already used in the third book of *Academica*. While reading that work again during his journey, he has realized his mistake, and has sent Atticus a new preface with the instruction to cut out the old and paste in the new (*tu illud desecabis, hoc adglutinabis* (16. 6. 4)). This model of literary production gives us a strange insight into Cicero's working methods, and suggests at the very least that his depiction of himself to Atticus, as one getting up in the middle of the night and filling his time with writing to block out his pain, should not be taken as the method of one whose main thought was for the coherence or consistency of his output.[16]

---

[16] *Ad Att.* 13. 38; 13. 39 (he goes only reluctantly to Rome, so preoccupied is he with writing); 13. 45 (Atticus' suggestion that Cicero spend his days *in philosophia explicanda* ('explicating philosophy') is redundant; he is already doing that). *Ad Att.* 13. 32. 3 also refers to separately written *prohoemia* (prefaces), as does 16. 6. 4: Steinmetz (1990*b*). Cf. *Philippic* 2. 20. A number of the letters in this book refer to the large-scale rewrites to which the *Academica* was subjected: Griffin (1997). Butler (2002), 109–23, discusses much of this material.

A similar insight can be gained from an at first sight rather commonplace comment in the prologue to *Tusculan Disputations* 1, where Cicero compares the disputations, essentially philosophical improvisations on chosen themes, to the rhetorical declamations through which he gained his expertise in political and forensic rhetoric.[17] The discursive, rather rambling quality of the discussions, whatever coherence they may gain from their thematic focus, convey once more the idea that Cicero's compensation was literary composition itself, the act of writing. It is difficult, in this context, to sustain a claim that the dream of achieving the status of a guru provided Cicero with much emotional sustenance; that it was not the details of the writing, not the particular arguments that he was conveying, so much as simply having a large-scale project to distract him, and a structure within which he found some kind of purpose, however fruitlessly, to express himself.

This is the context within which we need to consider the portrait of Roman institutions, of the ideology of the late Republic, that emerges from Cicero's writing. For the works which I discuss in the following chapters it is hard to escape the conclusion that whatever Cicero's ambitions for his philosophy may have been, it was bound to act as an expression of his marginalization, as a vehicle for the frustrations of those ambitions which had provided a sense of purpose to his career, even to his life. These works are produced because writing is needed to fill a void, and because once the idea of a complete philosophical curriculum presented itself, that curriculum demanded completion. The motivation, and the frenzy of production, do not suggest that we should be looking for confident renditions of Roman ideology, putting Cicero firmly at the centre and making his achievements the norm. Most clearly, the almost impossibly ambiguous picture that emerges, in *Brutus*, of the position of orators at Rome, is an indicator of a despair both at the course of Rome's past history and at its future potential.[18] It is reasonable to see in it the reflection of Cicero's own personal sense of failure, and of the uniqueness of his own place in Rome's history; a slightly stronger

---

[17] *Tusc. disp.* 1. 4. 8. The paragraph contains further highly ambiguous matter on the relationship between rhetoric and philosophical method; see below.

[18] Steel (2002–3), 207–11, describes *Brutus* as a suicide note.

argument is that Cicero's grief manifests itself in a particularly ironic attitude to Roman institutions and history. To support this argument requires, of course, detailed readings of the texts, so further discussion must be deferred. The central question, however, is this: how consciously did Cicero produce such a negative vision of Rome? How far did his obsessive writing bring with it an unreflective desperation which produced an unwittingly frantic and at times anarchic vision of Roman institutions? *De divinatione* provides, I shall argue, an even more helpless picture of the viability of Roman tradition, and by examining that work it is possible to find at least a partial answer to the question of how aware Cicero was of the desperate quality of parts of his presentation of Rome. Compensation is not a neglected concept in the study of Cicero's last works. By outlining it in this way, rather more fully than usual, I want to test how far it can help us approach the texts in detail, to prepare the ground for those readings which will shed some light upon Cicero's vacillation between irreconcilable visions of Rome's identity, and of his own role within that city.

The ultimate form of compensation which literature grants, of course, is the immortalization of the author, a theme very familiar in ancient literature. As we shall see, Cicero's doubts about his ability to effect change at Rome find a parallel in his difficulty in putting down on paper a picture of himself as a successful statesman. Certainly, the voice of Cicero comes across consistently as of one who could provide a model for a way of acting in politics at Rome; but just as with Cicero's vacillations about the nature of Roman history and institutions, so with his self-presentation, it is hard to escape the view that he realized that he was a voice crying in the wilderness. In his depiction of the role of rhetoric at Rome, we shall find that Cicero was under no illusions about the partial grasp of power that rhetorical skill could bestow within Roman history. In his exploration of that history, he uses his stylistic expertise not, as in his speeches, to present an impenetrable front for the supremacy of his own views, but rather to sustain the possibility of the argument both for that supremacy and also for its undoing: rhetoric has the potential to steer Rome to greatness, but the opposite potential also exists. This double-sided or dialectical presentation is not the result of a deconstructive reading; it relates closely to Cicero's philosophical values: his engagement with the traditions of the Academy. The form of commemoration that Cicero chose may contain elements of a positive relationship between self-presentation and a philosophical message; but the kind of writing, the concern about any possible influence, and the anti-dogmatic impulse of the Academy make a different view of Cicero's philosophy more compelling.

THE USEFULNESS OF ACADEMIC SCEPTICISM

Cicero's preference for Academic scepticism comes across as being a matter of personal affinity, of affection for a body of literature and a group of educators, and in particular for the image of a way of doing philosophy; ultimately, it must be Cicero's enjoyment of reading Plato which lies at the root of his loyalty to the Academy, as also for his ambition to write his philosophy in a manner that, of the available models, resembles Plato most strongly.[19] Although the Academy will not, in the end, provide a conclusive answer to the extent of Cicero's self-awareness, it does provide a more detailed context and support for my image of Cicero as open-minded as to the success either of his own philosophical ambitions or of Rome's capacity to function as a well-ordered state. Academic affiliation marks Cicero out in comparison with other leading philosopher-politicians of his day, such as Cato or Brutus, whose public Stoicism was a central part of their character as politicians. This affiliation could, of course, also be said to characterize his political action: just as the Academic philosophical position was recognizable through a disdain for a dogmatic position, so the classical historical account sees Cicero as a political vacillator.[20]

---

[19] Poncelet (1957); Zoll (1962); Puelma (1980); Lévy (1992).

[20] The beginning of the damnation of Cicero for political vacillation was the ground-breaking biographical encyclopaedia of Wilhelm Drumann (published between 1833 and 1844), whose notoriously critical volume on Cicero had a great influence on Theodor Mommsen, who in turn forbade any alteration to that article in the revisions of the encyclopaedia when undertaken in the early twentieth century (1899–1929). See the introduction to the 2nd edn., Drumann (1929), pp. viii–xi; Fuhrmann (2000); Yavetz (2001) contains a neat summary of the issues. For the wider ideological context, Girardet (1983), 227–31.

Nevertheless, Cicero's choice of philosophical approach is an important aspect of his writings and, since the philosophy of the late Academy remains something of a specialist interest, I shall describe it in a little more detail here.

The most detailed evidence for the state of the Academy during the period while Cicero was writing comes, of course, from Cicero's own writings, and most explicitly from the *Academica*, where he sketches the history of the Academic philosophical traditions, and from *De finibus*, where Cicero applies Academic principles to the Epicurean and Stoic ethical systems.[21] The history of this philosophical school was not, in Cicero's representation, a harmonious one; nor was it marked by a consistent approach even to the basic questions of philosophy. Cicero's response to this diversity was, as scholars now generally agree, to pick and choose between different aspects of Academic thought, which reflected his experience of various teachers. Throughout his exposition of the Academic position, it is clear that Cicero is not simply reproducing the thought of just one teacher; rather, he is working to develop his own brand of philosophical discourse, in which the merits of many different philosophical positions, including those of different representatives of the Academic tradition, are compared, and in which the reader is, in the process, constantly being presented with conflicting arguments.[22] As he expressed it, rather flippantly, in a letter to Atticus concerning the composition of the *Academica*: *o Academiam volaticam et sui similem. modo hunc modo illuc* (*Ad Att.* 13. 25. 3) ('O the Academy, inconstant and like itself: now going in one direction, now another').[23]

---

[21] On Cicero and the Academy, most accessible and comprehensive is Brittain (2001), which, although dedicated to examining Cicero's teacher Philo, paints a full picture of the Academy in Cicero's time, analysing in great detail Cicero's own evidence for it. Weische (1961) is still useful. Glucker (1978) contains much of specialist interest, but pp. 31–90 and 98–120 provide a manageable narrative. See too Barnes (1989); Görler (1990*b*).

[22] There are a number of important contributions on Cicero's eclecticism: Glucker (1978); Görler (1974) now conveniently synthesized by Leonhart (1999), 76–88; Nickau (1999).

[23] In his 1825 translation of the Atticus correspondence, William Heberden (1825), *ad loc.* puts in a footnote to this sentence hinting at a connection between Cicero's Academic affiliations and a general disposition to vacillation. Interestingly, in 1825, this flexibility did not demand editorial disapprobation.

One of the most revealing statements concerning the influence of the Academy on Cicero's own methodology can be found in the prologue to *De natura deorum*, where he explicitly discusses the question of philosophical dogma, and how best to pass on philosophical knowledge.[24] The passage strikes right to the heart of the Academic legacy (one of suspending judgement), and also to the problematic quality of Cicero's own approach.

> qui autem requirunt quid quaque de re ipsi sentiamus, curiosius id faciunt quam necesse est; non enim tam auctoritatis in disputando quam rationis momenta querenda sunt.   (*De natura deorum* 1. 5. 10)

> Those who want to know what I myself think on any particular question are being more curious than is necessary; for it is not the weight of authority so much as that of reason that should be looked for in an argument.

The contrast here is between *ratio* (reason) and *auctoritas* (authority): on the one hand, a remarkable profession of faith in the absolute power of reason to convince through argument, and on the other, a sense that the authority of the speaker ought to play no role in that process. The contrast explored above between philosophy and 'real life' can be observed here in a different form, perhaps rather better resolved. Cicero was ambivalent about the potential of philosophy to change the state, and seems to waver between optimism and a pessimism based upon the apparent disjunction between politics and the world of ideas. But here, in a purely philosophical context, he is resolute: only argument counts, authority does not.[25] Of course, such a presentation raises immediately the question of the relationship between the argumentative skills of philosophy and those of rhetoric, a relationship discussed in more detail below, and one that is clearly crucial to Cicero's definition of himself as a figure of (non-)authority at Rome.[26] Of course, the main point of these words is that they warn us not to expect Cicero's philosophy to contain a clear statement of his views, a warning which scholars still find it hard to take seriously;

---

[24] See also above, p. 4.

[25] In the very different context of *De officiis*, a more dogmatic work, he establishes at the start a special structure based on his own *auctoritas* and the juniority of his son (*quod et aetati tuae esset aptissimum et auctoritati meae* (*De off.* 1. 4)).

[26] Michel (1960) offers an exhaustive treatment.

but to justify ignoring it would require remarkable special pleading for a kind of double irony in this passage, to which there is no need to resort.[27]

The prologue continues by giving the context for the historical development of this non-authoritarian form of philosophy, one that, nevertheless, depends upon a series of authority figures.

non enim hominum interitu sententiae quoque occidunt, sed lucem auctoris fortasse desiderant; ut haec in philosophia ratio contra omnia disserendi nullamque rem aperte iudicandi profecta a Socrate, repetita ab Arcesila, confirmata a Carneade usque ad nostram viguit aetatem; quam nunc prope modum orbam esse in ipsa Graecia intellego. quod non Academiae vitio sed tarditate hominum arbitror contigisse.

(*De natura deorum* 1. 5. 11)

When men die, their opinions do not perish with them, though perhaps they do shed the light of their author. This is the case for that method in philosophy of arguing against every position, and of making no positive judgement on any matter. Originated by Socrates, revived by Arcesilaus, and reinforced by Carneades, it has flourished right down to our own period. In Greece itself, I understand, it has now been more or less abandoned. That can be explained, I think, not in the failure of the Academy, but in the slowness of mankind.

The argument is not perhaps quite what it first appears, and I am not convinced that Cicero's logic here is particularly tight. He sets up the ideal philosophical activity as something that deliberately goes against the notion of the authority of the philosopher; and none of the figures he mentions in this genealogy of the Academy undertook the step that Cicero himself is now taking, of committing their

---

[27] Steinmetz (1989) is the clearest statement of this view of Cicero. Although he cites the devotionally sceptic opening of the very early *De inventione* 2, Steinmetz represents two distinct philosophical phases: the works of the 50s, in which Cicero was not a sceptic, but was writing to put across his own views on rhetoric, law, and the constitution, and those of the 40s, where he returned to his original home. There is no evidence to support this interpretation outside the dialogues themselves, of course, so Steinmetz's evidence is his sense that Scipio and Crassus are just mouthpieces. It is the resistance of modern readers, rather than a particularly objective reading of Cicero's works, that make it seem likely in the first place that he would adopt a dogmatic approach. For a more plausible view of the difference between the two periods, see Classen (1989), 186: Cicero's public would not be ready for more detailed doctrinal discussion.

philosophy to writing.[28] What, however, in this presentation, is the role of the *sententiae* (opinions) of individuals? They can evidently live on, and here we are dealing again with the notion of posthumous compensation with which Cicero was clearly preoccupied. The crucial stage in the argument comes with the word *ut*, which introduces the comparison with the method of the Academy. The Academy is proof of Cicero's contention of the potential of *sententiae* to remain immortal, but how does the Academy's dialectical method preserve those very *sententiae*? It is certainly not, it would seem, by allowing opinions to become concretized into philosophical doctrine: all that these philosophers leave as their legacy is a sceptical process of argumentation, the demise of which Cicero clearly regrets. Some kind of tradition has been established, a tradition which depends only to a certain degree upon the figure whose opinions it can also convey. But by undertaking to write down his philosophy, Cicero is taking a step in the immortalization of his opinions that is precisely the opposite of the non-authoritarian technique that he finds so attractive in the Academy.

There is an unsolved tension here between a desire for the preservation of an individual's opinions and a recognition of an appealing purity in the non-doctrinal processes of philosophy. This tension is, in fact, exactly the same tension which made up the debate about how to continue the legacy of Socrates/Plato which dominated the Academy.[29] I shall argue in the following chapters that Cicero, as it were in response to this contradiction, goes out of his way to prevent himself emerging through his philosophy as a figure of authority. Clearly there is wide variation between different works, but particularly in discussing the relationship between ideas, institutions, and history at Rome, Cicero's approach, in spite of some moments where he clearly does take a stand, is to allow arguments to do the work, and to insist, as he suggests here, that the philosophical synthesis should

---

[28] I am grateful to the audience of a paper read at the Project Theophrastus conference in Leeds in 2003 for helping me clarify this passage. Throughout the opening of *De natura deorum* Cicero is in any case preoccupied with philosophical genealogies: Runia (1989), 29–33. The listing of variant doctrines (citing their written accounts) with which the dialogue proper begins is clearly in some kind of imaginative contrast to this depiction of philosophy as an emphatically oral activity.

[29] Annas (1992).

take place in the mind of the reader, rather than as a clear reflection of the opinion of the author. This is not to say that those who wanted to could not detect Cicero's views; as I have suggested, Cicero is clearly aiming in some degree to leave his mark. But that is not the manner in which the philosophy is presented; and if read in that manner, much of the sophistication of Cicero's philosophizing is lost.[30]

So it remains to be seen how far Cicero's adoption of a sceptical tendency within the Academic tradition could possibly serve the political ambitions he held out for his writings.[31] Surely a more dogmatic philosophical style would have suited his polemic more forcefully, and enabled his philosophy to emerge with a clearer voice as the work of a campaigner and reformer, one whose thinking could actually achieve the kind of changes to the political climate that his second preface in *De divinatione* suggest he was aiming at. The problem with dogmatic philosophical posturing, as practised by Cato and Brutus, however, was, by the time Cicero was writing *De divinatione,* fairly obvious. It did not produce politicians who were capable of surviving in the real political conditions of Rome, in spite of Cicero's clear ambitions for Brutus. It was, as Cicero makes clear in his letters, far too far removed from the Roman context, essentially too foreign, to be capable of the integration necessary to obtain anything like a consensus of political ideas. These are the terms in which the whole of Cicero's translation of

---

[30] At *De leg.* 1.13.39, uniquely, Cicero explicitly wishes that the Academy, with its disturbing approach to dogma, would shut up: *pertubatricam ... Academiam exoremus ut sileat.* See Weische (1961), 80–1. Unlike Weische, I do not regard this remarkable moment as a culmination of a method that generally characterizes the works of the 50s, but rather as a demonstration of how careful Cicero is to avoid dogmatism: he is making a pointed exception here, rather than stating his guiding methodological principle, and the remark comes not in isolation, but at the end of a passage where he has been attempting to smooth over the controversies *within* the Academy.

[31] Wilkerson (1988) gives a lucid account of how, focusing on the figure of Carneades, but resting heavily on Cicero, scepticism could be expressed in effective political rhetoric, something to which, at first sight, more dogmatic philosophical positions would be better suited. Lévy concludes his immense work with the suggestion that, in his refutation of dogmatism, Cicero was in effect resisting Caesar: 'Lorsqu'il cherche à réduire le *dissensus* des philosophes, c'est aussi la brisure de sa cité qu'il veut effacer. Lorsqu'il oppose le consensus à la fausse clarté d'une vérité individuelle, il réfute César tout autant que Zénon ou Épicure' (Lévy (1992), 634).

Greek philosophical discourse into Latin must be seen: as the attempt to negotiate a position for philosophy that would make it function in a Roman context. It is possible that Cicero saw, in his own brand of sceptical thinking, the right blend of moral even-handedness with indigenous Roman tradition that would enable philosophy actually to take root at Rome, in a way which the highly recognizable philosophical stance of Cato or Brutus would not. Furthermore, Cicero suggests that philosophical dogmatism itself could give philosophy a bad reputation, and that strong adherence to a dogmatic philosophical school was in some respects antithetical to the political texture of Rome. One of the constant impulses, therefore, in Cicero's philosophical writing is the exploration of Roman history and political institutions in terms of their potential to reveal the insights of Greek philosophy.

The rewriting of Rome as a philosophically coherent society is Cicero's attempt both to reform Rome and to demonstrate the necessity of philosophy. Rather than try to purvey a particular doctrine, Cicero applies a philosophical reading to Rome itself, putting philosophy into action by interpreting familiar material so as to make apparent its philosophical dimensions, and casting Rome as a city in which philosophy appears not as a foreign import which will appeal only to those with a particular interest in Greek culture, but as something with a more organic relationship with native Roman institutions.[32] In the chapters that follow, I shall examine, through close reading of a number of these works, exactly how Cicero brings about this re-characterization of Rome. In particular, I shall be analysing Cicero's representation of Roman history, which, in line with the philosophical programme I have just described, is reworked in such a way as to make Rome look like a philosophically fertile culture, and to produce a picture of Rome in which philosophical understanding can be seen to have a role to play. Because of Cicero's defensiveness about philosophy, and his preference for the Academic

---

[32] Griffin and Atkins (1991) spell this out with great lucidity, in the context of the unusually dogmatic *De officiis*. Lefèvre's analysis of that work's relationship to its model (Panaetius' *peri tou kathēkontos*) points out that even where following one Greek model quite closely, and even where that model was in fact written largely for a Roman readership, Cicero stresses the idea of philosophy as lived experience rather than as theory, and effectively produces a new kind of discourse. Summary: Lefèvre (2001), 189–216.

philosophical tradition, however, this reworking of history has a particularly complex quality: it needs to be able to sustain the weight of Cicero's philosophical project, but at the same time to look like a plausible reconstruction of Roman history and culture. By undertaking a detailed reading of the dialogues, it is possible to see exactly how Cicero manages to keep these at times contradictory impulses at work. The result, it will be seen, is an imaginative encounter with Rome's history and institutions which reveals a great deal about Cicero's understanding of Rome's past, and also about the manner in which that past can be rendered by writing.

PHILOSOPHY AND RHETORIC

A further, more deliberate strand in Cicero's thought, which lies behind much of his philosophical writing, is the consistent quest, visible in a number of the discussions about the kind of philosophy that he is aiming to establish at Rome, to harmonize his work as an orator with his work as a philosopher.[33] In this quest Cicero had a number of different role models, and a rhetorical approach to philosophical argument can be grafted on to the approaches to philosophy available to Cicero; he appeals both to the Peripatetic (i.e. Aristotelian) tradition and to the Academic tradition at different points for the notion that arguing on both sides of a question is an essential part not only of his philosophical method, but also of his rhetorical training.[34] The most well-known passage is that in

[33] On the Academic background to this harmonization, see Reinhardt (2000), with a full account of the scholarly controversies. *Part. orat.* 139 is another useful passage, equating the Academic approach to questions with that of the divisions necessary to construct a good speech.

[34] Fuchs (1959) stresses the centrality of dialectic as one of the orator's main skills, as well as providing a powerful account, with lengthy source citations, of philosophy's role in Cicero's struggle with mortality. On dialectic and rhetoric, Varwig (1991) is dense but stimulating. See too Granatelli (1990), 166–72; Nickau (1999), 22–6; Gaines (2002). As Granatelli points out, sometimes Cicero distinguishes between Academic and Peripatetic, sometimes he does not. Steinmetz (1990*b*), 146, suggests that Cicero began his late philosophical *œuvre* with little thought of its completion: the *Paradoxa stoicorum* is characteristic; with its rhetorical, rather than dialectical, manner of tackling philosophical problems.

Tusculan Disputations (mentioned above) in which Cicero explicitly designates philosophy as a kind of declamation, an evolution from the rhetorical exercises of his youth in a more adult guise.

hanc enim perfectam philosophiam semper iudicavi, quae de maximis quaestionibus copiose posset ornateque dicere; in quam exercitationem ita nos studiose [operam] dedimus, ut iam etiam scholas Graecorum more habere auderemus. ut nuper tuum post discessum in Tusculano cum essent complures mecum familiares, temptavi, quid in eo genere possem. ut enim antea declamitabam causas, quod nemo me diutius fecit, sic haec mihi nunc senilis est declamatio. ponere iubebam, de quo quis audire vellet; ad id aut sedens aut ambulans disputabam. itaque dierum quinque scholas, ut Graeci appellant, in totidem libros contuli. fiebat autem ita ut, cum is qui audire vellet dixisset, quid sibi videretur, tum ego contra dicerem. haec est enim, ut scis, vetus et Socratica ratio contra alterius opinionem disserendi. nam ita facillime, quid veri simillimum esset, inveniri posse Socrates arbitrabatur. sed quo commodius disputationes nostrae explicentur, sic eas exponam, quasi agatur res, non quasi narretur.   (*Tusculan Disputations* 1. 4. 7–8)

For I have always judged as perfect the philosophy which can speak about the most important questions with fluency and elegance. I have devoted myself so enthusiastically to practising it, that now I even dare to hold lectures (*scholae*) in the style of the Greeks. Recently in Tusculum after your departure, when several of my friends were there, I made a trial of what I was capable of in that kind of discourse. For just as before I used to do legal declamations (and no one did them for longer than I), so this is now the declamation of my old age. I would order them to ask what each of them wanted to hear; I argued about that topic, either sitting or walking around. And so I have composed five *scholae* (as the Greeks call them), in as many books. It happened in the following manner: when he who had said he wanted to hear about a topic had given his view, I then argued against it. For that is, as you know, the old Socratic method of arguing against another's opinion. Socrates thought that that was the easiest route to finding what was closest to the truth. But so that my disputations can be read more conveniently, I shall put them down not as if describing them, but as if the event is actually occurring.

This passage sheds a surprising light upon the whole philosophical project. It is methodologically unsound to extrapolate too far from what is clearly an explanation of the method of presentation adopted in this one work, and in particular from the persona of the rambling orator-turned-philosopher which Cicero produces for himself here to the rather different personae which he adopts in other works.[35] Nevertheless, this image of philosophical disputation as an extension of rhetoric is a strongly suggestive moment: it is hard to know how far this attempt to present philosophy as a thoroughly non-technical matter, and as simply the application of a well-organized argumentative capacity, would have struck Cicero's readers as a rather perverse over-identification of the orator with the philosopher.[36] Certainly, it is highly doubtful whether anyone would recognize the relationship between Cicero's practice here and the form of Socratic dialectic conveyed in Plato's dialogues. From another perspective, perhaps we should interpret the explicit identification of the two arenas as an indication of the individuality of Cicero's position, as a mark of how far his place as a pioneer of Roman philosophy could enable him to extrapolate from his own identity to understand the identity of these disciplines. Certainly Cicero could assimilate rhetoric with philosophy in a number of different ways, either more technical (arguing for similarities in the structure of arguments) or, as here, in a more general manner.[37] In his historical accounts of rhetoric, that generality becomes very broad indeed, and suggests that in the Roman context, the question of technical expertise may have been of rather limited relevance. The Academic background, however, undoubtedly provided Cicero with scope for exploring the boundaries between the different disciplines and, indeed, for looking outside them in his attempts to find a resonance for both philosophy and rhetoric within the fabric of Roman history.

Philosophy is a refuge from public life, as a response to grief, and at the same time undertaken with a tenacious allegiance, at least

---

[35] Henderson (2006), 192–203, esp. 192–3.

[36] Rubinelli (2002) argues that the assimilation of rhetoric and philosophy can already be traced back to Cicero's earliest treatise, *De inventione*. See Brittain (2001), 328–42, on Philo's version of this synthesis. He interprets this same passage as deliberate self-mockery, expressive of Cicero's anxiety at this disciplinary proximity (p. 338). But mockery relies on reading *senilis* as having the negative associations of the English word 'senile'; the close parallel of *De senectute* 11. 38, where Cato describes his historical labours in similar terms, makes clear that the word lacks automatic overtones of decrepitude.

[37] Michel (1960), 158–234, and Görler (1974) provide detailed readings examining the argumentative structures in their balance between rhetorical and philosophical.

in methodological utterances, to the sceptical Academy; a frantic spate of writing undertaken as a compensatory activity, and a further methodological attempt to assimilate philosophy to the more discursive forms of argument acquired through rhetoric. I shall argue in the case-studies that follow that all of these conditions produce an encounter with Roman institutions through philosophy that is inherently unstable and which does not allow the author to be easily identified either with individual arguments or with images of himself as a speaking character. Those studies will focus specifically upon the role played by history, since it is in history that, at least in some dialogues, Cicero looks to an external reality for some form of anchorage for the instabilities of his position. The integration of philosophy and rhetoric has its counterpart in a discourse about the place of rhetoric at Rome, and this is a question that Cicero treats historically, in both *De oratore* and *Brutus*. The anxiety about the relationship between philosophy and public life is tackled head-on in *De re publica*, the prologue to which is a direct discussion of this theme. In *De divinatione*, that same debate becomes both more specific (in its limitation to the matter of divination as an emblem of ritual continuity at Rome) and also subject to more extreme scepticism. In all these works, however, history plays an ambiguous role, and I shall end by arguing that precisely in its ambiguity, it is the perfect arena for Cicero's philosophy to express itself most fully: as dialogic, and as flirting with a scepticism about both historical knowledge, and the potential of philosophy to solve Rome's problems. But before those readings can be effectively undertaken, it is necessary to explore the reasons why such a procedure is so unusual as a reading of Cicero, and what the reasons are for a more dogmatic image of his philosophical endeavours, as far as his own aspirations to ideological authority through his theoretical works are concerned. Why Cicero's philosophy has been regarded, in spite of these conflicting impulses, as an essentially stable and confident body of work can be explained if we look at the traditions of reading through which our own understanding of those works has been shaped. These traditions go back to before the evolution of the modern academic disciplines, but they are also ones which particular trends in those disciplines have reinforced. To unthink them requires an understanding of them, and in the chapter that follows, I hope to provide a different way of thinking about the reception of Cicero. Reception can be a dynamic process of self-discovery, and I hope that it will facilitate a less authoritarian way of reading Cicero, one that responds to the concerns expressed in his own descriptions of his philosophical activity.

3

Reading and Reception

The picture I presented in the previous chapter is one which makes a close connection between the instability of Cicero's public career and the ambivalence of his philosophical endeavours. My concern in this book is to ascertain how far these instabilities can be observed when examining historical representation in the philosophical dialogues. The peculiar dynamics of Cicero's work with history are a neglected resource for the understanding of how history functioned at Rome, but their neglect is part of a wider process of interpreting Cicero's philosophy as essentially dogmatic. To see history in Cicero as something more than an inflexible tool to reinforce his own authority, one needs first to find a way to approach Cicero that looks beyond the simple paradigm that it was the aim of philosophy to provide authority. I hope I have shown convincingly, in the previous chapter, that Cicero's philosophical project is built upon ambivalence: ambivalence about the relationship between philosophy and life, about the relationship between rhetoric and philosophy, and the ambivalence which was integral to an Academic way of approaching philosophical questions. In examining particular works in the following chapters, I shall tackle in the proper context the more detailed question about how changes in circumstance between the works of the 50s (*De oratore, De re publica, De legibus*) and the late philosophical works can be judged to have affected the confidence of Cicero's ambitions for those works. In this chapter, however, I shall pursue a particular principle of interpretation: to understand what Cicero was thinking of when he represented Rome's past as he did, we need to divest ourselves as far as possible of those habits of reading which see literary interpretation and philosophical investigation as different activities, and try to recapture something of the spirit of the philosophical schools in which Cicero was immersed. Such a self-conscious procedure is necessary because of scholarly traditions which have influenced our understanding of Cicero, and which still act as an impediment to readings which are sensitive to the richness of his technique.

A good example is the passage from *Tusculan Disputations* I discussed in the previous chapter, in which Cicero appears to equate a relaxed form of declamation on a philosophical theme with philosophy itself. Many readers would, I suspect, be much less cautious than I have been in interpreting the voice of Cicero at this point as a clear statement of his desire to assimilate rhetoric to philosophy. The evident incoherence of the thought, and its inapplicability to much of his other writings, would be a sign not of the contingent quality of most of the positions which the voice of Cicero adopts in his works, but rather of a fundamental lack of coherence in his position. Such a reading rests, however, upon our own difficulty in accepting the manner in which Cicero uses representation, particularly self-representation, to allow a range of different possibilities to be explored; this range extends to a considerable variety in types of dialogue, from the most improvisatory (as represented in *Tusculan Disputations*) to the more tightly argued (e.g. *De natura deorum, De finibus*). Our own critical traditions are rather different from those in which Cicero was working. But they are not arbitrary; they follow dominant trends in the development of the academic disciplines of Classics and Philosophy and, although I do not think it is possible to speak of a standard reading of Cicero's philosophy, the readings that I will be putting forward in this book will appear unorthodox because they are not concerned to uncover any fixed philosophical position. On the contrary, they start from the assumption that Cicero is more interested in the suggestive quality of philosophical discourse than in getting his readers to accept his own views. Without spending unnecessary effort trying to establish exactly what is the consensus concerning Cicero's philosophy, therefore, I shall now sketch out some of the dominant currents which militate against the kind of reading that I am proposing.[1]

---

[1] For surveys of Cicero's reputation as a philosopher see Morford (2002), 95; and earlier, Douglas (1964); Powell (1995); MacKendrick (1989), 258–93.

VICARIOUS PLATO

The reading of Cicero's philosophy as philosophy in its own right, rather than as a guide to those Greek sources on which Cicero drew, has not accounted, at least in recent years, for a large proportion even of the scholarship on Cicero.[2] But the trends in reading Plato's philosophy, which is easier to survey, can serve as a model for the way in which Cicero's work is understood.[3] Plato was, of course, Cicero's most important philosophical role model, as well as one of his favourite authors and, although their work is hardly similar, different ways of interpreting the legacy of Plato were a central part of what distinguished various branches of the Academy. When writing his own philosophy, therefore, Cicero was situating himself firmly within a particular tradition of interpreting Plato, essentially one in which Plato's works re-enacted the aporetic quality of Socrates' own method of conversation. This aporetic quality, however, is one that has been largely suppressed by the academic study of Plato's philosophy, both in antiquity and during the evolution of the modern academic disciplines in which ancient philosophy has been interpreted. Two facts—first, that Socrates wrote nothing, and second, that Plato wrote dialogues—have bequeathed to readers of Plato an extraordinarily rich variety of possible perspectives for interpreting Plato's texts. But by far the most important impulse in reading Plato has been the desire to compensate precisely for the aporetic quality which the sceptical Academy, including Cicero, so valued.[4] Instead of sustaining what the sceptics saw as the guiding principle of Plato's writing, that the search for certainty or even knowledge was futile,

---

[2] As recently as 2001 it was credible for Lefèvre to begin his analysis of *De officiis* with effectively the same polemic that motivated Görler's quietly revolutionary work a generation earlier (Görler 1974): Cicero's philosophy has been treated as a source for the lost Hellenistic philosophers, not as original philosophy in its own right (Lefèvre (2001), 7–14). This polemic is by now so widespread in the scholarship, that it is not necessary for me to add to it; indeed, Leonhardt (1999), 9, declares it no longer relevant. Moreover, I am uncomfortable with the attempt to assess Cicero's 'originality', as if originality were something that could be proved. I have decided to focus more directly, therefore, on the traditions of reading which made his philosophy *seem* second-hand for most of the nineteenth and twentieth centuries.

[3] See Klagge and Smith (1992).   [4] Annas (1992).

and that the purpose of philosophical work was to explore the potential of arguments and, using a number of different techniques, many of Plato's readers over the centuries have been dedicated to revealing what Plato thought about a number of different issues. The concretization, which Cicero himself describes, of philosophy into different schools was the result of this turning away from the polyvalent approach to philosophy in which Plato's dialogues were, almost certainly, originally conceived.[5] As soon as philosophy became something that needed to be taught, the authority of the text became the central issue, and Plato's, in spite of his own reasonably clear misgivings about the nature of written authority, came ultimately to play the role of authoritative texts.[6]

The sophisticated awareness of the processes of philosophical dialogue which is now more common in reading Plato is much harder to find when we come to Cicero: the different significance of the two figures in the history of philosophy, has, I would argue, enabled the more innovative aspects of Plato scholarship to pass Cicero by, preserving a more technical approach to Cicero's philosophy, while allowing the conceptual framework for reading which was common to Plato for most of the twentieth century to persist. The habits of reading which more recent scholars of Plato have adopted, in order to move beyond more dogmatic traditions, have not been extended to produce more sensitive approaches to the dialogic aspects of Cicero's works. The central issue here is that of the polyphonic quality of the dialogues, and the attempt to translate that polyphony into clear philosophical messages.[7] There are different ways to account for

---

[5] Cicero lets Varro describe this development at *Acad.* 1. 4. 16–17. For detailed accounts of the controversies over scepticism at the time of Cicero, see Görler (1990*b*); Lévy (1992); Brittain (2001).

[6] The evidence for when this development occurred in the Academy, and how consistently it held sway there is complex and inconclusive; see Glucker (1978); Barnes (1989); Brittain (2001), 169–219.

[7] Those messages were, for Plato, often focused on the figure of Socrates: Kahn (1998), 3, gives a bleak assessment: 'In current English language scholarship on Plato, the belief still prevails that the philosophy of Socrates is somehow truthfully represented in Plato's entire writings'; see too pp. 88–90. New trends in reading Plato are represented e.g. by Rutherford (1995) and Blondell (2002), and anti-dogmatist approaches can be found as far back as the early publications of Gadamer (e.g. Gadamer (1934)). A breakthrough in English-speaking scholarship was Stokes (1986). The parallel between Plato and Cicero is not, of course, exact, there being no single Socrates figure which Cicero could be said to mediate.

the fact that this polyphony has been treated as a formal distraction from the real business of philosophy: the two most important must be the emphasis upon the analysis of philosophical topics rather than 'literary' readings of the dialogue, which is a hallmark of the way in which philosophy has largely functioned in the English-speaking academy (and beyond); and the fact that Cicero contains exceptionally important evidence for all philosophy after Aristotle, and thus plays a central role in conveying earlier writers' doctrines. Looking for them, of course, tends to lead to the neglect of Cicero's own interests, although, as I have said, in some of his late dialogues, reliable mediation of those doctrines was his main concern.

So in searching for the reasons why Cicero's philosophy is generally treated as less dialogically sophisticated than Plato's, we can look for some understanding in the traditions of reading Plato. Glucker has argued, on the basis of an extensive survey of English Plato scholarship from the start of the nineteenth century, that there were, by the end of that century, two competing approaches to Plato's dialogues: one (the dominant one, enshrined in the commentaries of Jowett) where Plato was regarded as a dogmatist, and his dialogues were read as elaborately encoded forms of philosophical doctrine, and the other (represented in the readings of Grote and others) in which Plato was seen as vacillating between idealism and scepticism.[8] The dominance of the dogmatist reading was the product not of a historically sensitive approach to Plato, but much more of a desire to integrate him into modern philosophical discourse, to make his teachings the foundations of an analytical philosophical tradition.[9] It has taken the best part of a century to make good the neglect, however, of the sceptical and idealistic traditions of reading Plato, and Glucker himself paints a rather dismal picture of the tenacious consequences of the eclipse of the demanding approach to reading Plato to which a better preservation of the sceptical methods of the Middle Academy might have led. Although the study of Plato is now looking at its own history to engage in a confrontation with, and partial liberation from these traditions, the same move has yet to occur with Cicero.

---

[8] Glucker (1996), building on Glucker (1987). Taylor (2002) tells a similar story. For the methodological implications of moving beyond this paradigm, see Gill (1996), as well as items cited above (n. 7).

[9] Stalkever (1992) gives a concise summary.

Cicero, of course, has never been regarded as a philosopher of the same importance as Plato, and there are too few who care enough about his methods to be able to generalize with any certainty about trends in reading his philosophy.[10] What is clear, however, is that the mind-set which approached Plato from the perspective of philosophical doctrine was not going to adopt a different approach to Cicero: hence the dominance of the vision of Cicero as a compiler of Hellenistic doctrines, whose literary methods do nothing more than garnish those doctrines to make them digestible for a public otherwise poorly catered for, those Romans who preferred their philosophy in Latin rather than Greek. If Plato himself was seen as the excessively modest disciple of Socrates, mediating his guru's beliefs in a manner designed to bring his readers to the true path, whose philosophy would have been a lot clearer if it had not been couched in elaborately woven dialogues in historical settings, this is all the more true for Cicero, who had no qualms about referring explicitly to his debt to various philosophical schools, and to his ambitions as a translator and mediator, and for whom, in some works, the process of compilation is so obvious (*De finibus, Academica*, or *De natura deorum*, for example). Of course, the ancient Platonists are as much to blame here as modern analytical philosophers. There is no doubt that it was easier, and more in tune with the times, to market Plato in the Roman world as a covertly doctrinal philosopher rather than as one whose main philosophical contribution is predicated upon the endless deferral of meaning. It is likewise clear that the transition from a sceptical to a more revelatory Academy was a turn which still cast a shadow over Cicero's own philosophical project, even if it had occurred some time earlier.[11]

---

[10] The range of approaches in Powell (1995) is indicative. Essays by Long (1995) and P. R. Smith (1995) discuss in particular how Cicero's rhetorical philosophy coincides with his relationship to the Academy (Smith) and to Plato and Aristotle (Long). Smith, however, is a good example of how modern preconceptions of how philosophy should be done can seriously distort Cicero.

[11] Essentially it was in the conflict between Antiochus of Ascalon and Philo of Larissa that the problem about scepticism and its relationship to the Platonic heritage came to a head, a conflict for which Cicero provides most of the somewhat intractable evidence: Glucker (1978), 27–39; Barnes (1989); Runia (1989), 32; Görler (1990*b*); Hankinson (1995), 116–20 and 137; Brittain (2001), *passim*. For a useful review article on the recent resurgence of interest in the sceptical tradition, see

It is easy to see, in such a context, how the philosophical contribution of Cicero would be seen to reside in the mediation of doctrines, and how the settings and structures of his dialogues would come to be regarded merely as window-dressing, different even from Plato, in that for Cicero there is not even the pretence that the dialogue form itself acts as a model of instruction in philosophical dialectic. It seems far-fetched to claim that Cicero intended the argumentative structures of his dialogues to be seen as models of philosophical method, particularly since for the most part those structures are often manifestly undisciplined.[12] Suggestive of a way of doing culture at Rome they may be, but this is a different discourse, separate from the philosophical ambitions of the dialogues.[13] In Cicero, in other words, the literary and the philosophical are treated, with some justification, as different activities, and the dialogic elements in the dialogues do little more than add a Roman flavour to the otherwise rather foreign quality of the philosophical arguments themselves. However, it is precisely this 'Roman flavour' which marks out the main difference between Plato and Cicero, and which demands a closer look at our traditions of reading. It is in the historical quality of this flavour, in the desire to integrate a dialogic approach to philosophy within a concrete Roman context, with a clear sense of not just philosophical but also political history, that Cicero was outlining a role for himself that was different from Plato's. One of the most revealing moments, where Cicero targets this very issue most clearly, is in the work which constituted his closest encounter with Plato, *De re publica*, also arguably his most audacious attempt to explore the potential of his own philosophical

Cavaillé (1998). The baldest argument for Cicero as a covert dogmatist is presented in the introductory reference work Johansen (1991), 490, where Cicero's earlier dialogues are designated as Aristotelian rather than Platonic, and the aim of the representation of different positions is to arrive at the right one—a deliberate eschewal, therefore, of the scepticism that Cicero at various points expresses. By contrast, Long (2003), 197–203, argues that Cicero's appeals to scepticism should not be over-stressed, while still allowing for a rich dialogic interpretation of his works.

[12] Görler (1974) and Leonhardt (1999) both do a good job of extrapolating method, but their readings have a certain artificially scholastic quality and do not seem to me to reflect what we know about Cicero's methods of composition.

[13] Such is the conclusion of Dyck's discussion of Cicero as a dramaturge: A. R. Dyck (1998).

agenda to provide something applicable to Rome. The work will be treated more fully in the next chapter, but as a test case in the integration of a Platonic approach to dialogue in the context of Roman history, I will look briefly at one key passage.

In *De re publica* 2, interrupting their discussion of the history of early Rome, the speakers pause to consider what it is that they (or rather Scipio, the main speaker) have achieved: a successful transition from a discussion of the ideal state based upon constitutional theory to one based on Rome's history.[14] Scipio's interlocutor Laelius remarks with delight that, unlike the Platonic Socrates, Scipio has not invented a theoretical state to explore his constitutional theory, but rather has bestowed philosophical insight upon Romulus, giving a theoretical explanation to decisions that he in reality made solely on the basis of accident or necessity. By suddenly having characters make an open comparison between themselves as speakers and the figures of Plato and Socrates, Cicero is providing his readers with a sense of ironic distance from the arguments of the dialogue. He is also undercutting the entire drift of the argument thus far: the argument that history and theory can be effectively interwoven. History has been used to guarantee the applicability of theoretical insights, and to make them directly relevant to the foundation of the city. The praise that Laelius grants Scipio is that, rather than remaining on the level of theory, as Socrates does in Plato, he uses history to support his argument. But at the same time, Laelius reveals the fact that this history had to be distorted in the process, and what happened by accident made to look as though it happened by design; and who is doing this distorting? Is it Cicero, who would in fact be the parallel to Plato, or is it Scipio, who ought to be the equivalent not of Plato, but of Socrates? So while, on the one hand, Cicero is substantiating a claim to utility, he is also exposing the fictional quality of his dialogue structure to an extent that goes beyond any of Plato's ironic moments. This is an emblematic passage for Cicero's entire philosophical output, since it establishes the

---

[14] *Rep.* 2. 11. 21–2. See Michel (1965); Büchner (1984), 188–91; Christes (1989), 39–43; Frede (1989); R. Müller (1989), 107–8; Fox (1996), 23–5. See also below, pp. 91–2 and 99–100. I am indebted to Niall Livingstone for drawing my attention to Plato's *Timaeus* in this context.

struggle between theory and practice as one between Plato and Cicero, between a way of doing philosophy that is historically grounded and one that is fundamentally idealistic.[15] At the same time, it shows us Cicero drawing his readers' attention to the processes underlying the production of a philosophical dialogue; in an open-ended manner, to be sure, but nevertheless one that will cause them to question the status of the arguments with which they are being presented.

The implication is that history has, as is obvious, an independent existence outside the fictional world of this dialogue, and that appeals to the authority of history within such dialogues are worthy of particular scrutiny. As we shall see in the chapters that follow, this is a point which Cicero makes over and over again. But because such historical references are a characteristic feature of Cicero's writing, they have been a particular casualty of the persistence of dogmatic readings of Platonic philosophy. In particular, the theoretical trends which persist in interpretations of Plato cannot really deal with the affront to the notion of universal transcendence that the use of history to support an argument brings with it.[16] To readers looking for what Cicero thinks about the Roman constitution, or about Roman history, moments such as this interchange between Laelius and Scipio are simply irritating irrelevances or, at best, moments of playfulness where Cicero nods, rather emptily, in the direction of the Academy. We need to readjust our perspective, to give greater priority to these moments, if we are to grasp more successfully how this very particular feature of Cicero's philosophy relates to his wider philosophical ambitions. Essentially Cicero develops, I will argue, a particularly Academic approach to the use of history to provide a foundation for philosophy. But in order to appreciate that better, we need to realize why it is that such a procedure for interpreting

---

[15] R. Müller (1989).

[16] As R. Müller (1989), 111, brilliantly puts it, 'Funktionalisiert man Theorie in der Weise, daß man sie der Faktizität des Bestehenden unterordnet, sie zu dessen Rechtfertigung einsetzt, dann büßt sie ihre kritische, den Status quo transzendierende Funktion ein'. ('If you functionalize theory by subordinating it to the factuality of what exists, and use it to justify that, then it loses that critical function by which it transcends the *status quo*'). This process is foreign to Plato, probably originating in Dicaearchus.

the dialogues comes across as unnecessarily elaborate. An inertia that keeps readers looking for Cicero's views, and which can be seen in part as the result of a dogmatic approach to Plato, does not provide a fertile basis for exploring moments where the dialectic between history and philosophy comes to the foreground.

This argument gains force if we pay a little more attention to the Platonic text upon which Cicero is drawing when he makes this glaring appeal to the superiority of a Roman historicizing philosophy over a purely theoretical Greek one: Plato's *Timaeus*. Cicero translated this work himself, although the only evidence for the date is internal to that text; at all events, he knew it intimately, and was aware of the manner in which even a mediation of it through translation would require modifications for a readership that had experience of later philosophical traditions.[17] At the start of *Timaeus* Socrates gives, in dialogue with the figure of Timaeus, an extreme condensation of the discussion of the ideal state in *Republic*, then expresses the wish that he could see the ideal state not just as a fixed image, like a painting, but like an actual body in motion, demonstrating its qualities by its interaction with other real states in war. Socrates' other interlocutors, Critias and Hermocrates, then promise to provide exactly that, and Critias appeals to an oral tradition of prehistoric stories, told to Solon on a visit to Egypt, and handed down to his grandfather. Cicero borrows this technique at the end of the prologue to *De re publica*, introducing the figure of Rutilius Rufus, who had supposedly related the dialogues of Scipio to Cicero and his brother when they were young men.[18] Plato is diligent in pointing out that the story/history which Critias tells (of Atlantis) never made it into the written record, since Solon was too busy with affairs of state to continue writing poetry, even though in Critias' own mind, the words he heard from his grandfather are imprinted indelibly in his memory.[19] So in spite of the speakers' desire for some

---

[17] See Lévy (2003), who puts it late, between *De natura deorum* and *De divinatione*.

[18] See below, pp. 88–9.

[19] *Tim.* 26c. Osborne (1996) gives a detailed account of the different kinds of authority within discourse at work in the dialogue. K. Morgan (1998) relates the work that the Atlantis myth does to a fourth-century mythologizing of history. She highlights the difference between Plato's thorough anti-historicism and Isocrates' interest in relating historical foundation myths to the present. K. Morgan (1998), 108.

kind of historical grounding for the theories of *Republic*, this grounding never occurs in a convincing form, the myth of Atlantis being a colossal red-herring in terms of a reliable basis in fact for the theoretical state of *Republic*.

Cicero is clearly drawing on Plato; as well as the direct comparison between Scipio and Socrates, the most obvious signal is the somewhat ironic glee with which Laelius greets the coincidence of theory and practice in Scipio's discourse.[20] But the differences are as relevant as the similarities: Plato's speakers appeal to a kind of historical tradition, but that tradition, as well as being non-literary, is also explicitly prehistoric: Solon's informant is an Egyptian priest who carefully describes the processes whereby the historical record at Athens has been repeatedly destroyed (although preserved in Egypt). Further, in spite of the assurance of Critias that the Atlantis story sprang to his mind during the conversations of *Republic*, as proof of those arguments (*Tim.* 25e–26a), the myth itself, narrated only briefly, has no perceptible bearing upon the conversations of *Republic*. Instead, the work takes an entirely different turn, as Timaeus produces an extensive elaboration upon a metaphysical system which can claim myth as its authority (*Tim.* 26e4), and which is excessive in its quest for a form of transcendent knowledge of a universal, mystical kind. By varying these ideas and, in particular, by imposing clarity upon a picture that in Plato is almost bafflingly elaborate in its setting up of different kinds authority for different kinds of philosophical insight, Cicero's appeal to Roman history is a signal of a certain degree of simplification: on one level, we know what history in *De re publica* is for: it provides empirical proof of the theoretical discussion of constitutions by grounding them in Rome's history. Scipio has done what Plato's Socrates has not managed and, in addition, unlike those Sophists whom Socrates disparages as rootless earlier on in *Timaeus*, he has restricted his argument to one state.[21] However, by recollecting the much more problematic arrangement of these ideas in the *Timaeus*, and by pointing out how artificial Scipio's appeal to history is, and how fundamentally

---

[20] A close echo of the manner in which the ancient story of Atlantis meets Socrates' demands for a concrete basis: K. Morgan (1998), 101–2.

[21] *Tim.* 19e; cf. *Rep.* 2. 22: *non vaganti oratione, sed defixa in una re publica*.

non-historical, Cicero is also inviting his readers to be wary of ironic undercurrents and, in particular, to be watchful for different sources of authority and different kinds of philosophical ambition.

The quest for transcendent philosophical truths, of which *Timaeus* is the most extreme case, is not much in evidence in Cicero's own philosophy; but in the contrast between the superficial appeal to history and the busy intertextual signalling of this double allusion to Plato (superficially *Republic,* less obviously, *Timaeus*), Cicero is drawing attention to the central struggle of this work, and of later ones: the struggle between history as a form of verification and philosophy as a form of thinking that aims to find a way beyond history to more universal truths. Such an interpretation is only possible, of course, if one approaches Cicero from an Academic perspective, and is likewise sensitive to the manner of reading Plato as itself a deliberation on competing discourses, rather than as a quest to find the master among all discourses which will embody the ultimate philosophical truths.

Few readers would press the ironies of this passage as far as I have done, but once the Platonic intertext has been taken into account, the issues with which Cicero is grappling become clearer, as does the complexity of the genuine attempt to bring in history as a form of philosophical validation. But this is a good example of where the appearance of an excessive pursuit of irony that might seem suited to Plato looks extreme in the context of Cicero. It is clear, however, that by engaging more directly with history, Cicero is, at the same time as challenging Plato, also borrowing something of his irony about the possibility of anchoring transcendence in a factual account. Interpretation of this kind goes against current trends in reading Cicero, even recent work which adopts a more literary approach to questions of authority. The studies of Krostenko and Dugan, for example, represent an innovative and dynamic approach to the reading of the treatises as literature.[22] But in both of these books, which build on earlier work on Cicero's rhetoric, Cicero's literary efforts are seen as directed towards producing a clear picture of his own values for posterity; the overlap between rhetoric and

[22] Krostenko (2001); Dugan (2005). See too Fantham's critique of Habinek (1998): Fantham (2004), 327.

philosophy becomes the clue to interpreting his treatises: like his speeches, they are working to put across a convincing and assured picture, in which, by virtue of persuasive language, Cicero's power is made to work within a social arena of which Cicero, in spite of his marginal social origins, had become the master. There are clearly virtues to this approach, but for me, the process of reading upon which it rests severely neglects the Academic context, and assumes that Cicero wrote his philosophy with the same self-assurance with which he undertook his forensic or political speeches. This is not a question that can be proved either way; but the occlusion of sceptical modes of reading seems to me to have nurtured the evaluation of the philosophical works as a positive form of self-advertisement, rather than as a collective call to self-scrutiny and scepticism, both about Cicero's own position and more widely, and about central aspects of Rome's political identity. The moment when Cicero effectively ruptures the fictional coherence of *De re publica* and reveals the problems of attempting to integrate a transcendent form of theoretical enquiry into a Roman context is a helpful reminder that, more generally, it is the aim of Academic philosophers to keep their readers thinking, rather than looking for an authoritative explanation of their authors' views.

Recognition of the power of the dogmatist reading is essential if we are to get beyond the notion that Cicero is using his philosophy to convey positive doctrines or to persuade his readers of the integrity of his own position. The pervasiveness of this approach cannot be stressed too much. If we are to come close to Cicero, we need to be clear that his view of the function of philosophical writing was different from the one with which we are familiar from modern philosophical traditions, and that, rather than thinking of dogma as the principal goal for the interpretation of philosophy, we need to subordinate this impulse. In reading these works, we should not be thinking 'What does Cicero think about the gods/virtue/ethics/politics?' or 'What does Cicero want us to think about them?', but rather we should be reading the words of his speakers as a dramatization of a philosophical quest. This should be the dominant mode of reading Cicero; that there are works, most obviously *De officiis*, in which Cicero does adopt a more dogmatic strategy, should not encourage us to think of the dogmatic current as the norm and to dismiss dialogic ambiguity as mere window-dressing. Even that work

adopts a style of discussion which is not so different from its predecessors, certainly not from *Tusculan Disputations*, a work that makes
a great deal more sense if interpreted as an experiment in a different
kind of declamatory oratory, rather than as a transparently autobiographical work in which the narrator can be treated as synonymous
with the first-person speaker of the different disputations. The traditions of dogmatic interpretation are strong, and they had already
taken root in Cicero's own time. They were not, however, exclusive,
and Cicero's practice is varied. We need to be aware, however, of our
own tendency in reading these works to underestimate the role of the
dialogue in removing certainty. Philosophical dialogue should be
understood not as encoded theory, but as an exploratory, sometimes
inspirational, meditation on the possibilities of philosophical
enquiry.[23] The Rome which emerges from such work is not a particularly positive place: it is certainly not the city of orators in which
Cicero is king, and in which the aim of the educational project is
to convince readers of the unproblematic supremacy of the world of
letters and of Cicero's mastery of that world.

FOUNDATIONS OF CICERO RECEPTION

The emergence of a dogmatic reading of Cicero's philosophy is itself
the result of a long evolution in ways of doing philosophy, and of
expectations of a philosophical text. These trends are perhaps related
more closely to the evolution of philosophy as an academic discipline than to an evolution in readings of Cicero. If, however, it
is legitimate to isolate as our central theme a general decrease in
sensitivity to the complexity of Cicero's philosophy, or a sense that

---

[23] Recently scholars (not writing in English) have gone much further in establishing a rigorous method behind Cicero's use of the dialogue form: Leonhardt (1999)
and Blößner (2001). Lévy (1992) brings Cicero's Academic scepticism once again
centre-stage (cf. Schmitt (1972)), but has had little impact so far. Brittain (2001)
demonstrates not only how deeply ingrained the sceptical approach to philosophy
was, but also the intense engagement with which the role of scepticism was debated.
Brittain's work makes clear how little room there is for a dogmatic approach to
Cicero, given his immersion in this tradition.

Cicero is by and large aiming to produce philosophical doctrine, rather than to encourage his readers to a process of inconclusive philosophical reflection, then it is possible to point to an almost causal connection with the way in which Cicero has in general been read in modern times.[24]

There is a large scholarly literature on the reception of Cicero, much of it concerned with the moments when individual scholars or thinkers adopted a distinct view of Cicero's role in their own attempt to reform their own disciplines.[25] It is Cicero as a founding authority, but also often as the instigator of a dramatic change, that provides a unifying theme to this history. It is difficult to generalize about a topic that is by its nature so diffuse, particularly since Cicero has been so widely read for so many centuries; so my aim here is simply to draw out some themes that shed light on the problems of interpretation that I have already described. The reception of Cicero is rather different from the reception of other Latin authors, for the simple reason that he was, from as early as Classical authors were read in post-Classical Europe, the principal source for the teaching of Latin as a language. He is, as a result, unusually closely integrated into the pedagogical processes in which all students of the Classical world are trained. His main educational function was to provide a model for Latin style, and the reading of his works, which emerged in

---

[24] I would sound a note of caution here: the idea that reception is a process governed by determinism and causality is tempting. It is difficult to resist suggesting, when writing about traditions of reading, that earlier readings have given rise to later ones in a manner that suggests an unbroken tradition, causally determined. All we can actually hope to do is to shed light upon some of the roots of our own preconceptions, and I hope the following survey does that.

[25] Charles Lohr's online bibliography, last consulted in July 2006, contains more than 200 items published before 1996, few of which are in English. The introduction to the website misleadingly suggests that the bibliography is concerned only with Cicero reception up until 1650; but this is not the case: www.theol.uni-freiburg.de/forsch/lohr/lohr-ch1.htm#cice The standard survey (which is partial in focus) is Zielinski (1912). Chevalier (1984) is a good example of the general trend: miscellaneous studies of the fate of Cicero at particular moments in different parts of Europe. Töchterle (1978) focuses on *De re publica*, but draws out the main currents in Cicero's role in education. Classen (2003) represents a new apex in the study of Cicero's speeches in the Renaissance. Cicero's role in rhetorical training in the sixteenth and seventeenth centuries is sketched by Freedman (1986). For orientation, Kennedy (2002), and on the fate of rhetoric more generally, Kennedy (1999), with chapters on the Middle Ages, the Renaissance, and Neoclassical rhetoric.

increasing numbers during the Renaissance, was determined to a large extent by their usefulness as tools for training in good Latin style and in constructing well-ordered argument, much more than for their content.[26] Rhetoric was one of the central areas of university curricula in the Middle Ages and, although this was before the circulation of more of his works from the fifteenth century onwards, Cicero was represented by *De inventione*, *Topica*, and *Ad Herennium*, at that time, thought to be by Cicero. With the rediscovery of more texts in the Renaissance, as well as with the expansion of humanism and the consequent broadening of educational perspective, Cicero became integral to the acquisition of a refined form of Latin, and became the cornerstone for the idea of a literary classicism, against the apparently more degenerate vernacular forms of Latin.[27] It is not an exaggeration to say that the entire notion of an educated literary discourse depended not just on writing like Cicero, but on thinking like him too.[28] Although the early church fathers and the gospels were also read for imitation, and Petrarch and others advocated a form of stylistic eclecticism, nevertheless, by far the most dominant figure in this discourse was Cicero, whose style continued to grow in popularity until attacked by Erasmus and his successors in the sixteenth century.[29] Their attack, however, did not really amount to more than an attempt to diversify Latin; Cicero's supremacy was barely touched.[30] There were always controversies about style, and it would be inaccurate to say that the Italian humanists and their successors were actually aspiring to sound like Cicero. All the same, he played a unique role, as a model of citizenship, as a political

---

[26] The survival of Cicero manuscripts is discussed in Reynolds (1986), 54–142. On the widely circulated *De amicitia*, Powell (1998).

[27] Grenler (2002), 236–48.

[28] Witt (2002), 24: 'Years of training oneself to filter ideas through a Ciceronian linguistic grid would ultimately affect how the humanists' [*sic*] thought and felt.'

[29] Murphy (1974), 106–23; Witt (2002), 344–5. On the distribution and publication of Cicero as printing arrived, see Murphy (2005), 521–30 (or pp. 256–65; there are two forms of pagination in this volume of reprints); 'Cicero' as a concept divorced from any actual reading of his work: p. 527.

[30] Streckenbach (1979) gives a detailed analysis of how Ciceronian Latin dominated language teaching material in fifteenth- and sixteenth-century Germany. See also Ockel (1991), 366–7; on Erasmus and followers, Croll (1969); Margolin (1990, 1991).

individual from antiquity, as a provider of a repertoire of technical materials (rhetorical, logical, and stylistic), and as the speaker of a profoundly impressive periodic form of Latin.[31]

Apart from the virtues of his style *per se*, there were other contextual reasons why Cicero was so successful in infiltrating both the classroom and the lecture-hall. Philosophical dialogues, in particular, made good language-teaching texts, since their dialogue structure simulates the language of conversation. Imitation of the speakers in *De amicitia*, *De officiis*, or *Tusculan Disputations* produced, it would seem, a discourse in which Ciceronian concepts could continue to be discussed, very much in the manner in which Cicero himself had envisaged; and crucially, the dialogic model would make Cicero's free play with different philosophical positions seem natural; no one educated in this method would easily fall into the trap of regarding one particular character as 'Cicero's mouthpiece'.[32] We need to remember that it was probably several centuries before the standardization of the vernaculars granted them the ease with abstract discussion that Cicero achieved in Latin. The training in Ciceronian Latin should not, therefore, be seen as an artificial or pretentious education aiming at producing an elitist discourse which could have been carried on with far greater inclusiveness had it been done in students' native languages; and as the reading of works other than the rhetorical textbooks began, Cicero himself began to emerge more clearly as a figure whose ideas, as well as his style, began to offer the possibility of acquiring real knowledge of Rome, as well as of Latin. Certainly, some time during the eighteenth century, linguistic politics shifted, and Latin, tainted by association with an ecclesiastical scholasticism, and resistant to the growth of nationalism, lost ground, and with it, the tradition of rhetorical education began to fragment.[33] But certainly during those many centuries in which Cicero was the uncontested king of the classroom, students were

---

[31] Witt (2002), 450–4.

[32] Mack (1984). The 'mouthpiece' metaphor is discussed in more detail in Chs. 4 and 7.

[33] Fuhrmann (1983), 17–19, 23; Ockel (1991), 368–70. It was *c.* 1800 that the first texts with commentaries were published, largely with the aim of assisting language study, and later on in that century that the commentaries shifted from Latin to the vernacular: A. R. Dyck (2002), 320.

trained by reading Cicero's work to speak like Cicero, and to recognize in his style the standard model for all educated discourse.

As such, he became a figure of unparalleled cultural authority—so much so that he must be thought of as a special case in the history of textual reception. The most exceptional aspect of Cicero's place is that his reception did not depend in any significant way upon the reading of his own writings, at least not in the sense that we would understand it. In spite of this systemic neglect of the content of his writing, it is clear that as a philosopher, the dialogic quality of Cicero's works was appreciated. Learning by imitation seems, at least in some educational systems, to have made heavy use of certain works: *Tusculan Disputations* and *De officiis* were particularly popular, texts which would be useful models more for declamation than for conversation; but others with a more dialogic quality were also read widely, most importantly *De natura deorum*, which gained popularity as its sceptical religious views became interesting, while *Academica* was instrumental, at least from the mid-sixteenth century, in the development of a thread of radical scepticism that culminated in the Pyrrhonists of the Enlightenment.[34] There are clear signs from early on that in writing their own philosophical dialogues in imitation of the Ciceronian models, writers had no difficulty in adopting the open-ended style which is characteristic of most of Cicero's works. The cultural authority of their model did not become transmuted into a sense of philosophical dogmatism until well into the nineteenth century, when, of course, philosophy itself had much more elevated aspirations to be able to achieve objective dogmatic results.[35] I have restricted this brief survey to examining the interface between the effects of Cicero's stylistic supremacy and the form of reading that Cicero's role as an educational resource is likely to have instilled. This must be regarded as the bedrock of Cicero reception: the fact that Cicero was used as a tool for generating more of a language that in part resembled his, in using his own works and the forms of his sentences, clauses, and arguments to provide a structure and models for a way of handling abstract ideas, and for learning how to talk about ethics and religion, as well as about language and style. Upon that bedrock, of course, there is a more

---

[34] Popkin (2003), 28–35.   [35] Schmitt (1972); Michel (1984); Ordine (1990).

specific image of Cicero as a republican, as a figure whose literary legacy provides a model for resistance to tyranny. This figure did good service at moments of constitutional tension in both England and France.[36] That ideological authority, however, was predicated upon a much more fundamental sense of Cicero's cultural authority, which, in its origins, was grounded in linguistic practice, and upon the universal study of Cicero as the principal mediator of the Roman world.

By the time of the Enlightenment, Cicero's reputation was, to say the least, controversial. The incipient mistrust of rhetoric made great strides in the eighteenth century, and this led to a demise in the appeal of Cicero's philosophical writings. His success as a working orator seems to have tainted his readers' ability to consider him seriously as a philosopher; the dominance of his speeches in the schoolroom was beginning to have the opposite effect from that intended once the distinction between rhetoric and philosophy, and the shift of philosophy into something like a distinct 'profession', became more firmly established.[37] Cicero's position here must have been particularly strange, since, on the one hand, the growth of professional philosophy brought with it a disdain for the pedantry of scholasticism; and on the other, philosophy was supposed to be relevant to life. This fitted well with Cicero's own intentions; but in practice, his inevitable association with the schoolroom and with Latin itself seems to have done little to ensure the perpetuation of his actual works. The development of the idea of a scientific form of

---

[36] Skinner (2002), 9–12; Bell (1994), 135, 171. Interestingly, Cicero's republicanism was an active disadvantage to his reputation as a model advocate in France (Bell (1994), 48–9, 198), an ambivalent reputation that deteriorated after the Revolution, when rhetoric was formally banned as a branch of education, precipitating the more concrete barriers between disciplines. Cicero only returned to the French political scene later in the nineteenth century under the influence of Anglo-American traditions of parliamentary debate: Douay and Sermain (2002). For the American version of a similar vacillation between authority and republicanism, Rahe (1994).

[37] Fuhrmann (1989, 2000); Bezzola (1993) traces in detail the demise in the reputation of rhetoric in the face of philosophy; van der Zande (1995), whose analysis of the popular philosophers who were the predecessors of Kant, demonstrates clearly the importance of Cicero as a model for a way of doing philosophy. For the sketch of an alternative version of the status of rhetoric in the eighteenth century, see J. Dyck (1991). His thesis, that rhetorical impulses were transmuted into the aesthetic philosophies of Romanticism, is interesting, but does not suggest continuity in rhetoric as a recognizable discipline.

philosophy, of course, constitutes a serious rupture in the survival of Cicero as a model for philosophy: this is expressed most clearly in the attitude of Hegel, for whom Cicero was almost an emblem of a kind of lazy, popularizing philosophy, which had nothing in common with the scientific philosophy which he himself was conducting.[38] Cicero is the explicit model for what Hegel calls *Populärphilosophie*, and became associated with a group of eighteenth-century philosophers from whom Hegel repeatedly distinguished himself.[39] Hegel was following a less-well-developed stance visible in Kant, who had already condemned philosophy in the Ciceronian mode as a branch of literature rather than philosophy, who had resolutely stifled the Isocratean and Ciceronian ideal of philosophical rhetoric, and whose ideas about rhetoric and style precluded him from taking much interest in Cicero.[40]

The eighteenth century is generally seen as the decisive era in which contact with Classical texts began to change. In Chapter 10, I shall devote some space to the discussion of one particularly useful

---

[38] Hegel's view of Cicero was not uniformly negative; he compared *De officiis* favourably to Confucius' teachings on the same subject (Hegel (1969–71), xviii., 114); he could also appeal to him as an authority figure, as when citing *Tusc. disp.* 1. 2 to rebut his critics in the preface to the 3rd edn. of his *Encyclopaedia* (ibid. xviii., 32). However, he took a particularly dim view of Cicero's relationship to the Greek tradition, accusing him (in his *Vorlesungen über die Geschichte der Philosophie*) of lacking a proper understanding of the relationship of philosophy to history (ibid. xviii., 34, 190); of mistaking his own confusion for Heraclitus' (p. 322); of reducing Socratic philosophy to a form of domestic debate (Haus- und Küchenphilosophie!), (pp. 445–6). Of course his greatest assault on Cicero's reputation came from the fact that he regarded the only ancient philosophers worthy of the name as Greek. He explicitly argued that Cicero's beautiful Latin style made real philosophical enquiry impossible, and that the attempt to do philosophy in the Middle Ages in that language resulted in the disastrous failure represented by the scholastic philosophers, whose Latin was unreadable (pp. 19, 541).

[39] *Populärphilosophie* is defined at Hegel (1969–71), xx., 263–7 (i.e. in *Vorlesungen über die Geschichte der Philosophie*); but the term had already been pinned on Cicero several times earlier in the same work (most emblematically in a section on Renaissance philosophers headed 'Ciceronianische Populärphilosophie' (pp. 20, 16–17)); see too ibid. xviii. 114; xix. 153.

[40] Bezzola (1993), 37–45; van der Zande (1995). Interestingly, Kant (who rarely mentions Cicero) could take a more positive view of popular philosophy, on one occasion making Cicero, Horace, Vergil, Hume, and Shaftesbury models for a kind of knowledge gained by profound acquaintance with the world, from which entry into real philosophy can be gained (Kant (1910–), ix., 47–8). On Kant's notorious anti-rhetoricism, see Vickers (1988), 201–4.

moment in the mediation of Cicero in this period, John Toland's prospectus for an edition of Cicero's complete works. Toland's essay demonstrates clearly the dynamics of authority, relating both to Cicero and to the notion of professional criticism, which can, at least by contrast, show up some of the characteristics of more dogmatic visions of Cicero which were to characterize his reception more recently. Toland is particularly useful because his treatment of Cicero reveals a particular approach to reading: one based upon a fundamental respect for Cicero's cultural authority, but one that is also alive to his methodological scepticism. In terms of the reception of Cicero, this constellation was unusual, both before Toland and after, since, as I have suggested, Cicero's cultural authority, being so fundamental a part of the educational curriculum, tended to make him into a figure who seemed in fact to be seeking that authority. Toland tackles this subject directly, ascribing to the authoritarian practices of the schoolroom a deeply engrained misunderstanding of Cicero as resembling the pedants and schoolteachers responsible for perpetuating his legacy.

An awareness of these different traditions, of the rise of dogmatic readings of Plato, of the danger, which had a long history, of Cicero's cultural authority becoming transformed into a vision of him as a dull, pedantic figure from the schoolroom, a workaday barrister, or a political vacillator is essential preparation for a reading of the dialogues which focuses directly upon their failure to provide authoritative positions, and their skill at destabilizing the easy identification of the utterances of the characters with the opinions of the author. It seems a reasonable hypothesis that as long as Cicero remained a model for stylistic imitation, and in particular while his dialogues were actually used as examples of conversational Latin, the dialogic quality of his works was readily accessible; students in any case were unlikely to be interested in the works in their entirety, and the kind of reading which imitation involves can be thought of as a kind of spoken dialogue, an encounter with the text that is oral and generative, rather than written and fixed. The aspirations of philosophy to become a more scientific discipline, and the parallel demise of rhetoric as a fundamental part of education, are clearly a watershed, but one that we can at least attempt to reach once we are aware of the potential problems that it causes. In the chapters that follow, I shall

argue that the path that Cicero himself marks out between philosophy and rhetoric, and their function within Rome, is a complex one
that demands close reading of the texts. It is complex not because it
involves a particularly rigorous form of argumentative structure or
philosophical method, but rather because it expresses in imaginative
form the difficulties presented by the reconciliation of those two
aspects of his life. The reconciliation of rhetoric with philosophy
shows Cicero struggling to overcome the contradictions of his public
career and his notion of a permanent legacy. Against this background, the focus of the readings that follow will be history, and on
how far representations of history can be made to support abstract
ideas or provide a foundation for a sense of identity. This identity is
that both of Cicero himself, but also of the city and people of Rome,
and we will observe how Cicero uses history to dramatize his ambivalence about theory, about the ability of Rome to foster the
organized forms of thinking which are necessary for the success of
both rhetoric and philosophy, and about his own success in using
those same theoretical discourses as the basis for his political career.
In these introductory chapters, I have shown both how far back in
Cicero's thought such ambivalence lies, and also how the traditions
of reading him have made it more difficult for us to appreciate it.
With that in mind, it is possible to turn to the study of individual
texts, and to focus upon how Cicero makes history reveal this same
ambivalence.

　　This approach rests upon breaking down the conventional scholarly
categories in which Cicero is normally analysed. There is no place for
the pervasive distinction between literature and philosophy, or even for
the distinction between historiographical and literary interests. That is
not to say that Cicero did not recognize such generic distinctions: it
is quite clear that he did, and that he conceived his periodic contemplation of historical work as being different from the philosophical
tradition to which he ultimately devoted himself.[41] However, the distinctions that Cicero makes between genres should not be conflated
with modern habits of interpreting those genres. The context of
Cicero's philosophy means that what we easily think of as literary
interests or philosophical interests are in fact inseparable; to undertake

---

[41]　See Fleck (1993) with synthesis of earlier scholarship.

an investigation of Cicero's philosophical position requires some of the techniques of reading normally associated with texts more conventionally seen as literary. Because of Cicero's place within the Academic tradition, and in particular because of his established fondness for Plato, it is the effect of the work as a whole which will produce Cicero's philosophical message, rather than necessarily any of the specific doctrines discussed within the work by any of the speakers. So an understanding of the philosophy requires an exploration of the formal qualities of the work as much as of the detailed analysis of the arguments.

CONCLUDING AND INTRODUCING

As suggested above, it is the purpose of these chapters to draw attention to the problems of approaching Cicero's philosophy, to dislodge some preconceptions about the character of his writing, and to provide preparation for the claims that will be made on the basis of the readings that follow. In summing up this process, therefore, I shall present, perhaps prematurely, some of the results of those readings. It is clear that beneath the comfortable and complacent quality of Cicero's writing, there is an urgency about the philosophical project that this complacency can conceal. The processes of dialogue, and the Academic method of leaving the reader to decide upon his own interpretation of philosophical difficulties, foster a suspension of judgement. Dialogues embodied in a philosophically informed group of elder statesmen contain an element of idealization that anchors the philosophy to particular moments in Rome's history (or in the present day); but such idealizations introduce an ironic quality to the use of history, as well as deriving the power of their idealization from it. These contrary impulses do not harmonize easily, and express the tension inherent in Cicero's position: he is committed to using philosophy to change the flavour of political culture at Rome, but in order to do so needs continuously to insist that such a political culture has already always existed. This is the reason why the philosophical dialogues are such an important place to look for Cicero's vision of Roman history. The Academic position allows for such a contradiction, but, as I shall explore in the following chapter, it is a contradiction that does not in practice produce an unequivocal political or moral programme which is easily graspable, or through which Rome can readily be transformed into a state organized along more philosophically inspired principles.

Cicero wanted his philosophy to be of practical use, but his own experience of the Roman political world exposed this desire as something that could always appear too idealistic. His gradual political marginalization has made his philosophy look like an attempt to provide an order for Rome's political culture which it in fact never possessed; but the obverse of this argument is the one adopted recently by some scholars who see precisely in Cicero's growing scepticism a resistance to the dogmatic and authoritarian style by means of which Caesar was able to sustain his dictatorship.[42] Either Cicero was attempting to provide a philosophical system for Rome which would make the chaos of actual Roman practice look like something that was amenable to reason, or his Academic leanings made his philosophy into a form of critique of Roman institutions, a critique which reflected his disappointment at his own failure to influence the course of events, and his sense of the impossibility of being able to make his own talents coincide with those valued by his peers. Neither of these possibilities, it seems to me, rules out the other; but, more problematically, it is difficult to find proof in either direction. Whether we read Cicero's scepticism as an attack on Caesar (veiled to us, presumably more obvious to his first readers), or whether it was a sign of his resignation at the impossibility of, virtually single-handedly, turning Rome into a culture where philosophical or theoretical work could be made to have an effect upon the course of the *res publica*, our answers will always be dependent upon how we read the philosophical works themselves. For this reason, an awareness of the traditions of reception in which we ourselves look at Cicero's philosophy is particularly pertinent. In the studies of individual works that follow, I argue that by focusing upon history in Cicero's dialogues we can come closer to a sense at least of what was at stake for Cicero in the representation of Rome as *a philosophically viable city.*

---

[42] So Strasburger (1990); Lévy (1992); and Krostenko (2001), 380–9.

The dialogic quality in Cicero's writing is something which has not been well preserved in the scholarly traditions via which Cicero has been transmitted down to the present day; but this has coalesced with other factors, essentially assessments of Cicero's political significance and (not unrelated) of his function in education. The dominant tradition in Anglo-Saxon scholarship is of Cicero as a conservative thinker; the German historical tradition sees him as politically incompetent, a hypocrite, and ultimately a poor judge of the institutions that he so copiously aimed to represent.[43] Recent studies from the USA, on the other hand, have resolved the tensions inherent in Cicero's project by asserting that rhetoric is power, and that Cicero's ambition is to ensure that he himself emerges from the theoretical texts as the ultimate wielder of that power. The studies of individual dialogues will make clear that, once Cicero's Academic training is understood as a hermeneutic tool for reading the dialogues, not only does the dogmatic ambition for the most part disappear, but, furthermore, Cicero's philosophy emerges as a powerful critique both of the political world in which he was working and of his own ideals to reform that world.[44] The presentation of contradictory positions does not aim, as in post-Hegelian versions of philosophical dialectic, at the production of a synthesis of views; rather, it presupposes the ultimate fallibility of any view (though there are certainly some positions, usually Epicurean ones, that are intrinsically more fallible than others), and points towards the reader, rather than the author, as the source of any likely synthesis or authoritarian standpoint. Modern habits of reading philosophy lead us to look to Cicero for an unequivocal statement of his own view of the world; but the dialogues themselves, studied in awareness of the fundamentally anti-authoritarian manner in which they were conceived, turn out to present us with a vision of Rome where tensions remain largely unresolved, and where even desirable philosophical outcomes are rendered relative, and subjected to an ironic juxtaposition with different, more cynical or realistic views.

---

[43] See Fuhrmann (1989, 2000).

[44] The clearest statement I have found of the dialogic conventions in which Cicero was working is the fairly inaccessible Michel (1977); his argument is clouded, however, by an overestimation of Cicero's quest for synthesis in his works.

4

Literature, History, and Philosophy: The Example of *De re publica*

AUTHORITY AND THE SETTING OF *DE RE PUBLICA*

To begin a detailed analysis of the interplay between formal, philosophical, political, and historiographical interests, we will look at one of Cicero's earliest big theoretical treatises, *De re publica*. It is a work that has survived only in fragmented form, and in that state it is brief and lacunose, and can convey only a hint of what must in its time have appeared as a particularly audacious and unique philosophical work. *De re publica* is a good example of how Cicero uses the potential of the philosophical dialogue form in order to produce a vision of Rome's constitution which, without being authoritarian or dogmatic, does suggest innovative ways of thinking about Rome which depend upon theoretical insights. At the same time, *De re publica* dramatizes, in a way that is best understood through a more literary kind of analysis, the problems of combining philosophical insight with traditional Roman political practice. The historical problems of representing Rome as a society which has a visible philosophical tradition are confronted, and we can see in this work from Cicero's first large-scale philosophical assault on central Roman institutions the beginnings of a discourse of scepticism about foundational uses of the past which is more fully developed in later works.

In the three major treatises from this period, *De oratore*, *De re publica*, and *De legibus*, Cicero is concerned to provide Rome with a theoretical framework which will give contemporaries a conceptual map and language to articulate their ideas about the commonwealth; his elaboration of the idea of the *princeps* in the lost portions of the last book of *De re publica* was possibly the one which had the clearest impact. In both *De re publica* and *De oratore* he makes use of a semi-fictional historical setting for the discussion, electing to place theoretical discussion in the mouths of characters who are, in varying degrees, unlikely to have possessed either the philosophical expertise or the argumentative skills for the debates which Cicero presents them as holding. The traditional reading, perhaps, is that the dialogue form is an inert convention, and that Cicero uses the form of philosophical dialogue simply out of a desire to produce a work of literary, as well as philosophical, merit; that the main speaker, Scipio, is a voice of unquestioned authority within the work, and that he can, by and large, be identified with Cicero himself. It is possible that Cicero's first readers were, like those dogmatic Platonists, going to make such an identification, and the pervasive modern approach to the dialogue has certainly followed that pattern: the narrative of Rome's history, for example, given by Scipio in *De re publica* 2, being treated as if it were actually Cicero's own historical account of early Rome, the carefully positive portrayal of monarchy, Cicero's own view on that subject.[1] Were the lost portions of the dialogue preserved, it seems unlikely that modern readers would be so committed to this approach, given the different castings adopted in later books, with different speakers taking on more prominent roles and Cicero beginning to employ that method which he developed (to different ends) more fully in works such as *De natura deorum, De finibus,* or *Academica.*[2] However, I shall argue below that there is sufficient evidence, both from a crucial letter

---

[1] For discussions of this view with regard to history, Cornell (2001); and monarchy, Frede (1989), 89–93.

[2] Steinmetz (1989), 7–8, takes the opposite view. He uses *De re publica*, in which he regards Scipio as the *Sprachrohr* (mouthpiece) of Cicero, as evidence that Cicero is adopting the method of arguing both sides of the question not in a spirit of Academic scepticism, but in the Peripatetic manner as a form of positive dialectic. I find this argument unnecessarily convoluted and remote from the experience of actually reading that work; nor is it consistent with what the other essays in that same volume tell us about Cicero's knowledge of the Peripatetic tradition, for which see also Fortenbaugh (2005). Nevertheless, the article is useful evidence for the persistence of the hermeneutics of the 'mouthpiece', and Steinmetz is not alone: see Johansen (1991) 490.

concerning the setting of the dialogue and from traces of a deliberate irony concerning the authority of the discourse within the dialogue itself, to see the main message of *De re publica* to be rather more than a reworking of the theory of constitutions. Although this would itself, in terms of Latin philosophy, have been a breakthrough, it does not seem to me that the drama of the dialogue is given sufficient weight if Cicero's main concern was just to provide access to Greek traditions of constitutional theory. The reading that I suggest takes more account of Cicero's interest in an Academic suspension of authoritative positions, but it also places at the centre the dialectic which dominates even the scarce extant portions of the work: between theory and practice, Greece and Rome, and Cicero's exploration of a role for Roman statesmen that negotiates this dialectic. Just as there is no straightforward resolution to this dialectic, so the dialogue itself works by suggestion, rather than by putting forward concrete suggestions or positions.

So in this and the following chapter, I shall be working on the basis that even at this stage in his career as a theorist, recovered from the trauma of exile but working in the shadow of the triumvirate, Cicero was expressing more than just a programme for the reform of the state: he was also working out the difficulties of his own position, and while confident that philosophy and theory could help Rome to develop along more positive lines, he was also aware of both his own political marginality and thinking about questions of authority and dogma which he spells out more clearly in later works. In particular, in both *De re publica* and *De oratore* (as well, to a lesser extent, in *De legibus*) the problem of authority is grounded in a reading of Rome's history: in *De re publica* what is at stake is the extent to which Rome as a whole can benefit from theoretical definition: justice, the statesman, and the constitution were all subjected to a discussion informed by philosophical currents which could with some plausibility be connected with the 120s BCE (extant portions mention Polybius and Panaetius).[3] In spite of some concern with his source material, Cicero is not only aiming to produce a degree of historical plausibility for his speakers: as I have shown, he also draws attention at points to the artificiality of his own historical edifice,

---

[3] *Rep.* 1. 10. 15; 1. 21. 34; 2. 14. 27.

most obviously when he makes these figures, themselves characters in a Roman version of Plato's *Republic*, refer openly to Plato.[4] Part of this deconstructive impulse is to strip away the conventions of the dialogue and reveal Cicero himself as the ultimate source of authority within the work. But a further aspect is the ambiguous presentation of Rome as a historical society: at times, one that will support the burden of philosophical investigation, but at other times, a city with an arbitrary historical development, providing only a shaky foothold for theoretical definition. Although *De oratore* was completed before *De re publica*, and can be thought of, in its exploration of the problems of talking about theoretical understanding of Rome, as a forerunner to it, I have decided to begin with *De re publica*, since it enables the more specific focus of *De oratore* on rhetoric to be seen within a wider context, something which will then be helpful in examining the much later work, *Brutus*, in Chapter 7.

Purely from its title, it is clear that Cicero was aiming to produce a Latin version of Plato's *Republic*, and this factor is a convenient way of focusing upon the nature of Cicero's ambitions. Although explicit reference to Plato does not occur extensively in the extant parts of the work (there are nine occurrences of his name), he is referred to at some crucial moments, usually in a manner that draws attention to the elaborate construction of Cicero's dialogue. So, for example, the first reference: right at the start of the dialogue, Scipio and Tubero discuss Plato's attribution of inappropriate cosmological speculation to Socrates, who is Scipio's model for not bothering about the heavens when matters on earth are pressing enough.[5] Already Cicero is making his readers aware of the possibility that characters within dialogues can be given inappropriate utterances: either Cicero is hinting that he will be aiming at greater verisimilitude in his portrait (Scipio won't be shown, as Socrates was, holding forth on matters for which we know he had no concern), or he is inviting the reader to be more generally aware of the constructed nature of the philosophical dialogue. The main function of Plato, as in this reference, is to be subjected to mild scorn for going about his philosophy in the wrong way. The clearest demarcation between Plato's republic and Cicero's is thus made clear by the speakers of the dialogue itself. Plato's republic

---

[4] See pp. 62–6.   [5] *Rep.* 1. 10. 15–16.

is an abstraction, while Cicero's speakers are concerned with the actual history of Rome.[6] Platonic hermeneutics, however, can be kept in mind when dealing with Cicero: in particular, the manner in which the historical narrative is understood will depend to a large extent on whether we think Cicero is writing history, whether he is himself even putting forward constitutional theory, or whether the historical narrative functions within a larger structure in which the utterances of the figures within a dialogue are different from the voice of the author of the work, and in which the philosophical significance of the work as a whole is different from the arguments that are contained within it.

The more theoretical parts of the work, in which Cicero discusses the notions of law and justice and outlines the character of the ideal statesman, are to a large extent lost, so my discussion will be limited here to the better preserved part of the work, where Cicero tackles the question of how to integrate political theory into the Roman context, and how to square Greek constitutional theory with the actual development of Rome in practice.[7] The tension that the dialogue explores is neatly foreshadowed in a letter to Atticus written some five years earlier, in which Cicero disparages the idealism of Cato in the Senate:

nam Catonem nostrum non tu amas plus quam ego; sed tamen ille optimo animo utens et summa fide nocet interdum rei publicae; dicit tamquam in Platonis πολιτείᾳ non tamquam in Romuli faece, sententiam. (*Ad Atticum* 2.1.8)

I am as fond of our Cato as you are: but in spite of his high-mindedness and patriotism, he can be a danger to the state: he gives his view in the Senate as if he is in Plato's republic rather than in the dregs of Romulus.

There is no sign that Cicero was already contemplating *De re publica* at this point, but we can observe his cast of mind: Rome, waste and all, is far removed from the intellectually and morally elevated, but entirely unreal, state of Plato's republic.[8] This is the tension that

---

[6] Most explicitly, *Rep.* 1. 46. 70 and 2. 11. 21–2. See above, pp. 62–3.

[7] As I have devoted some time elsewhere to a detailed discussion of Cicero's use of dialogue in *De re publica*, my discussion here will be brief. See Fox (2000).

[8] The word *faex* does not seem to refer to excrement until the modern period (Shackleton Bailey (1965, *ad loc.*) translates 'cesspool', whereas the image is probably connected with a less specific idea of waste); nevertheless, Cicero's use of it here and elsewhere (*Ad Q. fr.* 2, 9, 5: '*apud sordem urbis et faecem*'; cf. *Ad Att.* 1. 16. 11) makes it clear that it has highly pejorative associations. On Cicero's problems with Cato's excessive Stoicism, see Adamietz (1989), 10–11.

the speakers of *De re publica* explore; an important feature of their investigation is that Romulus emerges divested of the dregs which Cicero here so neatly associates with him, as an idealized monarch, an enlightened constitutional reformer, one who as it were by historical accident produced a state which turned out to manifest the best constitutional principles, even at the outset.[9] At the same time, we can find the germ of the idea which runs through Cicero's entire philosophical production: philosophy needs to be fitted to the Roman context, and in this letter a philosophical cast of mind is almost antithetical to the well-being of the *res publica*.

In the fragmentary prologue to the work, Cicero sets up the terms of the debate: there is no point, he claims, engaging in theoretical discussion of the best way to run a state if you are not in a position to put your theoretical insights to work by taking a leading role within government. Philosophers, therefore, need also to be political animals; and Cicero refers to his own period as a consul as proof that only by being capable of taking on the highest office was he in a position to put his understanding of statecraft to the service of the Republic. That was not simply a historical accident: Cicero had to make a concrete choice about his entire career, and in particular about the choice to pursue philosophy while at the same time progressing up the *cursus honorum* in a way that would enable him to guide the state at its moment of crisis. Philosophy, in other words, is action, not theory. In spite of the contribution that philosophy can no doubt make to an understanding of moral values, in one pithy phrase Cicero sums up his view: *virtus in usu sui tota posita est* (*Rep.* 1. 2. 2) ('the whole of virtue rests in the exercise of virtue'). This is pointedly expressed, but it is also an almost blinding challenge to conventional notions of philosophy at the start of a ground-breaking piece of theoretical work in Latin.[10]

The prologue gives way to the philosophical dialogue proper, and we know from Cicero's correspondence that his choice of speakers was made deliberately so as to remove from the dialogue the impression that Cicero wanted to produce a particularly authoritarian

---

[9] The clearest indication comes at *Rep.* 1. 11. 22, where Laelius points out that Scipio has found *ratio* (method) for Romulus' choice of the site for the city, whereas in fact his actions were motivated by accident or necessity: discussed above, p. 62.

[10] Blößner (2001).

discourse. Cicero wrote to his brother Quintus describing his latest thoughts on the composition of the dialogue, and reported that his friend Sallustius had suggested that he would have greater authority in putting across his own view of the state if, instead of adopting the form of a dialogue set in the past, he spoke in his own person.

ii libri cum in Tusculano mihi legerentur audiente Sallustio, admonitus sum ab illo multo maiore auctoritate illis de rebus dici posse si ipse loquerer de re publica, praesertim cum essem non Heraclides Ponticus sed consularis et is qui in maximis versatus in re publica rebus essem; quae tam antiquis hominibus attribuerem, ea visum iri ficta esse. (*Ad Quintumfratrem* 3. 5. 1)

Sallustius was listening when the two books were read to me at my place in Tusculum. He advised me that the arguments on those matters would have much greater authority if I myself spoke about the state, especially since I'm not Heraclides Ponticus, but an ex-consul, and one caught up in the greatest affairs of public life. He argued that what I attribute to men of such antiquity would look like it was made up.

Sallustius' argument, as we glimpse it in the letter, was that Cicero's own reputation would enhance the force of his arguments; in the mouths of figures from the previous century, readers would give less credence to the views expressed, because they came from characters for whom, by virtue of their antiquity, they were simply implausible. Cicero is still weighing up such questions when he comes to write *Academica* a decade later: the choice is between different characters from among Cicero's own friends to represent philosophical positions which they themselves were entirely incapable of articulating.[11]

Instead of following Sallustius' advice, however, Cicero chose to set *De re publica* in 129 BCE, shortly before the death of the principal speaker, Scipio Aemilianus, and to begin his characterization of that group of friends to whom he would return in later works (*De senectute* and *De amicitia*).[12] To abstain from capitalizing on his personal authority can partly be read as an Academic manner of doing philosophy, but this in itself does not account for the way in which Cicero goes on to exploit the historical setting of the dialogue. Cicero stuck to his guns in the face of Sallustius' sense that his ideas

[11] *Ad Att.* 13. 19. 3–5, from 45 BCE.
[12] On the 'Scipionic Circle' see Zetzel (1972); Forsythe (1991); Wilson (1994); on Scipio, Astin (1967).

would come across with more authority if he avoided the dangers of fictionalizing the past which the Scipionic setting brought with it. The vital question is whether, by opting for a historical setting that was evidently to some degree a fictional construction, Cicero was also aiming to concretize precisely that rejection of authority which seemed inappropriate to Sallustius. How far does this direct engagement with a form of philosophy that could distract its readers from the central authority of the author constitute a move by Cicero to ensure that his dialogue included more than a direct representation of his own views on the *res publica*?

As well as the specific moments where the characters refer to their own difference from Plato, the casting and setting of the dialogue raise the reader's awareness of the problems of the undertaking, problems which of themselves are historiographical in nature. Cicero's precedent for selecting a group of long-dead Roman statesmen was not Plato, but rather his near contemporary, Heraclides of Pontus, who located his philosophical discourses outside the immediate orbit of Socrates and Athens, using famous figures from history to put across a form of philosophical discussion that was, apparently, more accessible that Plato's.[13] From Plato, Cicero borrowed, and developed, the idea of the immediate temporal location: a short while before the death of the leading speaker, a device he also used in *De oratore*. Although the self-reflexive poignancy of the Socratic prison dialogues is lacking here, in placing Scipio's conversations about the state at a point just before his death, Cicero raises the idea that this conversation comes at an extraordinary time, perhaps even an epochal moment. How far this epoch represents the end of a particular way of thinking, or how far the conversations about the state are supposed to incorporate views which, with their protagonist, also belong to a bygone age, is an open question; but it is one that the setting of the dialogue itself seems to pose.[14]

---

[13] On what Heraclides' dialogues were actually like, see Gottschalk (1980), 6–12; Fox (forthcoming). Michel (1984), 10, points out (despite getting Heraclides' dates wrong) that it was for his emphasis on real political figures that Cicero selected Heraclides.

[14] A view first elaborated by Pohlenz (1931). Frede (1989) detects problems of this kind in the representation of monarchy; but rather than attribute them to Cicero, she posits a lost source which had a less positive view of monarchy than the one Cicero wishes to put across. Although a sensitive reading of the work, this article demonstrates perfectly the hermeneutic problems posed when desire to find Cicero's doctrine combines with the interest in lost Hellenistic sources.

Sallustius had clearly understood that Heraclides was Cicero's main model, and his objection was that this model was inappropriate to someone so closely involved in matters of state as Cicero: one, in other words, who would not need to use quasi-fictional statesmen from the past to imbue his ideas with political relevance.[15] Because Heraclides' works are not preserved, it is difficult to judge exactly what those familiar with him would have thought of Cicero's casting in *De re publica*, or how they would have judged the interplay between the *homage* to Plato and the form of dialogue recognizable from Heraclides. What little evidence there is suggests that Heraclides was a much easier read than Plato, and that his works had a fantastical element which included some rather far-fetched historical settings; the tyrant Gelon is certainly attested, the circle of Pisistratus slightly less well. By rejecting Sallustius' advice, and preserving at least a flavour of Heraclides, Cicero was choosing a form of dialogue that would actively engage his readers with problems about the nature and history of philosophical discourse at Rome, and about his own role in promulgating that discourse.

The transition between prologue and dialogue proper, for example, is made with the apparent proof that this dialogue on the state is not the fruit of Cicero's own ideas; nor is it something which should be thought of as particularly innovative in the present day, but rather as a historically reliable account of a conversation reported to Cicero and his brother (presumed to be the dedicatee of the work) by Publius Rutilius Rufus, who then appears briefly in the dialogue itself.[16]

nec vero nostra quaedam est instituenda nova et a nobis inventa ratio, sed unius aetatis clarissimorum ac sapientissimorum nostrae civitatis virorum disputatio repetenda memoria est, quae mihi tibique quondam adulescentulo est a P. Rutilio Rufo, Smyrnae cum simul essemus compluris dies, exposita ...   (*De re publica* 1. 8. 13)

But my argument is not setting up any particular new ideas, nor was it invented by me, but is a disputation that must be sought out again in

---

[15] Cicero refers again to Heraclides in relation to *De re publica* when discussing his casting of the *Academica*: *Ad Att.* 13. 19. 6.

[16] *Rep.* 1. 8. 13. Rufus does not speak in the dialogue, however, but is merely introduced as a *kōphon prosōpon*: *Rep.* 1. 11. 17. Cicero envisages a parallel role if he had introduced himself as a boy into the cast of *De oratore*: *Ad Att.* 13. 19. 4. See below, pp. 119–20.

memory held by men who were at one point in time the most famous and wisest of our state. It was once laid out for me and you when a youth by Publius Rutilius Rufus, when we were together at Smyrna for a few days …

Cicero is exploring the idea of giving the dialogue a reliable historical pedigree, and of the dynamic potential of removing his own authorial voice from the dialogue: by stating *nec vero nostra quaedam est instituenda nova et a nobis inventa ratio* … ('my argument is not setting up any particular new ideas, nor was it invented by me'), Cicero is evidently being provocative: an undertaking as bold and innovative as a Latin answer to Plato could hardly be this inert, second-hand dialogue; nor, however much trawling of collective memory, however much time Scipio spent with Panaetius and Polybius, could any such discourse be found in the conversations of Scipio. This ironic reading is certainly reinforced by the close echo of the ploy used by Plato in introducing the story of Atlantis in the *Timaeus*.[17] Sallustius' desire for Cicero to imprint his authority should be read as a forerunner to the passage from the opening of *De natura deorum* where Cicero rebuts the readers who want to know his own opinions; and, as we shall see, such appeals to evidently implausible historical sources are a feature too of *De oratore*, where even documentary sources are used for this purpose.[18]

The appeal to a historical authority, Rutilius Rufus, establishes a genealogy that is obviously spurious, and on that basis Cicero makes a transition: first we have the militant former consul of the prologue, vigorously arguing for his own history and personality to be identified as proof of the applicability of philosophy to public life; from there we move to the obviously idealized gathering of the great and the good from the previous century and their deliberations on the state. These deliberations are likely to be anachronistic, but they are also of a lesser order (at least for Sallustius) of authority than Cicero's own. However, unlike the work that Cicero hints he could produce if he were to speak in his own voice (revolutionary, new, and as individual as its author), this discourse is apparently safe: its authority derives from searching in memory for an age of former glory, and substituting the authority of the ex-consul for that of an idol of wider appeal, Scipio Aemilianus. Cicero takes refuge both

---

[17] See above, pp. 64–5.   [18] *De nat. deorum* 15. 10; see above, pp. 4; 45–6.

from an authoritarian position and from one of seeming to inculcate new ideas, by locating his analysis of the *res publica* in a fictionalized past.

The passage almost seems to presuppose two different readers (to whom, in order to clarify the argument, I shall allow a brief characterization): those like Sallustius, with a high opinion of Cicero's talents and a real desire to see what light his philosophical expertise can shed upon the problems of the state, and those who are more convinced by the revival of a discourse, given the authority of the names of this illustrious group of aristocrats, and who are not inspired by the thought of an ex-consul of dubious political credibility getting carried away by abstraction. Rather than commit to one of these audiences, however, Cicero's dialogue enables them both to coexist. No one could really expect Scipio and his friends to have held a discussion of this quality; nevertheless, they are not distracted by the intrusive novelty of the new Latin philosopher, holding forth on theory like some prosaic Lucretius. Likewise, those looking for philosophical insights would not be impeded by an obsessive desire on Cicero's part to produce a historically plausible discussion; they would, furthermore, be amused by the ironic references to Plato, and would appreciate Cicero's attempt to ground philosophical questions in Roman traditions, including the tradition of aristocratic *memoria*.[19] We find here the beginnings of an encounter with problems of self-positioning which become much clearer in Cicero's later works; in particular, the contrast between the energetic self-advertisement of the prologue and the benign narrative of the dialogue, in which the voice of the author can only occasionally be heard intruding at moments of gentle irony. These two forms of writing express a tension in Cicero's political and cultural position: genuinely captivated by the charisma and power of the aristocracy, driven to an Academic degree of detachment from fixed positions by his training, and politically and socially excluded, but trying to synthesize these into producing a new form of philosophical discourse which would please everyone, and not play to the prejudices of his enemies.

---

[19] More on *memoria* in Ch. 6.

BRINGING PHILOSOPHY INTO THE HISTORY OF ROME

Scipio and his friends represent a way of integrating philosophical insight with a particular conception of the Roman state, a conception which is historical, and which takes as its fundamental premiss the notion that Rome, in the development of her constitution, happened, by virtue of happy historical accident, to turn into a state which displays all the virtues of the constitution which Greek philosophers regarded as the most perfect: the mixed constitution.[20] After some evidently extraneous, but nonetheless significant, banter about the relevance of science and philosophy to public life, and the current state of the Republic, their discussion proper begins with a theoretical discussion of the best types of constitution, and essentially contains much of the same material as can be found in the discussion of the Roman constitution in Polybius. The three different types of single constitution (monarchy, oligarchy, democracy) and the theory of constitutional cycles are discussed before the speakers arrive at a provisional conclusion that the mixed form is preferable to any of the single forms.[21] Typical of Cicero's procedure is that, in laying the ground for the discussion, the speakers draw attention to their acquaintance with that same body of theory; Laelius, Scipio's closest associate and the character around whom Cicero builds his *De amicitia*, encourages Scipio to take the lead in the discussion of constitutions by referring to Scipio's habit of discussing constitutional matters with Polybius and Panaetius.[22]

... non solum ob eam causam fieri volui, quod erat aequum de re publica potissimum principem rei publicae dicere, sed etiam quod memineram persaepe te cum Panaetio disserere solitum coram Polybio, duobus Graecis

---

[20] Again, it is worth stressing that this was precisely the strategy of the discovery of happy 'historical' proof for the ideal city of *Republic* in *Timaeus*.

[21] The opening banter can be most easily understood as Cicero's way of giving an authentic sense of period to his dialogues, and here all three dialogues from this period are similar. There had been nothing like this written in Latin before: Fantham (2004), 50–1; and to see Roman statesmen disporting themselves like characters from Plato must have been startling.

[22] *De amicitia* is set shortly after the death of Scipio, thus soon after the dramatic date of *De re publica*.

vel peritissimis rerum civilium, multaque colligere ac docere, optimum
longe statum civitatis esse eum, quem maiores nostri nobis reliquissent.

(De re publica 1. 21. 34)

... I wanted this to happen not only because it was right that the most
powerful leader should speak about the *res publica,* but also because
I remembered that you used to talk frequently with Panaetius, in the
presence of Polybius—two Greeks most skilled in civil affairs—and that
you would bring much evidence together to prove that by far the best form
of state was that which our ancestors handed down to us.

By drawing attention to the writers on whom the following
account of the constitution is based, as well as granting historical
verisimilitude to the speakers, Cicero is also drawing the reader's
attention to the very problem of questions of verisimilitude within
such a setting. The device of source citation has the effect of providing an intellectual context for the theoretical discussion that follows.
It is a favourite strategy for stressing the possibility that the philosophical know-how attributed to these figures is not entirely the
product of his literary construction. The setting of the dialogue is
thereby brought closer to the philosophical discussion that then takes
place. Reminding the reader that Scipio had these learned Greek
friends, and engaged in debate about constitutional issues, Cicero is
making a claim for the plausible connection between the speakers of
the dialogue and the theme that they then discuss. However, in the
process, he is also drawing attention to the artificiality of the dialogue
form, and in so doing raises the possibility of implausibility much
more concretely than if the subject of Scipio's actual philosophical
education had never been mentioned. Given the stress in the prologue about the necessity of combining political experience with
philosophical awareness, the basis for the theoretical awareness of
the figures of the dialogue is important. They are clearly chosen
because of their fame as leading statesmen, and in the manner in
which Cicero represents them their historical significance responds
to the authoritative manner in which their discussion proceeds.
Indeed, Laelius' point here is one example of the same idea that
surfaces repeatedly in the dialogue in different forms: that theory and
practice magically coalesce at Rome. Just as the ancestral constitution
turns out, by happy chance, to be the perfect one (a theory, of course,
which Polybius elaborated at length), so Scipio's discussions with the

Greek theorists are harmonized with his authority as the *potissimus princeps*. Philus takes a slightly different angle a few lines later, by expressing the hope that Scipio's rendition will be richer (*uberiora*) than everything written by Greeks (*Rep.* 1. 23. 37). Scipio retorts that Philus is placing a particularly heavy burden upon him, only to be encouraged by Philus that *neque enim est periculum, ne te de republica disserentem deficiat oratio* ('nor is there a danger that eloquence will fail you when holding forth on the *res publica*').

Cicero articulates two different ways of combining Greek theory with Roman experience, one more reverential of Greek learning than the other; and this second one (Philus) then appeals to a highly rhetorical, almost discursive model of speech, to which Greek writings bear unfavourable comparison. The theory/practice dialectic is slightly altered to suggest that constitutional discussion by Romans will have a rhetorical quality, and be much more closely fitted to the authority of the individual speaker than is the case in the written traditions of philosophy practised by Greeks. Cicero is caught up here in the Academy's own struggle over the status of written discourse. It may be historically plausible that Scipio held conversations with Polybius and Panaetius in which their theoretical insights were made to work in harmony with an account of Rome's history offered by Scipio. The problems arise when such discourse has to be committed to writing, and all Cicero's ironic work with Plato and historical sources centres around that problem: how to render something that is easy to imagine in outline, as a conversation, into an extended written discourse. As a student of the Academy, he seems committed to undertaking that rendition in a manner which will keep alive the provisional, exploratory quality of oral discourse; Scipio will produce a discourse that is more pleasant to listen to than any dry theoretical tract that some Greek may have produced to be read.

Philus' appeal to Scipio's *oratio*, connoting a degree of spontaneity (like the *declamatio* of the *Tusculan Disputations*),[23] draws us into the other theme which preoccupied much of Cicero's philosophy, the extent of rhetoric's integration into the substance of Roman history. Even at this early stage in the philosophical *œuvre*, it is clear that in

---

[23] See above, pp. 51–2.

this passage, in the mirror held up by Laelius and Philus, we can observe Cicero outlining a role for himself as the orator statesman whose opinion on the state, so thoroughly informed by Greek scholarship, and still the organic product of a traditional political career, are going to be eagerly attended to. In this tribute to Scipio we can read Cicero as the statesman at the height of his powers discoursing with style on the Republic and harmonizing Greek philosophy with Roman history. However, this is a role with a great deal more *auctoritas* behind it if you are Scipio in 129 BCE than if you are Cicero in 54, hardly at this point the *potissimus princeps*;[24] but at the same time, there is a massive danger of overestimating Scipio's theoretical expertise. We can sense what advantage Cicero gains by not allowing his idealization of Scipio to be too obviously a veiled self-portrait. But beyond a directly political connotation, if we want to identify Cicero with Scipio, we must wonder how far this harmonization of theoretical and historical, together with its idealization of the constitution, can really apply to Cicero, or to his philosophical work. It will become clear by the end of this chapter that this is precisely the main thrust of *De re publica* as a whole: to display such a harmonizing history, but then to suggest that, however appealing as an ideal, it is something that at least needs to be worked for rather than taken for granted: and that, quite possibly, it is an idealization of Rome that belongs to a bygone era, an era, moreover, in which it can only at best be regarded as a somewhat excessive idealization.

This moment, where historical sources and the theme of theoretical and practical discourse are brought into view, is a good example of Cicero's exploitation of the dynamics of the dialogue form. The dialogue is certainly a historiographical curiosity: a kind of historical reconstruction, applying conventional devices to corroborate its reliability, that at the same time draws attention to the artificiality of its construction. The authority that the speakers do possess derives from their historical context: they are powerful figures from the past whom Cicero endows with intellectual coherence, but he then ironizes their historical credibility. This practice adds an extra layer to Cicero's sceptical methodology: as well as providing the kind of

---

[24] Fantham (2004), 1–15, on the precariousness of Cicero's position as he began *De oratore*.

philosophy that mediates enquiry rather than presents theory, Cicero is also making a comment upon how history itself can be used as an accessory to that type of philosophy. As well as removing the authority of dogma from the speakers, Cicero interweaves a thread of incredulity regarding his own historical reconstruction. History, in this process, is both the guarantor of authority and, at the same time, the place where that authority breaks down. The true implementation of theory thus becomes not the history of Rome itself, but that project which Cicero transfers to *De legibus*, the provision of an essentially timeless set of laws that negotiate the position between specific and universal in a way that is more easily accommodated to philosophical traditions.[25]

This account of the different layers at work in the construction of the fictional historical context for the speakers in the dialogue can appear rather abstract when described in this way. What prevents it from becoming simply a playful tool of literary composition is the fact that history itself is a vital part of the theme of the dialogue. The *res publica* that Cicero is describing is, as he frequently stresses, not some abstract philosophical notion, it is the state of Rome itself, and because of the historical setting, and the insistence of the speakers on grounding their discussion in the actual development of Rome, the question of history becomes tightly connected with the philosophical project as a whole. The arguments which the speakers themselves bring forward about the character of Rome are contingent upon presenting Rome's history in a particular way; in turn, this presentation is qualified by the ironic devices to which the historical setting of the dialogue itself is subjected. The result is that Cicero's scepticism takes on a historical dimension: a vision of Rome is brought forward in two historical fields, that of the speakers and that of their own account of Rome's past. That vision itself, like the theories that the speakers discuss, becomes the object of sceptical analysis, so that, ultimately, the reader is left with very little sense either of authority in theoretical questions or of the manner in which Rome's history should be conceived.

This process recurs in a very similar form in a number of Cicero's works. We can clarify how it works if we focus upon one particularly

<hr>

[25] Girardet (1983), *passim*, but esp. pp. 135–44.

important thread in the arguments of *De re publica*: the role of monarchy or, rather, the monarchic principle of government, in the *res publica*. The discussion of the simple forms of constitution is most interesting for the positive light in which monarchy emerges. Although Scipio repeatedly expresses his preference for the mixed form of constitution, the dialogue circles strangely around the issue of monarchy, Laelius not being content with Scipio's preference, and insisting that he select one of the single forms as well.[26] This leads into a protracted discourse on the merits of the monarchic principle within government, during which monarchy, rather than being treated as just one of a range of constitutional possibilities, is granted the status almost of a meta-constitutional principle. Cicero comes close to presenting an argument in which monarchy embodies the principle of government itself. In the account of the constitutional cycles with which the first book draws to a close, benign monarchy is seen both as the ideal single form and the one to which people most naturally turn at moments of political revolution. And once again, Scipio concludes by expressing a preference for monarchy as the best single form, second only to the mixed constitution.[27]

Scipio's closing arguments revive once more the question of Cicero's methods for philosophical dialogue. Scipio suddenly repudiates the role that he has taken on, that of the teacher addressing his pupils, and decides to turn the conversation away from theory, in which he is the acknowledged master, to a subject familiar to all, the actual historical development of Rome.[28] In this way, theory is jettisoned in favour of practice, and the discussion of the second book comprises the brief history of early Rome. Scholars are agreed that, as with the first book, there is a credible literary source for this narrative: that of Cato's *Origines*, which likewise dealt, in its first book, with Rome from its foundation to the Twelve Tables, the point at which it seems likely that Cicero's narrative once again gives way

---

[26] *Rep.* 1. 35. 54. That monarchy receives such detailed treatment may, of course, be, due to the loss of similar arguments defending each of the other single forms in the same way; but, given the rather polemic quality of Scipio's defence of monarchy, this seems unlikely.

[27] He repeats this preference once again in what looks like a digression on the cycle of constitutions within the historical narrative of *Rep.* 2: 2. 23. 43.

[28] *Rep.* 1. 46. 70–1. 47. 72.

to theoretical discussion.[29] The relationship between theory and practice, however, is more complex than simply shifting between one and the other. This becomes clear as the narrative of Rome's history progresses, where Scipio presents the rule of Romulus as providing the origins of Rome's famous mixed constitution, rather than as a monarchy in the conventional sense of the word. After the rape of the Sabine women, Romulus and his colleague Tatius set up an informal group of elder advisers and divided the people into tribes and *curiae*. After Tatius' death, Romulus paid more attention than ever to the advice of the *patres* (fathers), and they became a kind of senate. It is interesting to note that Scipio never actually describes Romulus' foundation of the Senate as a single political act. Rather, he gives three different angles: first, after the death of Tatius, power reverted to Romulus alone, except for the council they had set up together, known affectionately as the 'fathers' (*cum Tatio in regium consilium delegerat principes, qui appellati sunt propter caritatem patres* (*Rep.* 2. 8. 14)), and he made more use of its advice and its authority when Tatius was dead (*eo interfecto multo etiam magis Romulus patrum auctoritate consilioque regnavit*). Second: this experience brought him to the same insight as Lycurgus, that the power of one man to rule was better when joined to the authority of the elite :

quo facto primum vidit iudicavit idem, quod Spartae Lycurgus paulo ante viderat, singulari imperio et potestate regia tum melius gubernari et regi civitates, si esse optimi cuiusque ad illam vim dominationis adiuncta auctoritas. itaque hoc consilio at quasi senatu fultus et munitus et bella cum finitimis felicissime multa gessit. ...   (*De re publica* 2. 9. 15)

From that experience he first came to the same insight that Lycurgus had had a little earlier at Sparta: that in government by one individual with regal power, citizens could be better guided and ruled if the authority of each of the best men were joined to the force of his domination. And thus furnished with and relying upon this council, virtually a senate, he successfully fought many wars with his neighbours. ...

---

[29] See Cornell (2001), 46–8. At *Rep.* 2. 1. 3 we find Cato's *Origines* cited explicitly as a source (Cato himself is more frequently referred to just by name, as were Polybius and Panaetius in *Rep.* 1).

And finally: Romulus died after ruling for thirty-seven years, and in summing up his achievements, Scipio speaks of the two mainstays of the Republic: the Senate and the auspices (*cum ... haec egregia duo firmamenta rei publicae peperisset, auspicia et senatum (Rep.* 2.17.10)).

These three stages rather neatly demonstrate Cicero exploring the notion of historical idealization. At no point does Romulus, in one founding moment, actually produce a senate. At the same time, the comparison with Lycurgus reveals what is at stake. Lycurgus' actions were manifested in the establishment of a formal constitution, whereas Romulus' senate gradually evolved, becoming a formal body by the time of his death, but based upon the fruits of his own insights and experience, rather than any kind of plan. The language with which the different kinds of political power are described (*auctoritas, potestas, imperium*) of course stress the similarity with the political crises of the late Republic, so the resemblance between the political texture of Romulus' time and Cicero's is heightened.[30] At the same time, Cicero takes care that Romulus is not credited with excessive political wisdom, thus enabling the Senate to emerge almost organically from the pre-existing political order.

This caution, however, observable in small details, is not consistent in the narrative as a whole. By and large, the history continues to demonstrate the evolution of Rome as a gradual process, but this is one where developments are frequently described in such a way as to highlight correspondence with a theoretical preconception of what the best constitution, i.e. the mixed constitution, ought to look like. After the death of Tullus Hostilius (which occurs in a lacuna), for example, one speaker (presumably Laelius) remarks that in Scipio's account, the state is not just creeping, but flying towards becoming the ideal state (*neque enim serpit, sed volat in optimum statum instituto tuo sermone res publica (Rep.* 2. 18. 33)). The fact that Scipio's version of events (*tuo sermone*) is referred to draws attention once again to the constructed nature of the narration. As we have

---

[30] It is interesting to speculate on exactly how far Cicero's readers would have found the idea of a *regnum* conditional on the authority of others (*auctoritate consilioque regnavit*) an absurd paradox, or whether it was actually a recognizable constellation of concepts. Perhaps, indeed, the very idea of a monarchic rule that was so modified should itself be taken as an indicator of the primitive character of Romulus' proto-constitution.

seen, the most striking moment of obvious idealization, and simultaneous ironic deflation of that idealization, comes when Laelius
points out to Scipio that, like Socrates in Plato's *Republic*, Scipio is
attributing to Romulus' wisdom actions which would in fact have
happened by accident or of their own accord. I present that passage
this time in full, as it reveals a lot about both Cicero's ironic attack on
his own historical idealization and the afterlife of a scepticism which
originated in Plato's own dialogic technique.

tum Laelius: nos vero videmus, et te quidem ingressum ratione ad dispu-
tandum nova, quae nusquam est in Graecorum libris. nam princeps ille, quo
nemo in scribendo praestantior fuit, aream sibi sumsit, in qua civitatem
extrueret arbitratu suo, praeclaram ille quidem fortasse, sed a vita hominum
abhorrentem et moribus, reliqui disseruerunt sine ullo certo exemplari
formaque rei publicae de generibus et de rationibus civitatum; tu mihi
videris utrumque facturus; es enim ita ingressus, ut quae ipse reperias,
tribuere aliis malis quam, ut facit apud Platonem Socrates, ipse fingere, et
illa de urbis situ revoces ad rationem, quae a Romulo casu aut necessitate
facta sunt, et disputes non vaganti oratione, sed defixa in una re publica.

(*De re publica* 2. 11. 22–3)

Laelius continued: we do see, and realize that you have embarked upon a
new kind of argument, which is never in the writings of the Greeks. For that
leading philosopher, whom no writer has yet surpassed, found for himself an
empty space in which he could construct a state on the basis of his own
judgement. It may indeed be a glorious one, but it is far removed from the
lives and traditions of men. The rest of the philosophers ramble on about the
types and principles of states without any particular example or model of a
state. You seem to be going to do both: you have begun by attributing to
others what you have perceived yourself, rather than, as Socrates does in
Plato, constructing them yourself. Those decisions about the site of the city
which were made by Romulus either by accident or out of necessity you
attribute to theory, and you argue not in a speech that moves around, but
one which stays fixed in one state.

The crucial difference between Plato and Scipio is that Scipio has
chosen a historical city, rather than an ideal one. In the same manner,
the post-Platonic tradition of philosophy discusses states in theory,
rather than in practice. Crucially, Scipio is said to be occupying a
compromise position: using the history of Rome, but at the same
time shaping his narrative so as to draw out the congruency between

the ideal constitution and Rome's actual historical development. This apparently logical procedure, of course, falls victim to Cicero's ironic technique, since the comparison between Plato and Scipio instantly draws attention to the more obvious parallels between Cicero and Plato, and thus between Socrates and Scipio. It is Cicero who takes the next step in the Academic tradition of constitutional theory, not Scipio. And if, as I suspect, the historicizing of theory was obviously a powerful intervention in the Academic tradition, then the attribution of it to Scipio would be a particularly blatant form of idealizing exaggeration. By making a character in the dialogue provide a methodological statement so inappropriate to the fictional integrity of the dialogue, Cicero lays bare the artifice of his construction, and at the same time exposes the methodological flaw which is in any case apparent from the idealization of Romulus and the other kings. Scipio may be attempting to reconcile history with theoretical insights, but the result is a historical account that constantly raises exactly the suspicion which Laelius has voiced: this is not really history, but more the use of historical anecdote to demonstrate constitutional theory. This explains why the events that are narrated are not really described in much detail, and why constitutional theory is not brought to bear on the historical evidence with any precision.[31]

To summarize, Rome becomes the historical proof of the correctness of Greek political theory, demonstrating the excellence of the mixed constitution, and although the speakers in the dialogue acknowledge the happy accident, it is clear from their discussion that Rome's constitutional excellence is due not to theory, but to history; but at the same time, that history is not really history, but a narrative forced upon the traditional story in order to make it work as a verification for the theory. Cicero's historical account is history constructed around an *idée fixe*, with Rome being shown to manifest, through historical accident, the insights of Greek political theory. The purpose of this Roman history, therefore, cannot be to persuade

---

[31] Cornell (2001), 42–6, explores various factors lying behind the blandness of Scipio's narrative. Cicero suggests elsewhere (*De orat.* 2. 270; *Brutus* 299) that the real Scipio had an established reputation for Socratic irony; perhaps at this moment he is dramatizing a small piece of biographical information and making it work for a particularly pointed purpose.

Cicero's readers that it is literally true.[32] Rather, Cicero exploits the historical setting of the speakers to qualify their arguments, and the work as a whole presents an idealized version of Roman history which is clearly recognizable as such. At the same time, the speakers themselves are subject to a parallel idealization: their somewhat naïve faith in the rational development of Rome is tempered by their own acknowledgement that perhaps theory and practice do not always fit so neatly together. Nevertheless, the work as a whole expresses admiration for such an ennobling vision of Rome's history. There is no sense in which we can identify the historical narrative of Rome's early history as being Cicero's own history of Rome, but its purpose is clear: to represent one possible way of looking at Rome, a way which may have been possible in 129 BCE before Roman political life descended inexorably into a series of conflicts between generals incapable of keeping their megalomania in check. In particular, the idealization of the early kings is carefully placed by Cicero at a point in history when the almost automatic association of *rex* with *regnum* was susceptible to greater hesitation than in Cicero's own day. The notion that the kings of Rome were political *savants* who bequeathed to their successors the mixed constitution of the Republic, was one which, by the time Cicero himself was writing, would have been hard to sustain. Much easier would be an identification of monarchy with tyranny, and a sense of peril at the thought of a monarchic constitution. Scipio and his friends bypass this polemic, and are thus able to point, in a similarly idealizing fashion, towards the notion of the ideal *princeps* with which *De re publica* culminated.

This idealization of the ideal *princeps* corresponds both to the characterization of the speakers and, in particular, Scipio, and also to the brief sketch of the state of the Republic which occupies the very beginning of the dialogue, before the discussion of the state begins in earnest. There, briefly, Laelius laments the turmoil that followed from the death of Tiberius Gracchus, four years before the dramatic

---

[32] Cornell (2001) points out that Cicero was in fact ignoring a number of well-established traditions concerning early Rome which would have stood in the way of the political theories which he was exploring. His account is clearly not, therefore, a historical account of the kind that he would have produced were he writing straight history.

date of the dialogue, and describes Scipio as the only man who has the capacity to take charge of the state at this troubled point.[33] It is directly after naming Scipio as Rome's potential saviour that Laelius then turns and invites him to describe what he thinks is the best form of state (*quem existimet esse optimum statum civitatis*). The stage is set for a picture of Rome's constitution and history that reflects upon the characterization of the principal speaker as the leading figure at Rome.[34] The idealization of the benign early kings is most easily interpreted as an idealization which is proper to Scipio, and to the context in which he is speaking, surrounded by his most loyal supporters. Although there is a huge gulf between the powers of a king and the constitutional position apparently envisaged for the *principes*, there can be no doubt that, in the sanitized form in which they are presented in *De re publica* 2, the kings are intended as evocative models of benign government by individuals, exercised for the most part over a compliant and needy populace.[35] But one can only be so certain of this if one reads the history of *De re publica* 2 as ironic history, history presented in an awareness of the shaky basis upon which it is established.

This may have been Cicero's own view of the best way forward for the Republic, but he presents it as a kind of historical fantasy, a fantasy which manifests itself as such in the remarkable *Somnium Scipionis* with which the work ended. Such a staple of school curricula did this become, that the strangeness and freshness with which it must have struck its original readers are hard to recover. The fantastic quality, however, of the vision of the endless procession of the souls of the great, and the metaphysical elaboration of the notion of the posthumous incentives for selfless dedication to the earthly community, are all ways of reinforcing a message about commitment to the state which is not so much the fruit of theoretical labour

---

[33] *Rep.* 1. 19. 31.

[34] He is also presented as one impeded by the current political situation and the machinations of his enemies from making that contribution in the political arena: *Rep.* 1. 19. 31.

[35] The opening of Livy 2 is relevant here: there Livy makes it clear that the Roman people in their infancy needed the guiding hand of the kings in order to have the necessary maturity to be able to rule themselves. The idea is a variation on what Cicero implies.

as a summation of the inspiration which Scipio in particular has provided by working through the discussions of the previous books. This is an inspiration to participate in public life, but it is one that only in its most general terms can be taken as directly applicable to Cicero's own readers. Of particular importance is the major difference between this closing myth and Plato's myth of Er, a myth which, as is evidenced from the few fragments that remain of the portions of the book before the *Somnium*, the characters themselves discuss.[36] Er is a figure evoked solely for the purposes of the myth, and, like the rest of Plato's republic, he has no history. Scipio's history, on the other hand, is particularly clearly evoked, especially at the moment when the voice in the dream, Scipio Africanus, alludes to the younger Scipio's imminent death, and when the framework of the dream narrative is interrupted for Laelius and the dialogue's other characters to groan and exclaim.[37] This is the clearest indication of what is otherwise more vaguely expressed by the date of the setting: that Scipio represents a unique embodiment of civic virtues, one which may be inspirational, but has also perished.[38] In casting his closing myth in this form, Cicero is once more pointing to the crucial difference from Plato: the historical contingency of philosophical views and the necessity, when dealing with concrete political circumstances, to modify theoretical discussion accordingly. Certainly, the details of the foregoing constitutional discussion are subsumed by the metaphysical quality of the representation in a manner that will effectively make Scipio's dream into a vision without history But, as I have said, Cicero is quite pointed in interrupting this vision precisely to reinforce the historical point.

The work, therefore, cannot be said to represent Cicero's vision of the ideal republic, any more than the ideal state produced in Plato's *Republic* can be thought to represent a real political programme. There has, however, as I suggested in the previous chapter, been a powerful tradition of misreading Plato, in particular *Republic*, which has made it into a dogmatic work, the blueprint for an authoritarian state, most famously by Popper.[39] This tradition of misreading has,

---

[36] *Rep.* 6. 3.   [37] *Rep.* 6. 12.
[38] For expressions of Scipio's uniqueness, see e.g. *Rep.* 1. 21. 34; 1. 23. 37; 1. 47. 71.
[39] Popper (1945).

quite understandably, been just as effective in dampening the original complexity of a number of Cicero's works. *De re publica* does not provide a clear outline of the Roman state; what it does instead is confront the very question of how to combine an understanding of Rome's history with theoretical discussions of ways of making states work more effectively. If Cicero has a solution to this last problem, then it resides in the evocation of a particular form of self-reflexive political participation, as practised by the speakers in the dialogue. Even so, Cicero's speakers are clearly not historically accurate portrayals of the individuals whose names they bear, and the artificiality of their construction is made clear, especially at those places where they refer to themselves as being like figures in one of Plato's dialogues. There were, no doubt, in the later books (now too poorly preserved to be able to judge) moments when Cicero's own views on justice could be perceived between the lines. But, as a whole, the dialogue structure militates against any one particular argument being susceptible to the authoritarian reading which places Cicero's full weight behind it. Instead, Cicero dramatizes the very question of theory and practice in discussing Rome's constitution, and, while debating Rome in philosophical terms, makes clear his misgivings about any ultimate formula for Rome that rests too heavily upon theoretical models.

The debate is clearly central to the whole of Cicero's subsequent philosophical output; the essential Greek-ness of philosophy and the anti-theoretical current at Rome were counterparts to his own personal sense that philosophy was only a second-best to political action. However, in *De re publica*, Cicero provided, as far as we can tell, a complex encounter with this theme, and outlined ways in which, in spite of a strong tradition of distrust of theory, philosophy can still have a role to play: it aims to enable those who, in a purely traditional manner, have risen to the top of Rome's political structure, to exercise their power with greater awareness and a better sense of the intellectual context of even conventional views of Rome's development and character.

CICERO'S OWN VOICE: THE PROLOGUE

Is *De re publica*, therefore, a manifesto for a fundamentally conservative view of politics at Rome? Such a conclusion has prevented scholars from perceiving how strongly theory and practice coalesce in the work to emphasize repeatedly the power of great men to take control of affairs. The prologue to the work can be reread in the light of this interpretation.[40] Although it is tempting to see Cicero here exploiting the opportunity once again to glorify his consulship, the prologue in fact lays the ground for the exploration of history which takes place within the dialogue. Here, however, the message is unequivocal: history shows us what kinds of men we admire: ones who participate fully in the affairs of the state, putting its welfare above their own, irrespective of the rewards. The extant part of the work begins with a clear vision of history. We are in the apodosis of a conditional clause: the generals of the Carthaginian wars would not have been able to defeat the enemy who in the end got so close to the walls of Rome. From what follows, it is clear that the conditions that must have obtained for Rome to have been able to overcome successfully this period of peril were the selfless dedication of these men to public affairs, and their desire to put the interests of the state over their individual contentment. It soon becomes clear, with the words *ut isti putant* ('as those fools suppose') that Cicero is here in polemic vein. The vision of Rome's history that he is outlining is a direct attack upon what then emerges as an Epicurean view of how society ought to work, one in which individuals devote themselves instead to the cultivation of their own inner peace. This world-view is given more detail a few paragraphs later, as it becomes clear that Cicero is referring not just to a general Epicurean *Weltanschauung*, but to particular writings which, even if they are not strictly speaking historical, provide the same kind of philosophical interpretation of history as Cicero is making here. These writers have gathered together, in learned and abundant prose, examples from history where the dedication of famous men to the good of the state has

---

[40] There now exists a splendid treatment of the opening chapters of the prologue: Blößner (2001).

resulted only in their own unhappiness (*illo vero se loco copiosos et disertos putant, cum calamitates clarissimorum virorum iniuriasque iis ab ingratis inpositas civibus colligunt* (*Rep.* 1. 3. 4)).

The examples of Miltiades and Themistocles follow, so that:

... nec vero levitatis Atheniensium crudelitatisque in amplissimos civis exempla deficiunt; quae nata et frequentata apud illos etiam in gravissumam civitatem nostram dicuntur redundasse; nam vel exilium Camilli vel offensio commemoratur Ahalae vel invidia Nasicae vel ...   (*De re publica* 1. 3. 5–6)

... and there is no shortage of examples of the fickleness and cruelty of the Athenians to their most talented citizens; behaviour that, though born and repeatedly practised by them, is even said to have spread into our most serious-minded civilization; recollection is made of the exile of Camillus or the affront offered to Ahala, the envy of Nasica...

The contrast between the cruel and fickle Athenians and the *gravissimi Romani* is most striking, as is the notion that civic ingratitude, almost like a sickness, has spread across the sea from Greece to Italy. As far as I am aware, no one has actually identified the writing that Cicero has in mind here; there is nothing as detailed as this in Lucretius, but from the rejection of the standard Roman evaluation of the virtues of public service, we can get a sense of the discourse against which Cicero is directing his polemic. However, it is clearly a recently produced work, since Cicero then tells us that he himself has been cited as an example of the ingratitude that was his reward. The philosophers he has in mind are as heedless of the conditions which granted them the political stability necessary for their own meditations as they are considerate of the losses which Cicero himself suffered.[41] It is no accident that in this list of great Romans, the last name on the list is that of Marius, and that Cicero comes next.

We find out more about the Epicurean theories after a lacuna: the disturbed and dangerous world of politics is not the place for a wise man; he can perhaps take part if the times or necessity demand it (*si eum tempus et necessitas coegerit* (*Rep.* 1. 6. 10)). Cicero's argument, again referring to his consulship, is that lifelong devotion to the *res publica* is essential to provide the expertise needed should such an emergency arise. These introductory arguments, which Cicero concedes have been long (*Rep.* 1. 7. 12), draw to a close with a kind

---

[41] *Rep.* 1. 3. 6.

of compromise: the *scientia rerum civilium* (≈ knowledge of civil affairs) must be among the accomplishments of any wise man, apparently an argument aimed at convincing Epicureans that even if participation in politics is not essential, wisdom itself does require the study of civic society as it is constituted.

The prologue, then, presents a dialectic, one which, ostensibly, requires for its resolution the detailed philosophical investigation to which it is merely the prologue. The dialectic concerns competing ways of conceiving of the life of the individual: according to the Epicurean model, that life, while naturally connected to the social world, is determined by values intrinsic not to that world, but to standards of wisdom and happiness measured according to the individual. *Otium* is where life's potential will find fulfilment. History is the record which proves the solidity of these arguments; it demonstrates the impossibility of acquiring tranquillity through public life, so the task of philosophy is to encourage its adherents to negotiate their way to a better existence, a way out of history. Cicero presents an alternative vision both of history and of philosophy as far as it deals with the aims of the individual's life. Nature has given human beings a desire for virtue and an instinct to defend the common good that overrides all considerations of *otium* or pleasure, *voluptas*.[42] What history demonstrates is the manifestation of this same principle: that a striving for virtue for the sake of the common good is an ingrained characteristic, and that history provides not just a collection of inspiring examples, but also a demonstration of the order of things.

It is simply not possible to break the pattern of history, and the desire to develop a form of wisdom that is independent of history is a manifestation of folly. It should be the task of philosophy to accentuate the lessons of history and to find an explanation for them, to provide an understanding of what is worth pursuing in public life which will enable it to continue on its course. The proverb of Xenocrates is cited early on: his disciples would do of their own accord what they were commanded to do by law. Law enforcers, magistrates, therefore, are superior to philosophers, in that the social

---

[42] *Rep.* 1. 1. 1: *unum hoc definio, tantam esse necessitatem virtutis generi hominum a natura tantumque amorem ad communem salutem defendendam datus, ut ea vis omnia blandimenta voluptatis otique vicerit.*

effect of their wisdom is greater. There is no judgement or evaluation
of the historical precedents that Cicero uses. Clearly the naming of
Rome's past leaders is itself the expression of veneration; there is no
suggestion here that the leaders of the future need be different from
those of the past. The progress of the state, however, is assumed, and
the continuity between past and present is enshrined in the notion
that states themselves are by nature organized so as to work towards
harmony between citizens. The dissenting philosophers are like those
who are trying to divert the course of nature, a course which is
already running and cannot in fact be held back.[43]

So the role of philosophy is simply to interpret politics and inspire
the continuation of the political practice inscribed in history. One
could construct a plausible reading of the remainder of what survives
of *De re publica* to suggest that, as far as a philosophical message is
concerned, this is as much as Cicero will in fact go on to say. However,
such an argument ignores all of the complexities and detail of the
presentation of Rome which the dialogue itself produces. The idealization of Scipio and his friends, and their idealized, essentially
optimistic vision of Roman history as a progression of great men,
do provide an elaboration of the conception of politics which he
outlines in the prologue; but, as we have seen, that idealization is
frequently enough exposed as such, and in particular the theoretically
over-laden depiction of early Rome is quite clearly a narrative dis-
tanced from that which Cicero, were he writing outside the frame of
the dialogue, would be minded to give. If there was a 'message' which
De re publica had to impart about Cicero's view of Roman politics,
it would read something like this: 'for our great-grandfathers, it was
still possible to imagine that Rome's history would develop along the
same path that it had previously followed. The leading representatives
of the leading families would continue to uphold family traditions,
respecting constitutional practice, and developing the state through
the exercise of their duty. Since that time, of course, we have seen
that Rome has an intrinsic constitutional weakness, in that the constraints upon the abuse of personal power do not function properly;
although the mixed constitution does temper the monarchic aspects
of Roman government, it does not do so effectively. We need some

[43] *Rep.* 1. 2. 3.

other way of conceptualizing this constraint. Nevertheless, Rome's history does provide many models of how great men did form the state: let us see if we can deduce some kind of political principle from their abilities and powers. Perhaps this can then provide us with a model of personal political power which will contribute to stability rather than undermine it.' Of course, Cicero's faith in Academic philosophical method makes the whole notion of a 'message' for a philosophical work untenable, and I have provided this sketch as an illustration of the kind of thing that I think more dogmatically inclined readers might make or have made of *De re publica*. This conception of Rome's history, and of the potential of philosophy to influence it, is much more complex and ambiguous than the one found in the prologue.

History, then, just as it is for proper historians, is the arena in which the dilemmas of the present are worked out, using the material drawn from the past. *De re publica*, however, uses both the historical setting of the dialogue and the historical narrative of early Rome to do this. The speakers of the dialogue represent an intermediate stage between the idealized origins of the city and the political problems of Cicero's own day. These dilemmas are explored using a philosophical method that does not produce a clear solution, for such a solution would involve breaking out of history, which, Cicero seems clear, is neither possible nor desirable. Concluding the prologue, and justifying the relationship between his own career and the production of this treatise, he says:

quibus de rebus, quoniam nobis contigit, ut iidem et in gerenda re publica aliquid essemus memoria dignum consecuti et in explicandis rationibus rerum civilium quandam facultatem non modo usu, sed etiam studio discendi et docendi [lacuna] (*De re publica* 1. 8. 13)

On these matters, therefore, since it befell me on the one hand to pursue a course of action worthy of memory when I was active in politics, and on the other to possess a certain facility for explaining theories of civilization, not just on the basis of my experience, but also through my love of learning and teaching . . .

It could be said that the whole of Cicero's impulse to write *De re publica* rests upon these clauses, but his situation is not just the inspiration; it is also crucial to the way in which the work is constructed: the interplay between theory and practice so that neither ever in fact takes precedence over the other. At the same time, the inescapable issue of memory and immortalization is touched upon. This constitutes the centre of Cicero's conception of history, and it is this which prevents the theoretical insights, however distorting, from allowing the dialogue to depart too excessively from the details of Rome's historical development. In this respect, *De re publica* is an important basis for Cicero's later works. The role of historical anecdote, as we shall see, is often to produce a philosophical discourse that, while closely articulated with regard to philosophical tradition and even technical argument, never strays far from the familiar, and often, as a result, fails to develop its own technical momentum. At the same time, theory is always tied to history, and has no reasonable basis without it. Nevertheless, when it comes to writing that history itself, we observe a different side to Cicero's scepticism. History may provide us with examples of ideal behaviour, and is both the testing-ground for and proof of the truth of those ideals. But because we need, at the same time, to narrate Rome's history, we can never be sure that that narration is not itself constructed around those ideals.

5

History with Rhetoric, Rhetoric with History: *De oratore* and *De legibus*

De re publica demonstrates a sophisticated handling of historical material: it presents an idealized historical narrative of early Rome, articulated by figures who are themselves somewhat idealized, and the whole is presented to Cicero's readers as a way of applying theoretical insights to Rome's constitution and institutions that have a purchase in Roman culture. To grant this purchase historical validity requires a stretch of the reader's imagination, and an extension of the conventional terms in which Roman history is conceived: Scipio and his friends are brought to life as a gathering of sophisticated *savants*, and granted a kind of potential intellectual authority which Cicero decided to deny himself. In the process, he represents them producing a discourse about history that has its own historical specificity, in particular in its unambiguous promotion of monarchy, but is also characterized by an easy, fluent argument. In two other works from the same period, *De oratore* and *De legibus*, we find more detail about Cicero's thinking: in particular, concerning the relationship between rhetoric and history. As I suggested in the previous chapter, one of Cicero's main concerns is with grounding different ways of talking about Rome in different historical periods. This is the fundamental process for his exploration of the social context of rhetoric (as opposed to the technical dimension), and it is one which has ramifications both for his representation of history and for his discussion of rhetoric.

History in *De re publica* is used as a way of giving an argument a kind of representational value: readers are less concerned about the bare accuracy of the history of early Rome as Scipio presents it, because it lacks the unmediated endorsement of the historian. But at the same time, the symbolic value of the narrative is greatly enhanced by placing it in the mouths of Scipio and his colleagues, and the dialogue as a whole is more thought-provoking in its exploration of theory and history than if Cicero had attempted to present those same themes in a more straightforwardly didactic manner. The political ramifications of his approach, however, must also be considered: the idea of aristocratic *memoria* is one that grants considerable *auctoritas* to Cicero's characters, but at the same time, his over-characterization of them, and the vigour of his opening polemic, draw attention to his own literary skill, to his reforming zeal, and also to a playful ironization of the attempt to do something Platonic in Rome. Recent readings have stressed how Cicero attempts to define Rome in his treatises by developing a theoretical model which insists upon his own centrality to the processes of Roman history. He defines philosophy and rhetoric as discourses that are, if not indigenous, at least at home in Rome, and possess enough of a heritage for Cicero to be able to appear as a master, rather than a maverick.[1]

My reading of *De re publica* suggests that the process is not so straightforward: Cicero certainly provides enough material to come to such a conclusion; how far it would have appeared far-fetched to his contemporaries is an unanswerable question. But, more than that, the processes of dramatization and reconstruction are not carried out so as to reinforce his authority and occlude the problems of historical reconstruction. On the contrary, the dialogue is a much richer encounter with questions of history and authority than a simple teleology, culminating in Scipio as a cipher for Cicero, will allow; we certainly cannot identify Scipio's monarchy with Cicero's, but Cicero clearly wants that history and those ideas about the best *princeps* to prompt his readers to examine their own views of monarchy and its role in Rome's constitution. The other works belonging to this same period of productivity, *De oratore* (completed before *De re publica*) and *De legibus* (never completed) are much more concerned with their respective subject matters, and much of their main purpose was

---

[1] Dugan (2005), 76: 'Cicero had to present himself and his ideas as vested with the full authority of traditional Roman values'; p. 80: 'This mystification through idealization contributed to Cicero's own prestige.'

to provide an accessible discussion of law and oratory. Nevertheless, they also contain material which supplements most usefully the approach to history displayed in *De re publica*.

The historical framework that Cicero establishes in *De re publica* had been rehearsed in a similar form in *De oratore*, a work that was composed during the same period, and which can benefit from being read in the light of its companion dialogue. By applying the same kind of analysis to this work—in other words, being sensitive to both the historical aspects of the work and to Academic expectations of philosophical dialogue—it is possible to see *De oratore* in a new light: although its main purpose must still be to provide an introduction to rhetorical theory in Latin, the dialogue can also be read as a meditation upon the character of Rome itself.[2] By paying greater attention to the way in which *De oratore* functions as a representation of a particular moment in Rome's history, we can see the dialogue emphasize concerns more wide-ranging than its central topic: concerns about the nature of Roman political life, about the role of theoretical insights within that life, and about the understanding of the relationship between Roman history and the political concerns of Cicero's own day, which, of course provide the background against which the rhetorical theory needs to be understood. In essence I shall argue that, where as *De re publica* explores the possibility that great individuals constitute Rome's historical fabric, *De oratore* takes this theme in a different direction, and deliberates upon the role of rhetoric in the political competence of those leading individuals. This is a theme which Cicero tackles more directly in one of his later works, *Brutus*. Reading *De oratore* from this perspective gives more coherence to a similar interpretation of *Brutus*. In *Brutus* the debate about different kinds of theoretically informed life has taken on a much graver tone with Caesar's rise to domination; it is therefore useful to see how Cicero explores these themes in a context where the stakes are somewhat lower.

The reading of *De oratore* that follows will not focus much upon the details of the rhetorical theory, and in this respect will follow my procedure in discussing *De re publica*. For *De oratore*, because we have

---

[2] Fantham (2004) provides a full account of all aspects of this meditation; I hope that, within the context of the present work, there is still room for a more closely focused reading.

the complete work, the resulting interpretation may appear rather more one-sided than it does for *De re publica*, where elaborations upon the theoretical content rely heavily upon speculation about the lost portions of the work and possible sources for the various constitutional theories which Cicero discussed. Rhetorical theory does take up a large proportion of the work, so my decision to focus upon the apparently peripheral moments where that theory is given some kind of historical context may appear rather perverse.[3] However, there must also be room for the argument that the pervasive way of reading *De oratore*, as a technical treatise, overlooks some of its significance. *De oratore* 1 in particular is concerned largely with the function of rhetoric as a cultural and historical phenomenon, and with discussion of different approaches to rhetorical theory, rather than with technical matters, and presents an opportunity to evaluate rhetoric in general, rather than in narrower, practical terms. For this reason, my discussion of the dialogue will focus primarily on this book.[4] Although the details of the technical discussion are central to the dialogue—and in this part of it, we can see Cicero fulfilling his ambition of contributing to the development of a technical literature in Latin for the first time—at least as important as this discussion is the polemic, which can be found in so much of his writing, that will persuade his readers of the appropriateness of his theories to their own culture. As well as mediating rhetorical theory, Cicero is producing an account of Roman history that places rhetoric at its centre. The dialogue is the first of a number of attempts to do this, and although *Brutus* connects rhetorical skill with political power with greater singleness of purpose, this connection is first explored in detail in *De oratore*.

---

[3] Readers may, however, turn to Fantham (2004), esp. chs. 7–11.

[4] As Leeman and Pinkster point out, the function of *De oratore* 2 and 3 is more expository; dialectical struggles necessary to making such exposition possible occupy the first book. Although historical anecdotes continue to be important in the later books, more wide-ranging historical analysis is found in book 1. Leeman–Pinkster, i (1981), 12. On Platonic echoes and their ramification for the presentation of rhetoric in the book, see Schütrumpf (1988).

THE ORATOR AND THE STATESMAN

It is clear that well before this work, Cicero had been concerned about how best to conceive of the relationship between oratory and political activity at Rome. The fullest engagement can be found in *Pro Murena*, a speech delivered in 62 as part of the fall-out of the Catilinarian conspiracy. One might expect a speech from that period to display a rather more optimistic vision of the integration of rhetoric and politics than *De oratore*, written surely in a more defensive frame of mind after Cicero's return from exile. In fact, we find that Cicero recognized, even at the height of his political career, that there were difficulties in defining exactly how important the role of rhetoric was in Roman political life.[5] Murena, consul elect for the following year, had attracted a powerful trio of speakers in his defence (Cicero, Hortensius, and Crassus), an indication that these figures saw in Murena the resources necessary to ensure political stability in a successor to Cicero, stability which was seen to reside, and which was likewise a target for accusation, in the character and experience of Murena. So the defence of Murena (for electoral corruption against his rival, Sulpicius) is, within the narrow context of the consular elections of 62, a defence of a way of evaluating what Rome needs in its leaders, and in Cicero's formulation of these values we can see the evolution of what he presents in a more overtly theoretical form in his dialogues. The main thrust of his argument, given the polemical context, is obvious enough: the skills of the military man (Murena) enormously exceed in public importance the skills of the legal expert (jurisconsult Sulpicius). However, the choice of a career as an orator, which lies between these two other routes to political prominence, occupies an ambiguous position, and one which varies according to the rhetorical strategy of the context in which it appears.

Evidence for the prosecution claim that Murena had won the consular elections over Sulpicius by bribery rests on the claim that, on merit, Sulpicius would have won the election. Cicero sets out to demolish this case by contrasting the relative achievements of two men whose careers had been, in terms of ascent of the *cursus honorum*,

---

[5] I am grateful to Chris Pelling for encouraging me to think about this speech. I found the commentary of Adamietz (1989) very useful.

comparable, if not exactly parallel. He begins by accepting that the
two men had an equal expectation of success in the consular elections:
*summam video esse in te, Ser. Sulpici, dignitatem generis, industriae
ceterorumque ornamentorum omnium quibus fretum ad consulatus
petitionem adgredi par est. paria cognosco esse ista in L. Murena....'*
('In you I see, Servius Sulpicius, the greatness of your family, your
hard work, and all the other accomplishments which it is right to rely
on in seeking the consulship. I know that those same qualities are
equally found in L. Murena. . . .').[6] However, after tracing the parallels
between the two men further, Cicero proceeds quite unequivocally to
denigrate Sulpicius' legal calling, and to emphasize the central place of
military skill in Roman history. After a deliberately over-humorous
contrast between life in the field and life in the forum (*te gallorum,
illum bucinarum cantus exsuscitat; tu actionem instituis, ille aciem
instruit* ('the song of the cockerels rouses you from sleep; him, that
of the trumpets; you start up a case; he musters a battle line')), Cicero
drives home his point with a eulogy of the pivotal role played by war
in the production of the myth of Rome: *ac nimirum—dicendum est
enim quod sentio—rei militaris virtus praestat ceteris omnibus. haec
nomen populo Romano, haec huic urbi aeternam gloriam peperit, haec
orbem terrarum parere huic imperio coegit* ('I have to say what I think:
the virtue of military activity is far above all others. This granted the
reputation to the people of Rome and eternal glory to this city; this
forced the world to obey her'); and so on.[7] He then proceeds further to
devalue legal expertise, pointing out that in spite of being fitted in all
that would qualify him as *dignissimus* for the consulship, Sulpicius
can derive absolutely no *dignitas* whatever from his legal work; it is
not the route to the consulship, an office for which Sulpicius had to
wait another decade.[8]

   He sets up a standard for measuring the relationship between intellectual pursuit and politics: *omnes enim artes, quae nobis populi Romani
studia concilient, et admirabilem dignitatem et pergratam utilitatem
debent habere* ('For any arts which foster the affection of the Roman
people for us must have a *dignitas* worthy of admiration and a usefulness which they find particularly pleasing'). The central clause is very
revealing: Cicero wants to imagine an immediate connection between

---

[6] *Pro Murena* 15.   [7] Ibid. 22.   [8] Ibid. 23.

the gift of political power by the people to their leaders and the qualities that those leaders display. *Dignitas* and *utilitas* become the two alternatives routes for achieving appreciation by the public, and both have a distinct affective dimension: *dignitas* awakens *admiratio*; *utilitas* is recognized as being something that elicits feelings of gratitude. In a strange turn to the argument, this definition of political power then allows Cicero to move, in a very brief space, and in a logic that is not particularly lucid, from praising the role of the military commander to insisting upon the centrality of rhetorical skill in Rome's leaders.

gravis etiam illa est et plena dignitatis dicendi facultas quae saepe valuit in consule deligendo, posse consilio atque oratione et senatus et populi et eorum qui res iudicant mentis permovere.   (*Pro Murena* 24)

Serious and full of public respect is that capacity to speak which has often been of value in selecting a consul; it is able through wisdom and rhetoric to sway the minds of the senate and people and of those men who judge cases.

Here the choice of the orator as consul (and consul as orator) has an avowedly self-referential quality and, for the purposes of Murena's defence, to drive a wedge between the work of the orator and the work of the jurisconsult seems a perverse tactic.[9] Cicero's tribute to Sulpicius in *Brutus*, in which he is one of the very few living figures to be discussed, and the only one to be praised explicitly in Cicero's own voice, shows just how perverse; there, not only his legal wisdom but also his skill in arguing cases is highly praised.[10] Nevertheless, Cicero pursues this very argument: jurisconsults are failed orators: only the *imperator* and the *orator bonus* can bring men to the highest point.[11] The passage involves an elaborate defence of the public significance of rhetorical skill, even where the character of his client does not particularly demand it. And by having to demarcate so precisely between legal and rhetorical expertise, he in fact only draws attention to the disparity between the military and rhetorical routes to success. The ambiguous place of rhetorical achievement in Rome is, despite

---

[9] *De orat.* 1. 56. 238–57. 245 makes a similar case that legal knowledge is useless without eloquence, but the broader argument is the promotion of rhetoric rather than the definition of political success.
[10] *Brutus* 151–7. Fantham (2004), 112–13.   [11] *Pro Murena* 30.

the propaganda it receives here, something which, even in his most accomplished manner as a defence lawyer, Cicero is unable entirely to occlude. The same question, about where to place orators in describing Rome's political life, is central to *De oratore* 1.

The setting of *De oratore*, like that of *De re publica*, has a powerful influence over how the dialogue progresses. In *De re publica* the choice of speakers enabled Cicero to present an optimistic vision of Rome's history as a procession of great men, and to present the political process at Rome as an arena of enormous potential for men of talent and commitment.[12] This view of history compensated for the clear anxiety in the preface about the political world of Cicero's own day, and the potential for political theory to be able to do much to change it. There are clear similarities to the setting of *De oratore*: just as Scipio died shortly after the dramatic date of *De re publica*, so Crassus, the most charismatic character in *De oratore*, died of a chill not long after the dramatic date of the dialogue. The device is a clear signal of the nostalgia with which Cicero depicts these leading statesmen of his youth. Within a few years of the dialogue, Antonius too would be dead, in this case murdered.[13] Cicero's target audience would, presumably, have needed no prompting to be sensitive to the particular flavour of this historical setting, but we need to explore its connotations more deeply.

One particularly useful letter makes a good starting point: ten years after completing *De oratore*, Cicero wrote to Atticus concerning the casting of the *Academica*, which he had just finished.[14] In order to comply with Atticus' desire that Cicero grant some homage to Varro, he has altered his usual practice of not using living speakers in his dialogues. Essentially the letter is an extremely compressed discussion of the role of the author in the historical dialogue form, and the attribution of different arguments to different figures. Against Atticus' advice, Cicero has preferred, once the decision was made to use living figures, to appear in the dialogue as himself and take an active

---

[12] Hall (1996) examines the ideological function of Cicero's representation of his speakers; see also Fantham (2004), 50–3; 71–7.

[13] Fantham (2004), 237–9.

[14] *Ad Att.* 13. 19. 3. On the different editions of *Academica* (the letter refers to the second version), Griffin (1997).

role, rather than just appearing as a *kōphon prosōpon*, the mute character on the stage of a Greek tragedy. He approves this practice when the setting of the dialogue is historical, and gives as examples the works of Heraclides of Pontus and his two dialogues *De re publica* and *De oratore*. He then points out that he could not in any case have spoken in *De oratore*, since it took place while he was a boy. On the other hand, it is unclear, given that *De re publica* is located a whole generation before his birth, what exactly Cicero's point is here. He may just be alluding to the practice of using a *kōphon prosōpon*, or more generally to the use of a historical setting that excludes the author as a speaker.

si Cottam et Varronem fecissem inter se disputantis, ut a te proximis litteris admoneor, meum κωφὸν πρόσωπόν esset. hoc in antiquis personis suaviter fit, ut et Heraclides in multis et nos sex de re publica libris fecimus. sunt etiam de oratore nostri tres mihi vehementer probati. in eis *quoque* eae personae sunt ut mihi tacendum fuerit. Crassus enim loquitur, Antonius, Catulus senex, C.Iulius, frater Catuli, Cotta Sulpicius. puero me hic sermo inducitur, ut nullae esse possent partes meae.   (*Ad Atticum* 13. 19. 3–4).

If I had made Cotta and Varro discuss it between them, as you advise in your last letter, mine would be the *kōphon prosōpon*. That is elegantly done when dealing with characters from antiquity. It is what Heraclides did in many of his books, and I did in my six *De re publica*. Then there are my three *De oratore* with which I'm extremely happy. There **too** the characters are such that it would have required me to be silent. For Crassus is talking, Antonius, the elder Catulus, and C. Julius, Catulus' brother, Cotta and Sulpicius. The conversation is held at the time when I was a boy, so that there could not be any role for me.

The crucial word here is *quoque* (italic). It must here signal an additional argument: as well as the general practice of setting dialogues in the past, and thus removing the voice of the author altogether, *De oratore* is a special case, where, in addition to the general use of historical figures, the actual casting or time frame itself precludes the author taking a voice. It might be thought strange that Cicero should make no reference here to Plato, since his dialogues almost all follow this pattern, but instead refer to Heraclides. Whereas Plato worked almost entirely with Socrates and various interlocutors, some of whom were well-known philosophers, others just friends, Heraclides evidently selected characters of political and historical weight, and made them do philosophy. The artificiality of the construction is thus not in doubt, but as is clear from *De re publica*, the notion of the compatibility of theory with political practice is in many respects the driving force of the dialogue. Later in the same letter, referring again to *Academica*, Cicero makes it clear that the kinds of arguments he presents can involve deliberate miscasting:

haec Academica, ut scis, †cum† Catulo, Lucullo, Hortensio contuleram. sane in personis non cadebant; erant enim λογικώτερα quam ut illi de iis somniasse umquam viderentur. itaque ut legi tuas de Varrone, tamquam ἕρμαιον adripui.   (*Ad Atticum* 13. 19. 5).

This treatise on the Academy, as you know, I had given to Catulus, Lucullus, and Hortensius. Obviously the arguments did not fit the characters, for there were sophistications greater than those men could ever be thought to have dreamt of. And so when I read your letter about Varro, I seized on the idea like a godsend.

This is not to say, however, that we can always assume the casting to be as improbable as Cicero suggests here (and he then proceeded to rewrite the dialogue using different characters), and, as will emerge, he goes to some pains to justify a number of the more technical aspects of his speakers' expertise with reference to written sources. However, the letter is good evidence for reading *De oratore* and *De re publica* in much the same way: as dialogues where the historical figures themselves contribute a particular flavour to the work, and where Cicero himself is playing quite deliberately with the tension between the verisimilitude of the speakers' arguments, their own reputation as political figures, and the requirements of the philosophical or technical material that is being conveyed.

Cicero's retrospective pleasure at his achievement in *De oratore* provides an impulse for exploring what exactly the particular gains of his historical setting are. In the analysis that follows, I shall argue that Cicero is particularly careful in the dialogue to tackle one central question: how far is rhetoric an essential part of Roman political life? For Cicero, this was of course the burning question of his career, and is, perhaps as a result, the place where his polarization between the life of *otium* (in which he writes philosophy) and the life of *negotium* (in which he practises politics) breaks down. Cicero was aware of the extent to which his rise to the consulship was due to his success in the courts, and to building a reputation upon his ability to control and influence a crowd in challenging legal and political settings. The tension between his lack of *auctoritas* as a relatively obscure *novus homo* and that rhetorical ability is expressed powerfully in the opening of his first surviving speech, the *Pro Sexto Roscio Amerino* ('In Defence of Sextus Roscius of Amerina'), delivered under the dictatorship of Sulla, and a direct challenge to Sulla's most powerful henchman Chrysogonus. By virtue of his obscurity, Cicero can take on a challenge which deterred more prominent individuals, and the rhetorical confidence of the speech is effectively a manifesto for a more egalitarian form of political activity, one which relies upon education, and thus rhetorical skill, rather than family contacts or hereditary access to office. Cicero comes into the public eye, as he himself describes in the autobiographical section of *Brutus*, as a fully competent orator, and the speech demonstrates the effectiveness of rhetoric in producing a public career at Rome. However, the theoretical elaboration of his own experience, towards the end of his career, repeatedly draws attention to the atypical quality of Cicero's achievement. In that same part of *Brutus*, Cicero compares himself with the other candidates for the consulship; he stood alone not just when it came to basic rhetorical expertise, but also when it came to the wider study of literature.[15] The tension between Cicero's evaluation of the importance of rhetoric in his own career and the environment in which he exercised that skill sets up a dynamic which I will explore in more detail in the remainder of this chapter, and pursue also in Chapter 7. Essentially this is a tension between different visions of Rome's political culture and, by extension, history. I shall argue that in an implementation of his Academic outlook, Cicero brings before his readers two contradictory visions of Rome: one in which rhetoric is a central aptitude for the great men who have produced Rome's history, and one in which it is a peripheral accomplishment with no intrinsic connection to the development of Rome's historical destiny. As in *De re publica*, the contradiction between these two visions is never resolved, and *De oratore* ultimately leaves readers to make up their own minds as to how far a vision of Rome in which Cicero occupies centre-stage is an accurate

---

[15] *Brutus* 322.

description of Roman history, or how far it is wishful thinking on Cicero's part—a failed, self-conscious attempt to glorify his own career as an expression of something which has the potential to exist in Rome, but in reality does not.

COMPETING VERSIONS OF ROME'S HISTORY: CHARACTERIZATION AND HISTORICAL RECONSTRUCTION

In this section, I shall discuss in more detail the manner in which Cicero characterizes the three main characters who dominate the dialogue: Crassus, Scaevola, and Antonius. These figures are used to embody different ways of looking at the relationship between rhetoric and history at Rome, but Cicero's practice is a lot more sophisticated than one that makes the figures into mouthpieces for particular theoretical standpoints or interpretations of history. Instead, he uses the dynamic potential of the dialogue and an enhanced awareness of the problems of characterizing individuals from history, in order to produce a range of different views of Rome's past which cannot readily be synthesized. As the letter discussed in the previous chapter makes clear, the question of *auctoritas* was one of which Cicero was particularly aware with regard to the casting of his dialogues. The characters in both *De oratore* and *De re publica* are clearly chosen because of their reputation, their *auctoritas* as figures of political significance. In the case of *De re publica*, we have seen how the cast of the dialogue presents a kind of prehistory to the political problems of Cicero's own day. Scipio and his friends can hold an optimistic vision of the potential of Rome's great men to take control of the state in a benign manner precisely because they are situated at a point in history where the full horrors of such a vision, in the form of the civil wars which characterized the Marian and Sullan dictatorships, had yet to occur, and where the balance between individual ambition and the collective government of the Republic had not degenerated unequivocally into a fear that powerful individuals necessarily extinguished the power of their peers.

The speakers of *De oratore* are different: they are chosen not because their vision of Roman history belongs to the final moment of a tradition, but because they are pioneers: pioneers of rhetorical excellence, who, like Scipio and his friends, are created by Cicero to embody ideals which are clearly projections of Cicero's own ambitions, but which contain a balance, in their own historical context, between plausibility and manifest idealization. Just like the characters in *De re publica*, Crassus, Antonius, and their circle express this balance in the production of competing visions of Roman history. Whereas *De re publica* explored the tension between different visions of the potential of Rome's history to support an idealization of the monarchic principle, in *De oratore*, rhetoric, and its role in Rome's history, is the central theme. Comparison with *De re publica* makes it clear that what might otherwise look like decorative scene-setting in the opening parts of *De oratore* is in fact material organized around one of the important polemic aims of the entire work: the positioning of rhetoric as a central institution in the development of Roman political life.

The central problem is made clear in the work's preface: Cicero is responding to a request from his brother Quintus, the work's addressee, to produce a treatise on oratory, and counters Quintus' request with an expression of what has led him to desire to meet it. Cicero's interest has been awakened by contemplating the reasons for the comparative lack of good orators in Rome's past: ... *cur plures in omnibus artibus quam in dicendo admirabiles exstitissent* (*De orat.* 1. 2. 6). He continues: *quis autem dubitet, quin belli duces praestantissimos ex hac una civitate paene innumerabiles, in dicendo autem excellentes vix paucos proferre possimus?* (*De orat.* 1. 2. 8) ('There is no doubt that we can easily find almost innumerable eminent military leaders from this one state, but hardly any who excel in speaking'). Rome is thus characterized as a nation rich in statesmen and warriors, but lacking in orators.

This interpretation is developed shortly afterwards, in a sketch of the development of Rome as a world power which integrates the development of rhetorical education with the expansion of Rome's influence. The benefit of an established *imperium* was *otium*, and the youth of Rome devoted itself to rhetorical glory: *nemo fere laudis cupidus adolescens non sibi ad dicendum studio omni enitendum putavit* (*De orat.* 1. 4. 13). The initial lack of instructional material was soon compensated by the growth in popularity of an education acquired from Greeks, or in Greece. Oratory flourished at Rome, and the rewards for those individuals who excelled were great then, as they are now: *gratia, opes, dignitas* (personal favour, wealth, status). But notwithstanding the richness of native *ingenium*, the number of famous orators from the past is small. The explanation of this state of affairs lies in the subject itself; excellence in rhetoric demands a total command of a wide range of *artes*. However, Cicero's own treatise on rhetoric will modify this demand for a Roman audience: *neque vero ego hoc tantum oneris imponam nostris praesertim oratoribus, in hac tanta occupatione urbis ac vitae'* (*De orat.* 1. 6. 21). The real business of the Roman courts and Senate already places such demands upon politically active men that it is unreasonable to suppose that they will have in addition time to increase their theoretical knowledge. Cicero will therefore sift the enormous quantity of Greek theory, and include only what the greatest men have thought relevant (*non complectar in his libris amplius, quam quod huic generi, re quaesita et multum disputata, summorum hominum prope consensu est tributum* (*De orat.* 1. 6. 22)). He does not object to Greek theory, but knows that his brother will excuse him if he grants greater weight to Romans with a reputation for eloquence than to the authority of Greeks: *dabis hanc veniam, mi frater, ut opinor, ut eorum, quibus summa dicendi laus a nostris hominibus concessa est, auctoritatem Graecis anteponam* (*De orat.* 1. 6. 23).

The cultural stereotype is clear and familiar: the Romans are conceived of as great and powerful, the Greeks as learned but politically insignificant, their capacity for theoretical elaboration an expression of the comparative triviality of their political culture.[16] But we must not let familiarity obscure the strangeness of Cicero's position. There has been a marked shortage of Roman orators, in spite of a huge interest in rhetoric. The traditional political institutions at Rome have favoured the growth of oratory and brought in a flood of learned Greeks to teach it. However, although Greeks understand rhetoric better, there is no point attempting to adopt their standards wholesale for Rome, for the

---

[16] For a useful recent summary of the cultural stereotype in Cicero with copious bibliography, see Zetzel (2003).

political conditions at Rome will not accommodate them. The standards of what is relevant for Rome will be set not by Greece, but by those
summi viri at Rome, whose very paucity, at least as accomplished
speakers, was the motivation for Cicero's initial decision to write a
work of rhetorical theory.

So, while evoking an account of Rome that emphasizes the supremacy of eloquence, the applicability of rhetoric, and the suitability
of Rome as a potential breeding ground for future orators, Cicero
at the same time spares no blushes in stating openly that Rome's
historical development hitherto has not constituted such a breeding
ground. Even in the opening preface of the work, it is clear that Cicero
is dealing with a contentious and complex historical problem: the
popularity of rhetoric has not been matched by a corresponding
success in producing effective or memorable orators, and in spite of
historical conditions that have promoted rhetoric, political power
at Rome has not corresponded to rhetorical excellence; in spite of
the high rewards rhetoric can bring, we can deduce that those rewards
have been reaped by surprisingly few. As the inspiration for a treatise
aimed at promoting a new, more culturally appropriate form of rhetorical theory, this makes perfect sense: Cicero's theoretical ambitions
recognize a situation which requires remedial action, in the form
of an accessible digest of the essentials of Greek theory. As an analysis,
of Rome's character and historical development, however, the tensions
are unresolved. What, therefore, is the basis for supposing that
the arguments of his speakers are likely to be convincing as a historical
analysis? And is that even what Cicero has as his aim?

One of the keys to understanding the role of history in the work
comes in the opening exchanges of the dialogue, as Crassus and
Scaevola propose competing evaluations of the significance of rhetoric.
Crassus begins with a grandiose and authoritative statement of the
importance of rhetoric as a constant feature of human society, clearly
designed as itself something of a rhetorical show-piece, which culminates in a plea to the younger members of the gathering to dedicate
themselves further to the pursuit of rhetoric. Rhetoric, he claims, sets
men apart from beasts, and is the mechanism for the wise and ordered
government of all states. Scaevola's response is unexpected, and vital
for our enquiry. His arguments against Crassus set up a distinction
between the practice of statecraft and the practice of oratory, which

Crassus' speech had sought to elide. He strikes at Crassus' generalities about *humanitas*, and sets up a distinction between different kinds of society. Early Rome, he argues, was categorized by an absence of rhetoric; it was not by means of *eloquentia* that Romulus gathered his people around him or organized intermarriage with the Sabines, but rather through *consilium* and *sapientia*. In short, challenging ejaculations (designed perhaps to make clear that good ideas do not require stylistic ornamentation to be effective), he rejects the notion that eloquence can be equated with good government, arguing instead that Rome's history is characterized by the wealth of its *consilia* (sensible ideas, wise counsel), the absence of *verba* (words) (*omnia, nonne plena consiliorum, inania verborum videmus? (De orat.* 1. 9. 37)).

Moreover, eloquent men have been responsible for more harm than good; the Gracchi can be contrasted with their father. He was *homo prudens et gravis, haudquaquam eloquens* ('a wise and serious man, barely articulate'), and in that capacity, the salvation of the state (*De orat.* 1. 9. 38). His sons, on the other hand, employed their eloquence to destroy the *res publica*. A knowledge of Roman law and custom (*leges veteres moresque maiorum*), augury, religion, *iura civilia*; these things operate independent of eloquence. Scaevola's next reproof is more technical, referring to the Greek philosophical rejections of rhetoric going back to Pythagoras, Democritus, and Socrates, all insisting on the distinction between rhetoric and true wisdom. It is this part of the argument that Crassus picks up on, stating familiarity with that debate and advancing the terms of the discussion. His response to Scaevola essentially turns into an extended display of his detailed familiarity with different positions within Greek philosophy concerning the relationship between an ability to speak authoritatively on any issue and a genuine understanding of that issue. But Scaevola's evocation of a Rome without rhetorical skill is left uncontested, and it clearly has a central place in Cicero's thoughts. These two visions of the place of rhetoric present us with two alternative versions of Rome. One is characterized by natural wit, traditional wisdom, and the practice of good government. The other sees all these achievements as part of a teleological process, whereby the current dominance of interest in rhetoric is no more than a more explicit form of what has always been present, if undefined. The latter, represented in Crassus' arguments, is essentially an argument for the synthesis of theory with practice; the former sees technical expertise and practical wisdom as two different things, potentially, but not necessarily, complementary.

The conflict between Crassus and Scaevola essentially expands a disagreement between Cicero's and Quintus' views on rhetoric, referred to with almost incomprehensible compression in the preface: *ego eruditissimorum hominum artibus eloquentiam contineri statuam, tu autem illam ab elegantia doctrinae segregandum putes et in quodam ingenii atque exercitationis genere ponendam* (*De orat.* 1. 2. 5) ('I think that eloquence belongs to the accomplishments of the most learned men; but you think it should be removed from the elegance of learning and regarded as a type of natural faculty and practical skill). Essentially this is a dispute about the right kind of theory with which to discuss rhetoric: either as a branch of philosophy, with its own moral and ethical implications, or simply as a matter where practical instruction is all that is required, and where the cultivation of the gifts of the individual marks out the highest ambition of any theoretical enquiry. In the view that Cicero here ascribes to Quintus, rhetoric lacks wide-ranging social and political connotations, and should be dealt with as a primarily practical form of knowledge. In Cicero's own view, these practical elements need to be seen within a wider social framework. The conflicting historical visions of Crassus and Scaevola transfer this theoretical debate on to the historical plane. Scaevola sees rhetoric as a social accomplishment that might adorn political activity, but which is wholly independent of its essential, historical character. Crassus, on the other hand, makes rhetoric into the guiding principle of all human activity. If one had to choose which of these two analyses is more compelling as a piece of history, it would have to be Scaevola's, and by leaving Scaevola's anti-rhetorical analysis uncontested, Cicero suggests that he has a great deal of sympathy with it as a historical analysis. But as an idealization that has the power to effect some kind of political progress at Rome, Crassus' view of Rome as an essentially rhetorical culture is much more compelling. It is, at the same time, manifestly rather bad history. As we have come to expect, from Cicero's general dialogic practice, however, there is no resolution of this dilemma. In particular, Scaevola's conception of a society devoid of rhetoric acts as a necessary pre-condition to the establishment of a discussion of rhetorical theory that is appropriate to Rome.

It is vital that, in spite of the powerful appeal to the development of philosophy which constitutes Crassus' refutation of Scaevola's position, Scaevola's arguments derive ultimately not from philosophy, but from historical anecdote. Such anecdote is hard to refute. And as the dialogue progresses, and in particular by the time we come to the discussion of the production of rhetorically effective history in *De oratore* 2, the relationship of hard historical fact to persuasive arguments derived from a sense of what is probable, becomes highly opaque. In Scaevola's evocation of a history of Rome where rhetoric has no role to play, we find the negative pole for the conception of rhetoric which dominates the dialogue: rhetoric as the life-blood of Rome, and Rome as a place where not only can the ideal orator thrive, but where the discussion of that ideal has a connection with the political and intellectual conditions in which he is to operate. Scaevola's history is history as unadorned fact, history almost in opposition to the world of ideas. Wisdom and good counsel operated, from Romulus to the Gracchi, as forces independent of theory. The theoretical discussion which Crassus' refutation sets out to promote depends upon a different view of history, one where the political and the philosophical are two sides of the same coin, and where the continuation of the dialogue depends upon a demonstration of that history in action. In laying the ground for the exposition of rhetorical theory that takes place in books 2 and 3, Crassus needs to demonstrate, in his own use of theory, that he, as a historical character, can himself act as a refutation of the society without rhetoric that Scaevola evokes. He himself becomes an emblem of the integration of philosophy and rhetoric at Rome, and the validity of his position depends, therefore, to a large extent upon him functioning not just as a transparent fiction, a screen for the projection of Cicero's own theoretical preoccupations, but as a manifestation of a historical process that did in fact take place at Rome. Only in this manner can the spectre of Scaevola's image of Rome be finally driven out. It will become clear, however, that what Cicero ultimately settles for is a compromise: the re-creation of a plausible Crassus, with plenty of room for an essentially playful ambiguity concerning the nature of his reconstruction and the relationship between past and present in the vision of an integration of rhetoric and history at Rome. The casual manner, of course, in which many critics refer to Crassus as Cicero's mouthpiece vastly underestimates the complexity of Cicero's concerns in producing this representation.

Thus, in his protracted discussion of the state of Greek rhetorical theory, Cicero goes to excessive lengths to demonstrate Crassus' theoretical expertise. His speech is littered with references to Greek thinkers and teachers from the generation before Cicero's birth, and simultaneous to the main thrust of the dialogue, which is the exploration of these different theories, runs another argument, in which Crassus' own expertise becomes the object of attention. Using a technique that resembles the one by which the speakers in *De re publica* draw attention to their philosophical friends and sources, Cicero makes Crassus, then likewise Scaevola and Antonius, justify their acquaintance with a wide range of rhetorical theory and theorists. The aim is to make the presentation of rhetorical theory adhere to a coherent vision of Roman political history. Crassus and his colleagues are dramatic embodiments of the idea of Rome as a fertile breeding ground for rhetoric—as, in short, the antecedents to Cicero himself. Just as in Scaevola's evocation of a Rome without rhetoric, however, Cicero never allows the alternative view of Rome to be silent for long.

After Crassus, responding to Scaevola, has stated at length his view that the expertise of the successful orator rests not just on technical mastery of his own field, but on that of a large number of related disciplines, Scaevola once more expresses scepticism concerning Crassus' over-idealized view of rhetorical practice. His short speech is a perfect encapsulation of a number of Cicero's favourite devices. Scaevola begins, a smile on his face, by drawing attention to Crassus' own excessive rhetorical skill, pointing out that he has both managed to accept Scaevola's separation of rhetoric from other arts and, at the same time, to turn those same arguments on their head and make the orator master of them all.[17] Cicero is here relativizing the authority of Crassus, drawing attention to the artificiality of his arguments, and in particular to the potential distortion of philosophy which rhetorical skill can accomplish. He then, as if to sharpen the focus of this critique, refers to a conversation which he himself had with the rhetorician Apollonius, whom he met when taking up the office of praetor on Rhodes, concerning the philosophy which Panaetius had taught him. Crassus' speech is, he says, more serious than that of Apollonius, but is essentially the same, in that it attributes the needs of all different kinds of learning to rhetoric.

---

[17] *De orat.* 1. 17. 74.

irrisit ille quidem, ut solebat, philosophiam, atque contempsit, multaque
non tam graviter dixit, quam facete, tua autem fuit oratio eiusmodi, non ut
ullam artem doctrinamve contemneres, sed ut omnes comites ac ministras
oratoris esse diceres.   (*De oratore* 1. 17. 75)

Indeed, he laughed at philosophy, as he always did, and expressed his contempt,
and made a lot of points that were amusing rather than serious. But your speech
was of a different sort: not that you despise any skill or branch of learning,
but that you say that all are companions and hand maidens to the orator.

The mention of this specific conversation, firmly located as to date
and place,[18] emphasizes Scaevola's credentials as a statesman capable
of theoretical discourse, while also reiterating the indiscriminate
hegemony of Crassus' definition of oratory. This problem of such
a hegemony is clarified in the next sentence. By defining rhetoric so
broadly, says Scaevola, Crassus is setting up an ideal which has never
been fulfilled historically. Even if Crassus himself were able to embody this idea of oratory as a form of universal wisdom, he would in
the process become such an exceptional figure that, in the process, he
would detract from the repute of those lesser orators who had
acquired their reputation through a rather less lofty conception of
what rhetoric consists in.

quas ego, si quis sit unus complexus omnes [i.e. artes], idemque si ad eas
facultatem istam ornatissime orationis adiunxerit; non possum dicere, eum
non egregium quemdam hominem atque admirandum fore, sed is, si quis
esset, aut si etiam unquam fuisset, aut vero si esse posset, tu esses unus
profecto; qui et meo iudicio, et omnium, vix ullam ceteris oratoribus (pace
horum dixerim) laudem reliquisti.   (*De oratore* 1. 17. 76)

If there were ever any one man who could embrace all these arts, and the same
man could join to them that faculty of producing a most finely worked speech,
I cannot deny that he would be a particularly unusual individual and worthy of
admiration. But that man, were he to exist, or if he ever had existed, or indeed if
he could exist: you, in short, would be he. You are the one who, in my
judgement and everyone else's, has scarcely left any room for praise for other
orators (they will excuse me for saying so).

Scaevola, rather incongruously, has become the character who stands
up for the integrity of philosophical knowledge against that of

---

[18] See Leeman–Pinkster, *ad loc.* and *ad* 1. 11. 45.

rhetoric, trying to keep philosophy and rhetoric apart. And once again he reinforces the notion that Crassus' idealization of oratory infringes not only the more common understanding, but also the very terms in which the excellent orators of the past have themselves been judged. The standards set by Crassus, in other words, are based upon that same methodological procedure which, if we recall the objection of Scipio and his friends to the ideal republic of Plato, was explicitly rejected in *De re publica*: namely, the divorcing of theoretical knowledge from its historical context. Elaborating upon Scaevola's earlier rejection of rhetoric, Cicero here suggests that, by setting up the discussion of the ideal orator as the goal of his dialogue, he will necessarily be violating historical veracity. The crucial words of Scaevola are *si etiam unquam fuisset* ('if indeed he ever had existed'). The existence of this orator as a historical phenomenon is in itself enough to undermine what little trace of rhetorical excellence the orators who have in fact existed have been able to acquire. Crassus' ideal will undermine any actual reputation (*laus*) that they have in reality been granted. So here, Scaevola not only protects the integrity of philosophy from being subsumed as a branch of rhetoric; he also demarcates the ahistorical ideal of oratory (that will form the object of the ensuing discussion) from the historical reality of rhetorical tradition at Rome.

Cicero makes similar play with the conflict between historicity and the needs of rhetorical theory in the figure of Antonius, most pointedly when referring to Antonius' own rhetorical handbook, a work which is made to bear not just the burden of proof of the verisimilitude of Antonius' character in this dialogue, but also, by extension, the lack of verisimilitude which Cicero's portrait of him exposes. In *Brutus*, Cicero makes Brutus describe the work as *illum de ratione dicendi sane exilem libellum* ('that really rather scanty booklet about the theory of speaking').[19] It becomes, in Antonius' own narrative, a piece of writing that somehow got published against his wishes (*De orat.* 1. 21. 94). It is also referred to by Crassus to encourage Antonius to supplement his writing with a proper presentation of his views on the acquisition of rhetorical excellence (*De orat.* 1. 47. 206). Picking up on this, Antonius describes it in a little more detail as a work

---

[19] Fantham (2004), 90, presents the evidence for its character.

based upon his own practical experience, rather than one derived from learning.

> neque enim sum de arte dicturus, quam nunquam didici, sed de mea con-
> suetudine; ipsaque illa, quae in commentarium meum rettuli, sunt eius-
> modi, non aliqua mihi doctrina tradita, sed in rerum usu causisque tractata.
>
> (*De oratore* 1. 43. 208)

> For I am not about to talk about the art which I have never learnt, but about
> my own practice. Those very things which I have recorded in my handbook
> are of that sort, not handed on to me by any study, but employed in practical
> affairs and in court cases.

This book embodies the whole conflict facing Cicero in his use of the historical dialogue setting. He wants his theoretical conversation to appear at least to some degree plausible in the mouths of his speakers. That Antonius did write a handbook of rhetorical theory is a cornerstone in his attempt to retroject some kind of theoretical interest in rhetoric back to a period before his birth. The contents of that work, which was presumably also available to Cicero's readers, were clearly of a very different kind to the philosophically competent character whom Cicero here presents. By characterizing that book here as one in which the fruits of experience, rather than the products of *ars* or *doctrina*, can be found, Cicero finds a compromise position, one in which Antonius can function both as a figure with an interest in rhetorical theory and as one for whom rhetoric is a practical discipline, one which, unlike philosophy, does not require technical instruction. This is the same position represented by the one directly attributed sentence from the booklet: *disertos me cognosse nonnullos, eloquentem adhuc neminem* ('that I had known several accomplished speakers, but as yet not one truly eloquent).[20] The sentiment strikes once again at the historical dilemma which confronts Cicero: rhetorical skill of the kind which he is hoping to define and promote is, and was at the time of his speakers, not a feature of the Roman political scene.

At the start of *De oratore* 2, we find ourselves in another prologue, and Cicero immediately draws attention to what is in fact one of the

---

[20] *De orat.* 1. 21. 94; cf. 3. 49. 189, where Antonius expresses astonishment that he has now, at last, found (in Cicero's Crassus) the truly eloquent man of whom he had previously despaired.

most striking features of the discourse which has just concluded: its artificiality. The new book opens with Cicero recalling to Quintus the opinion that was common when they were young, that both Crassus and Antonius had only the most rudimentary grasp of rhetorical theory. The gesture is very striking, given the excessive dependence of the previous book upon the demonstration of a high degree of theoretical knowledge. This contradiction is, however, an essential part of Cicero's technique, in that, even though the prologue then continues to justify Cicero's decision to credit his speakers with theoretical understanding, and to provide, as it were, a set of footnotes to justify the state of their knowledge, the starting point is a moment where the detailed theoretical understanding is shown to be entirely Cicero's own, and his attempt to ground it in the grandees of his early youth is shown to be no more than a desperate idealization.[21] The philosophical awareness which Crassus in particular demonstrates constitutes, therefore, a vacillation between several different voices: Cicero wants to reconstruct as accurately as he can the intellectual world of his childhood, discussing even relatively obscure teachers of rhetoric or philosophy in some detail. We should look upon this as a serious attempt to provide a kind of intellectual history which conveys information useful to Cicero's readers, and which fulfils the wider function of locating the development of rhetorical education firmly in its historical context. On the other hand, by putting this reconstruction in the mouths of figures for whom such knowledge is, to say the least, improbable, Cicero draws attention to the difficulties of the process of reconstruction itself. In this second prologue he ultimately justifies his choice by pointing out that at least it can be verified that Crassus and Antonius were effective speakers; and he compares them to other figures he might have chosen, Servius Galba or Gaius Carbo, about whom he could have made up anything he wished, *nullius memoria iam refellente* ('with no-one's memory to contradict him').[22] As in *De re publica*, the historical setting of the

---

[21] See Leeman–Pinkster, ii (1985), 186–8, who give a masterfully concise discussion of Cicero's careful play with the tension between historicity and fiction.

[22] *De orat.* 2. 2. 9. In spite of these reservations, Cicero does give a quite detailed account of both men in *Brutus*, in the case of Galba, relying explicitly on the oral testimony of Rutilius Rufus, who was, it will be remembered, the supposed informant

dialogue is of central importance to the communication of its ideas; and even though much of the second and third books are taken up with the more ahistorical matter of rhetorical theory, Cicero is still preoccupied with the question of historical validation for his speakers. As I have said, that is a validation which is both granted and, at the same time, withheld.

HISTORY AND ORATORY IN *DE ORATORE* 2

The most notorious part of *De oratore* 2, at least as far as Cicero's interest in historiography is concerned, is Antonius' discussion of the stylistic qualities appropriate to historical writing (*De orat.* 2. 12. 51–15. 64). The section has been interpreted as demonstrating that Cicero regards historical writing as no more than a branch of rhetoric.[23] Although it is hardly necessary to engage in a detailed refutation of this view, the polemic does to a certain extent dominate scholarly discussion of the section, and I will therefore take this opportunity to apply the principles of my approach to reading Cicero, in order to move the argument beyond a position such that Cicero is either criticized for failing to separate history adequately from oratory or is defended from this charge. By looking at the section in the wider context not just of the arguments of the part of the dialogue in which it occurs, but also as part of an engagement with the theoretical relationship between history and rhetoric in Cicero's writing generally, it is possible to arrive at a reading which advances our understanding of Cicero, rather than

for the conversations of *De re publica: Brutus* 85–9; and for Carbo, there was also evidently reasonable oral testimony, as well as speeches preserved in written form: *Brutus* 104–6.

[23] See Leeman–Pinkster, ii. 249–52, who direct much of their fire against Wiseman (1979), who in fact makes little use of *De oratore*; contrast Woodman (1988), 78–116, taken up by Fantham (2004), 147–52. Petzold (1972) is authoritative on many aspects of Cicero and historiography; he attributes to generic differences the conflict between Cicero's view of serious history as culminating in the orator-statesman, and the rather different requirements for autobiographical memoir. See too Kessler (1983), 31, who sees this passage as an exception to widespread neglect of historiography in ancient rhetorical theory. Kessler also points out that Petrarch's copy of *De oratore* did not contain 2. 51–60, which were only discovered in 1421: Kessler (1983), 32.

just entrenching our own prejudices in partial readings of individual voices within more polyphonous texts.

Antonius introduces historical writing as an example of the kinds of discourse which have as a rule been left untouched in the conventional accounts of rhetorical theory. This argument is two-sided. On the one hand, Cicero seems to want to compensate for the absence of a discussion of historical writing in rhetorical treatises and, on the other, to be arguing for a greater role for the study of history in the formation of the ideal orator. Once again, the role played by the characterization of the speaker in the attribution of the arguments is ambiguous. Antonius lists a canon of Greek historians, some of whom he does no more than name, while for others he does offer a brief characterization of their stylistic virtues. These characterizations are deliberately diffident: qualifications such as *mea sententia* ('in my opinion'), *ut me quidem, quantum ego Graece scripta intellegere possum* ('as far as I can understand written Greek'), *ut mihi quidem videtur* ('as it seems to me, at least'), densely punctuate the already quite laconic account. When Antonius has finished, Caesar draws attention to Cicero's strategy, by asking Catulus to join him in dismissing those (among them, presumably, many of Cicero's readers who would be fully alive to the irony of this moment) who claim that Antonius does not read Greek (*De orat.* 2. 14. 59). Antonius responds to this by describing his own reading of the historians, as a kind of amusement for his leisure, one which enables his own style to absorb something of that of his models, without him needing to undertake a deliberate study of their technique (*De orat.* 2. 14. 60–1).

Cicero would seem to be allowing Antonius' knowledge of the Greek historians to be historically incredible, but at the same time making him act once again, this time in the particular area of historical education, as a model for the combination of rhetorical expertise without a cumbersome body of theoretical discussion. One vital sentence reads: *sed ne latius hoc vobis patere videatur, haec dumtaxat in Graecis intellego, quae ipsi qui scripserunt voluerunt vulgo intellegi* (*De orat.* 2. 14. 60) ('in case you think this view should apply more widely, I only understand from the Greeks what they who wrote them wanted to be understood by the common reader'). He then goes on to distinguish such discourse from philosophical (too obscure) or poetic (in a different language); so that the reading of history in Greek becomes an easy pastime for the general reader, being a fundamentally non-specialist form of writing. Cicero here strikes a compromise in his characterization of Antonius: he has prepared us already for the notion that his theoretical understanding goes beyond the evidence presented in the surviving handbook; in this particular example, Antonius' acquaintance with Greek literature is allowed as a possibility, but qualified by the brevity and diffidence with which the Greek material is discussed. Antonius discoursing upon the Greek historiography may appear historically unlikely, but Cicero goes to considerable pains to draw attention to this unlikelihood without sacrificing the requirements of his argument.

The main argument here, then, is the consistent demarcation of history from the main traditions of rhetorical theory, a demarcation reinforced shortly afterwards, when, concluding the discussion of history, Antonius moves to the next topic by pointing out that there are other areas too where a vital aspect of rhetorical practice remains untouched by the conventional divisions of theory: *in eodem silentio multa alia oratorum officia iacuerunt, cohortationes, praecepta, consolationes, admonita*...(*De orat.* 2. 15. 64) ('in that same silence lie many other duties of the orators: exhortation, precept, consolation, admonition...'). History is presented, therefore, as an area of general education which is not generally the subject of rhetorical theory, but which is an essential part of the education of an orator. What Antonius has learnt from Greek historians comes in the form both of knowledge of the past and in terms of a general improvement in style, one that occurs in much the same way as a suntan when one is walking outdoors (*De orat.* 2. 14. 60). It is, therefore, experiential (or empirical) rather than theoretical education.

The prominence that scholars have attributed to this passage as a clue to Cicero's own views on historiography appears, in this light, to assign too much weight to a subject which appears within the dialogue as explicitly marginal. History is included here because it is not normally a part of rhetorical treatises, and moreover we are precisely in a part of our own treatise where marginal processes generally are being discussed. The stylistic qualities appropriate for the historian are tackled briefly, right at the end of the section, and once again as proof of the general exclusion of this material from the treatises. The end of the discussion picks up on the beginning; the Roman historians with whom the speakers in the dialogue are familiar—the latest of whom is also the most sophisticated, Cloelius Antipater, who was also a teacher of Crassus[24]—are characterized as producing bare narratives of events, scarcely touched by rhetorical expertise. Cicero provides an important potted history of Roman historiography here, one that has, in its basic shape, been little challenged: history at Rome began with the keeping of yearly records; these developed into literary annals, whose authors' only stylistic aim was clarity of expression.[25] In contrast to the situation in which the Greek historians were working, Roman eloquence was confined to specific rhetorical contexts, legal and political, and therefore history is deliberately set up as a realm that was, traditionally, non-rhetorical. Even without making Antonius have recourse to the analysis of Roman culture as one that was in essence non-rhetorical—without arguing, in other words, that Fabius Pictor wrote so plainly because he reflected a general stylistic plainness characteristic of all early Roman efforts at literary production—Antonius does describe a form of historical writing at Rome, where the model, unlike in Greece, was a simple, unadorned narrative, immune from rhetorical influence. He thus evokes once again the spectre of Scaevola's vision of a pristine form of Roman self-expression, where rhetoric took the form of a later adornment, something acquired from Greece, without in so many words pointing out that the Roman historians were reflecting a general absence of rhetorical skill common to all forms of expression at Rome in the era preceding that of the dialogue.

Contrary, therefore, to the interpretation which sees this passage as a sign that Cicero wants to reduce historiography to a branch of rhetoric, what we find is that Roman historiography, in careful contrast to Greek, is delineated by Cicero as a genre where rhetorical influence is a later accretion. It is true that in Greece, too, there was an early phase in which writers such as Hellanicus, Acusilaus, and others wrote in a manner comparable to that of Pictor and Cato (*De orat.* 2. 12. 53); but the subsequent development represented by

---

[24] *Brutus* 102.
[25] See Frier (1999); Chassignet (1996); Wiseman (1994), 1–4, offers some resistance.

Herodotus and Thucydides has yet to occur at Rome. Antonius regards rhetorically enhanced historiography as a desirable outcome, but never suggests that the stylistic qualities of the Greeks are the result of a distortion of their fundamental task. He elaborates, in other words, upon the analysis given at the start of the discussion by Catulus, responding to Antonius' question, '*qualis oratoris et quanti hominis in dicendo putas historiam scribere?*': '*si ut Graeci scripserunt, summi*' inquit Catulus; '*si ut nostri nihil opus est oratore; satis est non esse mendacem*' (*De orat.* 2. 12. 51) ('What kind of orator or a man of what kind of skill in speaking do you think writes history?' 'If you mean write it like the Greeks have done, one of the highest skill,' said Catulus, 'if as our Roman ones, there is no need of an orator; it is enough that he is not a liar'.)' The present tense of *scribere* is central, as is the perfect tense of *scripserunt*.[26] Antonius is asking not about Catulus' vision of ideal historiography, but rather for an evaluation of the rhetorical qualities of existing historiography as they bear upon his view of the role of rhetoric within the genre in the two cultures. Greek historians have displayed the highest rhetorical skills, while their Roman counterparts have been merely truthful recorders of the past. The discussion continues as a plea for a greater cross-fertilization between Greek and Roman practice, in much the same way as the more mainstream body of Greek rhetorical theory is adapted for Rome, orators being capable of learning from historians, on a stylistic level as well as in terms of their ability to converse authoritatively about the past.

There is, therefore, a parallel between this discussion of historiography and the wider vision of rhetoric within Roman culture that I have examined above. Once again, two alternatives are presented, historiography with or without rhetoric, just as history itself can either display rhetorical accomplishment or not; but this time they are differently situated. Antonius and Catulus describe the state of historical writing in their own day, Antipater acting as a signal of a development that for Cicero's readers would be continued in the development of historiography in the predecessors of Sallust, Licinius Macer, or Valerius Antias,

---

[26] Translations can distort the status of this discussion e.g. '... do you think it requires to write history' (Watson (1889), 234); 'Very great indeed, if you're talking about Greek historiography' (Woodman (1988), 76).

for example.[27] However, in contrast to the ambivalent view which the dialogue as a whole expresses about the necessity for believing at least in the possibility that Roman politics from its very beginning was carried out by, and produced, men of rhetorical ability, there is little faith here that the recording of that history followed a similar trajectory. Roman historiography is unequivocally non-rhetorical, and it is a striking gap in Antonius' argument that the simple connection is never explicitly made between the general absence of rhetorical skill and the work of the Roman historians. Instead, historiography is carefully distinguished from those areas of Roman culture where rhetoric did flourish, namely politics and the courts, and what are almost the rules of the genre of historiography: lack of rhetorical enhancement.

This is the perspective from which we should interpret the repeated complaint about the absence of theoretical treatments of historiography. Historiography needs rhetoric, and rhetoric needs historiography; Greece presents a satisfactory historical development. But what has gone wrong at Rome? Once again, Cicero steers clear of the obvious interpretation, that the absence of rhetoric in historical writings was simply a reflection of an absence of rhetorical skill endemic in Rome as late as the period in which the dialogue is set. But the elaborate manner in which the discussion assumes that rhetoric and historiography are at Rome generally discrete genres, with neither theoretical nor practical contact with each other, needs to be understood as part of Cicero's careful characterization of his speakers, and of the historical setting of the dialogue. Just as in *De re publica*, the central topic of monarchic rule is discussed in a manner which deliberately bypasses the dictatorial trends of political events subsequent to the date of the dialogue, so for the more peripheral topic of historiography, *De oratore* presents a view of the simple, unadorned nature of historical writing which is linked firmly to the fictional world of the dialogue, and which reflects neither Cicero's own views of the needs of historical writing nor the development of the genre by Cicero's own day. Indeed, the choice of Cloelius Antipater as the most recent figure mentioned is most striking.

----

[27] See Wiseman (1979), 117–21; Chassignet (1999); Kierdorf (2003). Fantham (2004), 154, points out that Catulus wrote his own historical work (*Brutus* 132); Antonius' grim assessment is thus hardly a compliment to his interlocutor.

Other historians could have been used; the most obvious candidate is C. Fannius, a character given lively characterization in *Brutus*, and who also takes a walk-on part in *De re publica*.[28] He would, however, represent a form of rhetorically elaborate historical writing which would disrupt the requirements of the dialogue that Roman historiography should be presented as a genre where rhetorical influence was minimal; furthermore, as we discover in *Brutus* (102), Antipater was Crassus' teacher, although how much of his rhetorical skill he could have acquired from such a teacher is impossible to say: Antipater is surely being used here as a symbol of prose simplicity and simultaneously in order to foster the sense of a nascent intellectual *coterie* at Rome at this time.[29]

Rhetoric, therefore, occupies an ambiguous position in historical writing: from Cicero's vision of 91 BCE, it could provide much needed enhancement, something which would increase its popularity among orators, and therefore among the political elite generally. This enhancement, of course, is the key to the notion of rhetoric distorting the main task of history: namely, the truthful recording of events. But I hope that my analysis has shown that Cicero is occupied at this point with themes more closely related to those of the rest of the dialogue. Most importantly, the discussion of rhetoric in historical writing needs to be read as an expression of the wider ambiguity concerning the position of rhetoric at Rome: either an essential part or a desirable enhancement. In the case of historiography, Cicero adopts an analysis carefully grounded in its historical context. Historiography was, at this point, both theoretically and practically, divorced from rhetoric. He refrains from suggesting that this divorce was the result of a general neglect of rhetoric at Rome. If from this we want to deduce a theoretical position regarding historical writing (questionable though that desire itself might be), it would have to be that historiography and rhetoric are mutually beneficial. It is clear, however, that Cicero is determined to approach

---

[28] *Rep.* 1. 18; *Brutus* 99–102; (but see Douglas (1966), *ad loc.*, for Cicero's problems identifying the historian of whose work Brutus had produced an *epitome*) and Chassignet (1999), pp. xxxiii–xl.

[29] Fantham (2004), 71–7. At *De leg.* 1. 2. 6, Antipater is an object lesson in bad style, mocked by Atticus for his crude and bristling style that ought to have served as a warning to subsequent historians, but regrettably did not. Lucius Sisenna, another potential candidate for a more elaborate form of historiography, was probably too young to figure in the dialogue; and, just like Antipater, Cicero uses him too as an example of how poor Latin historiography was, this time in *Brutus* (228).

the question from its own historical perspective, as an encounter between disciplines which, at the point where the figures in *De oratore* stand, has yet to reach its full potential.

DE LEGIBUS

At the opening of *De legibus*, Cicero includes an account of the position of Roman historiography similar to that given by Antonius, and the presence of such a discussion is perhaps the strongest support for laying such a heavy emphasis upon problems of historical representation in these three works. The works all have their genesis in the same period, and they represent three different, but complementary, approaches to the technique of philosophical dialogue. *De legibus* has, in terms of its Platonic model, a more obvious affinity as a companion piece to *De re publica*, and indeed, the characters in that work (Cicero, Atticus, Quintus, Cicero) undertake their discussion of laws in full awareness of the discussion of Scipio.[30] A more significant overlap for our purposes is the very fact that *De legibus* opens with a protracted discussion of the problems of writing Rome's history, the absence of a thriving tradition of historiography at Rome, and the specific question of whether or not Cicero is himself in a position to fill that gap. The subject matter takes account both of the discussion of *De oratore* and of the account of Rome's early history in *De re publica* 2. This triangular relationship between the three works can be understood if we bear in mind that while the other two were completed and published in fairly quick succession, *De legibus* was never finished, and Cicero took it up and worked on it again during the last years of his life.[31] It thus seems possible that it contains more pointed responses to the earlier works, and in particular that Cicero is exploiting the differences between the three different castings. By adopting the 'present' and by speaking himself, he was following the suggestion

[30] *De leg.* 1. 9. 27; 2. 10. 23; 3. 5. 12, etc. These references to Scipio bring with them more of the same playfulness regarding the dialogue form which is the basis of my reading of *De re publica*. The fictionalized friends of Cicero treat the fictionalized Scipio as their own discursive antecedent.

[31] *Ad fam.* 9. 2. 5 refers to reworking, but the evidence is not conclusive: Rawson (1973), 337–8.

rejected for *De re publica*; but he is still clearly developing the possibilities of applying the same kinds of ironic potential to the dialogue without the extra dimension of historical distance. The clearest indication is the remarkable moment when the characters wholly rupture the illusion of a self-contained world and comment on the conventions of the philosophical dialogue form directly.[32]

A more pervasive theme is the relationship between this text and *De re publica*, in that these speakers, Cicero, Atticus, and Quintus, openly refer to Scipio's discourse on the state as being their inspiration for a discussion of laws, laws which, at one point, are defined as those of that same Scipionic republic.[33] The opening of the work entails an oblique glance at the historical idealization of *De re publica*. The speakers begin by setting the scene for their discussion, in the vicinity of a tree which the speakers (in the first instance, Quintus and Atticus) identify as Marius' oak tree, a tree which Quintus describes as a product of *ingenium* rather than agriculture, in that the oak has become famous through Cicero's poem *Marius*. Shortly afterwards, Atticus presses Marcus as to whether he was following an earlier account of Marius' planting of the tree; Marcus responds by rebutting the question, by asking Atticus in turn about the topographical traces for the apotheosis of Romulus, an episode which was treated as a test case of the veracity of written historical sources in *De re publica*.[34] Different laws apply to poetry and to history (*intellego te, frater, alias in historia leges observandas putare, alias in poemate (De leg.* 1. 1. 4)), a maxim of considerable significance when we come to consider Cicero's treatment of his poetic account of his own consulship in *De divinatione* (see Chapter 8). The speakers give up trying to find a basis in fact for such legendary material, a process which was, however, vital to the semblance of historical underpinning to which the speakers in *De re publica* subject their account of early Rome. Instead, they focus their discus-

---

[32] *De leg.* 3. 11. 26. I will deal more fully with this passage in Ch. 8 (see below, pp. 228–31), since its context is a discussion of Cicero's own career, and the ironic moment is best understood as another layer in Cicero's self-representation.

[33] *De leg.* 2. 10. 23. The speaker is Marcus himself, and it is ambiguous whether this is the historical Rome, the Rome which Scipio conjures up in *De re publica*, or an ideal state somewhere between: Powell (2001).

[34] *Rep.* 2. 10. 20. See Wiseman (2002), 338–42, 353.

sion on Cicero's own possible role as a historian of Rome. The change of subject, however, is more significant: it involves a move away from questions of fiction, veracity, and the reliability of sources, to deliberate instead upon history as the sign of a flourishing national literature, as an opportunity for stylistic excellence.

There is a close similarity in the arguments here and those presented in *De oratore*: Greece again has set a standard for historiography which Rome has yet to meet, and Atticus in particular compares the potential that Cicero's stylistic mastery would have to rectify the situation, again listing the most prominent Roman historians and drawing attention to their stylistic shortcomings. From this point on, the momentum for the argument comes from reaching the main topic of the dialogue, Marcus' legal deliberations; but the trajectory is interesting: writing history acts as a bridge to the idea of holding forth on law, since both might be appropriate occupations for a senior statesman with the spare time on his hands granted by old age. There is a foreshadowing here of the introductory material to *Tusculan Disputations*, in that Atticus draws attention to an increased gentleness in Marcus' style, one which is, he says, not very different from that used by philosophers (*cotidie relaxes, ut iam oratio tua non multum a philosophorum lenitate absit* (*De leg*. 1. 4. 11)). The characters together outline the context of legal discussion, like the philosophy of *Tusculan Disputations*, as an activity associated with a less energetic form of discourse than the full-time political and forensic work of a younger man's career.[35] History, however, is an undertaking for which Cicero does not have the time required:[36] it cannot be produced in an improvisatory manner in response to prompting from clients (like legal opinions), or, as in *Tusculan Disputations*, questions from the philosophically curious.

History emerges rather badly from this encounter: it is a task to which, were Cicero to set his mind on it, he would doubtless be able to contribute his stylistic expertise; he would also shed light on two major events of recent times: his own consulship and the achievements of Pompey.[37] As we shall see in the next chapter, the idea that retired statesmen write history that includes an element of

---

[35] *Tusc. disp.* 1. 4. 8. See above, pp. 51–2.   [36] *De leg.* 1. 3. 9.
[37] *De leg.* 1. 8. 3.

self-commemoration was standard for historiography in the Republic; but it is precisely for this refusal to write history that this passage is useful. And as a supplement to the other works of this trio, it seems to serve precisely to draw attention to Cicero's failure to engage with a conventional historical narrative; the closest that Cicero comes to historiography is through his poetry, or through his style. In this sense, the opening of *De legibus* is programmatic: but what is interesting is the decision to begin *De legibus* with such a discussion, given that the dialogue itself contains very little material of historiographical interest, either in terms of the treatment of specific laws or in terms of the historical dimension of the dialogue form. Perhaps the opening simply takes this form in order to undermine any endorsement of the historical narrative of *De re publica*; equally, the similarity to the critique of Roman historiography in *De oratore* suggests that Cicero may be exploiting the setting of the dialogue to endorse that critique, and even to update it, including figures (Licinius Macer and Cornelius Sisenna) who are more recent than those mentioned by Antonius. At any event, it is certainly not material that is demanded by the subject matter of *De legibus*, and serves to draw attention to the fact that, whatever Cicero's encounter with historiography will be, it will not fit the conventional pattern. The elaborate play with historical material in both *De oratore* and *De re publica* demonstrates Cicero's engagement with history, but the opening of *De legibus* clearly lays down the boundaries of that engagement.

CONCLUSIONS

When interpreted with an eye to its dialogic qualities, without insisting upon a hierarchy among the different speakers in the dialogue and subordinating one voice to another, *De oratore* emerges as a thoughtful meditation upon the potential of rhetoric at Rome, rather than as an attempt to impose a particular view of rhetoric. My approach to the text may appear to represent a form of unacknowledged deconstruction, in that it focuses on minor moments of apparent contradiction and presses them to a conclusion which is more extreme perhaps than a natural reading of the whole work will allow, deliberately ignoring that sense of a determining authority which the work is generally thought to possess, the character of Crassus working as Cicero's mouthpiece. This criticism is only justified, however, if we start from the premiss that the treatise does have a totalizing ambition and a particular theory about how rhetoric functions at Rome. Cicero's unambiguous aim is to produce a rhetorical treatise that, particularly in books 2 and 3, makes available in Latin a body of technical material. The emphasis in book 1, though, is to outline the cultural background and possible audience for whom that material is being mediated, and here those moments of contradiction are vital to the production of the main thrust of the work. Cicero is most careful to allow for the contingent quality of his project, and not to silence the difficulties which the introduction of theory to Rome will bring with it.

Rome, understood as the history of the city and of the men who make up its political elite, is described in this work as a place which certainly has a potential to accept the theoretical contribution which Cicero is making, but *simultaneously* as a place where Cicero himself is a historical anomaly, someone attempting, in a deliberate theoretical intervention, to change the value of Rome's history. These incompatible views coexist, and thus provide a more elaborate context for the rhetorical handbook which Cicero produces. Once again, a comparison with *De re publica* is useful: there, Cicero's essentially reforming agenda is expressed as an abstract principle of leadership apparently derived from Rome's own historical development; nevertheless, the workings of the dialogue reveal the idealizing dimension of the historical account, and thus the optimistic and essentially unreal quality of Cicero's reforming agenda. In spite of the emphasis in the dialogue on the predominance of the practical over the theoretical, Cicero's contribution will always be a theoretical one: if he is fortunate, there will be practical consequences. *De oratore* is very similar. There is no doubt that a rhetorical treatise will find an audience at Rome (though it may be a small audience); but in a sense, theoretical work will always run against the grain of Roman culture. In the parts of the text I have discussed above, we can see Cicero experimenting with different margins of error, different points on a scale on which Roman hostility or openness to rhetoric can be measured. Most interestingly, in the discussion of the role of rhetoric in producing historical writing, Cicero raises the question of whether, given different kinds of historians, the history of Rome could be made to look more like the history of Greece: would Rome produce, in the years following the dramatic date of the dialogue, a Thucydides? Cicero's readers would surely have been tantalized by this prospect, and *De legibus* suggests that it was a task that he might himself have fulfilled (though I think that an ironic reading of that potential is more probable). As a result of the loss of all direct remains of any possible candidates, we cannot judge whether any of the historians contemporary with Cicero would immediately have struck his readers as good examples of a more polished, rhetorically experienced prose. Whatever the solution to that particular puzzle, rhetoric's contribution to history needs to be considered within the context of this particular work: Cicero focuses once again on the difference between Greek and Roman literary traditions. For a discussion of *De oratore*, the central point is that the absence of rhetoric in historiography is part of a general picture of Rome as a society without rhetoric; those unadorned chroniclers of early Rome are one component in the complex dialectic to establish the rhetorical complexion of the city, a dialectic which, on the one hand, requires a certain native tradition to provide Cicero with a genealogy, but, on the other, accepts that this genealogy is itself in the service of the aims of the particular dialogue, a necessary part of Cicero's reforming didactic programme. There is without doubt a rhetorical quality to this use of history, but we will need to examine more examples of Cicero's practice, looking at his later philosophical work, before that quality can be properly evaluated. First of these will be *Brutus*, the dialogue in which Cicero treats more directly the theme of history and genealogy which he had already exploited in *De oratore*.

In the following chapter, I will sketch the context in which Cicero's encounter with history takes place. As far as *De re publica* and *De oratore* are concerned, that context suggests that the traditions of Roman historiography do not harmonize well with Cicero's sceptical and rhetorical tendencies. Nevertheless, the engagement with history which we have seen in these works can be read as an active response to those traditions; Cicero does to a certain extent want to colonize historiography, or at least to leave his own mark upon it. But that mark is, as *De re publica* and *De oratore* show, one that neither endorses traditional forms of historical narrative, nor accepts a role for history simply as a place where ideological analysis of Rome receives an uncritical foundation. Both dialogues use history to contextualize their arguments, and both do it in a manner which, rather than simply using history to validate or verify, instead generates more complexity of argument. In *De re publica*, the dynamics of historical representation challenge readers to engage with the difference between the constitutional issues preoccupying Scipio and his friends, and those caught up in the very different circle represented by the first triumvirate. In *De oratore*, perhaps in a manner more personal and of less pointed political urgency, the interplay between different historical periods produces a general historical reflection on the status of rhetoric at Rome, one in which opposing visions of Rome's rhetorical culture exist side by side. The context for this ambivalent and pointed use of historical material is the established relationship between a form of government based on hereditary patterns of office holding and a form of record keeping which stresses familial continuity and a prestige dependent upon continuity. The context is particularly important here, since the crucial question in reading Cicero is whether he simply allows himself, as one standing outside these aristocratic structures, to be awed by them, and to attempt to substitute his own narrative of history in order to supplant them, or whether he engages with them in a more active manner. In bringing rhetorical theory into that arena, Cicero is actually experimenting with a bold claim: that a change in an individual's style—an education in rhetoric, in other words— could have a general effect upon the way in which public discourse worked at Rome. As with *De re publica*, that claim is likely to be less contentious from the comfort of a fictionalized dialogue, and it is useful to have a charismatic group of aristocrats to explore it. When Cicero comes to look more directly at Rome's history in those terms, in *Brutus*, the negative potential of that history emerges more clearly; but we need to bear in mind that in all the works from this period, the texture of politics that emerges from Cicero's theoretical works is excessively benign. The reality of political life in this period was more violent, and the structures of political debate were unlikely to make the niceties of rhetoric particularly relevant to the actual wielding of political power.[38] We are in a poor position to judge how far matters of style could be reasonably related to those of power; but fortunately, in his ironic expression of both sides of this dialectic, Cicero does much of our work for us. In his continued negotiation with traditional ways of looking at Rome's history, and his evocation of Rome as a rational society in which rhetorical theory could perhaps flourish, he gives us a sense both of Rome's potential and of the forces which prevent that potential from being realized.

---

[38] So, e.g., Mouritsen's account of the *contio*, which points out how little potential there may have been for effective rhetorical communication before a mass audience: Mouritsen (2001), 53–6: what rhetoric could do was to keep already existing support networks functioning. The implication is that its relationship to the power that established those support networks in the first place is unclear. This view is clearly extreme; see Morstein-Marx (2004), 7–12, and *passim*, for a treatment which brings 'mass oratory' firmly back to the centre. At the very least, the continuation of this debate should make us cautious about assuming a match between Cicero's ambitions for the orator and the actual valences of political power, and allow for the possibility that Crassus' idealizations may have appeared as far-fetched as some of Scipio's.

6

History and Memory

In terms of paucity of evidence, one of the most awkward themes in this book is the relationship between the vision of history that can be found in Cicero's writings and the accounts of history to be found in the work of his contemporaries and successors: scholars have explored the relationship between the mainstream canon of Roman historiography and Cicero's work with history, but that attempt has generally restricted itself to questions of knowledge: how Cicero carried out his research, what he knew about the past, and what his views on historiography were, rather than looking at his own historical representations.[1] The difficulty relates to the quality of the evidence that Cicero provides: in some respects, it is much fuller and more abundant than other evidence; but it is not, of course, historiography in the conventional sense. As *De legibus* makes clear, Cicero wanted to demarcate his work about history from that of full-time historians, his closest encounter with that arena being, at least in that particular moment of self-portrayal, his historical poetry. There are several serious obscurities that prevent us from fully understanding the connection between Cicero's engagement with historical representation and the norms of existing historiography. Regarding the critique of existing historiography in *De oratore* and *De legibus*, for example, the long period of revision and lack of completion of *De legibus* make any connection with the historiography of Cicero's own day a matter of pure speculation. Leaving aside the historians whose works have not survived, it might be possible to see veiled attacks on Caesar in Cicero's despair at the state of Roman historiography if

---

[1] Rawson (1972); Fleck (1993); Brunt (1997).

we imagine Cicero still working on that section of *De legibus* in 46 BCE. Certainly, like those historians openly criticized, Caesar's commentaries were written in a style of which Cicero would not really approve, but the complexity of the evidence makes it impossible to conclude that Caesar is a target for criticism.[2] Beyond that, there is a lack of any substantial survival of the texts written by Roman historians before this period, and the evidence for many of those authors comes from Cicero, who, we have seen, is inconsistent even over quite large points of style between different accounts.

So we are lacking context in which we can judge how Cicero's work with history would have appeared to his first readers, how much it drew upon existing techniques, and thus also what its influence might have been. This would be problematic enough if Cicero were actually writing history, but the situation is worse: we are looking for parallels and a context for an imaginative reworking of history in a form of philosophy that is also clearly influenced by rhetorical practice. What kind of relationship can we establish between Roman historical consciousness and the ironic manner of working with history that Cicero provides? The expected answer is that history at Rome was a conservative force, characterized by a powerful moralizing and exemplary tradition, and that if Cicero was indeed doing anything other than simply reinforcing those impulses, then this is his unique contribution, one that results from a desire to distort history in favour of himself, in an attempt to make rhetorical and philosophical interest look as though they belong to Roman tradition.[3] This chapter will explore this area. I shall argue that the

---

[2] Caesar's commentaries are likely to have started to appear after *De re publica*; Büchner (1980), 204–5. On Caesar's style and its critics, see Kraus (2005). I am inclined to read the praise of Caesar's minimalist style at *Brutus* 262 as mildly ironic, at the least. Although Sallust doesn't seem to have started to dedicate himself to writing full time until after 44, there must at least be a possibility that some of his work had appeared before 46, the date of the supposed revisions to *De legibus*.

[3] See Morstein-Marx (2004), 78–107, on the concretization of history as a marker of a shared public ideology to which rhetoric could effectively appeal. Habinek (1998), 89, contrasts Cicero with Horace: 'Whereas Cicero, both through the performance of a myth of Roman legitimacy and through his philosophical expropriation of the cultural capital of conquered Greece ... seeks to localize authority in an expandable but always Romanocentric aristocracy, Horace is here seen to enact a more polyvalent model of cultural authority.' It is the aim of this chapter to question so close an identification of Cicero with the reinforcement of authority through history.

picture of an exemplary history is indeed powerful, but that it is not necessarily inflexible. Indeed, in Cicero's own comments upon the use of memory, we can observe a way of thinking about the past that makes his historical work seem less idiosyncratic and, at the same time, provides a different way of examining the polarity between rhetoric and history.

It is one of my more contentious claims that in his exploration of ambiguous and ironic ways of working with history, Cicero provides the best evidence for a tradition of producing a kind of historical writing that simultaneously includes an ironic critique of its own methods, a tradition that culminates in Tacitus. I will explore this in more detail in Chapter 9, after looking at two of Cicero's last works, *Brutus* and *De divinatione*, in which the ironic exploitation of historical material seen in *De re publica* and *De oratore* rises to a higher pitch. *Brutus* must bear much of the weight for the argument that Cicero wanted to shape history in his own image; I shall argue that, as in the earlier works, Cicero fails to grant history that kind of authority. In order to support that argument, it is necessary first to understand how the mechanisms for granting authority to the past functioned in the late Republic. Rawson identified some time ago a scepticism on Cicero's part concerning historical evidence, combined with a desire to get historical research working for higher moral and educational aims, which set his work apart from the antiquarian researches of Varro and Atticus.[4]

These ideas can be taken further when the argument and narrative of the dialogues are given greater prominence. In *De re publica* and *De oratore*, history is precisely the place where clear-cut theoretical distinctions seem to break down, and where theories can both find support through precedent but also have that support removed: the competing representations of Rome from the start of *De oratore* provide perhaps the easiest example, but the ambiguous representation of monarchy in *De re publica*, with its profound political consequences, is a better one, in that it shows how important historical ambiguity is in advancing a complex argument about the nature of the Roman state. If history was generally conceived as the discourse from which foundations for arguments, institutions, or ideas was derived,

4 Rawson (1972), 37, 43.

we need to know whether Cicero's exploitation of a destabilizing foundation has parallels, or, indeed, whether we are looking in the wrong place for our understanding of history's role. In exploring Cicero's own elaboration of the idea of *memoria*, I shall be suggesting that the use of history in this period was much more about creating an effect than about finding validation in the past. It is a delicate balance, since both aspects are important. But the political implications of historical representation do suggest that in appeals to historical foundation the focus was on the effect, in the present and the future, rather more than upon the past. There is little doubt that Cicero's work with history is idiosyncratic, but it can also be located with reasonable precision as a response to the aristocratic traditions of commemoration and exemplarity which characterized historical consciousness at Rome. Once that is understood, it becomes easier to see how later readers of Cicero might have responded to the creative potential which Cicero draws out in his adaptations of these ideas of exemplarity and commemoration, and how the ironic approach to history could in fact have been more widespread.

EXEMPLA AND CONSERVATISM

The main trope by which history functions in Cicero, both in the speeches and in the philosophical works, is that of the historical *exemplum*, the figure from history who, by virtue of being dead, is able to provide a model for the living.[5] In Cicero's speeches, historical *exempla* functioned, obviously alongside other rhetorical weapons, as

---

[5] Cicero himself seems to have defined this exemplary quality particularly clearly in his first major philosophical work, the lost *Hortensius*. In the speech given by the politician-turned-historian Lucullus, evidently in praise of his own literary metier, he remarks: *unde aut ad agendum aut ad dicendum copia depromi maior gravissimorum exemplorum, quasi incorruptorum testimoniorum, potest?* (Fr. 27 = Nonius, p. 315. 23) ('from where can we derive a greater store of the most weighty examples, as incorruptible evidence, both for doing and for speaking?') and *unde autem facilius quam ex annalium monumentis aut bellicae res aut omnis rei publicae disciplina cognoscitur?* (Fr. 28 = Nonius, p. 275. 34) ('from where can the whole nature of war or science of the state be better known than from the records of the annals'). Fragments are numbered from Straume-Zimmerman (1976); see her comments on pp. 74–8, 229.

a means to achieve particular political results.[6] The exemplary quality of the past brought with it a framework in which political questions could be examined, and indeed in which debates about appropriate kinds of precedent could be held; the enduring quality of *exempla* is clear, but so also is the flexibility with which individual historical examples could be characterized.[7] Demandt goes so far as to assert that in antiquity, the role of historical precedent can be detected in almost every single political decision.[8] It is clear that there is more at stake here than a 'simple' model of exemplarity in which, as Thucydides defines it, human activities will always follow a pattern determined by human nature.[9] In their tendency to think historically about all kinds of moral and political issues, the Romans (like the Greeks) lived in a thought-world rather different from our own: and the main difficulty which this difference presents is that of appreciating the extent to which what for us is an intellectual or academic interest in history could exert such a powerful force upon political decision making, even upon the development of a sense of individuality, as we can in effect observe in much of Cicero's own writing.[10] Projected more broadly, and given dramatic realization, this exemplary quality also characterizes the historical representation of the philosophical dialogues: the 'Scipionic Circle' and the speakers of *De oratore* are Cicero's attempt to supplement his theoretical endeavours with a layer of charisma derived from the exemplary

---

[6] An impressive successful analysis of how historical examples achieve concrete political ends can be found in Demandt (1972), 30–40. Demandt's analysis of *exempla* leads to a division between a *popularis* and a patrician way of treating historical precedent (primarily in the context of Cicero, *Pro lege Manilia*).

[7] J. Oppermann (2000), 300–1, gives a neat summary.

[8] Demandt (1972), 11.   [9] Thucydides 1. 22.

[10] Demandt (1972), 14, remarks that Cicero represents the zenith for a kind of historicist thinking at Rome. It should be borne in mind, however, that there are philosophical positions available which would dismantle the firm distinction between lived and textual experience upon which the separation between history and politics or identity ultimately rests: see, e.g., Stierle (1973), with Fuhrmann (1973). One approach centres on the role played by metaphor in expressing lived experience: Ankersmit (1994) gives a full treatment in the context of historiography; see Franke (2000) for a summary of the revival and extension of metaphor with extensive bibliography; Paul Ricoeur is particularly relevant; for Ricoeur, identity itself is produced out of the same kind of relationship with time upon which narratives depend; see Sweeney (2002, 2004) for a cogent summary and critique. Waddell (1988) scrutinizes so-called constructivism from within a similar tradition.

quality of these famous characters. As we have seen, however, their exemplarity is severely circumscribed, and the view of history which they themselves articulate is even more contingent if we are looking for an uncomplicated idealization. Work on the use of *exempla* in rhetoric, however, suggests that we would be mistaken to think that exemplarity demands consistency of interpretation: *exempla* draw on models capable of a range of interpretations. The exemplary function remains constant, but individual examples are capable of meeting the needs of a variety of different arguments.[11]

This way of dealing with history is particularly characteristic of Rome. Greek writers, by contrast, tended to use what we think of as mythical material for similar purposes, and the characterization of Rome as a society lacking a highly developed mythology can be balanced, or even explained, by the quasi-mythical function which history plays in Roman explorations of their identity.[12] In terms of an exploration of the details of Cicero's historical representation, how-ever, we need to lay particular emphasis upon one central set of questions: How far does the exemplary quality of history bring with it a kind of inflexible conservatism? Must the past always be used to provide authority for the present? And if so, is this authority by its nature something that will always affirm the greater power of the past over the present? Is there also a more specific political flavour to this conservatism? Is the exemplary use of the past always bound to reinscribe the traditional authority of the Roman aristoc-racy, whose public careers intersected closely with the traditional mechanisms for recording and referring to the past? In my readings of *De re publica* and *De oratore*, I have argued that the past can be used more flexibly, and that Cicero is playing with notions of authority and idealization in a way that leaves his readers space to reflect

---

[11] Brinton (1988) examines the argumentative function of *exempla* in parts of *De finibus* and *De officiis*. For an exhaustive account of how historical *exempla* function in Cicero's letters, see J. Oppermann (2000). David (1980) is stimulating, esp. pp. 67 and 84–6, where *exemplum* is characterized both as an impetus for direct imitation in the form of the repetition of behaviour, and as something that, in providing a model for imitation, can lose its relationship with the original: some *exempla* are little more than empty names. The introductory essay to the same volume (Berlioz and David (1980) is also worth consulting. Fuhrmann (1973) added a level of sophistication to the debate which has not been as influential as it deserves to be.

[12] Fox (1996).

upon the present and develop their own thinking. The open-ended, provocative argument corresponds, of course, to Cicero's Academic philosophical perspective, and in his integration of that perspective to Rome, Cicero draws upon the dynamic potential of history. In the subsequent chapters, I shall go further, and argue that under Caesar's domination, Cicero's ideas developed further: he became more overtly cynical both about the potential of history to have a positive effect upon Rome's political situation and about his own earlier optimism on this very question. In this chapter, therefore, I shall be exploring how his openly interrogatory approach to history coincides with what we can piece together about the context in which his conception of the past was formed: in particular, the strength of the exemplary character of the past, and how amenable it was to complex or multi-layered development.

IMAGINES, FUNERALS, AND THE HISTORICAL RECORD

The most important piece of contextual material which sheds light on this process must be Polybius' description of the funeral practices of the Romans in his day. Polybius' account forms part of his general discussion of the characteristics of Roman society in the sixth book; he stresses in particular the stability of Rome's political constitution, the superiority of Rome to Carthage, and the military institutions which have contributed to Rome's great success. The description of the funeral rites is part of this same exposition of Rome's unique cultural virtues: the veneration given to dead ancestors grants Roman society a powerful sense of cohesion, binding the living to the dead, and promoting imitation of the dead as a means of ensuring a continuity of virtue.[13] Young Romans are inspired in particular by the vision of the long procession of ancestors.[14] Polybius even

---

[13] Habinek (1998), ch. 2, gives a masterful account of the emergence of Latin literature as a form for aristocratic social cohesion, including excellent analysis of Polybius and Cato. See esp. pp. 50–4.

[14] The text of the Loeb translation can be conveniently consulted at http://penelope.uchicago.edu/Thayer/E/Roman/Texts/Polybius/6*.html, from which translation, I quote here.

reproduces the process whereby this particular ritual intersects with written historiography: he describes how the funeral masks of distinguished ancestors are brought out at each new funeral, and the masks put on by living relatives, even wearing clothing appropriate to the rank of the mask's model; and how the reincarnated family assemble on ivory chairs to surround the speaker of the funeral oration. That oration in turn recounts the achievements not just of the deceased, but of all the represented ancestors, in this manner, reinforcing and retelling the traditional stories associated with the family:

> By this means, by this constant renewal of the good report of brave men, the celebrity of those who performed noble deeds is rendered immortal, while at the same time the fame of those who did good service to their country becomes known to the people and a heritage for future generations. But the most important result is that young men are thus inspired to endure every suffering for public welfare in the hope of winning the glory that attends on brave men.   (Polybius, 6. 54. 2–3)

Polybius' stress is on the patriotic benefits of this institution. He reinforces that stress in the next sentence by claiming that the overwhelming impression of such noble deeds is one of self-sacrifice, particularly for the good of Rome. He then proceeds to recount the story of Horatius Cocles, in essence reinscribing exactly the same tribute to historical continuity and heroism which he has just described. His own retelling of the Horatius episode is of the kind that we might reasonably assume to have made its way into a funeral oration; the old tale is designed in this context to inspire Polybius' readers with the same zeal for patriotic self-sacrifice as the audience to such an oration, and we should remember, of course, that Polybius' readers would have lacked the familiarity with this story which the millennia of schoolroom extracts from Livy have given it in our own minds. A central part of Polybius' description of the context for such historical *exempla* is the aristocratic milieu: it is the core families of the Roman elite, with their shared traditions of office holding, ancestor masks, and public funerals that are responsible for the continued circulation of this discourse of historical exemplarity.

The aristocratic context, implicit in Polybius, is given specific emphasis by Cicero at *Brutus* 61–2, where he describes how the funeral orations themselves are preserved for reuse:

ipsae enim familiae sua quasi ornamenta ac monumenta servabant et ad usum,
si quis eiusdem generis occidisset, et ad memoriam laudum domesticarum
et ad illustrandam nobilitatem suam. (*Brutus* 62)

For the families themselves would preserve them like memorial trophies,
both for use, if anyone of the same *gens* died, and for the commemoration of
the glories of the house, and to make clear their nobility.

He goes on to point out how unreliable information stored in such a
context tended to be, one of many indirect tributes in the work to the
historical researches of Atticus, whose *liber annalis* is repeatedly
referred to, and in which such frauds of historical tradition were
presumably revealed. What is important is the extreme proximity
between notions of preservation of heritage, bloodline, and public
advertisement. This is an aristocratic world with a monopoly on
historical memory that was not just about passive continuation of
tradition, but rather about the propagation of its own social position,
nobilitas, through public display, including the display of historical
narrative given in speeches. *Imagines* and historical narrative, therefore, both cluster around the performance of the funeral rites: there is
an intimate connection between death, commemoration, and the
incorporation of the individual into a tradition of public glory.
These are all themes which have an important function in Cicero's
own historical thinking. Most pointedly, we can think of the emphasis upon the last days of Scipio and Crassus in the *De re publica*
and *De legibus*, to be reworked in the more complex struggle between
the living and the dead in *Brutus*. More generally, Cicero himself is
clearly, and more so as his literary production intensifies in the last
years of his life, preoccupied with transcending his own mortality,
and with articulating a historical framework which would help him,
unaided by aristocratic trappings, to transcend it.

ANNALES: LIVING THROUGH HISTORY

In a manner congruent with the production of historical narrative
through the funeral procession, the annalistic structure of the Roman
calendar also provides a framework for thinking about the past
which expressed the need for display of an aristocracy keen on

stressing the synonymity between hereditary position and public good.[15] The passing of years was marked in terms of their leading political offices, legal and political decisions, and events of religious or sacred significance (including strange portents). There were several different kinds of chronicle lists which followed an annual structure and which contained different types of information: the lists of consuls; the lists of military triumphs, the annals held by the high priests.[16] Dates, it must be remembered, were not numbers but the names of the two consuls: these individuals became the articulation of time. The fact that they are individuals, whose names give access to their own individual careers (at least where they are recorded) provides the fundamental structure for how the Romans conceived of the past: as a political process, contiguous with the present, in which the highest political achievement, the leadership of the Roman state, is in itself the measure of passing time.[17] Scholarship in this area has recently widened its focus to include the study of biographical funerary inscriptions, which integrate the lives of individuals into a shared social framework based on the intersection between individual and collective memory.[18] Fundamental, however, is the shift that occurred with the coming of the Empire. The centralization of power in the hands of Augustus not only placed the senatorial elite in a different position from the traditional patterns in which institutional or social success were measured, but also changed those patterns themselves.[19] The summation of the republican way of thinking must be Augustus' forum of Mars, which gave monumental expression to the idealized heroes of Roman history, making *imagines* into three-dimensional busts and the oral telling of

---

[15] *De orat.* 2. 52–3. Petzold (1999), 252–65, gives an exhaustive account of the history of the annals form up until the late Republic. Frier (1999) and Fuhrmann (1987) examine the historical conditions in which the accounts themselves were retained and supplemented. See also Wiseman (1979*b*), 9–26.

[16] Nicely summarized by Oakley (1997), 22–30; Kierdorf (2003), 9–17. For Tacitus' ironic handling of the annals structure, see Henderson (1998), 257–300.

[17] Oakley (1997), 38–62, presents a neatly categorized account of the different kinds of information available in the annals.

[18] See Koortbojian (1996); Beard (1998), esp. 87–94; and Eck (1997), esp. 78–81; Habinek (1998), 51–2.

[19] See Beard (1987); Wallace-Hadrill (1987); and now especially useful Gowing (2005), 7–27. On the enormous breach in understanding which post-Caesarian material gives us in general: Schneider (1998), 64–8.

the individual's deeds into a concise written inscription.[20] Cicero is a vital point of reference in the development of this tradition, most obviously in his laments for the disappearing Republic, but also in his meditations upon the role of memory in the constitution of the orator or upon the role of *mos maiorum* in general.[21] Any consideration of this topic will always begin with the extraction of memorable appeals to *mos maiorum* from his speeches, and will see his theoretical pronouncements on the requirement for historical knowledge in rhetoric (e.g. *Orator* 120; *De orat.* 1. 201, 2. 36) as simple extensions of this same desire to express and promulgate an essentially conservative vision of the necessity for political action to take place within boundaries imposed by the *mos maiorum*.[22]

Orator 120 is both succinct and revealing: the orator needs historical knowledge (*cognoscat etiam rerum gestarum et memoriae veteris ordinem*), of the kind that Atticus has been helpful in compiling. Cicero has two arguments to substantiate this exhortation. It is part of becoming a mature adult to realize the relationship between the past and present, and, of course, *exempla* add authority and pleasure when introduced into any oration.

nescire autem quid ante quam natus sis acciderit, id est semper esse puerum. quid enim est aetas hominis, nisi ea memoria rerum veterum cum superiorum aetate contexitur? commemoratio autem antiquitatis exemplorumque prolatio summa cum delectatione et auctoritatem orationi affert et fidem. (*Orator* 120)

To be ignorant of what happened before you were born is to remain always a boy. For what is the lifetime of a man, unless it is connected with the lifetime of older men by the memory of earlier events? Moreover, the commemoration of antiquity and the production of *exempla* bring, along with the greatest pleasure, authority and credibility to a speech.

---

[20] On the forum, see Rich (1988); Spannagel (1999); Gowing (2005), 138–45. On *monumenta*, Kraus (1994) on Livy 6. 1. 2.

[21] The account of Häussler (1965), 168–74, is still worth consulting on this aspect. Pina Polo (2004) gathers the evidence for the relationship between developing historiography and *mos maiorum* with great clarity. Gowing (2005) gives a profound examination of the ramifications of this nostalgia in early Imperial literature, with many thoughtful observations on Cicero.

[22] The most thorough exposition of this historicist thrust in Cicero's entire œuvre is Vogt (1935).

The argument here is rather more nuanced than it appears on first reading. Male maturation can occur only if *memoria* can take its proper place within the life of the individual: linking him, as he grows older, to previous generations and their own memories of events. The point about the pleasures that *exempla* bring to oratory is really a separate idea, complementary rather than contradictory (and introduced by *autem*); but the connection is left implicit: it is the display of historical knowledge by the orator in the use of *exempla* that will show to his audience that he is not only a man of substance, but also one who can be trusted: one who has, in other words, successfully adopted the shared value system which Roman history perpetuates. Behind this inspirational account lurks a strange shadow, the stupid man, who has grown old without making the necessary connection with previous generations.[23] If pressed in detail, there is a certain vagueness about Cicero's use of the word *aetas*, in particular the relationship between *aetas hominis* and *aetate superiorum*, the hypothetical individual man and his elders, by whom, as he grows older, he is connected by virtue of sharing their age. These might be older men of the next generation, so that as the young man matures, he is able to talk to them about events that they have both witnessed; or they might be the collective dead, with whose deeds each properly aware Roman citizen will be connected, simply by virtue of *memoria*.[24] But we do not need to decide between these two alternatives: Cicero is giving here a striking evocation of a form of historical continuity of which the specific rhetorical expression (the use of *exempla*) is only a small token.

Whether such a purple description of the necessity for historical knowledge should be read as a parallel to other passages in works of the same period which stress the enormous public utility of philosophy, or whether Cicero here is touching on something that would have

---

[23] The portrait of Curio in *Brutus* is a useful point of comparison. Curio, interestingly an orphan, has such an appalling memory that he could neither remember earlier passages in his own speeches when he delivered them, nor even, when he wrote a philosophical dialogue, be consistent about events within it. He was also very poorly acquainted with poetry or history: *nullum ille poetam noverat, nullum legerat oratorem, nullam memoriam antiquitatis collegerat* (*Brutus* 214).

[24] Being a *puer*, even when fully mature, is not always negative: Leigh (2004), 325–6, with the example of *De orat.* 2. 22.

been of more recognizable appeal as a characterization of a Roman historical consciousness is in absolute terms hard to argue; Cicero's most explicit deliberation on the topic comes in the *Pro Archia*, his defence of the citizen rights of a Greek poet from almost twenty years earlier, in which he stresses the enormous significance of posthumous fame as an incentive to political participation. But because, of course, the arguments are designed to sway the case in favour of Cicero's client, they may well be more exaggerated and more motivated by the occasion than those in *Orator*.[25] But in any case it is beyond dispute that an appreciation of the relationship between past and present, and a sense that real authority in the political arena could be gained by a display of historical awareness, were central features of the political scene in the late Republic.[26] Cicero's own extensive use of *exempla*, as well as the overwhelming historicist propaganda of the Augustan regime, suggest that we can lay more weight on Cicero's ideal of the grown-up citizen as one who derives at least some of his *auctoritas* from his connectedness with history. Of course it suits the arguments advanced in this book to imagine an audience fully alive to the political potential of historical representation, so I will not continue to labour this particular point. Connectedness to the past, however, is clearly the basis for any more specific analysis of the uses to which historical representation could be put.[27]

In their origins, the *Annales* were another means of symbolic display in the hands of the aristocracy, and the dominant view of the evolution of Roman historiography is that the number of great families who succeeded in shaping the records to exaggerate their own importance became smaller rather than larger as the Republic progressed.[28] One can only speculate about the experiences of a *novus homo* entering a public arena where historical discourse had such a particular flavour. Cato the Elder had followed this path well over a century earlier, and his response was the production of the first proper prose history in Latin, the *Origines*. In it, he also criticizes the

---

[25] *Pro Archia Poeta* 19–30; Dugan (2001*a*); S. H. Smith (2002), 22–4.

[26] Morstein-Marx (2004), 71–83.

[27] As Habinek pithily puts it, 'The *mos maiorum* is something you know, but also something you do': Habinek (1998), 54.

[28] Büchner (1980), 252; studies of the Aemilii and other minor dynasties in Wiseman (1998) could be said to corroborate this picture.

Annales, although it is not clear whether the focus of the complaint was more ideological or narratological.[29] For Polybius there is no problem in extrapolating from family pride to national patriotism, and both his history and Cato's were clear in the emphasis on collective Roman identity expressed as the communality of family traditions. Both, however, derived their perspective, and their sense of a need to mediate Rome through historical narrative, from the fact that they themselves stood outside this tradition. Less ambiguous is the fact that early Roman historians were always men of action who were moved to write down the events in which they themselves were involved.[30] Self-advertisement combined with glorification of Rome for a wider audience was therefore the basic assumption when producing history, and it seems reasonable to suppose that negotiating the balance between identification with individual families and identification with Rome was not going to cause any fundamental alienation from the idea of the value of history itself.

Sallust provides the best evidence here, in particular in the speech in which he makes Marius (hero alike of the *popularis* cause and of both Cicero, the next consular *novus homo* from Arpinum, and Caesar) take issue with the tokens of historical precedent, the *imagines*, by which the aristocracy set so much store.[31] Sallust, another *novus*, was in no sense inhibited by his veneration for aristocratic models of historical representation (as I shall argue further in Chapter 9). But when Sallust makes Marius hold forth on the role of *imagines*, he nevertheless bows under the weight of tradition in recognizing the value of the *imago* as a token of historical continuity and social power. Although Marius has to substitute his own military achievements for the traditional pedigree of ancestral *imagines*, his rhetoric revolves around the idea that he himself has a closer connection to the traditions of the Roman nobility than that corrupted

[29] Fr. 77 (Peter); Marincola (1997), 236; Mellor (1999), 13–14; on scepticism about the *Annales*, Wiseman (2002).

[30] Marincola (1997), 77, 181–2 (on *commentarii*); Oakley (1997), 13–108, surveys the annalistic tradition; on particular authors, Ogilvie (1965), 7–17; more succinctly, Forsythe (2005), 60–4; Fantham (2004), 152–9. L. Morgan (2000), 54–6, on their participation in historic events.

[31] Sallust, *Bell. Jug.* 85. See H. Flower (1996), 16–31, for a thorough treatment. Leigh (1995), 207–212, on the substitution of battle scars for *imagines*. Pina Polo (2004), 165.

present-day incarnation of the nobility itself. The *novus*, therefore, is able to establish himself, at the point at which he takes up his consulship, as the genuine heir to the tradition of consular achievement, sifting the aristocratic tradition to produce a vision of genuine *nobilitas* based not upon blood, but upon achievement and dedication to the state. Sallust here is a useful supplement to what Polybius shows us about the conflation of Roman and dynastic glory. By the time of Sallust, and probably much earlier (if, as H. Flower argues, Sallust was able to get some reliable information about Marius' actual speech), that ideological position was one that was available for parodic reworking.[32] But even while making *imagines* act against the nobility, Sallust still stresses the relationship between past and present as one of continuity and inspiration—as, of course, he does more explicitly in his prologue to the same monograph.[33]

MEMORIA

The symbolic display of historical material brings with it not just questions of ideological position, but also questions of historical veracity. In the works explored so far, a central role is taken by the concern with historical sources in the production of competing versions of Roman culture, and in the dynamic interplay between arguments valid in Cicero's own day and a retrojection of those arguments into the past. *Memoria* ought to be the guarantor of historical veracity, but in Cicero's exploration of it, the symbolic significance of memory is more important than any factual basis.[34] The mutability of historical *exempla* in rhetoric, as well as the surviving narratives of Sallust, Livy, and Tacitus, all suggest that at Rome, readers were much less concerned about consistency in this respect,

---

[32] H. Flower (1996) 19.   [33] Sallust, *Bell. Jug.* 1–4.

[34] *Memoria* thus takes on some of the role which more easily lies within the scope of *fama* (reputation, rumour), a concept which became particularly important for Tacitus; see S. H. Smith (2002). At *Post red.* 3 Cicero seems to present *fama* and *memoria* as almost synonymous: *quod enim tempus erit umquam, cum vestrorum in nos beneficiorum memoria ac fama moriatur?* ('when will the time ever come when the memory and fame of your good deeds towards me will die?').

and that the imaginative function of history was more important than the question of sources.[35] However, it is my aim to advance this argument a little further, by considering how far the concept of memory itself actually expresses not just the recording of events, but also their representation and perpetuation. As such, it can still fulfil its function without an excessive concern for the factual basis of that memory.

Returning for a moment to Cicero's account in *Brutus* of the preservation of historical memory in the funeral oration, we can define more exactly the traditional function of *memoria*:

ipsae enim familiae sua quasi ornamenta ac monumenta servabant et ad usum, si quis eiusdem generis occidisset, et ad memoriam laudum domes-ticarum et ad illustrandam nobilitatem suam. quamquam his laudationibus historia rerum nostrarum est facta mendosior.					(*Brutus* 62)

For the families themselves would preserve them like memorial trophies, both for use, if anyone of the same *gens* died, and for the commemoration of the glories of the house, and to make clear their nobility. However in these celebrations of glory the history of our own deeds has been made more deceitful.

Next he lists the kinds of distortions that have been recorded in these very early examples of oratory at Rome. In articulating the criticism in these terms, he sets up a contrast between the communal interest (Rome, and knowing about its past: *res nostrae*) and the advantages of propaganda to particular families. The exemplarity of history is not vitiated by fiction; the fabrications of particular families, how-ever, are an incentive, particularly in proximity to the mention of the *liber annalis* of Atticus, to strive for a more reliable, and simultan-eously more collective, form of historical inspiration. These speeches are the earliest available to anyone interested in the development of oratory at Rome, and the fact that Cicero's main concern is not with their style (a theme which he momentarily abandons), but with their fictitious quality, is good evidence of the interplay between rhetoric and history in *Brutus* which will be the subject of the next chapter; the history of rhetoric at Rome is in effect inseparable from the rhetoric of history, and funeral orations are a central part

---

[35] The standard formulation is to regard this interest in the mutability of history as a sign of a rhetorical mentality: most clearly put by Woodman (1988).

of the latter. The function of the speeches, however, the *memoria laudum domesticarum*, is one that does not in any sense depend upon the actual memory of a particular event, since, as Cicero goes on to make clear, such events are frequently imaginary.

Memoria, therefore, can be seen as a process aimed at producing a particular effect, rather than one determined by a causal process of actual recollection. Such a view of memory is the key to the inspirational but flexible manner in which historical *exempla* function: apart from the general edification which citation of historical precedent involves, *exempla* open up the possibilities of argument rather than close them down. The implications of the word *memoria* require closer scrutiny: *memoria* is always looking both towards the historical referent and into some undefined moment of future reading. As such, it becomes a useful tool in the production of historically inflected argument aimed at creating a particular effect. This formulation may appear rather abstract; concrete evidence is, of course, the copious historical *exempla* in Cicero's speeches, where there is a clear assumption that history provides a shared system of values through which the orator can seek to promote a consensus within his audience, while at the same time, individual *exempla* are in effect a constant reinterpretation, or at least *re-presentation* of familiar material.

The exemplary quality of history is, moreover, directly linked to the sense of self which motivates participation in public life. In spite of their ambiguous play with history, there is no ambiguity about the educational objectives of Cicero's philosophical works, *De re publica* and *De oratore* included: they are to inspire, and to add significant detail and vividness to that sense of connectedness to history that mere *exempla* only hint at. This vividness does not depend upon historical accuracy, however, so much as upon the power of the historical evocation to strike at the preoccupations of its readers, and to exhort them to measure their own conceptions of the *res publica* by that projected from the past. The moral imperative that comes from history is for those learning about these figures to measure their own conduct in terms of the perpetuation of their own reputation, as Polybius' account of the funeral oration suggests. The examples of Cicero's preoccupation with his own posthumous reputation are so many that they cannot be listed here; we need only recall what a powerful emphasis Cicero's first biographer, Plutarch, placed upon that preoccupation as a guiding motivation in his life.[36] But this was certainly a rule which all Cicero's rhetorical appeals on the subject suggest would find a ready identification with his audience.

One good example shows him appealing to Caesar's sense of his reputation. In *Pro Marcello* Cicero presents Caesar with the prospect of posterity's wavering judgement: Caesar needs to realize that his actions at this point in time may evoke dispute among the living, but that far more important will be the reputation that he achieves among future generations. Those yet to be born, moreover, will be far more objective than those currently alive, and if Caesar is to earn a reputation that is both positive and enduring, he needs to assess himself by their standards of objectivity. This insistence upon the distant future as the place where *memoria* has its true audience is particularly significant:

sed nisi haec urbs stabilita tuis consiliis et institutis erit, uagabitur modo tuum nomen longe atque late, sedem stabilem et domicilium certum non habebit. erit inter eos etiam qui nascentur, sicut inter nos fuit, magna dissensio, cum alii laudibus ad caelum res tuas gestas efferent, alii fortasse aliquid requirent, idque uel maximum, nisi belli civilis incendium salute patriae restinxeris, ut illud fati videatur fuisse, hoc consili. servi igitur eis iudicibus qui multis post saeculis de te iudicabunt et quidem haud scio an incorruptius quam nos; nam et sine amore et sine cupiditate et rursus sine odio et sine invidia iudicabunt.   (*Pro Marcello* 29)

But unless this city is made stable by your decisions and actions, your reputation will wander long and wide, but will have no stable and secure home. There will be among those still to be born as much as amongst us a great controversy, as some will bear your deeds to heaven with their praises, others perhaps still feel a lack: of this, most of all: unless you extinguish the fire of civil war with the salvation of the fatherland, so that that (i.e. the war) seems like the product of fate, while the extinction seems like the product of wise counsel. Therefore pay heed to those judges who will judge you after many centuries, and who indeed will most likely be more incorruptible than we; for they will judge without love and without greed, and again, without hatred and without envy.

---

[36] Plutarch, *Cic.* 24. 2; *Comp. Dem. Cic.* 2. 3.

The passage is particularly remarkable for the manner in which these closing phrases foreshadow Tacitus' famous declaration that he wrote his history *sine ira et studio*. Although Tacitus manages to find, among Cicero's quartet of absences, two new cognate terms which he has not used, it seems inconceivable that this memorable sentence was not in his mind when he produced his own, equally memorable formulation. An examination of the relationship between the two passages is highly instructive.[37]

sed veteris populi Romani prospera vel adversa claris scriptoribus memorata sunt; temporibusque Augusti dicendis non defuere decora ingenia, donec gliscente adulatione deterrerentur. Tiberii Gaique et Claudii ac Neronis res florentibus ipsis ob metum falsae, postquam occiderant, recentibus odiis compositae sunt. inde consilium mihi pauca de Augusto et extrema tradere, mox Tiberii principatum et cetera, sine ira et studio, quorum causas procul habeo. (Tacitus, *Annals* 1. 1)

But the successes or failures of the Roman people are recorded by famous writers; and fitting geniuses were not lacking for writing about the times of Augustus, until they were deterred by rising sycophancy. Histories of Tiberius, Gaius, Claudius, and Nero written while they were alive were, out of fear, fictitious, after they were dead, written under the influence of recent loathing. Whence came my idea to write little about Augustus, only the final things, and to move quickly on to the principate of Tiberius and other subjects, without anger and enthusiasm, the causes of which are remote from me.

At first sight it looks as though the echoing of Cicero's phraseology simply signals a disjunction between two different discourses: Tacitus' ambitions as a historian to write without bias, without expressing his personal opinion, and the reputation of posterity against which Caesar's political actions will be judged. To realize the connection, however, will enable us to understand better the way in which the notion of the judgement of posterity functions, and Cicero's formulation actually makes it easier to interpret Tacitus accurately. Tacitus' anxiety about bias is not a fear that his account should be seen to express his own opinion, but rather that he should seem to be too closely involved with the figures whose history he is narrating. They are sufficiently far back in time for his personal judgement not to be

---

[37] Luce (1989).

clouded by any sense of excessive personal involvement. *Sine ira et studio* does *not* mean that he will not be judging the character of the period that he is narrating, just that his opinions will not be the result of a personal involvement with the characters and events. There is no contradiction, therefore, between the highly opinionated manner in which Tacitus portrays the Julio-Claudians and this expression of high-minded detachment, except, of course, in the implicit identification of every example of defective imperial behaviour as in some sense a foreshadowing of Domitian, where personal feelings of enmity would clearly make such detachment impossible for Tacitus. But we must not overestimate Tacitus' irony here; the incentives to distort recent history are seen as personal engagement with the historical subject.

Cicero threatens Caesar with a similarly disengaged panel of judges, men who will not be involved in the network of affection and personal advantage which clouds the judgement of those directly witnessing the events.[38] Caesar is being confronted with a version of his own *memoria*, and it is one in which Cicero is placing particular weight on one decisive act: the distinction between *fatum* (fate) and *consilium* (counsel, i.e. here a deliberate decision) enables Cicero to extricate Caesar from a damning responsibility for the civil war, so long as he takes action to end it: that will be the manifestation of decisive action which will create unanimity among both living and future critics, amongst whom historians must be numbered. Caesar will be able to change the plot of his own history. By virtue of one considered action, he can ensure that he is seen as a historical agent rather than a creature of destiny. The processing of *memoria* which the production of a historical account entails, will, for Tacitus, produce a form of objectivity which endures over time: this same process of working at one's own posthumous reputation to ensure the persistence of a record in the face of which personal involvement will recede, is crucial to Cicero. *Memoria* is directed to the distant future, where partiality, in the sense of personal advantage or disadvantage, the network of carefully negotiated personal relationships which

---

[38] There is a paradoxical opposition here between the notion familiar from Polybius onwards that it was precisely such personal involvement that could best guarantee historical reliability. See Marincola (1997), 63–86; L. Morgan (2000).

make up the texture of political life at Rome, is no longer an issue. It is in the context of such a view of posterity, and of *memoria*, that Cicero seeks to perpetuate so vociferously the record of his own consulship, but also, more broadly, his obsessive publication of speeches, letters, even pamphlets explaining his own political decisions.[39]

The quantity of his literary production, and perhaps in particular the detailed self-justification of some of his letters, can be seen as an attempt to make up for a lack of a decisive standpoint from which to judge the success or failure of his career. Although the consulship could have provided that, it is my belief (one which I will explore in more detail in Chapter 8) that the experience of exile made it impossible for Cicero to sustain his faith in that as sufficient by itself to guarantee his reputation. I will examine his letter asking the historian Lucceius to bring him into the historical record in Chapter 9. But to any future historian, Cicero in any case provided instead an enormous quantity of evidence, some of it (particularly in the letters, also in some speeches) deliberately targeted so as to dismiss the detractions of his own enemies as envy, but much of it producing a complex and contradictory image that still presents challenges to any historian. But, taken in this context, historical writing is obviously the most direct manner of ensuring the continuation of one's own reputation, and of putting it out of reach of the politics of envy or favour. The story about Rome which Cicero tells, however, as we are discovering, refuses to adopt the authorizing position which the traditional forms of Roman historiography entailed.

But, rather than judging the ambiguities of Cicero's position against an imagined standard of historical representation where only one version of events is possible, his rejection of a stabilizing account of the past needs to be seen in the light of the flexibility of the exemplary tradition, and in terms of the clear emphasis upon the educational or imaginative function of historical representation. In this context, it is worth returning briefly to Cicero's unfavourable comparisons between Greek and Roman historiography.[40] Although scholars conventionally see this contrast as being about levels of rhetorical expertise, it also makes sense to read it as a complaint about the inadequate realization of history's educational function.

---

[39] Marincola (1997), 172.   [40] See above, pp. 136–40.

The elaborate rhetoric of Hellenistic historiography may be what Cicero has in mind here, a form of historiography which laid particular emphasis upon engaging its readers. Cicero's ambiguous comment about the *commentarii* of Caesar, that he has provided the raw material for someone else to write the history (*Brutus* 262; see above, p. 150) certainly suggests a separation between the true purpose of history and the recording of the past in which Caesar has engaged. It is a back-handed compliment to Caesar that he is so skilful in his employment of a brief, plain style that he has in effect deterred anyone else from writing up his accounts in a fully-fledged *historia*. It is not adornment that would make *commentarii* into *historia*; Cicero's speakers turn back to the rhetoric of the dead before they tell us explicitly what it is, but the general discussion of the style of historians in the dialogue makes clear that Cicero regards it as the role of the historian to engage his readers and employ his style to educate and to edify.[41] As Atticus is made to put it regarding the story of the death of Coriolanus: *concessum est rhetoribus ementiri in historiis, ut aliquid dicere possint argutius* (*Brutus* 42) ('it is permitted for orators to lie in their histories in order to be able to express something more pointedly'). It is not entirely clear why orators would be writing histories; perhaps this is just a revealing slip on Cicero's part, which conveys rather more about his views of historiography than the argument demands. But the point about the requirements of the argument is as relevant to the use of historical examples in rhetoric as it is for argumentatively sharpened historiography.

Hellenistic historiography in particular (and the Coriolanus episode gives rise to a comparison between Thucydides' account of Themistocles, and later, more embroidered ones by Clitarchus and Stratocles) seems to have acquired a high level of self-consciousness concerning the advantages of dramatic representation, and to have presupposed a sophisticated relationship between reader and subject matter. The best evidence for a conscious moral dialogue between the

---

[41] The comparison of Cato's *Origines* with the works of Philistus and Thucydides (in contrast to the more high-flown Theopompus) (*Brutus* 66, cf. 294), of Hortensius with Timaeus (*Brutus* 325), and the contrast between Thucydides and Clitarchus/Stratocles (*Brutus* 42) all suggest that Cicero was fully aware of the resources of Greek history not just for style *per se*, but for the role of style in making history into compelling reading.

readers and writers of history is Dionysius of Halicarnassus, who produced his essays on Thucydides and historiography (*Thucydides*; *Letter to Pompeius*) some time after Cicero's death. But there is enough evidence from Polybius' polemics with his predecessors, and from other scattered fragments, to show that at least from the fourth century onwards, Greek historiography was undertaken in full expectation of a critical reception that revolved primarily around the educative and political relevance of different forms of historical representation, at least as much as, if not more than, around problems of sources. It is within this context that Cicero's sense of the power of written historical legacy developed, just as it makes sense of his complaints about the primitive state of Latin historiography.[42] If history is going to be deserving of the name, and not simply remain at the level of bare annals or *commentarii*, it needs to animate *memoria* and enhance its function. Cicero's engagement with this topic confirms one central idea: that *memoria* is concerned with representation and effect, and that it is the function of the memory of the past to bring a positive influence to bear on future generations.

HISTORICAL REVIVAL; THE BOUNDARY BETWEEN POLITICS AND METAPHOR

The strange cultural practice of historical revival at Rome can benefit from a brief consideration in this light. Again, it is under Augustus that the full ramifications of this theme are most evident; a central historical problem for Augustan historians is how far what appears to modern eyes to be a blatant exploitation of a symbolic system could in fact have functioned effectively as an engine of social change; we tend to think that ideology follows, rather than propels, political movement, and the success of Augustus is in this sense a puzzle,

---

[42] Luce (1989), 21–3, on the change of climate later in the fourth century. M. A. Flower (1994), 42–62, effectively demolishes the orthodoxy that all Hellenistic history was somehow Isocratean; but cf. Dionysius of Halicarnassus, *Letter to Pompeius* 6, defending Theopompus against charges of *psychagogia* (sensationalism). K. Morgan (1998), 104–8, is useful on Isocratean history as charter-myth; Candau Morón (2000), esp. 459–61.

one that is only partially resolved by accepting the mechanistic explanations which build on what Tacitus tells us were the reasons for his popularity.[43] The boundary between historical revival and a living historical tradition is narrow: are the attempts to pass land-reform legislation, which caused repeated unrest throughout the first century, for example, to be seen as deliberate appeals to revive the reforming strength of the Gracchi, or were they just further, continued demonstrations of an ideology that looked to the Gracchi for a foundational inspiration? The difference depends upon our understanding of ideology, and how it intersects with the writing of history. The trial of Rabirius on a charge of *perduellio*, in the year of Cicero's consulship (63), is the most challenging example, and Cicero's own participation as defence makes it especially interesting.[44] In its cynical exploitation of historical revival, and its interweaving of contemporary power struggles with appeals to obsolete institutions and distant historical precedent, it presents a challenge to modern notions of the neat separation between history and politics, even between narrative and law. The trial depended upon bringing to justice, on a long obsolete charge of a particular kind of treasonable murder, an old man who had supposedly committed the act (killing the notorious Saturninus) thirty-seven years earlier. In essence a struggle between senatorial and populist factions for control of the legal system, the trial was brought to a halt by a supporter of the senatorial cause raising a flag on the Janiculum, the standard mechanism for declaring the closing of the centuriate assembly (which at this point was, according to Dio, voting on Rabirius' appeal), but nevertheless something of a theatrical stunt.[45]

The episode is most remarkable for the apparent cynicism with which the protagonists exploited historical material, as if they were aware both of its power and of their own ability to fashion it for

---

[43] Tacitus, *Annals* 1. 2. For recent reassessments of 'the Roman revolution' see the essays in Giovannini (2000); succinctly on Augustus' powers, Cotton and Yakobson (2001).

[44] Fuhrmann (1981) was the initial impetus for my thoughts on the implications of revival, and for a consideration of this trial; for more detail and evidence, Bauman (1996), 42–5; Morstein-Marx (2004), 24–5, 109–10, with discussion of the scholarship; briefly Forsythe (2005), 194, and historical 'reduplication', 346–7.

[45] Dio Cassius 37. 26–8.

political ends. Those who revived the charge, with its archaic form of court (the *duumviri perduellionis*) were able to use historical rituals to push a fierce political struggle to the point where only the application of further archaic ritual prevented the capital punishment of Rabirius. Dio is clear, however, that the court was brought into being in a manner that actually violated historical precedent.[46] The revival was not undertaken with any particular diligence or need to stick closely to prescribed forms, and by the same token the political purposes of the revival were entirely clear.[47] In spite of the obvious absurdity, however, Rome was drawn into what looks to us like an elaborate historical charade. Nevertheless, it is clear that cynical political manœuvring does not satisfactorily account for the effectiveness with which this appeal to ancient law could give rise to such an important crisis in public affairs. Rather, the episode demonstrates particularly well that the processes of living within a historical tradition, and of displaying and perpetuating historical anecdote as a means of reinforcing political status, do not represent a self-contained discourse of historical consciousness, unique to the aristocracy. Rather, it shows that the boundaries between historical knowledge, and in particular the display of that knowledge, and socio-political power were differently drawn at Rome. As well as the numerous Augustan revivals, the most striking manifestations of this different arrangement were the 'fatal charades' in which historical narratives were, in the early Empire, acted out in the gladiatorial arena.[48] Although the stakes were much higher in these executions, or in Rabirius' trial, than they are in Cicero's writings, what all share is the idea that historical representation has ramifications which go far beyond the literary, and that, indeed, the record of life or events in historical representation is a process without secure closure. Just as *memoria* can look into an ever-receding future for its effect, so too the memory of past lives or practices can suddenly leap out of the book and into the lives of new generations—in the case of Rabirius,

---

[46] Ibid. 37. 27. 3.

[47] As Cicero's defence speech demonstrates. Cicero invokes a wide range of Roman history to demonstrate that the revival represents an aberrant return to tyranny, and challenges his opponents with his own genealogy of true popular feeling: *Pro Rab. perd.* 10–14.

[48] Coleman (1990).

with most unwelcome consequences. Cicero's attempt to contain those consequences, in his defence of Rabirius, consists in part in the presentation of a better genealogy for *popularis* politics, and in the restriction of brutal judicial practices in a period in Rome's past (the tyranny of Tarquinius Superbus) with which the historical consciousness of his audience would be disinclined to identify, if not recoil.[49]

We are dealing here with a politics built upon competing historical narratives, a situation, when so formulated, perhaps not so unknown in modern societies. As my earlier peek at the origins of Roman historical tradition suggest, those same narratives were responsible for providing a structure in which different versions of ancestry could be articulated and contested. The contestation, however, could characteristically combine the cynical exploitation of history with an endorsement of its effectiveness. Intellectual sophistication and faith in the mythic properties of history could coexist quite happily. The ironies here of the account of Romulus' deification in *De re publica* 2, where Cicero plays an elaborate game with the historical credulity both of the speakers in the dialogue and of his own readers, express the same kind of double awareness that we can imagine when the flag on the Janiculum drew Rabirius' trial to a close.[50] It is a double standard that scholars of Roman religion are beginning to be comfortable with, but which has not as yet had great impact in the study of historiography.[51] Cicero's own death is not irrelevant here; the brutality of the act is not just a sign of flexible boundaries between literary and political, and of the potential for metaphors to be made concrete; it is also an invitation to consider the effort to transcend his mortality as a response to that same tendency.[52] Bearing in mind the representative focus of *memoria*, I would argue that in the late Republic history was precisely the arena in which contested notions of identity were worked out, and that although intensely retrospective, and in

---

[49] *Pro Rab. perd.* 13: the archaic form of words associated with the punishment for *perduellio* is quoted, and directly attributed to the tyrant.

[50] *Rep.* 2. 10. 17–20; see Fox (1996), 18–19.

[51] Feeney (1998) explores a similar argument in the field of Roman religion. *De divinatione* is the best (and most studied) evidence for a similar attitude regarding the rituals of divination. See below, Ch. 8.

[52] See Butler (2002).

that sense conservative, there is plenty of evidence that historical representation, rather than a dead realm in which ideas or institutions were given validation, was a changing and dynamic discourse, in which the gaze was more resolutely directed towards the effect of the past upon the present and the future. In this context, Cicero's own play with history, both foundational and destabilizing, is a manifestation of the evident difficulty of achieving a satisfactory consensus about the identity of Rome, and a creative encounter with that difficulty that provides a unique insight into the difficulties of achieving an authoritative vision of Rome.

Historical consciousness in our own societies is so complex, the relevance of the past so disputed, and the continuity between past and present so difficult to define, that it is hard to find ways of describing the Roman obsession with the past that convey what is most characteristic of it: its conjunction of conservative and radical impulses, its capacity to represent the distant past as though fixed and conventional, while at the same time experimenting with innovative forms of historical representation. *The Aeneid* is perhaps the most immediate example: seemingly rooted in clichés of primitive simplicity and early heroism, it both breathes new life into those clichés and entirely overturns them by the freshness of its interpretation, as well as by its disturbing and inconclusive vision of Rome's history as one of epic struggle. The apparently conservative ideology of Augustus is another well-known case: the pose of historical revival enabled Augustus to embark on a type of social and political engineering without precedent in antiquity.[53] These Augustan ways of dealing with the past do not constitute a breach with earlier generations. In the writings of Sallust, it is clear to see that history is a potent medium in which to explore the tension between progressive and conservative, and that in the figure of Marius, conventions concerning Roman social norms are there in order to be debated, overturned, and freed from any sense of historical fixity. In Cicero's philosophical deliberations with history, we can see the same processes at work. Furthermore, in his complaints about the shortcomings of Roman historiography, we should detect not the imperialist fervour of the rhetorician seeking to colonize an alien discourse,

---

[53] Fuhrmann (1987).

but rather the philosopher and politician aware of the enormous role
of history in already providing an arena for political engagement at
Rome. The absence of stylistic charm is a missed opportunity to give
that discourse sufficient appeal to reach a readership wider than those
with a specialist interest in tradition. This was the same readership
that he envisaged for his philosophy, and when that philosophy dealt
with history readers could reasonably be expected to be excited, rather
than deterred, by a dynamic representation of the past that did not
occlude the processes of its own inception. In this respect, Cicero was
the founding father of a tradition of ironic historiography, and his
philosophical exploitation of history actually mined the same vein
which Tacitus was later to find so fruitful.[54]

[54] See Ch. 9.

7

Brutus

From the foregoing chapters, it will be clear what the themes will be for the examination of Cicero's late dialogue on rhetoric, *Brutus*, the first work to be discussed in which the influence of Caesar's dictatorship is felt. Written in the wake of the final defeat of the Pompeian cause, with closure of the courts and the oppression of the Senate which Caesar's monopolization of power brought with it, the work is a strange account of the place of rhetoric at Rome, and a more personal deliberation on the central question: what style of man is most suited to exert political control at Rome? The work is not defeatist in tone, but neither is it a particularly effective demonstration of the centrality of rhetoric at Rome, even though it contains some naked self-advertisement for Cicero, for his rhetorical style, and for his way of doing political discourse. The work is long and episodic, and it lacks the theoretical focus of either *De oratore* or *De re publica*, both of which can be seen as direct antecedents to it. As such, it is hard to decide whether the mourning for the loss of the rhetorical skills of the Republic, the attempt to provide a genealogy for the career of Cicero, or the evident failure of that genealogy takes the upper hand. It is not just because the end is missing that this work lacks closure: it also fails to tell a coherent story. There are regretful qualities to the work, and to some extent the apparent demise of the Republic led Cicero to record its historical orators as if they were a species facing extinction.[1] However, when looked at in the light of a continuing story about the history of Rome, begun in *De oratore* and pursued in *De re publica*, *Brutus* can usefully be read

---

[1] The analysis of Gowing (2000) is particularly strong on the commemorative aspects of the work. For a general introduction, Narducci (2002).

as a deliberation not just on the nature of rhetoric at Rome, but on the attendant problems of writing that history, both in terms of the possible benefits of an idealized history that would grant a sense of purpose to Cicero and a desperation that Cicero's own position is a unique one, which Rome's structures have not fostered.[2]

BEGINNING *BRUTUS*

In order to begin a more detailed examination of the work, I will start with the prologue and the introductory section in which the three speaking characters, Cicero, Brutus, and Atticus, manœuvre in preparation for the main body of the work. In spite of its title, *Brutus* begins with an extended tribute to Hortensius, Cicero's only real rival for rhetorical supremacy at Rome, whose death sparks off deliberations on the eclipse of rhetoric under Caesar. These deliberations, and the prologue as a whole, are written in an entirely different voice from the rest of the work, and are the best evidence for understanding the political dimension of the history which follows. The story of the conflict between different possible ways of categorizing a public career at Rome is one which takes its lead in the prologue from the situation of Cicero's own life; but the version here is not simply a predictable struggle between an idealization and a rejection of rhetoric, or between an actual historical success in terms of political power and a wished-for success achieved by speaking. Rather, Cicero's language in the prologue, in particular his ambiguous use of military metaphors, indicates a more complex picture, where rhetoric has a potential which is at times enormous, at other times bound to be frustrated. We need to look carefully at the images that Cicero employs here, and

---

[2] Once again, Dugan (2005) provides a helpful reading, but one fundamentally different from mine. So on p. 172: 'The *Brutus* presents itself as an opportunity for Cicero to gain some degree of mastery over history's paradoxes and caprices.' On p. 199: 'the inevitable conclusion of the *Brutus*' basic historical premises is that Cicero himself is the culmination of the tradition he traces in the work.' In a sense this is true, but I would dispute the use of the word 'inevitable', and suggest that Dugan misplaces the function of the ironic moments to which he himself gives detailed attention.

at the implications of the images for the conceptual framework which Cicero establishes to discuss the development of oratory at Rome.

The prologue is focused upon Hortensius, Cicero's long-standing colleague and his only challenger for the position of Rome's leading orator. Hortensius' death, Cicero argues, was timely, since he avoided experiencing the extinction of public rhetoric under Caesar's regime. The pain that Cicero himself feels in these changed circumstances is precisely the one which Hortensius was spared, that of seeing rhetoric silenced and the power of the orator to control public affairs eclipsed by that of military power (*arma*). However, Cicero makes a great deal more out of Hortensius' death: to begin with, the fact that he mentions it at all, and beyond that, the notion that in some way his death is the occasion which gave rise to the present dialogue. Hortensius had died in 50 BCE, several years before Cicero can even have conceived of writing such a dialogue; but in his prologue he treats his grief at Hortensius' death as though that emotion in itself were an impetus to produce this work. Death, or grief at that death, is in fact a springboard for Cicero to deliberate upon a number of key themes: most obviously, that of the dead orator. Almost all the orators who come to be discussed in the following dialogue are dead,[3] but the notion of the dead orator has much wider, almost symbolic ramifications. The death of Hortensius prompts a meditation on the question of the effect of the dead upon the living, and upon the question of the legacy of individuals:

sed quoniam perpetua quadam felicitate usus ille cessit e vita suo magis quam suorum civium tempore et tum occidit cum lugere facilius rem publicam posset, si viveret, quam iuvare, vixitque tam diu quam licuit in civitate bene beateque vivere, nostro incommodo detrimentoque, si est ita necesse, doleamus, illius vero mortis opportunitatem benevolentia potius quam misericordia prosequamur, ut, quotienscumque de clarissimo et beatissimo viro cogitemus, illum potius quam nosmet ipsos diligere videamur. Nam si id dolemus, quod eo iam frui nobis non licet, nostrum est id malum, quod modice feramus, ne id non ad amicitiam sed ad domesticam utilitatem

---

[3] The exceptions are Marcellus and Caesar, and Cicero puts an evaluation of their oratory in the mouths of Brutus and Atticus, and much earlier in the work (*Brutus* 150–7) Servius Sulpicius Rufus, whose virtues are extolled by Cicero and Brutus. These moments give the secondary characters their only real opportunity for the kind of critical discussion which 'Cicero' monopolizes for the rest of the work.

referre videamur; sin tamquam illi ipsi acerbitatis aliquid acciderit angimur,
summam eius felicitatem non satis grato animo interpretamur. (*Brutus* 4–5)

He experienced a particular enduring happiness, and departed his life at a
time more suited to himself than to his fellow citizens; he died at the point
when it was easier to grieve for the Republic than, if he had lived, to come to
its aid; he lived as long in our society as he could well and happily do so; so
we should grieve at our own discomfort and loss, if we must, but we should
look upon the opportunity of his death with good wishes rather than pity. So
that, whenever we think of that dearest and most blessed man, we may seem
to love him, rather than ourselves. For if we are grieving because we cannot
enjoy his company, that is our own ill fortune, which we should bear with
moderation, in case we seem to experience it not out of friendship but for
our own private utility; but if we grieve as if some disaster has happened to
him, we do not recognize with sufficient gratitude his great good fortune.

This elegantly expressed argument centres on the dichotomy between
the benefits that accrue to either the self or others. Hortensius' death
is a blessing to him, and it is a form of solipsism to misconstrue one's
own grief at his death as pity for him; it is, in fact, pity for ourselves.
Cicero here is weighing up the degree to which private emotions can
be conflated or kept distinct from moral conclusions that can be
discussed in a public discourse such as this one. He warns his readers
against confusing a sense of personal loss with an evaluation of the
significance of the dead person; it is only a benefit that Hortensius is
no longer alive, for he is spared the sight of the Republic in its present
condition, a sight that tortures Cicero in the same way that he would
be tortured if he were unable to restrain his identification with
Hortensius, to fail to demarcate his own sense of loss from any
sense of what was actually good for Hortensius: nothing bad has
happened to him. Any disadvantage or grief resulting from his
demise is a private matter (*domesticam*): Hortensius was fortunate
to have failed to witness the end of oratory; but the extinction of the
Republic is something that elicits grief from another source, one
where there is no decorum in restraining one's emotions. But in
spite of Cicero's attempt to distinguish between his own sense of
grief at Hortensius' death and a form of grief which recognizes more
objectively the actual fate of the deceased, the whole point of this
opening presentation is precisely to conflate those two areas, by
making the death of Hortensius into a symbol of the extinction of
oratory at Rome which Caesar's dictatorship has brought with it, and

to display, with a certain philosophical and stylistic sophistication, a kind of grief that will find collective recognition.

Moving on from the passage quoted above, Cicero expands upon the reasons why it is better for Hortensius to be dead, and thus brings the argument around precisely to that form of self-pity which he has warned against in this passage. The admiration he feels for Hortensius is extended, in much the same language, to include men not just from Rome but from any state, to whom an honourable old age was permitted. That blessed state is contrasted with the situation where military force has been employed, and in particular military force of an inappropriate kind:

equidem angor animo non consili, non ingeni, non auctoritatis armis egere rem publicam, quae didiceram tractare quibusque me assuefeceram quaeque erant propria cum praestantis in re publica viri tum bene moratae et bene constitutae civitatis. quod si fuit in re publica tempus ullum, cum extorquere arma posset e manibus iratorum civium boni civis auctoritas et oratio, tum profecto fuit cum patrocinium pacis exclusum est aut errore hominum aut timore.   (*Brutus* 7)

I too am tortured in spirit that the *res publica* does not need the weapons of good counsel, genius, authority, which I had learnt to handle, to which I had grown accustomed, and which were proper as much to a man prominent in public life as to a civilized and well-ordered society. If there was ever a time in the *res publica* when the authority and rhetoric of a good citizen could wrest the weapons from the hands of angry citizens, it was at exactly that point that either by men's mistakes or fear that the advocacy of peace was precluded.

The contrast is between the *arma* of the Caesarian regime and those metaphorical *arma,* of *consilium, ingenium,* and *auctoritas,* which were Cicero's particular achievement, the result of his own education (*didiceram*). In a well-ordered state, these 'weapons' are what make it possible for the good man to function, to exercise his power within the state for the purposes of peace, even, where necessary, enabling him to bring an end to violence, to bring his angry fellow-citizens to lay down their arms. The striking phrase *patrocinium pacis* encapsulates the tight connection between rhetorical capacity and political action: to be able to use his experience and skill as an advocate for the cause of peace would have been the culmination of Cicero's entire career. As I argued in Chapter 5, Cicero had long been wrestling with the dilemma of the orator's relationship to the military commander, and here that dilemma is in a sense resolved, but with the full-scale defeat of rhetoric.[4]

Importantly, this whole argument depends upon the particular historical moment. The interpretation which Cicero gives of the times in which he is living is a crucial factor in the historicizing of rhetoric which occupies the rest of the work. But in the repetitive structure of the ensuing history, it is easy to forget what is at issue in this characterization of the *res publica*: it is not just the capacities of individuals that make up history. It is possible to construct, as Cicero attempts to do in *Pro Murena*, the argument that makes rhetoric into the cornerstone of the Roman public career, the *cursus honorum*. But looking back over the lists of those men who have achieved in the political arena, the relationship between that achievement and rhetorical skill is not evident. The tension that characterizes the following dialogue is foreshadowed in this prologue. What Cicero's genealogy actually needs to explain is not the supremacy of his own rhetorical achievements, but rather their failure to be effective in the face of weapons, human failure, or fear, and what that failure tells us about the character of Rome. He continues now to focus upon the disappointments at the end of his career, expanding upon the contrast between the growth in his rhetorical confidence and the extreme circumstance in which it became powerless:

ita nobismet ipsis accidit ut, quamquam essent multo magis alia lugenda, tamen hoc doleremus quod, quo tempore aetas nostra perfuncta rebus amplissimis tamquam in portum confugere deberet non inertiae neque desidiae, sed oti moderati atque honesti, cumque ipsa oratio iam nostra canesceret haberetque suam quandam maturitatem et quasi senectutem, tum arma sunt ea sumpta, quibus illi ipsi, qui didicerant eis uti gloriose, quem ad modum salutariter uterentur non reperiebant.   (*Brutus* 8)

And so it happened to me, of all people, that, although other things were a much greater cause of grief, that I should instead have to grieve for this: having reached a time of life when, after the highest achievements, I ought to have been taking refuge in the harbour, not of laziness or apathy, but of a controlled and respectable retirement, when my oratory was going grey and had a certain maturity, almost an old age; at that point, weapons were taken

---

4 See above, pp. 115–18.

up, and those men who had learnt how to use them gloriously, would not find a way to use them for public safety.

The repetition of vocabulary from earlier in the passage is quite striking: Cicero is a victim of circumstance (*accidit*); we should not imagine that anything dreadful had happened to Hortensius (*acciderit*). Cicero had learnt (*didiceram*) to handle the weapons of authority; these unnamed figures had learnt (*didicerant*) to use weapons for glory. This fixation on certain central concepts and terms continues as the prologue draws to a close, introducing the dialogue proper:

itaque ei mihi videntur fortunate beateque vixisse cum in ceteris civitatibus tum maxume in nostra, quibus cum auctoritate rerumque gestarum gloria tum etiam sapientiae laude perfrui licuit. quorum memoria et recordatio in maxumis nostris gravissimisque curis iucunda sane fuit, cum in eam nuper ex sermone quodam incidissemus.   (*Brutus* 9)

And so those men seem to me to have lived particularly fortunate and blessed lives, in other states too, but particularly in our own, who could properly enjoy their authority, the glory of their past achievements, as much as their reputation for wisdom. The memory and recollection of these men was especially pleasant amidst our own extremely serious anxieties, when recently we hit upon the subject in the course of a conversation.

This collective blessedness parallels the rather hyperbolic depiction of Hortensius' own enormous personal happiness; the *cum ... tum* contrast in the penultimate sentence reasserts the polarity between intellectual gifts (*laus sapientiae*) and the authority and glory of political achievement. In both respects, the maturation of Cicero's rhetoric has not been rewarded by a dignified withdrawal from public life, but by enforced silence in which the intellectual gifts and the record of public achievements can have no public effect and produce no personal satisfaction. *Gloria* is something which Caesar had formerly achieved; it is something that dead men were able to enjoy. It is also something which bound Hortensius to Cicero while they worked together (at the very start of the work).[5] The central themes of the rest of the work are being trailed: the appropriate use of

---

[5] *dolebamque quod non, ut plerique putabant, adversarium aut obtrectatorem laudum mearum sed socium potius et consortem gloriosi laboris amiseram* (*Brutus* 2) ('I grieved not because, as people thought, I had lost an adversary or critic of my reputation, but rather an associate and colleague in my work of glory').

education in the formation of effective statesmen at Rome; some learn to achieve glory through intellectual gifts, others through arms. *Auctoritas*: how it is acquired, whether it can be put to good political effect, and, crucially, its relationship to *oratio*. The picture of Cicero's growth to political maturity is of his gradually achieving a pinnacle of stylistic *auctoritas*. His *oratio* has acquired the power of a grand old man. But this has not led to the expected political or social consequences.

Memory and recollections are a real pleasure, an escape from the terrible turn of events. The sense of grief at the death of Hortensius is resolved into something which takes that particular topic and makes it into something more general: the contemplation of a better way of life which *all* those no longer alive can be thought to have enjoyed. The naturalness of the transition, reinforced by the idea expressed by *incidissemus*, that the conversation we are about to overhear was a spontaneous one, masks a stark historical diagnosis:[6] only the dead are fortunate, and the only manner in which pleasure can be achieved in these troubled times is through memory. In the light of the previous chapter, it is worth noting the pairing of *memoria* and *recordatio*. If one has to distinguish between the nuances of these two words, then *recordatio* lays more emphasis upon the processes of producing a written account of the past, whereas *memoria* is concerned with the reputation of the dead and the continuation of that reputation. The purpose of recollection, therefore, is both the compensation for pain and the perpetuation of a lost way of life. However, we shall observe in the course of the dialogue that Cicero is unable to maintain such an extreme view of the relationship between the past and the present, as of the supremacy of rhetoric as a measure of political achievement. Indeed, the question of the inclusion of *only* dead orators becomes itself the object of discussion, some of it quite light-hearted.[7] But more importantly, it emerges that this position of

---

[6] Cicero's phrasing is surprising, but actually rather exact: *ex sermone quodam* suggests that the conversation was already under way when it turned toward the *memoria* of the orators. At the start of the dialogue itself, he does then include an opening introduction (including reference to the *liber annalis*, Brutus' own writings (his *De virtute*) and allusion to Cicero's own literary production). See Douglas (1966), pp. ix–xi.

[7] Dugan (2005), 208–9.

total despair at the loss of the Republic, in particular at the loss of the possibility of fruitful employment for the skills of political oratory which Cicero has just outlined, cannot be sustained, for one clear reason: it rests upon an idealization of Rome's history which is clearly untenable. Those dead men are doubtless fortunate in escaping the tyranny of Caesar, but it is far from clear that the reasons for that are the foreclosing of the arenas for them to exercise their eloquence. If they are to be envied that they are dead, it does not follow that rhetoric played the same role in allowing them to fulfil their potential as it did for Cicero and Hortensius.

THE MAIN FEATURES OF THE HISTORY

It is tempting to see the catalogue of orators as an attempt to provide a teleology of Cicero's own rhetorical achievements, a celebration of his own place as the culmination of a tradition of rhetoric at Rome, and an attempt to enforce Cicero's own *auctoritas* through the production of a written history that will compensate for the frustrations of living under a dictator.[8] Needless to say, I shall be arguing that such a reading overlooks the obvious ironies through which Cicero evokes a rather different picture of his place in Rome's history. Another useful pointer from the prologue is the reference to *De re publica* and to Atticus' *Liber annalis*. The former is said to have inspired the latter, and the latter in turn to have given rise to the present work.[9] In addition, reference is made to a text produced by Brutus (*litterae*) which has been presumed to be his *De virtute*.[10] Cicero conjures up an elaborate conceit of mutual inspiration, of which the present work is somehow the fruit, the characters in the dialogue referring to the very work which gives them a voice. The researches of Atticus were prompted by the historical aspects of *De re publica*: so the present work can be thought of as a continuation of that project facilitated by the extra resources which Atticus' labours have made accessible. That the response to a treatise on Stoic

---

[8] So the excellent account of Rathofer (1986).   [9] *Brutus* 19.
[10] Douglas (1966), p. xi.

virtue should be a genealogy of Roman oratory is indeed remarkable: in both these instances, Cicero is making pointed reference to the function of history. The current undertaking, the first, apparently, since *De re publica*, and certainly written before Cicero conceived his project of a complete philosophical curriculum, continues the emphasis in *De re publica* upon history as the realm of practical, rather than theoretical, wisdom, but the expression of that wisdom is presented, with an almost perverse consistency, to be rhetorical prowess. The work will thus clearly build upon both *De oratore* and *De re publica*, resting upon Atticus' researches, and presenting an alternative vision of public virtue and consequent public success, one fitted more to Cicero than to Brutus.

So we can see this history as an attempt to substantiate the central question of *De oratore* 1: how far is it historically accurate to regard rhetoric as a fundamental factor in the life of the Republic? Although the work evidently gives a history of Rome, or rather Romans, in these terms, it also continually keeps the question open as to how far what these men actually achieved was achieved by means of rhetoric. The main body of the work, after an extensive sketch of the history of rhetoric in Greece, is a monologue by Cicero, beginning with Rome's earliest history (as in *De oratore* 1), attributing rhetorical skill of different kinds to a long succession of named individuals, and attempting to characterize different individuals in terms of their verbal style. Of course, as well as substantiating, Cicero also leaves space for a more sceptical view. Thus, from Cicero's perspective, it would be convenient if rhetoric did indeed occupy this position; that would justify his work, and would validate not just his rhetorical publications as authoritative expressions of actual political influence, and his copious deliberations on the nature of rhetoric, and on the best type of orator for the Roman context, would be given a basis in history. But, rather than providing a positive genealogy for Cicero's own aspirations, *Brutus* actually tends more to the repudiation of any such genealogy. The dialogue does produce a historical narrative that makes rhetorical performance the measure of historical events; but, in line with Cicero's own despair at his own marginalization, at the same time leaves even less doubt than *De oratore* that this is a hopeless fantasy, and that Rome's history is one of rhetorical ineptitude. Even in the main historical catalogue itself, Cicero's method is not to idealize the rhetorical skills of his speakers—at least, not consistently. Here is one typical example:

et quoniam Stoicorum est facta mentio, Q. Aelius Tubero fuit illo tempore, L. Paulli nepos; nullo in oratorum numero, sed vita severus et congruens cum ea disciplina quam colebat, paulo etiam durior ... [ ] ... sed ut vita sic oratione durus incultus horridus; itaque honoribus maiorum respondere non potuit. fuit autem constans civis et fortis et in primis Graccho molestus, quod indicat Gracchi in eum oratio.   (*Brutus* 117)

Since the Stoics have been mentioned, Quintus Aelius Tubero belonged to that period, the grandson of Lucius Paullus. Not to be counted as an orator, his way of life was severe and of a piece with the philosophy which he cultivated, even a little harsher ... (there follows an account of a legal judgment where Tubero was not swayed by family loyalty)... but as he was in life, so in speech: harsh, untrained, rough; and so he was not able to respond to the high ranks of his ancestors. But he was a solid and brave citizen, and a particular annoyance to Gracchus, as Gracchus' speech against him shows.

The aim of this catalogue entry could certainly not be said to overestimate the role of oratory in the history of Rome, and if it grants a teleology to Cicero, then it is a teleology based upon negative examples, an ambiguous possibility which the speakers in the dialogue also raise.[11] But typical of the method of the dialogue is the application to a written source, where one exists, and to the central feature: the attempt at a stylistic characterization of the particular speaker. As the work comes closer in time to the present, of course, the degree of detail and the range of critical vocabulary both increase. But, as we shall see when we come to consider those moments where this methodology is itself brought under scrutiny, the evidence supplied in anecdotes such as this one is overtly ambiguous: it is not clear whether there is any point at all in thinking about Tubero in rhetorical terms. It seems to have little bearing upon his function as a citizen. Rather, the description raises questions about the place of oratory at Rome, the same questions as were raised in *De oratore* 1. Cicero does suggest that it was the lack of rhetorical skill that limited Tubero to a lower position in life than the one for which his birth had destined him: higher achievement would have been within his grasp

---

[11] e.g. *Brutus* 122–3: the publication of Cicero's speeches has stopped people reading those by earlier orators.

if he had been able to transcend his oppressive adherence to Stoicism, which here, rather pointedly, given the prominence both of Brutus' Stoicism and his love of a plain style, is seen to militate against reaching the highest level of success.

If a historical process such as this is supposed to produce a genealogy for Cicero's own position, then that genealogy cannot really be thought of as a happy foundation. So even without considering the more extreme moments where that genealogy is subjected to ironic deconstruction, we can see that there is an intrinsic tension: again, it is between competing narratives of Rome. But we are one stage further on than in *De re publica* or *De oratore*: as well as asking whether or not Rome was a breeding ground for orators, *Brutus* is also asking how that question should itself be answered, how the history of rhetoric at Rome should be written. The significance of such an openly ironic piece of historiography is considerable, and the interplay between careful historical research and sometimes excoriating irony, not only make *Brutus* into a fascinating proof of the sophistication of Cicero's historical thought; the work also provides a problematic model of the relationship between rhetoric and history which cannot easily be made stable.

The opening of the narrative of Roman history reprises some of the material that we encountered in *De oratore*, with such similarity of argument that one has to suspect that Cicero's position was already familiar to his closest readers. The first example of oratory at Rome that Cicero discusses is L. Brutus, the founder of the Republic, and ultimate ancestor of the eponymous character of the dialogue. Recollecting Crassus' arguments from *De oratore*, Cicero hypothesizes that *oratio* would have been an essential factor in the expulsion of the kings. The surrounding context, however, is interesting. Cicero begins his account by stressing the difficulty of assessing Roman orators in comparison with Greek ones:

sed veniamus ad nostros, de quibus difficile est plus intellegere quam quantum ex monumentis suspicari licet.   (*Brutus* 52–3)

But let us move on to our own men. It is difficult to understand more about them than can be guessed at from the historical record.

The exact meaning of *monumentis* is hard to grasp: presumably it refers to the historical record, but it is unclear what exactly the process is by which rhetorical capacity can be grasped (or even guessed) from a *monumentum* (or the *monumenta*, plural), and that indeed would seem to be Cicero's point here. The word *suspicari* returns again in a dense list of somewhat later statesmen from the third century—so frequently, indeed, that the accumulated weight of so much suspicion leads to an explicit conclusion:

sed eos oratores habitos esse aut omnino tum ullum eloquentiae praemium fuisse nihil sane mihi legisse videor; tantum modo coniectura ducor ad suspicandum.   (*Brutus* 56)

That they were regarded as orators, or that at that time eloquence was held in high regard, I don't indeed seem to have read anywhere: I am only led by conjecture to suspect it.

The change that then occurs in the structure of the dialogue is between orators for whom there is some explicit mention of rhetorical skill in the sources and those for whom it can only be deduced from their actual deeds; *monumenta* would therefore seem to be records of action, not words, rhetorical activities, or even the facts of speeches made. We are brought rather vividly face to face with the entirely non-rhetorical quality of the Roman historiographical tradition. These are the records which Atticus has been assembling: *monumenta* is the word used of them in the context of Greek chronology.[12] But, as the dialogue tells us, the product of his labours was characterized, if by diligence, also by brevity.[13] This is almost a chronicle: it provides the substance of history, but that substance does not extend to rhetoric.[14]

Corresponding to this problem of the sources, the main speaker, Cicero himself, constantly draws attention to the difficulty either of characterizing statesmen as orators or of attributing rhetorical expertise to those whose reputation rests on political activity. Cato

---

[12] *post hanc aetatem aliquot annis, ut ex Attici monumentis potest perspici, Themistocles fuit* (*Brutus* 28) ('a few years after this time came Themistocles, as can be perceived from the *monumenta* of Atticus').

[13] *nempe eum dicis, inquit, quo iste omnem rerum memoriam breviter et, ut mihi quidem visum est, perdiligenter complexus est* (*Brutus* 14) ('You are, of course, talking about that book in which this man has brought together the complete memory of events, briefly, and as it seems to me at any rate with great care').

[14] Cicero mentions the *Annales* as joyless reading matter in the *Letter to Lucceius*, discussed below, pp. 256–63.

appears initially as the watershed, the point from which written records become reliable. There are, however, speeches that have been preserved in particular noble families; they have had a bad effect on the historical record, since, in their zeal to glorify particular families, they are free in their invention of false triumphs, honours, and genealogies (§62).[15] We must surely here remember the words of Atticus from §42, that in Cicero's own judgement, orators are permitted to fabricate history in order to strengthen their argument.[16] Shortly afterwards, in the assessment of Cato, Cicero deplores how little known his 150 surviving speeches are, how little influence they have had upon Latin oratory in comparison with Greek models (§68); they are, he claims, the first written speeches to survive that are worth reading, *dignum lectione* (§69). The problem of relying upon such preserved speeches is tackled head on at §§91 ff., where the ironic interpretation is certainly possible, that Cicero has deliberately overestimated the expertise of Servius Galba (a contemporary of Laelius and Scipio), disregarding the evidence of the preserved speeches in favour of a more flattering reputation based on the memories of P. Rutilius Rufus, who also acts as the putative informant for this period in *De re publica*. A small touch of drama signals the significance of this point:

atque etiam ipsum Libonem non infantem video fuisse, ut ex orationibus eius intellegi potest. cum haec dixissem et paulum interquievissem: quid igitur, inquit, est causae, Brutus, si tanta virtus in oratore Galba fuit, cur ea nulla in orationibus eius appareat? quod mirari non possum in eis qui nihil omnino scripti reliquerunt.   (*Brutus* 90–1)

'And I even see that Libo himself was no child, as can be gathered from his speeches.' When I had spoken, and had paused briefly, Brutus said, 'So what is the reason, if there was such great merit in Galba as an orator, why none of it appears in his speeches? I cannot be surprised at that in the case of those who have left nothing whatever written.'

Cicero replies with a useful explanation of the different processes by which speeches make the transition from oral to written. But central to the dialogic technique, with which we are by now familiar,

---

[15] Suerbaum (1996–7) gives a full account of the literary/non-literary distinction from the perspective of Roman historical traditions.

[16] See above, p. 170 and below, p. 199 n.

is that this moment allows conflicting interpretations to emerge: Galba and the others are being idealized in the face of the evidence, or perhaps it is just that the written evidence does not really reflect the true quality of the rhetoric. Brutus' laconic comment, that he cannot be disappointed by the disparity between Cicero's praise and the reality where no written speech exists, makes clear, I think, which side of this dialectic the reader is being pushed to accept as more realistic. For this brief moment, the possibility arises that rhetorical skill resides elsewhere than in language and expression, is a matter of personal charisma and delivery, and therefore not amenable to the kind of stylistic analysis to which Cicero has, from *De inventione* onwards, been committed. The central presumption that textual analysis, reading, and imitation are the mainstay of rhetorical training is at risk. Nevertheless, it is of the nature of Cicero's dialogues to move swiftly on and to leave such problems hanging in the air. Without going so far, it is clear that the provenance of the information for this catalogue of orators is an important topic; it mirrors the changing nature of historical evidence for early Rome and, in particular, the necessity to elaborate upon that evidence by conjecture. In spite of the threats offered by Brutus' scepticism, the purpose of those conjectures, however tentatively they may be offered, is to reveal the presence of effective oratory throughout the history of the Republic.

But as well as the problem of the evidence, there is a further problem imposed by the form of the work itself; as the dialogue progresses, the fussing over evidence gives way, as the figures discussed become those known personally to Cicero and Atticus, to a similar fussing about who should, or should not, be counted as an orator. In a sense, this is the same debate, but the nature of the available evidence, actual human recollection, changes its quality. At *Brutus* 181, for example, when dealing with orators of the same period as those who appear in *De oratore*, Cicero confesses:

atque ego praeclare intellego me in eorum commemoratione versari qui nec habiti sint oratores neque fuerint, praeteririque a me aliquot ex veteribus commemoratione aut laude dignos.   (*Brutus* 181)

I am fully aware that I have become involved in the commemoration of men who were neither regarded as orators, nor actually were such, and that sometimes men of olden times who deserve commemoration or praise have been passed over by me.

This is both a problem of lack of evidence and a problem about the criteria of selection. The principle becomes established that Cicero has to make the minimal evidence work far too hard in order to construct a coherent history of rhetoric at Rome; but at the same time, we are presented clearly with this working. The apparent digressions into anecdote are not in fact digressions; they are Cicero displaying the material with which he has to work (much of it, presumably, the product of historical gossip); the displaying of the working, however, does not do much to round out the edges of the picture of oratory at Rome that emerges.

Cicero's openness about what is possible on the basis of the evidence becomes much greater as the work continues, and in this he is aided by the dialogue structure, in particular by the figure of Atticus, who is presented as holding the view that what Cicero ought to be doing is demonstrating the glory of Roman oratory. Atticus has fallen into a trap that was laid for the reader at the start of the dialogue, and as such he functions perfectly as a decoy reader; we need to be aware not to fall into the same trap. The trap, indeed, was to ignore the main topic with which this discussion was introduced: certainly, the subject of the dialogue is introduced, albeit rather loosely, as being the history of rhetoric at Rome—*de oratoribus: quando esse coepissent, qui etiam et quales fuissent* (§20) (about orators: when they began to exist: who they were and what they were like)—but perhaps we should, it transpires at this rather late stage, have paid more attention to Cicero's opening argument, one familiar from *De oratore*: that no art is more difficult than oratory (§25). The tension between these two impulses, and the fact that, however problematic, the work has taken the form of a historical narrative with minimal interruption, has given rise to the situation where certainly Atticus, and quite possibly we as readers, have mistaken Cicero's plan. We are soon to be put right, as he reveals clearly the pitfalls of idealizing the function of rhetoric in Roman political life.

IRONY IN THE CHRONICLE

At §§242–4, we come to one particularly significant moment—indeed, a moment of considerable structural importance in the architecture of the dialogue, since it is from this point on that the tussle over who should and should not be included in the work becomes considerably more intense. By §244, Cicero has finally driven Atticus so far in his lurid account of a collection of particularly idiosyncratic speakers, men with questionable morals, grating shrill voices, provincial accents, or manic manners of speaking, that he bursts in, accusing Cicero, in colourful language, of really scraping the bottom of the barrel in his treatment of politicians as though they were orators. The last of these, Quintus Arrius (made famous for his affected aspirates by Catullus) is a figure of such ridicule that he elicits a sharp response from Atticus. Arrius is characterized as someone who, despite very low birth (*infimo loco natus*) and a total lack of any gifts (no *ingenium*, no *doctrina*), managed to achieve a high level of wealth and status through his work as an advocate, even though apparently entirely ill-fitted for the rigours of a legal career.

tum Atticus: tu quidem de faece, inquit, hauris idque iam dudum, sed tacebam; hoc vero non putabam, te usque ad Staienos et Autronios esse venturum.   (*Brutus* 244)

Then Atticus said, 'Now you really are draining the dregs, and have been for a while, but I kept quiet. But I really didn't think you would ever get as far as the Staienuses or Autroniuses.'

Arrius, it seems, is not even worth mentioning; Staienus and Autronius reappear a little later in Brutus' mouth as emblematic anti-orators. But it is, at first sight at least, unclear whether, by *usque ad Staienos et Autronios esse venturum*, Atticus is referring to chronological progression or to conceptual progression in terms of the scope of Cicero's inclusive catalogue: how far can you diverge from the normal definition of the term and still count as an orator? As the dialogue has moved forward in time, it has now approached the dramatic present, and from this point on the particular question of the inclusion only of dead orators becomes once again an obtrusive theme—so obtrusive, in fact, that it can almost be regarded as a signal from Cicero that we are dealing with a particularly significant idea, one that demands extra attention from his readers. Cicero's response to Atticus' outrage gives him an opportunity to enunciate again a recurrent topic:

non puto, inquam, existimare te ambitione me labi, quippe de mortuis; sed ordinem sequens in memoriam notam et aequalem necessario incurro. volo autem hoc perspici, omnibus conquisitis qui in multitudine dicere ausi sint, memoria quidem dignos perpaucos, verum qui omnino nomen habuerint, non ita multos fuisse. (*Brutus* 244)

I said, 'I don't think you would regard me as slipping because of any desire for personal advantage, especially concerning men who are dead: but following the sequence I necessarily come to the memory of acquaintances and contemporaries. But I want this to be understood: when all are collected who dared to speak before the crowd, there will be few indeed who are worthy of memory, but even fewer who have any kind of reputation.'

Since no favours of any kind can be received from the dead, Cicero cannot be suspected by his interlocutors of exaggerating their merits in the hope of personal gain; that is the idea that lies behind the defence against *ambitio*.[17] However, it is more revealing that what Atticus has perceived as an act of praise, Cicero turns into a simple act of compilation. His intention is to make a record of oratory, even including those orators whose memory is not in fact worth preserving. Indeed, we must be inclined, therefore, to regard the idea of '*venturum esse*' as one of desperation; as has recently been suggested, Staienus was in fact born before 109 BCE, and had been exiled from Rome in the 70s.[18] It is the extreme degree of his rhetorical incompetence, rather than his place in the chronological sequence, that qualifies him for Cicero's list, then exciting the ridicule of Atticus. So instead of this detailed compendium of great Roman speakers aiming to act as a monument to oratory at Rome, it can be supposed to be acting as the opposite: a monument to the paucity of great oratory at Rome. In this context, the barrier to discussing the living takes on a further level of meaning:

hoc loco Atticus: putarem te, inquit, ambitiosum esse, si, ut dixisti, ii quos iam diu conligis viverent. omnis enim commemoras, qui ausi aliquando sunt stantes loqui, ut mihi imprudens M. Servilium praeterisse videare. non, inquam, ego istuc ignoro, Pomponi, multos fuisse, qui verbum numquam in publico fecissent, quom melius aliquanto possent quam isti oratores, quos colligo, dicere; sed his commemorandis etiam illud adsequor, ut intellegatis primum ex omni numero quam non multi ausi sint dicere, deinde ex iis ipsis quam pauci fuerint laude digni. (*Brutus* 269–70)

---

[17] This is in essence the same accusation of personal interest that otherwise accompanies professions of freedom from historical bias. See above, pp. 167–8. *gratia* is what the historian Lucceius claims to be immune to, and what Cicero urges him to give in to in producing a eulogistic account of his consulship. See below, p. 258.

[18] Ryan (1999).

At this point Atticus said, 'I would think that you were aiming at political advancement if, as you have said, those men whom you have all this time been listing were alive. For you commemorate all who have at any point had the courage to stand up and speak, to the point that you appear to me foolish to have passed over Marcus Servilius.' 'I am not so unaware, Pomponius', I replied, 'that there are many who have never spoken a word in public, who could speak better on occasion that those orators whom I list. In commemorating them, I am following this idea: so that you can understand first of all how many from the whole number did not dare to speak; and then from those, how few were actually worthy of praise.'

Here again, the death of the speakers is a guarantor against the danger either of being seen to want to gain favour or, its obverse, to be thought to be exercising personal bias against an individual. The implications of *memoria* here correspond closely with the account in the previous chapter. *Memoria* should be the reward of those whose reputations can be judged without self-interest. It is vital to Cicero's project that the genealogy of Roman orators is by this standard objective. Rather, therefore, than using Atticus' chronicle to provide a structure aiming at teleology, we must conclude that Cicero is adding an extra dimension to that chronicle: the assessment of rhetorical competence. But that does not mean that he will thereby provide a teleological story about Rome's history: the self-interest of such an account is too firmly visible within the work, and the requirement for a more objective assessment too constant a theme. It is possible to argue that Cicero is made to stand out as a unique figure in Rome; but, as we have seen in the prologue to the work, such uniqueness will not provide Cicero with comfort.

At §279, Cicero announces his intention of tackling the one remaining orator, Hortensius himself, whose memory provided the impetus for the start of the work, and who returns as a structuring theme again at the end. Discussion of Hortensius, however, is deferred by a long digression on Curio and Calvus, and a further, much longer digression, prompted by the mention of the latter, on Atticism.[19] Although scholars have paid a great deal of attention to the picture

[19] The passage is one of the most important pieces of evidence for the controversy, in which Cicero himself clearly played an active role, concerning the use of Greek models for oratory at Rome, under what Cicero characterizes as the misleading slogan of *Attice*, in the Attic style. For a thorough account of Atticism, see Wisse (1995); Swain (1996), 20–56; Narducci (2002), 408–12; less technical is Whitmarsh (2005), 41–54; see too Kennedy (1989), 235–41; May (1990).

of Atticism here, the emphasis that I would place is more upon the opportunity which Cicero takes to produce a vivid picture of the central substance of the entire work: the exact manner in which rhetorical excellence operates within political reality. In emphasizing the uselessness of Atticism, he evokes with great clarity a picture of Roman rhetoric as a dramatic interaction between a speaker and the crowd, which suddenly gives the stylistic carping and comic caricatures of the previous selection of speakers an entirely different quality, and forms the climax to the dispute about the Attic style, a dispute settled by depicting the most essential features of rhetorical success in action:

volo hoc oratori contingat, ut cum auditum sit eum esse dicturum, locus in subselliis occupetur, compleatur tribunal, gratiosi scribae sint in dando et cedendo loco, corona multiplex, iudex erectus; cum surgat is qui dicturus sit, significetur a corona silentium, deinde crebrae adsensiones, multae admirationes; risus, cum velit, cum velit, fletus: ut, qui haec procul videat, etiam si quid agatur nesciat, at placere tamen et in scaena esse Roscium intellegat. haec cui contingant, eum scito Attice dicere, ut de Pericle audimus, ut de Hyperide, ut de Aeschine, de ipso quidem Demosthene maxume. sin autem acutum, prudens et idem sincerum et solidum et exsiccatum genus orationis probant nec illo graviore ornatu oratorio utuntur et hoc proprium esse Atticorum volunt, recte laudant. est enim in arte tanta tamque varia etiam huic minutae subtilitati locus. ita fiet, ut non omnes qui Attice idem bene, sed ut omnes qui bene idem etiam Attice dicant. sed redeamus rursus ad Hortensium.   (*Brutus* 290–1)

These are the conditions I want for the orator: that when it is heard that he is going to speak, the seats on the benches are taken, the platform full, the clerks are helping to allocate and vacate space, the crowd is of all types, the judge is alert. When he who is to speak rises, the signal for silence will come from the crowd; then frequent expressions of agreement and many of admiration. A laugh when he wants one, tears when he wants them, so that anyone seeing it from far off, even if he doesn't know what the case is about, will know that he's doing well and that a great actor (lit. Roscius) is on the stage. If these conditions apply, be assured that he is speaking in the Attic manner, as we hear about it for Pericles, Hyperides, Aeschines, and most of all, Demosthenes. But if they approve of a sharp, sensible and at the same time pure, unadorned, and restrained type of speech, and do not use any of the grander rhetorical ornamentation and want that to be a property of the Attic orators, then they are right to praise it. For in so widely varied an art there is even a place for that delicate refinement of taste. So it will be that not all who speak in the Attic manner speak well, but that all who speak well speak in the Attic manner. But let us return again to Hortensius.

Cicero here is circumventing a more technical discussion about style by actually imagining the orator in action, and using terminology to describe the features of a plain oratory that is deliberately neither technical nor in any sense derogatory (with the possible exception of *exsiccatus*, literally 'dried up'). Likewise the comparison between the orator and the actor, and the general sense of the relationship between oratory and theatre, loads the argument heavily in favour of thinking about rhetoric as a performance, rather than, as we have come to expect, a matter for analysis in terms of language. Perhaps this is the key to overcoming the contradiction of different kinds of evidence for rhetorical performance in the past, the solution to how written evidence might in fact not be capable of capturing the act of speaking as experienced by an audience. But Cicero does not allow the point to be reinforced any further, moving, through this attempt to steer the conversation back to Hortensius, into yet another digression, this time one with even greater ramifications for the understanding of the whole work than that on Atticism.

Instead of accepting that Hortensius should now receive their attention, Atticus interrupts Cicero. His speech is worth detailed comment, so I break it up:

aliquotiens sum, inquit, conatus, sed interpellare nolui. nunc quoniam iam ad perorandum spectare videtur sermo tuus, dicam, opinor, quod sentio. tu vero, inquam, Tite. tum ille: ego, inquit, ironiam illam quam in Socrate dicunt fuisse, qua ille in Platonis ex Xenophontis et Aeschini libris utitur, facetam et elegantem puto. est enim et minime inepti hominis et eiusdem etiam faceti, cum de sapientia discepetur, hanc sibi ipsum detrahere, eis tribuere illudentem, qui eam sibi arrogant, ut apud Platonem Socrates in caelum effert laudibus Protagoram Hippiam Prodicum Gorgiam ceteros, se autem omnium rerum inscium fingit et rudem. decet hoc nescio quo modo illum, nec Epicuro, qui id reprehendit, assentior. sed in historia, qua tu es usus in omni sermone, cum qualis quisque orator fuisset exponeres, vide quaeso, inquit, ne tam reprehendenda sit ironia quam in testimonio. quorsus, inquam, istuc? Non enim intellego.   (*Brutus* 292)

'Several times I have tried,' he said, 'but I did not want to interrupt. But now, since your speech seems to be looking to its conclusion, I think I shall say what I think.' 'You do that, Titus,' I said. He said, 'That irony, which they

say Socrates possessed, and which he uses in the books of Plato and
Xenophon and Aeschines, I do find witty and elegant. For it is the mark of
a man who is not only devoid of stupidity, but at the same time witty, to
deny his own wisdom, when wisdom is being discussed, and to attribute it
to those who claim it for themselves: so Socrates in Plato praises Protagoras,
Hippias, Prodicus, Gorgias, and the rest to the skies, but makes himself
out to be ignorant on all matters and uneducated. Somehow this suits him,
and I don't agree with Epicurus, who criticizes it. But in history, which you
have used in your whole speech, when you lay out what kind of orator
each man was, I wish you would see that irony is just as much to be criticized
as it is in legal evidence.' 'What is your point exactly?', I said. 'I don't
understand.'

First we should remember that Cicero uses exactly the same phrase, *ut
apud Platonem Socrates*, at *De re publica* 2. 11. 22, the moment where
he draws attention to the fictionality of the arguments by which Scipio
has idealized Romulus into functioning as an ideal monarch.[20] In the
earlier work, Laelius accused Scipio of disingenuously adopting the
cover of the conventions of Socratic dialogue to pass off his own
arguments as those of the subjects of his narrative. Atticus' accusation
is rather more multi-layered. Here again, the mention of the very
form of philosophical dialogue in which these characters are themselves appearing draws the readers' attention to the idea that they
function as literary representations, and that their arguments are the
works of their author, rather than necessarily historically accurate:
Atticus is careful to talk about Socrates' reputation, his character as
represented by these authors, rather than the irony which Socrates
himself expressed. So we begin to think about the distance between
the real Cicero, author of the work and experienced orator, and the
Cicero as represented in this dialogue, and Atticus too draws attention
to Cicero's other activities: irony is no more at home in the courtroom
than it is in the philosophical dialogue. Hearing this argument, of
course, we become aware of a further level of irony, since Cicero's own
speeches provide abundant evidence of irony in that context too; it
was Atticus who, much earlier in the work, conceded that for orators,

[20] See above, pp. 62 and 99–100. In that context as well, he employs the word *fingere*,
and we can recall its use too in the letter to Quintus which describes Sallustius'
objections to using a historical dialogue form: ideas would *seem to be made up*.

the requirements of argument will enable them to lie about history where necessary.[21]

The courtroom provides here, then, somewhat problematically, the standard for the delivery of reliable evidence. Atticus' main argument is to attack the presence of irony in history and, in so doing, seems for the first time to be labelling as history Cicero's assessment of the orators of Rome. We should remember here that it is Atticus' work as a historian that determines to a large extent his function in this dialogue, so that when he appears here springing to the defence of history against irony, he does so in the character that Cicero had already drawn for him earlier on, as the most devout author of Roman history (*rerum Romanarum ... auctorem religiosissumum* (*Brutus* 44)). Atticus seems here to be extending quite deliberately his definition of what constitutes history in order to encourage Cicero back into the bounds of sensible, non-ironic discourse: it *is* history to lay down who the orators of Rome were and what their qualities were, and this is as serious a task as Atticus' own history, or Cicero's own work in the legal setting. Cicero's expressed lack of comprehension here (*non enim intellego* ('I don't understand')) clearly heightens the irony even further, as we sense Atticus' indignation and what then emerges as Cicero's indifference to it.

non enim intellego. quia primum, inquit, ita laudavisti quosdam oratores ut imperitos posses in errorem inducere. equidem in quibusdam risum vix tenebam, cum Attico Lysiae Catonem nostrum comparabas, magnum me hercule hominem vel potius summum et singularem virum—nemo dicet secus—sed oratorem? sed etiam Lysiae similem? quo nihil posset esse pictius. bella ironia, si iocaremur; sin adseveramus, vide ne religio nobis tam adhibenda sit quam si testimonium diceremus.   (*Brutus* 293)

'I don't understand.' 'Because first of all', he said, 'you have so praised certain orators that you might mislead those less experienced. Indeed in some cases I could barely stop myself laughing, when you compared our Cato to Attic Lysias; god knows, he's a great man; the greatest, unique even. No one would disagree. But an orator? Like Lysias even? Than whom no one could be more polished? It is lovely irony if we are joking, but if we are talking

---

[21] *Brutus* 42: *quoniam quidem concessum est rhetoribus ementiri in historiis, ut aliquid dicere possint argutius* (see above, p. 190); although being ironic in giving evidence and lying about the past in order to make a point in a forensic speech are congruent rather than identical.

seriously, take care that we remain as respectful as if we were giving evidence in court.'

The recurrence of the word *religio*, applied earlier to Atticus' devotion to history, and again the unstable appeal to reliability in the legal setting (*testimonium*) show us how Cicero is fixing on particular ideas: the reliability of evidence, the appropriate attitude, one of devotion, which that evidence demands.[22] Atticus states that the catalogue of orators we have heard falls far short of these standards; it is, in fact, a joke.

Atticus' attack on Cicero's procedure continues for some time. He accepts that Cato should be admired as a citizen, a senator, a general, and a virtuous man, but not as an orator. And he reserves particular scorn for the earlier comparison of his *Origines* with Thucydides and Philistus: here was a man who had barely any idea of what it meant to speak with stylistic elaboration (*nondum suspicantem quale esset copiose et ornate dicere*). After a similar critique of the account of Galba, he repudiates the earlier picture of Scipio and especially Laelius. Here Atticus accuses Cicero of misleadingly representing the reputation (*laudes*) of the man's life through his oratory: when divested, the speeches themselves are not worth reading (*Brutus* 295). The process visible in the presentation of Tubero is being scrutinized, although in the case of Tubero, Atticus' criticism is barely necessary. Soon the speakers of *De oratore* come into view (after Carbo and the Gracchi), and although not disputing this time the basic evaluation, Atticus here accuses Cicero of an exaggeration which is pure irony (*haec germana ironia est*), in particular in the claim that Cicero himself had learnt from a speech by Crassus (*Brutus* 296). The culmination of this energetic argument is a fundamental subversion of the entire process of the catalogue of orators up to this point:

---

[22] Another striking phrase echoed from earlier on to similarly suggestive effect is *minime inepti*: it was applied to Cotta at *Brutus* 207, in surprise that a man so sophisticated should have been content for an inferior oration composed on his behalf by L. Aelius Stilo (one of Varro's teachers, his forerunner as an antiquarian) to circulate under his own name. Cicero seems preoccupied with notions of false attribution and of the substitution of voices. Cotta's published oration is not in fact by him; by contrast, Sulpicius (with whom Cotta is paired) never got round to writing his speeches down. In the later occurrence of the words, we are talking about that supreme example of the unwritten voice, Socrates. Again, the artificiality of the present dialogue is very apparent.

nam illud minus curo quod congessisti operarios omnis, ut mihi vide-
antur mori voluisse non nulli, ut a te in oratorum numerum referrentur.

(*Brutus* 297)

I'm less concerned about the fact that you have piled up all these labourers,
so that I feel that there are plenty who would happily have died to be
included in your account of orators.

The minor orators listed, therefore, rather than the major figures on
whom disagreement is possible, themselves vitiate the entire project,
since it is they, not those for whom sensible evaluation of proven
rhetorical skill is viable, that make up the bulk of the catalogue. This
is the working out of the dilemma of *De oratore* 1: the absence of
rhetorical gifts among Roman statesmen, but harshly brought up to
date. The *memoria* which Cicero so generously doles out to the dead
is one that would make many of the living wish they were dead. In a
passage of similar ironic significance, Cicero has already claimed that
he would not deal with orators who were still alive (*Brutus* 231), a
point upon which all debates about the date of the composition
of the work are based.[23] However, as far as the true historian is
concerned, being dead does not permit a confusion of stylistic and
civic gifts of the kind that Cicero has apparently been perpetrating.
Even though we saw (in the example of Tubero) that the catalogue
itself has been equivocal in granting the status of orator to all and
sundry, Atticus here strikes both at a number of prominent individuals and at the general process, in order to suggest that a clear
distinction has to be maintained between a man's significance for
the state and his level of rhetorical achievement. The danger of this

---

[23] Hendrickson (1962), 4–7; Douglas (1966), pp. ix–x. That this evidence should
perhaps not be taken at face value does not seem to have occurred to any scholar. It is
worth exploring the possibility that the work appeared as part of Cicero's later
philosophical production, and that the date of composition was not actually identical
with the date of the fictitious conversation that makes up the dialogue (46 BCE); the
ambiguous position of the Battle of Thapsus, in which some of the figures mentioned
have died, while others are still alive, would suggest that Cicero is producing a more
elaborate fiction: a retrojected picture of what a conversation about oratory in the
shadow of Thapsus might have been like, from a standpoint a year or two further on,
but vague as to the exact date. From the later perspective of a Rome actively
dominated by Caesar, the despair of the speakers (e.g. *Brutus* 22–3) looks wistfully
tolerable, and the conversation, which includes some frank discussion of Caesar, has
an element, as in the earlier dialogues, of *après moi le déluge*.

argument is apparent: Cicero himself, with a few select others, becomes a freak of history.

It is worth considering briefly how the breach between past and present upon which the dialogue is predicated relates to what is, in effect, the obverse relationship in *De re publica* and *De oratore*. In those dialogues, the historical context of the speakers was itself the focus for a form of idealization. Here, however, in a dialogue set in the immediate present (*nuper* (*Brutus* 9)), and a present which has been characterized as one where the *res publica* barely exists, the same ideals can be found, but they are embodied in the conversation of the speakers, in their discussion of dead orators (including, of course, those same characters already familiar to Cicero's readers from his previous writings). But this form of embodiment turns out to be a great deal less stable than any which is possible on the basis of speaking characters taken from history, a point made particularly sharply by the highly ironic manner in which the main speaker in the dialogue (Cicero) allows himself to be characterized.[24] Furthermore, the projected future which is only implied in the early works, the imminent deaths of the principal speakers of both, and a significant change in the fortunes of the Republic (rather more concrete for Scipio than for Crassus) has a parallel in *Brutus*, and that parallel in its turn strengthens my interpretation of those earlier works.

The final sections of the work consist of a lament that Brutus' own rhetorical and political gifts will be wasted, given the demise of the Republic to which Cicero has already so often referred; and Cicero makes a clear connection between his sense of wasted potential, and his now completed genealogy of rhetoric at Rome: *nonne cernimus vix singulis aetatibus binos oratores laudabilis constitisse?* (*Brutus* 333). ('Don't we observe in every single period, that scarcely two orators worthy of praise existed?'). The sentence represents the most extreme pole of the anti-history of Roman oratory which has, it now transpires, made up the entire work. But the voice of Cicero here must surely be read ironically, and cannot be allowed to stand as a clear statement that the entire previous catalogue has in fact been drawn up only in order to demonstrate the validity of such a negative claim.

---

[24] For a sensitive account of Cicero's autobiographical digression, see Charrier (2003).

Nevertheless, Cicero has only just urged Brutus in the strongest possible terms to extricate himself from the rabble that make up this catalogue (*ut te eripias ex ea quam ego congessi in hunc sermonem turba patronorum*, (*Brutus* 332)); and the final argument of the whole work presents those pairs of orators, hesitating to draw the obvious, but in many respects evidently implausible, conclusion that with the death of Hortensius, the only other figure who could function as Cicero's partner would be Brutus. Just as a reminder, Calvus, whose name Brutus introduces as a springboard for Cicero's entertaining diatribe against the label 'Atticist', was clearly far from being the frigid speaker whom Cicero here characterizes; Quintilian and Tacitus both make clear that he was widely read and admired, and in his *Dialogus* Tacitus draws attention to the unusual venom of Cicero's disdain for the style not just of Calvus, but also of Brutus (*Dialogus* 25. 6).[25] The Calvus of *Brutus* and the Brutus of *Brutus* are exaggerated portraits that, on the one hand, make the identification of Brutus as the future salvation of Roman oratory possible. On the other hand, the evident exaggeration makes it clear once again that the voice of the dominant speaker demands qualification. And the despairing Cicero, for whom Rome never held more than two good orators at a time, is clearly not the only Cicero which this work brings forward.

CICERO'S SELF-PRESENTATION

One of the most striking features of Cicero's self-presentation in the dialogue concerns the arguments about style which make up the diatribe against the Atticists. There is no doubt that Cicero was sincere in his consistent ridicule of those who attacked his own rhetorical style as being too florid and advocated instead a barer style which they, according at least to Cicero, attempted to market as closer to the models of Attic oratory.[26] The question of style, however, takes on a

---

[25] Douglas (1966) on *Brutus* 283, and Jahn and Kroll (1962), p. xix, assemble the evidence.

[26] *Orator* is the best evidence.

much wider significance in the context of a dialectic about rhetoric in Rome's history, and in particular Cicero's own evaluation of his place in that history. His style, after all, is what, in accordance with the method adopted in the dialogue for the discussion of other orators, gives him his place. Here May's brief insight that Cicero sets up a parody of Atticism in order to undermine the strength of the polemic in favour of his own style takes on a much wider significance.[27] That parody, in fact, expresses on the level of style the same argument about the acquisition of status which has characterized the entire history. Status and political power can certainly be idealized in terms of ambitions about style: the picture of the theatrically brilliant orator who, regardless of the actual verbal constitution of his speech, is able to sway the crowd, and who overcomes any quibble about Atticism or ornament generally by virtue of some vaguer form of verbal charisma—that character can be seen as someone whose political capacities match their ability to project their own style, their own self-image, for the good of the state. In this scenario, all effective speakers can follow in the footsteps of Pericles or Demosthenes, even if they do not in reality produce such high-quality rhetoric. However, that picture is a rather irrelevant ideal, given the general despair about the status of most of the orators discussed in the work.

In his autobiographical excursus, Cicero reinforces the close relationship between personal qualities and rhetorical style. His striking account of the decline of Hortensius is a good example: he decided that, after the consulship, he could afford to let himself go, and he became a less energetic, less cogent orator as a result.[28] And at the very close of the work, Cicero laments how little all his immersion in the teachings of the Academy has helped him if, after all, he is not so very different from all the other orators that Rome has produced.[29] The desire to make rhetorical technique into the basis of political or judicial success is sincere; but it more or less fails in the face of the character of the rhetorical scene at Rome. Cicero returns to the place where he began, imagining himself as a victim of history, someone to whom things have happened (*si mihi accidisset ut numerarer* (*Brutus* 333) ... ('if it befell me to be counted ...'), but, rather symbolically

---

[27] May (1990); cf. Innes (1978), which, again briefly, points in the same direction.
[28] *Brutus* 320, cf. 327.   [29] *Brutus* 332–3.

for us, the apodosis of this conditional sentence is lost as the text breaks off. Technique, it appears, is no guarantee of the effect that the projection of style will have, and the ephemeral success of the individual speech is no guarantee of a reputation. That can only come from the judgement of posterity or, in the case of a speech, from the written record which, as we have seen, is not always good evidence.[30] Paradoxically, the only point of real comfort in the grim assessment of the death of oratory with which the work ends is one that Cicero derives from Brutus' own treatise, and it is pointedly included:

tamen ea consolatione sustentor quam tu mihi, Brute, adhibuisti tuis suavis-simis litteris, quibus me forti animo esse oportere censebas, quod ea gessissem quae de me etiam me tacente ipsa loquerentur, mortuo viverentque; quae, si recte esset, salute rei publicae, sin secus, interitu ipso testimonium meorum de re publica consiliorum darent.   (*Brutus* 330)

However I am sustained by the consolation which you, Brutus, offered me in your most charming epistle. There you advised me to be brave, because I had done things which would speak for themselves about me, even if I were silent, and would live when I am dead. If they had worked out well, the preservation of the state, or if they had not, its demise would bear witness to my wise decisions regarding the Republic.

This is the opposite pole of the decades of publishing speeches and works aimed at improving Latin rhetoric: the actions which, totally independent of Cicero's gargantuan literary output, will speak out without any need for him to elaborate or justify them. This is the form of political success that transcends style entirely, and relies upon a non-verbal form of reputation. It is a useful consummation of the anxieties about where real political power resides that have been visible throughout the work, and it is far from a happy synthesis of a quest to work endlessly to improve one's own style, the trajectory which Cicero's autobiography describes, and the political and rhetorical context in which that labour takes place.

Can we look, therefore, for some kind of message beyond these contradictory signals about the power of the orator, and his ability to affect it by study and attention to style? Rathofer (1986) argues,

---

[30] At *Brutus* 328, Cicero says that one of Hortensius' written speeches does bear out the reputation which Brutus granted it when delivered.

persuasively, that the organizing principle of *Brutus* is the pedagogical stance towards Brutus, and that the criticisms of particular orators function within a closely argued praise/blame model aimed at isolating the ideal virtues of the orator, and that the work aims to exert Cicero's own *auctoritas* and see it manifested in Brutus' future career. The work therefore is a literary-critical one, but one where literary criticism has a concrete historical and political dimension. As an educative work, it purposefully leaves a place for the true culmination of rhetoric at Rome to occur; it is for Brutus to achieve (§§155–8). Cicero's main aim in writing *Brutus* is therefore to get the real Brutus under his influence, to coerce him into seeing the world through Cicero's eyes. Rathofer may be right here; but his analysis also leaves open the very real possibility, one to which he himself points when drawing attention to the evident gap between the ideal picture of the Brutus of the dialogue as a gifted orator and the conclusive evidence of other historical sources which make exactly the opposite point (§§271–3), that the figure of Brutus is, rather, a parallel to the general idealization of rhetoric at Rome which Cicero's history produces. It is an idealization that, as we have seen, displays equally clearly its own reverse image: in Atticus' expectation that a list of orators will be a list of *good* orators and in Cicero's tendency to exaggerate the comic failures of many of the politicians of whom he speaks. If Cicero is presenting Brutus with an authoritative discourse on politics and oratory, we are also made aware that this is a long shot: and for those acquainted with the frigid rhetoric of the real Brutus (Tacitus, *Dialogus* 21; Quintilian, 10. 1. 23), the disparity between Cicero's expectations of Brutus and the likelihood of their fulfilment must have been striking. In short, Rathofer's analysis lays rather too much weight upon the closing sections of the work, the lament for the opportunities lost to Brutus, and not enough upon the imaginative dynamics of the historical account itself. Within that, the competing views of how rhetoric might or might not be of benefit to the state are rather less neatly amenable to a clear resolution.

If, to close, we step back a little from the specific arguments and presentation of history in *Brutus*, and think more generally about the impact of reading the work as a whole, we must become aware of what a strange, and at points, frantic piece of writing it is. And what is, in fact, the substance of Roman history which emerges from the detailed criticisms of the Roman orators? Rhetoric here is display of personality; in flagrant contradiction of Cicero's own theoretical writings, which operate on the assumption that erudition, study, practice, and above all a detailed understanding of the technical principles of style, and of the structure of sentences, arguments, and speeches, is what counts, the overwhelming impression left by the Roman orators is of figures who, with varying degrees of felicity, leave behind an impression of *themselves* through their speeches. The style *is* the man, and although it has recently become fashionable to look upon this as a positive process, whereby orators fashion their own identities as a way of consolidating their personal power, what Cicero tells us in *Brutus* is that style is, rather, the manifestation of being trapped in history.[31] Rome's orators have not mastered their own personalities and achieved a degree of autonomy through careful study and application; even Cicero himself has to resign himself at the end of this work to the possibility that the climate of rhetoric has granted him no influence. There are not now, nor have there ever been, a sufficient number of colleagues who care enough about style to grant even Cicero a place as a rhetorical role model. If the evocation of rhetorical excellence that transcends debates about style is one that assimilates rhetoric to theatre, then the diligence and study which have characterized Cicero's own work are redundant.

Rhetoric in *Brutus* is, by a paradox with which we are by now familiar, both a product of that history and a way of escaping it. Perhaps Cicero's tribute to the consolation of Brutus was genuine, but in the light of the continuing quest to produce so much material as a written legacy, later readers at least are bound to look at the idea of *me tacente* ('myself silent') as being ironic. The work as a whole is, as we have seen, characterized by its direct engagement with the theme of ideal histories and their ironic demise: Atticus' words *haec germana ironia est* ('that is pure irony') should be taken as an emblem of the entire project to observe an ideal of stylistic progress, and political success predicated upon it, in Rome's past. These arguments are here tied closely to the lament for the Republic which is so prominent at the start and the end of the book, but references to *De re publica* draw our attention to the fact that this is a process already

---

[31] Gleason (1995); Dugan (2005).

explored in that work: the quest to provide theoretical underpinning for the *res publica* and the doubt that this can ever truly reflect historical reality. Nevertheless, as I have hinted in my presentation of it, there is considerable humour in *Brutus* and, particularly because of its episodic structure, a clear potential for the Academic reading to prevent the competing visions of Rome from demanding a clear synthesis, whether this is an optimistic one, reinforcing Cicero's authority, or a pessimistic one, in which that authority is seen to rest not on words, but on deeds. And, as in the context of those words, the genuine grappling with sources of historical evidence, the texture of Rome's historical record, is, as in *De re publica* and *De oratore*, an essential part of the process.

8

Divination, History, and Superstition

DIVINATION AND IDEOLOGY

In *De divinatione* Cicero tackles one of the fundamental institutions of Roman political life, the series of fortune-telling rituals which traditionally accompanied many of the crucial political and military processes of the Roman state. Although divination might, at first sight, seem like a marginal theme in the history of Rome—compared, say, to the struggles between factions, the vicissitudes of electioneering and patronage, or the court or senate-house battles which characterized the political process of the late Republic—Cicero's decision to dedicate a separate dialogue to the topic of divination suggests that it has an importance that belies that appearance. Divination becomes, in Cicero's treatment, a testing-ground for the fundamental relationship between the human and the divine orders: it is represented as the mechanism by means of which humans are able to harmonize their decisions with a sense of divine will. But instead of being a measured debate about the possibility of foreknowledge or the reliability of different methods of prediction, *De divinatione* turns out to be a strangely personal exploration of Cicero's own relationship with the institutions of the Republic, and a fundamentally bleak encounter with the impossibility of reconciling philosophical self-awareness with traditional ways of conducting public life at Rome. It is this personal quality which has made me think it important to include the work here, while not discussing other works with related themes (such as *De fato* or *De natura deorum*).

The dramatization of two opposing philosophical positions, using the characters of Cicero himself and Cicero's brother Quintus, produces a vision of Cicero's own engagement with Rome's history—in particular, recent history—which is much less nostalgic than that found in *De re publica* or *De oratore*. But by fixing on the historical dimension of the dialogue, and building on the examination of history in those other works, we can reveal once more the same kind of vacillation between an integrative, optimistic vision of Roman history and institutions and its opposite, one of Rome as a city lacking cohesion, in which neither the virtues of individuals nor the good will of the gods have left their trace in the historical record. This is a related, though not identical, dialectic to the one which characterizes Cicero's views on the role of rhetoric at Rome; the relationship is closer with *De re publica*, although *De divinatione* projects a much more overtly negative picture of the potential of Rome to disturb any optimistic notions of Roman destiny.

In the dialogue, we can chart some elements of Cicero's own complex representation of Rome, and in particular his ambivalent relationship with history and tradition.[1] In reading this dialogue, it is essential to remain aware of Cicero's philosophical strategy, which is represented prominently in the prologues to both books. The division into two books makes the strategy particularly easy to grasp, and for this reason the dialogue is a rich source for analysing the effect of the particular approach on the presentation and dramatization of a topic of central importance to the way in which Roman political life was conceived. The contrast between the two books is sharply drawn; each book is essentially a monologue by one speaker (first, Cicero's brother Quintus, then Cicero himself, hereafter referred to as Marcus), each with a methodological preface, describing from different perspectives Cicero's philosophical position. In the first prologue, Cicero outlines the approaches of the different philosophical schools to the topic of divination, summarizing the main trend as a series of vacillations between scepticism and credulity. He is careful to distinguish between Epicureans and others, in setting up a distinction which is returned to at the end of the work, and which acts as a specific limitation upon Cicero's own scepticism: namely,

---

[1] There are two important articles in which similar accounts of this work can be found: Krostenko (2000); Schofield (1986). See too Beard (1986). A less detailed but still balanced assessment is given by Goar (1968).

that one may doubt belief in divination, but this is independent from belief in the gods. Only rarely in the dialogue are signs and portents discussed seriously as messages from divinities, in the very specific context of the Stoic position that beneficent divinities express their beneficence through omens and by granting humans the power to know the future (e.g. 1. 6. 10; 1. 38. 82); rather, such signs are treated, in book 1 as revelations that emanate from the divine order, and in book 2 as haphazard events that could be mistaken as such. This, in essence, is, the dialectic which structures the whole of the work, and the principal material in which the dialectic is explored is the historical anecdote. These anecdotes are thereby subjected to two different interpretations, and a large number of the anecdotes that Quintus discusses in book 1 are then in turn tackled by Marcus in book 2.

The interpretations can be summarized as follows: either the relationship between premonition and event is proof of an ordered, predictable universe, or the opposite is the case, and what looks like a premonition is in fact just another random occurrence.[2] Cicero, in other words, is contrasting two different world-views, one which stresses order, regularity, and the continuation of tradition; the other which stresses accident, disorder, and the arbitrary quality of tradition. Given the enormous dominance in the work of historical anecdote, we can further distinguish between the two books in terms of their ideological emphasis. History in Quintus' view becomes proof of the harmony between natural and divine forces, and the deeds of their human agents. In Marcus' view, such a harmony is illusory, and what history in fact teaches us is that good or bad luck are simply random outcomes which we are powerless to foresee or to influence. We are faced, in other words, with a choice between a radical historical agenda for the presentation of Rome, where past regularities are no guarantee of future ones, and a conservative one, where in spite of an absence of a positive theory of causality, we can be certain that things have tended to follow a predictable course, and will continue to do so.

---

[2] Succinctly put at *De div.* 1. 6. 13: *est enim vis et natura quaedam, quae tum observatis longo tempore significationibus, tum aliquo instinctu inflatuque divino futura praenuntiat* ('for there is a certain natural power, at times through observation of signs over a long period, at other times through some instinct or divine inspiration, which predicts future events'). See below, pp. 234–5.

In line with Cicero's general representation of history as a continuum, a process in which he and his contemporaries are the latest agents in the drama of Rome's fate, the dialogue makes rapid transitions between historical events separated by centuries. The earlier stages of Quintus' argument are worth a brief description: he lays out a moderate philosophical approach based on the idea that it is the results of prophetic events that should be examined, rather than their causes, and thus repudiates in advance arguments of Carneades (later taken up by Marcus) that prophetic occurrences should be dismissed because they cannot be explained. Next he proceeds to give extensive quotations from Cicero's own poems, first his translation of Aratus, then, at greater length, his *On his Consulship*. The final quotation concludes with a rhetorical question, challenging Marcus, on the evidence of his own poetry, to refute the moderate attitude to divination that Quintus has thus far espoused.[3] Following this train of thought, Quintus then refers to the reliability of the auspices during the time when Marcus himself was an augur, and then, with a similarly easy sidestep, introduces King Deiotarus as an example of successfully heeding omens. And so begins a series of anecdotes taken from all eras in Roman history, designed to demonstrate, on the basis of results, that inattention to omens leads to disaster, obedience to them to success, and that therefore, whatever their cause, it is undeniable that they are an effective mechanism for ensuring the harmony between historical event and the divine order. Before moving on to the topic of dreams (which likewise focuses mainly on historical material), Quintus, discussing the Delphic oracle, points out that to deny its veracity would be to pervert history (*id quod negari non potest nisi omnem historiam perverterimus* (*De div.* 1. 19. 38))—a clear enough statement, as a culmination of this part of his argument, that the proof of a prophetic or divinatory order is history itself.

---

[3] This is carefully, if laconically, argued: Marcus' deeds, and what he has himself written, in fact confirm the position laid out by Quintus: *tu igitur animum poteris inducere contra ea, quae a me disputantur de divinatione, dicere, qui gesseris ea, et ea, quae pronuntiavi accuratissime scripseris?* (*De div.* 1. 13. 22) ('Will you therefore be able to bring yourself to speak against my arguments, you who have both done these things, and have most accurately written down what I have pronounced?'). The use of *pronuntiavi* here is particularly witty: Quintus is using the very language of divination to describe his philosophical position, predicting, perhaps, the demolition of both in the second book. Krostenko (2000) lays particular weight upon the role of Cicero's poetry in his interpretation of the dialogue.

Marcus' refutation likewise makes history into the place where theories of fate and providence are tested, but of course the argument on divination is reversed: the same material, and many of the same examples, demonstrate the disconnectedness of the real world from any providential power. Deiotarus, for example, illustrates the arbitrary quality of fate, against which any illusion of prediction is useless, and likewise the destruction of the Roman fleet in the first Punic War would have occurred just the same, whether or not the inauspicious auguries had been ignored.[4] The workings of fate, therefore, are beyond human ingenuity to perceive or to predict; and although natural phenomena have an observable regularity, history does not follow any such pattern. In spite, therefore, of the apparently rather narrow focus of the philosophical topic which Cicero has chosen for this dialogue, the work acquires a different and rather richer significance if we focus on its use of history, and look at it in the light of the series of historical encounters which Cicero has already produced. To be able to substantiate the claim that, rather than being predominantly concerned with divination, this work is more a dramatization of a dilemma central to the identity of the Republic, requires a considerable readjustment of our expectations. This readjustment can be justified, however, if we think in more detail about how the reception of Cicero has distorted much of his original emphasis upon the Academic approach to philosophy, and militates against a reading which treats the work not as aiming at either a defence or an attack on divination, but as a piece of philosophy characterized by the representation, and indeed dramatization, of those philosophical positions.

OBSTACLES TO AN IDEOLOGICAL READING OF THE DIALOGUE

There are two major challenges to the interpretation of this dialogue, and they are closely connected. The first comes in finding the appropriate approach to evaluating the dialectic between the two

---

[4] Both anecdotes are treated both to a cursory dismissal and then to a more detailed treatment at a later stage in the argument. Deiotarus: 1. 15. 26–7 and 2. 8. 20, further elaborated at 2. 36. 76–37. 79. The lost fleet: 1. 16. 28–9 and 2. 8. 20, further at 2. 33. 71.

opposing interpretations; the second relates to the appropriate recognition of the historical dimension of the dialogue. Once the first of these is solved, it becomes much easier to understand why Cicero makes such dense use of historical anecdote and, more importantly, what the effect is of Cicero's own self-presentation in the dialogue: a self-presentation which rests upon a particularly rich experimentation between different ways of thinking about history, both as lived and as a written phenomenon. In this way, the aim of my discussion of *De divinatione* is to show that the main focus of the work is not divination, religion, or even philosophy, but the presentation of an accessible and lively discussion of something for which Cicero had no name, but which we can clearly perceive to be ideology itself. History, in the form in which it is used in this dialogue, is being examined for its ability both to contain and to justify a sense of a political world order. Different kinds of historical proof, from his own poetry, to anecdotes derived from an annalistic tradition, to his own experiences as a politician and participant in the civil wars, are all looked at in terms of a question which was to become central to the Augustan presentation of the past: is there a sense of progress and order to the way in which events at Rome are unfolding, or are they just arbitrary? The dialogue has the potential, therefore, once its philosophical conventions are properly understood, to gives a particularly direct insight into the workings of ideology at Rome.

In order to reach this point, it is essential first to dispense with the deceptively obvious reading of the work which sees it as propagating religious scepticism, the character Marcus as representing Cicero's views, and the refutation of the arguments of Quintus as the message of the dialogue.[5] In this analysis, Cicero himself emerges as a rabid rationalist with only the most minimal respect for the cultural traditions which the character of Quintus so carefully represents in the first book. There are, however, few arguments in favour of this position.[6] I will return later to the clear methodological statement with which the dialogue ends, and which provides the solution to this difficulty. Although this statement is, as I say, unequivocal, it is easy,

---

[5] See Schäublin (1985), 161.

[6] Nevertheless, scholars occasionally still espouse it. Thus Harris (2003), 27: 'Attempts to show that Book 2 of *De divinatione* does not represent Cicero's views ... are to be firmly rejected'; he then cites a list of evidently misguided scholars.

given the traditions of interpretation that operate when we read Cicero, to ignore. So I want to deal first with these traditions, and then return to the solution to the dialectic between rationalist and traditionalist, once its reception has been better understood. In this manner, the very significant ideological implications of this dialectic can themselves be apprehended more directly.

To read the arguments of Marcus the rationalist as convincingly trouncing those of Quintus the traditionalist is to reinscribe a set of traditions in the reception of Cicero which have obscured many of the original resonances of his philosophical writings. The fundamental premiss of this tradition is that Cicero uses characters to act as his mouthpieces. Naturally, in *De divinatione* it is not difficult to read the character of Marcus as representing the views of Cicero. But in other dialogues with more far-fetched casting, one does not need to seek far in any commentary to find one dominant character described as Cicero's mouthpiece; Crassus in *De oratore* and Scipio in *De re publica* are obvious examples. Cicero in *Brutus* is a rather different case, where the fictional quality of Cicero's speaking persona plays a less powerfully determining role. In German, a slightly different metaphor is used, that of *Sprachrohr* (literally, speech-pipe: the speaking tube formerly used on ships, etc.). Mouthpiece and *Sprachrohr* are metaphors, however, metaphors which act, as often, as an excuse for a lazy interpretative technique, which in turn has a different tradition behind it. In the mouthpiece metaphor, and in its extension into a method for reading Cicero's dialogues, we can see at work the traditions of reception which I described in Chapter 3. To summarize and extend my arguments there, we can see that the traditions of reception have an effect not just on the general manner in which Cicero's philosophy is judged but, more importantly, upon the possibilities of reading individual dialogues. The conceptions of what Cicero's philosophy is for, what the reasons are for reading his work, and how Cicero himself is regarded all have an effect upon how individual works are interpreted. The idea that Marcus in *De divinatione* 2 is a mouthpiece for Cicero rests on a particular idea of how sophisticated Cicero is likely to be in his approach to writing philosophy: how accomplished his use of self-irony, and how much appreciation of that irony can be expected from his readers. Further, we need to bear in mind the wider notion of how clear the philosophical message of the work will be seen to be: Is Cicero expected to produce a particular position on divination, or is his philosophy more open-ended? The traditions discussed in Chapter 3 certainly explain why we are over-inclined to find Cicero using his philosophical characters as mouthpieces.[7] In the process we under-estimate the role of the sceptical philosophical tradition and, as a result, pay little attention to the dynamics of the dialogue, which can themselves express a more complex vision of ideological dilemmas than the conventional mouthpiece metaphor allows for.[8]

The insistence that somewhere a mouthpiece can be identified will, of course, restrict the potential reach of the dialogue to arguments of this kind. However, with the abandonment of the mouthpiece model for reading the dialogue, it is possible to engage with the ideological issues of the dialogue more directly. As I have indicated, these are in fact quite obvious, and are quite sharply presented, challenging the reader to find a compromise between two essentially irreconcilable visions of Rome's history and identity. Furthermore, once the dia-logue has been liberated from the constraints imposed by the sup-position that it represents Ciceronian dogma, it turns out to be a particularly clear place for appreciating how history, politics, and literary production intersect to produce an ideological discourse which expresses Cicero's own complex relationship to political power. This dialectic follows the pattern already familiar in *De re publica* and *Brutus*; but because of the narrow focus of the work on one central state institution, and the absence of any preoccupation with rhetoric, the ideological aspects emerge more strongly.

PERSONA, PHILOSOPHICAL AUTHORITY, AND THE AUTHOR

To substantiate these conclusions, let us continue to examine *De divinatione*, first making a comparison with another pair of dialogues

---

[7] This is essentially the same conclusion as Schofield (1986).

[8] Of course, the mouthpiece metaphor is no longer as prominent as it was: Levene (2004) and Fortenbaugh (2005) are good examples (and there are others) of recent work in which, although the detailed reading of Cicero is not the main purpose, the dialogic framework is nevertheless treated sensitively.

from the same period, *De senectute* and *De amicitia*. These dialogues are clearly conceived as a pair, and in the prefaces Cicero provides clear guidance as to how we should evaluate the fictional quality of the dialogue. In *De senectute* he explicitly states that he is making Cato act as the embodiment of his own views on friendship. He closes the preface, which treats briefly the notion that philosophy is a consolation in old age, with the words: *iam enim ipsius Catonis sermo explicabit nostram omnem de senectute sententiam* (*De sen.* 1. 3) ('Now, then, the speech of Cato himself will unfold my whole view of old age'). These words follow the acknowledgement that such arguments as Cato derives from immersion in Greek philosophy may seem discordant with what we can ourselves read in his own writings; but Cicero feels that they are justified by Cato's established enthusiasms for such work in his old age. Even here, then, Cicero is being deliberately ambiguous: first of all he suggests that he is aiming at something like historical verisimilitude in his characterization of Cato, but then he suggests that he will in fact just be using him to express his own *sententia*. The preface to *De amicitia* adds another layer. There Cicero describes how he has been rereading *De senectute*, and confirms that in retrospect the choice of Cato was particularly appropriate, since it lends his words an almost mysterious grandeur:

genus autem hoc sermonum positum in hominum veterum auctoritate et eorum illustrium plus nescio quo pacto videtur habere gravitatis: itaque ipse mea legens sic afficior interdum, ut Catonem, non me, loqui existimem.

(*De amicitia* 1. 4)

Furthermore, this kind of discourse seems, for some reason, to have more weight when located in the authority of men of old, especially famous ones. So when I read my own words, I am now and then so affected that I think that Cato, not me, is speaking.

A cynical reading, which I think for us is the easiest, would recall Cicero as the master of forensic *prosopopoeia*, and regard his appeal to *gravitas* as somewhat disingenuous. But this is to set up an illusory polarization between rhetoric and sincerity, and in any case leaves unanswered our problem as to where Cicero expects us to find authority within these works.

Paradoxically, this return after a decade to the constellation of speakers in whom Cicero invested his more overtly political treatise on the state is an opportunity for him to dwell more upon nostalgia and atmospheric anecdote, and the expected complexity of philosophical debate, which the anxiety in the preface about the characterization of Cato leads us to expect, never takes place. Cato and Laelius wear their philosophical technicalities lightly, and are more easily readable using the mouthpiece metaphor than are the arguments of the *De divinatione*, even though those come from the mouths of Cicero and his brother. What is clear, however, is that Cicero is aware of the question of authority and characterization, and that characterization can be used as much for its emotive power (*afficior*) as for its role in producing a vision of a philosophical culture at Rome (not to mention the experimentation with different arguments or perspectives, admittedly less of an issue in these dialogues).

I referred in Chapter 2 to Cicero's own ambivalence about the relationship between philosophy and public life, and it is in this area that a solution to the complexities of *De divinatione* can best be found. After all, in philosophizing about divination, Cicero is bringing two apparently different worlds face to face. The copious prefatory material and, in particular, the fact that the two prefaces are so different make it clear that something both awkward and necessary is being undertaken: a confrontation between Roman and Greek traditions of wisdom and knowledge. The second preface, in particular, is useful in this respect. It consists of a catalogue of the works that Cicero had produced by this point (only *De fato*, *De officiis*, and *Topica* post-date *De divinatione*), summarizing their subject matter and characterizing them as a coherent project aimed at establishing philosophy in Latin as a realm which can stand independent of Greek sources. Why should Cicero feel that *this* dialogue was the appropriate place for a summary of his complete philosophical work? The explanation lies in the self-justificatory quality of his explanation: the philosophical works are a resource not just for Cicero himself at a time when political engagement is impossible, but educating even only a few of his prominent contemporaries will lead to a potential improvement in the condition of the *res publica* (2. 2. 5–7).[9] The work of the dialogue may, by virtue of its rather specific subject

---

[9] See above, pp. 33–5.

matter, be hard to square with these ambitious aims. How central, in the end, are theories of divination to a philosophical curriculum? Cicero seems at first sight to have chosen a particularly trivial moment to spell out his educational ambitions. But if we return to the details of the argument, the case becomes easier. The contrast between the two books of the dialogue, it will be recalled, is between two different world-views. They differ among other respects in the manner in which they apply philosophical insights to what might usefully be called political memory at Rome. In other words, Cicero and Quintus represent two incarnations of that vision of a philosophically informed public life to which Cicero alludes in the second preface. Quintus' view is one that relies upon Stoicism to harmonize a philosophical system with traditional practices. Marcus, by contrast, takes a much more sceptical approach, and his claim to be acting in support of traditional practice is much more tentative. At the conclusion of his speech, and of the dialogue itself, he restates an absolute distinction between *religio* and *superstitio*, which must be entirely rooted out. What remains, he concedes, is the wisdom of preserving ancestral customs and the order of the universe, which in its beauty and unchanging power, must compel veneration.

nec vero—id enim diligenter intellegi volo—superstitione tollenda religio tollitur. nam et maiorum instituta tueri sacris caerimoniisque retinendis sapientis est, et esse praestantem aliquam aeternamque naturam, et eam suspiciendam admirandamque hominum generi pluchritudo mundi ordoque rerum caelestium cogit confiteri.   (*De divinatione* 2. 72. 148–9)

However—and this is a point I want to be properly understood—because superstition must be rooted out, that is not to say that religion is rooted out. For it behoves the wise man to preserve the institutions of our ancestors by retaining the sacred rites and ceremonies; and the beauty of the world and the order of the heavenly bodies compels me to confess that there is some superior and eternal nature, that humans must respect and wonder at.

But this sense of reverence for a natural order is rather out of place from what precedes it. Without summarizing arguments of book 2 in unnecessary detail, we can find a particularly cogent example by looking at the event of Caesar's death from near the start of book 2. In the preface to the book (2. 2. 1), Cicero hints that this, presumably in catapulting him once more into the centre of public affairs, has caused an interruption to his plans for a complete philosophical curriculum (he calls it a *causa gravior*, a more serious reason). Quintus has referred only briefly to Caesar, and although to some extent Caesar is introduced simply as another example to prove the reliability of divination (in this case, the auspices), the details of this appearance do establish the terms of reference for the treatment in book 2. But as we shall see, Caesar is used not just to prove or disprove the reliability of divination. Quintus introduces Caesar as proof of the rather specific contention that at the moment of sacrifice, the bodies of the victims (specifically their internal organs) can swiftly change state, and that this change can be a response to divine forces (in this case, *vis quaedam sentiens, quae est toto confusa mundo* ('a certain sentient power which pervades the entire world')—a Stoic form of divinity in other words). The proof that Caesar provides concerns two sacrifices: the first on the day when he appeared in a purple robe and sat on a golden throne, when the sacrificial ox contained no heart, and on the next day, when the liver (I presume once more of an ox) had no head.[10] These omens came from the gods not to enable Caesar to prevent his death; but rather, simply to foresee it (*quae quidem illi portendebantur a dis immortalibus ut videret interitum, non ut caveret* (1. 52. 119)).

When, in a quite different context, Marcus takes up the topic of Caesar in book 2, it is strange to observe that he actually repeats Quintus' arguments: not those concerning the nature of the auspices, which he entirely ignores, but those concerning the futility of foreknowledge, which he exaggerates to the point where the earlier emphasis is entirely changed. He is engaged in an energetic series of anecdotes designed to show the essential futility of Stoic ideas of fate to an understanding of Roman history. Foreknowledge of fate is effectively useless: it is manifestly not the case that divination has had any impact on the outcome of history, whether you are talking King Deiotarus, the first Punic War, or the second: Cicero, clearly enjoying this rabid rhetoric, pokes fun at the sacred chickens, and produces some fine syllogistic apothegms:

ubi est igitur ista divinatio Stoicorum? quae, si fato omnia fiunt, nihil nos admonere potest, ut cautiores simus; quoquo enim modo nos gesserimus,

---

[10] Plutarch, *Caesar* 63, reports the missing heart, as well as a large number of other omens which Cicero does not mention (but not the aberrant liver). It is interesting that the moral that Plutarch derives from these portents (death may be more easily foreseen than prevented) is not far from the point which Quintus makes.

fiet tamen illud, quod futurum est; sin autem id potest flecti, nullum est fatum; itaque ne divinatio quidem, quoniam ea rerum futurarum est.

(De divinatione 2. 8. 21)

So where is that divination of the Stoics? It cannot in the least warn us to be more careful, if everything happens according to fate; for however we act, that which will happen happens. But if, on the other hand, it can be turned aside, there is no such thing as fate: so there can be no divination, since divination is of things that are to come.

His argument can then continue: *atque ego ne utilem quidem arbitror esse nobis futurarum rerum scientiam* ('indeed, I do not think that knowledge of future events is even useful to us'): Priam, Crassus, and Pompey, ordered to emphasize the increase in the magnitude of their tragic reversal, are the examples of how, had their doom been foreseen, they would have felt no joy in their great achievements. In one splendid sentence, Marcus presents Caesar as a butchered corpse whose life would have been a torment, had he had foreknowledge of the manner of his demise:

quid vero Caesarem putamus, si divinasset fore ut in eo senatu, quem maiore ex parte ipse cooptasset, in curia Pompeia, ante ipsius Pompei simulacrum, tot centurionibus suis inspectantibus, a nobilissimis civibus, partim etiam a se omnibus rebus ornatis, trucidatus ita iaceret ut ad eius corpus non modo amicorum, sed ne servorum quidem quisquam accederet, quo cruciatu animi vitam acturum fuisse? (*De divinatione* 2. 9. 23)

Or what do we think about Caesar? If he had foreseen, that in the Senate, most of whom he had appointed, in Pompey's Senate-house, in front of the statue of Pompey himself, with so many of his own soldiers looking on, he should lie there slaughtered by the most noble citizens, some of whom had been granted the highest honours by him? Slaughtered in such a manner that not even his friends, not even a slave would approach his body—with what a tortured spirit would he have lived his life?

The passionate juxtaposition with Pompey (whose death is described immediately before in similarly emotive terms) and the focus on the physicality of Caesar's death at first sight give this argument about the futility of divination a strong materialist, anti-sentimental basis. The reality of the shattered body, untouchable even to slaves, is a powerful weapon against any fanciful metaphysical system.

There are paradoxes lurking, however, which make what is a refutation, if not of fate itself, at least of any idea of knowing it, seem more about the demands of the particular argument than about the provision of a clear theory. Most obvious is the fact that, as we already know from Quintus' account, Caesar had already been warned about his death, a theme which evidently grew in importance as the cult of Caesar developed, as the accounts of Plutarch and Suetonius demonstrate, but which was evidently sufficiently clear even so soon after the event. The argument that would fit Priam, Crassus, Pompey, and Caesar rather better would run: even with foreknowledge, these great men pursued their sense of destiny undeterred by superstition. That, certainly, was a mentality with which Vergil would endow Aeneas; it would surely have struck Cicero's readers as more plausible than this fundamentally unheroic idea of Pompey or Crassus unable to derive any pleasure from their achievements because of their fear of death. It is fear of death which preoccupies Cicero directly in *Tusculan Disputations* 1, admittedly completed before Caesar's death, but nevertheless a sober reflection of what was surely in these last years visible to Cicero himself, and something where the consolations of philosophy were particularly pertinent.[11] There is no trace of these discourses here, however, as pleasure at a sense of achievement stands in for the resolution or sense of political mission that ought to characterize devotion to the *res publica*.

Cicero's scepticism can be seen at its most destructive on the subject of dreams, one of the subspecies of divination with which the subject is introduced in the first preface (1. 2. 4). Marcus' repudiation of the prophetic power of dreams rests on a number of different arguments, one of which gives us a hint about how to read the ideological overtones of this extreme rationalism. Marcus swiftly deals with those many dreams that Quintus had derived from historical tradition, pointing out that in fact we know nothing about them, and then enters into an energetic internal dialogue in which a theory of dreams in fact rather different from the one which Quintus earlier proposed is swiftly brought forward, and equally swiftly refuted. The theory, ascribed to Democritus, is described as follows:

quem enim tu Marium visum a me putas? speciem, credo, eius et imaginem, ut Democrito videtur. unde profectam imaginem? a corporibus enim

---

[11] He refers explicitly, after the mention of Priam, to his lost *De consolatione*, a collection, he says, of *gravissimi exitus*.

solidis et a certis figuris vult fluere imagines; quod igitur Mari corpus erat? 'ex eo,' inquit, 'quod fuerat.' ista igitur me imago Mari in campum Atinatem persequebatur? 'plena sunt imaginum omnia; nulla enim species cogitari potest nisi pulsu imaginum.' quid ergo? istae imagines ita nobis dicto audientes sunt, ut, simul atque velimus, accurrant? Etiamne earum rerum quae nullae sunt? quae est enim forma tam invisitata, tam nulla, quam non sibi ipse fingere animus possit, ut, quae numquam vidimus, ea tamen informata habeamus, oppidorum situs, hominum figuras? num igitur, cum aut muros Babylonis aut Homeri faciem cogito, imago illorum me aliqua pellit? omnia igitur quae volumus nota nobis esse possunt: nihil est enim de quo cogitare nequeamus; nullae ergo imagines obrepunt in animos dormientium extrinsecus, nec omnino fluunt ullae; nec cognovi quemquam qui maiore auctoritate nihil diceret.   (*De divinatione* 2. 67. 137–9)

Which Marius do you think appeared to me? His likeness, I believe, and *imago*, as Democritus thinks. Where does the *imago* come from? He has it that *imagines* flow from solid bodies and actual forms. Which body of Marius therefore was it? 'From that which had existed.' So that very *imago* of Marius was pursuing me to the plains of Atina? 'All things are full of *imagines*, for no likeness can be thought of unless inspired by *imagines*.' What? Are those *imagines* so attentive to our speech that as soon as we like, they run up? Even of those things which don't exist? For what shape is so unheard of or so unreal that the soul cannot itself produce it, so that we can clearly perceive the forms of things which we have never seen, the sites of cities, or the appearances of men? It can't be the case that when I think of the walls of Babylon or the face of Homer, some *imago* from them is striking me. Therefore everything we like we can imagine, for there is nothing about which we are not able to think. Therefore, no *imagines* force their way from outside into the souls of sleepers, nor do any flow in any way; neither have I ever known anyone say nothing with greater authority (i.e. than Democritus).

There then follows a theory of the soul which explains dreams as the manifestation of the soul's own energy, a theory, of course, which refutes any concrete relationship between external occurrence and mental process. We are here in a very different world from that of Cicero's much better-known disquisition on dreams, the *Somnium Scipionis*, which made up the closing mythological flourish to his most single-minded attempt to define the Roman state in philosophical terms.[12] The insistence on his ridiculing the power of the *imago*

---

[12] Scholars think that the apparition of Urania which constitutes the long quotation from *De consulatu suo* in *De divinatione* 1 is also to be interpreted as a vision in a dream. See Hose (1995), 463–4.

recalls to me too the discourse of the *imagines* as the ancestor masks, most clearly represented in Sallust's speech of Marius from the *Bellum Jugurthinum*.[13] Cicero too had dreamt of Marius in the example which he is discussing here. These are no more than suggestive connotations, but there is no doubt that the rampant dismissal of Democritus as a philosopher with plenty of *auctoritas* but nothing to say, and the repudiation of the traditional view of an *imago* as a form possessed of particularly vibrant spiritual and political energy, leaves the reader wondering what is left of any of the socially integrative spirituality from which those other texts derive their ideological force.[14]

A world without *imagines* conjures up the possibility of an entirely rational universe in which any metaphysical connection between individuals is repudiated. Social bonds are maintained for the sake of tradition, but those traditions are not the manifestations of any underlying philosophical or religious system. It makes an enormous difference to what we think Cicero is doing in this dialogue whether we regard the arguments of the second book as the expressions of Cicero's mouthpiece, or whether we read the two books as somehow complementary to each other, and look outside the dialogue for a resolution of the two positions. This, quite clearly, is the Academic position to which the work appeals at the very end, a position which, as Cicero came to make increasingly clear, regarded doctrine as the antithesis of real philosophy. The last words of the work are a statement of allegiance to this approach, which, even given a reading sceptical that any words spoken in philosophical dialogue can be regarded as having a direct validity, seem only minimally encoded. The relationship between the traditions of the Stoics and those of the Academy are contrasted so explicitly at the end of the work that the passage demands lengthy citation:

'perfugium videtur omnium laborum et sollicitudinum esse somnus. at ex eo ipso plurumae curae metusque nascuntur; qui quidem ipsi per se minus valerent et magis contemnerentur, nisi somniorum patrocinium philosophi

---

[13] Sallust, *Bell Jug.* 85, with 5; see above, pp. 162–3.

[14] Kany-Turpin and Pellegrin (1989), 233–42, point out that Cicero avoids any of the more complex arguments from Aristotle about dreams that might disrupt the coherence of his rationalist polemic. They also conflate 'Marcus' with Cicero.

suscepissent, nec ii quidem contemptissimi, sed in primis acuti et conse-
quentia et repugnantia videntes, qui prope iam absoluti et perfecti putantur.
quorum licentiae nisi Carneades restitisset, haud scio an soli iam philosophi
iudicarentur. cum quibus omnis fere nobis disceptatio contentioque est, non
quod eos maxume contemnamus, sed quod videntur acutissime sententias
suas prudentissimeque defendere. cum autem proprium sit Academiae
iudicium suum nullum interponere, ea probare quae simillima veri videan-
tur, conferre causas et quid in quamque sententiam dici possit expromere,
nulla adhibita sua auctoritate iudicium audientium relinquere integrum
ac liberum, tenebimus hanc consuetudinem a Socrate traditam eaque inter
nos, si tibi, Quinte frater, placebit, quam saepissime utemur.' 'mihi vero',
inquit ille, 'nihil potest esse iucundius.' quae cum essent dicta, surreximus.

(De divinatione 2. 72. 150)

'Sleep seems to be a refuge from all toils and cares. But out of it very many
cares and fears are born. Certainly of themselves they would be of less
account, and would be more disregarded had not the philosophers taken
them under their protection. I'm not talking about the lowest-grade philosophers either, but particularly the sharpest ones, who can see all the consequences and objections to their arguments; those, in other words, who are
regarded as the purest and most accomplished philosophers. If Carneades
hadn't held out against their lack of restraint, I imagine they would be now
judged to be the only philosophers. My whole debate and polemic is with
these men, not because I hold them especially in low esteem, but because they
evidently defend their arguments with the greatest acumen and wisdom. But
since it belongs to the Academy to interject no judgment of its own, but
rather to accept those things which seem closest to the truth, to compare
explanations and to disclose what can be said for each argument, but by
failing to exert its own authority, leave the judgement of the listeners intact
and free, we will cling to this custom handed down from Socrates, and make
use of it ourselves as often as possible, if that, brother Quintus, is agreeable to
you.' 'To me', he said, 'nothing could be more pleasant.' That said, we arose.

The interpretation of dreams is made here into the testing-ground of
the philosophical schools. Only the resolute scepticism of Carneades
has stemmed the seemingly unstoppable success of Stoic views of the
nocturnal emergence of *imagines*. In their hands, sleep has been
robbed of its innocence. But Cicero is slipping here from the immediate context to a more general evaluation of philosophy, and it is
clear to see that (once again) he takes a resigned and rather pessimistic
view of the unpopularity of the Academic tradition. Evidently the
Academy represents an unfashionable branch of philosophy; it is also

likely that Cicero is here signing off the work with a warning against taking either the argument in favour of divination or the opposing argument as one which he himself is willing to endorse (though even this analysis is not unproblematic in itself; see below). Of less obvious but equal importance is the implication that allegiance to a particular philosophical school can have a powerful effect upon one's perception of something as routine as sleep and dreams. It is clearly more than an incidental response to the drift of the argument that Cicero draws such conclusions as he does by summing up the philosophical attitude to dreams. As I have already suggested, *imagines* need to be read with a full awareness of their significance; but, more than this, Cicero is exploring different approaches to the role of philosophy in life, which is of course part of a much wider discourse about the point of philosophy which runs through the whole of the late philosophical project.

This final shift in the argument of the work in fact appears somewhat forced; how do we move from a discussion of dreams to an evaluation of the relative merits of conflicting schools of philosophy? But the argument does make sense if we bear in mind that the different philosophical schools are being evaluated here not just for their arguments, but for the kind of *Weltanschauung* that they demand. The Stoic approach, however highly developed its intellectual virtues, and however pervasive its influence, requires a kind of allegiance which Cicero presents as undesirable. The doctrinaire quality that causes Marcus at the end of this work to express his preference for the Academic tradition so strongly is brought to prominence in the idea of the person who has in fact surrendered to a pervasive fatalism, where any occurrence that appears as random or strange immediately receives interpretation, and where that interpretation will always manifest the workings of higher powers as they go about expressing their destiny in the experience of mankind. As we know from Lucretius, it is precisely the defence of the arbitrary impulse which characterizes the Epicurean world-view; what Cicero suggests here is some way from that position; but it is clear that by casting the Stoics as occupying almost the whole popular philosophical scene, he then presents the alternative world-view not as a different set of philosophical arguments, but as a different approach to philosophy altogether.

This apparently unequivocal expression of allegiance to what is seen at the same time as an unpopular and marginal form of philosophy is an ambivalent moment. On the one hand, the Stoic theory of dreams has been roundly defeated by Marcus' arguments in book 2; on the other, the Academic position has not presented us with an alternative—rather, it has emerged from the arguments of book 2 in the guise of a thoroughgoing scepticism. At this final stage, the ground seems to shift, and Academic philosophy is characterized not as a scepticism about supernatural forces, or solely as the repertoire of critical devices developed to show that the Stoics were betraying their Socratic heritage. Rather, the Academy allows a healthy scepticism about philosophy itself, which has the potential both to unite Marcus and Quintus and to keep them talking. We are being encouraged, having consistently been presented with compelling arguments against superstition, to keep, after all, an open mind, and to regard the exchange between Marcus and Quintus as an educational exercise in itself, one designed not to produce so much clarity regarding the central theme, as a general heightened awareness. It is even possible that Cicero is presenting two versions of the Academy here, one more fiercely focused on scepticism with regard to the Stoics than the other.[15] The one with which the work ends lays emphasis on philosophy, but as an experience of debate, rather than a tool for indoctrination; and by ending the dialogue and making the speakers depart with this agreement, Cicero shows that this experience is one that is bounded in time. This discussion of divination is now complete, but what lessons readers should draw is not prescribed. Their philosophical education continues beyond the bounds of the dialogue itself, and the future tenses of the verbs in the final sentence point to a continuing series of future dialogues in the same vein—an idea, of course, that is clearly to be read metaphorically, given that we already know that Cicero's philosophical project is near to completion. There is a clear poignancy in combining this vision of the perpetuation of a Socratic form of open-ended philosophical work with the knowledge that Cicero himself would not be writing much more philosophy.

---

[15] I do not think it is possible to graft these two versions on to the debate about Cicero's wavering allegiance to the Academy; it strikes me that the image of the Academy as involving a non-dogmatic version of continuous dialogue is one that resides principally in Cicero's imagination, and the one he refers to in the prologue to *De natura deorum* as already dead in Greece. Its roots may lie in his nostalgia for Philo, while the anti-Stoic version is more strongly attributable to Carneades.

Despite the apparent clarity of the allegiance to the Academy here, we need to remain aware of the fictional quality of Cicero's presentation. Even though at the close of the dialogue the character of Marcus seems to be presenting us with a critical position from which to judge the arguments presented thus far, it would be risky to take this as too literal a proof of Cicero's own unalloyed allegiance to the Academic approach. We need to be particularly aware of the dangers of conflating the rigorous scepticism characterized by the frequent appeals to Carneades, both by Marcus and by Quintus, with the Academic openness of mind which is advocated at the close. In signing off the work, Cicero deliberately avoids identifying himself as the speaker of the second book, and if there is a moment where, in appealing to the Academic tradition, we can sense particularly strongly the figure of Cicero working as the mouthpiece of the author, then this needs to be balanced by the contradiction between an Academic approach and the doctrinaire rationalism of the character Marcus. In the light of this quasi-sphragis, a deliberate placing of his authorial seal at the end of the work, the structure of the work as a whole becomes clear. We are presented with a set of contrasts: two different ways of looking at divination, historical tradition, and social practice, and two different ways of integrating philosophy into an area where political and social institutions have previously granted it little access. We are not being asked to select one of these alternatives as superior to the other, and this explains why the arguments of Quintus are presented at such length, and, in a neater form, why the speakers agree at the end to follow an Academic approach and to continue with their discussions in the future. The mouthpiece reading is in fact redundant.

A passage from *De legibus* 3 provides useful support for Cicero's technique here. It is the place where Cicero most blatantly fractures the conventions of the dialogue form, by making his speakers not only refer to Platonic conventions but do so in terms of the actual course of their own argument. Marcus is holding forth on the excellence of the institution of the tribunate, in response to vivid criticisms by Quintus, who first of all expresses energetic paranoia about the endless conspiracies of the tribunes against both himself and Marcus; he culminates by pointedly declining to comment on Pompey's restoration of the full powers of the tribune (in 70, after they had been curtailed by Sulla in 81). Marcus retorts by defending

Pompey, even to the point of presenting himself as a martyr to the very power that Pompey had restored. Pompey only did what was best for the state, and the power which Clodius exercised in bringing about his exile was not supported by the people; things would have been a lot worse if it had been, but even then, with the entire *populus* roused against him, Cicero would have gone calmly into exile.[16] Cicero bestows on Quintus the role of the righteously indignant, furious at the machinations of Clodius, the failings of the constitution that could grant him such opportunities, and, barely implicit, those of Pompey to protect Cicero. Marcus takes the more conciliatory position, respecting the ancestral wisdom of the constitution, and accepting his exile, in a way, of course, as we know from the letters, that was far from historically accurate. The juxtaposition of these two dramatically opposed depictions of Cicero's own political fate, is resolved (or rather not resolved) by the following ruse:

sapientis autem civis fuit causam nec perniciosam et ita popularem, ut non posset obsisti, perniciose populari civi non relinquere. Scis solere, frater, in huius modi sermone, ut transiri alio possit, dici 'admodum' aut 'prorsus ita est'.
Q. haud equidem adsentior, tu tamen ad reliqua pergas velim.
M. perseveras tu quidem et in tua vetere sententia permanes?
A. nec mehercule ego sane a Quinto nostro dissentio, sed ea, quae restant, audiamus.   (*De legibus* 3. 11. 26)

It was for the wise citizen not to abandon disastrously a cause which in itself was not dangerous, and was so close to the people that it could not be resisted, to a populist citizen. You know, brother, that in conversations of this sort, in order to change to another topic, it is usual to say 'quite so' or 'that is the case'.
Q. But I don't agree in the slightest. But by all means go on to the rest of the topic.
M. Are you sticking resolutely to your old opinion?
A. By god, I agree completely with Quintus. But let us hear the rest of the argument.

So Marcus is appealing to the conventions of Socratic dialogue in order to prompt Quintus to accept his view of things; but Quintus continues in polemic vein, only to be supported by Atticus, who has not spoken since the topic of the tribunate was introduced (*De leg.* 19). A resolution is thus averted, but not before Cicero has managed

---

[16] *De leg.* 3. 21–6.

to provide plenty of opportunity for readers to wonder at the boldness of his irony, and to begin to reflect what the purpose of these conflicting visions of the tribunate might represent.

Needless to say, I think it would be a gross distortion to insist that the quasi-autobiographical account of the exile, evoking a Cicero so selfless that he could have accepted an even more desperate form of banishment than the one he in fact could accept only with such difficulty, should be privileged over the paranoid ranting of Quintus. It would be just as inaccurate to attempt to resolve those views into an account of what the real Quintus, Marcus, or Atticus thought about the rescinding of Sulla's legislation. But rather than pursue that argument further, I will just reinforce the parallel with *De divinatione*, and point out how, even in an earlier work, Cicero was working with forms of self-representation, conflicting narratives of his exile, and deliberate subversion of the dialogue form. The full ramifications of that process can be better understood if we look more closely at the role of self-presentation in *De divinatione*. Cicero, even when working in the present, is not embarrassed to let the fictional persona bearing his name merge into an implausible version of himself; in *De legibus* he presses the boundaries of the dialogue form in order to reinforce Quintus' and Atticus' position, and to remove from his readers any stable footing for adjudicating between these two different projections of his own history. The explicit reference to the dialogue conventions can also be read as a moment of genuine self-congratulation at handling the convention so effectively, producing so much drama, even to the point of insulting Pompey, on an apparently rather dry subject, and then again containing it. The swift change of topic is characteristic of such moments, where conflicting arguments are pushed to their limits, and then left: the end of *De natura deorum*, as of *De divinatione*, is another good example.

HISTORICAL ANECDOTE, IDEOLOGY, AND INTERTEXT

I have already suggested that there is a noticeable intertextual element in the closing section of *De divinatione*. Intertextuality also plays a large role in *De divinatione* 1, since Quintus' discourse is embellished extensively with quotations from Latin poets. In this context, the long extracts from Cicero's own poetry are particularly interesting: his translation of Aratus and, more importantly, the poem on his consulship.[17] The passage quoted from this last is extensive, and can be reinterpreted in the light of my emphasis upon the ambiguity of the philosophical message of the dialogue as a whole. By dwelling on poetry, and in particular upon Cicero's own interweaving of the poetic and the political in that poem, Quintus is sneakily preparing the ground for the arguments of Marcus that follow. He presents Marcus in advance with his own texts as a way of persuading the readers of the evidence of Cicero's own credulity regarding omens. The shock, therefore, of the rationalist refutation that occupies book 2 is correspondingly greater. If we are looking for an understanding of what ideological model Cicero wants this work to sustain, we cannot overlook the fact that there are multiple Ciceros. As is pointed out in the preface to *De divinatione* 2, Cicero has a theory of textual compensation whereby his philosophy takes the place of politics:

quod cum accidisset nostrae rei publicae, tum pristinis orbati muneribus haec studia renovare coepimus, ut et animus molestiis hac potissimum re levaretur et prodessemus civibus nostris, qua re cumque possemus. in libris enim sententiam dicebamus, contionabamur, philosophiam nobis pro rei publicae procuratione substitutam putabamus.   (*De divinatione* 2. 2. 7)

When this [tyranny] occurred to our state, then I began to renew these studies, deprived as I was of my former duties, with the aim as much as possible of relieving my spirit of worries, and of being of use to my fellow-citizens in what way I could. For in my books, I delivered my opinion, I carried out my legal pleading, and thought that philosophy stood in for the management of the state.

---

[17] Aratus: 7. 13–9. 15; *De consulatu* 11. 17–13. 22 = Fr. 6. There are also quotations from Cicero's *Marius* (1. 106 = Fr. 20); a few from Homer (Frs. 23, 26, 27); ?Euripides (Fr. 45); a tragedy involving Hecuba and Cassandra, variously attributed to Accius or Ennius: 31. 66. On the Aratus, see Jocelyn (1973), 80–2, which is preoccupied with Cicero's putative sources. Puelma (1980), 148, points to Cicero's models for long verse citations: Plato, but also Dionysius (the Stoic) and Philo; Jocelyn (1973), 66, singles out Aristotle and Theophrastus and at p. 77, Crantor and Chrysippus. As well as poetry, the work contains a good store of similarly evocative references to earlier Roman historiography; on one example, Wiseman (1979*a*).

This notion of substitution bears closer scrutiny: it ought not to be read as meaning that Cicero is using his philosophy to put across a particular political programme. In the present context, it suggests that books themselves can take on the different personae which Cicero himself had needed in his political career. Particularly evocative is the pointed wording of *substitutam putabamus*; even in this moment of apparently candid reflection on his behaviour during Caesar's rule, Cicero is allowing for a further subsequent change of attitude, one following Caesar's murder, where perhaps even the comfort of his previous tactic has to be abandoned. Hence too the odd ambiguity of the consistent use of the first-person plural in the passage: the calamity which affected the state was not just Cicero's, but it is unlikely that the recourse to philosophy in a crisis can refer to anyone but him. But here, in retrospect, there is even a hint that he felt this position too to be provisional, perhaps even slightly disingenuous: 'I used to think', or even 'I liked to think, under those circumstances, that philosophy was a substitute for politics'. The situation that 'we' are now in is left unclear; but what does emerge is a sense of a mutability in Cicero's different public roles. And just as Cicero's political activities were diverse, so were his literary ones. The consulship itself is not the same as the memory of it which Cicero's poem leaves behind: textual records of that event can, as we know from the *Letter to Lucceius* (discussed in the next chapter), take on a variety of different forms. What matters is not the particular set of arguments or beliefs, but rather, the effect of the particular work in question.

The contribution which Cicero makes to the Republic through his texts, however, is not one that rests upon a single ideological programme. The image of himself which this work in particular leaves to posterity is diverse: we have not only the sceptical speaker of *De divinatione* 2 and the slightly desperate Academic apologist of the book's conclusion, but we also have the poet and translator cited by Quintus, who celebrated his own political achievements in a way which integrated them into traditional political values and a poetic language which is deliberately conservative and archaizing. The other poets cited by Quintus make the point: Ennius, Pacuvius, Accius. When Marcus closes the first book by commenting that Quintus has come well prepared for this debate (*praeclare tu quidem ... paratus*

Quinte venisiti (*De div.* 1. 63. 132)), it is not hard to read this as dryly ironic: Quintus has prepared not only his own arguments, but also a figure of Marcus, constituted in the copious poetic citations, who is bound to approve them. The enthusiastic dismissal of Quintus' celebration of a providential universe, with its fortunate interplay of historical and metaphysical, is a particular surprise against this context. And although anyone reading this work as a sequel to *De natura deorum* would to a certain extent take this easily in their stride, there is a particular sense in which the comparative lack of technical philosophy in this work, and the manner in which at crucial moments it seems to take in, through citation or through the publication catalogue, all of Cicero's non-forensic writing, does lead to the conclusion that we should be reading *De divinatione* as having its own point to make, one rather different from that made in *De natura deorum*. And that point is not about divination, but rather about the complex, and ultimately insoluble, problem of Roman public life and its representation. The celebration of Rome, the notion of order and political progress, is balanced by a sense of impending chaos and the collapse of previously secure belief systems. The contribution that philosophy will make in this context is not the restoration of those systems, not the propagation of a particular theory which will bring back the old certainties. Rather, it is the possibility of continuing to think and to discuss, in the tradition of Socrates, and in the process to alleviate anxieties: *ut animus molestiis levaretur.*

A central role is played in this process by literary self-reference, by the manner in which Cicero uses this dialogue not just to sum up his achievement in composing philosophy in Latin but also to incorporate so much of his own poetry. The question as to why this dialogue in particular should be the place where Cicero so deliberately catalogued his literary achievements must in part be answered by the fact that, as he makes clear, he knew that he had covered most of the philosophical curriculum that he had set for himself; the comparative triviality of divination as a philosophical topic, and the relative simplicity of the arguments concerning it, gives him space to incorporate more than usual an element of deliberate self-representation. Cicero took the simple opportunity offered by the circumstances of the particular work to sum up his literary achievements, at the point when he is turning once again from philosophy to politics; but his self-representation is not simple: in particular, the great length of the quotation from *De consulatu* makes clear that he wants to provide a wider circle of readers with another text of the poem, at a time in history when the significance of that consulship was surely not great, restating, but again in an oblique manner, his contribution not just to Roman politics, but to the whole manner in which those politics could be represented. Recalling the end of *Brutus*, Cicero is countering the notion of a silent Cicero whose works need no written testimony with this elaborately multi-vocal self-portrait, in which the integrative, poetic rendition of the great events of the consulship is presented, but then also cast into doubt.[18]

The republication of extracts from Cicero's poetry is such a prominent part of the earlier stages of book 1 that the manner in which the poetry is presented and, in particular, the way in which it is woven into the development of Quintus' argument demand closer examination. Quintus begins his argument with a somewhat ambiguous statement concerning the relationship between history, memory, and divination, which, although unclear in its ideological ramifications, provides a suggestive introduction to the extensive quotations that follow:

> est enim vis et natura quaedam, quae tum observatis longo tempore significationibus, tum aliquo instinctu inflatuque divino futura praenuntiat. quare omittat urgere Carneades, quod faciebat etiam Panaetius requirens, Iuppiterne cornicem a laeva, corvum ab dextera, canere iussisset. obervata sunt haec tempore immenso et in significatione eventus animadversa et notata. nihil est autem quod non longinquitas temporum excipiente memoria prodendisque monumentis efficere atque assequi possit.   (*De divinatione* 1. 6. 12)

For there is a certain natural power which foretells the future, sometimes through signals observed over a long period of time, sometimes through some sort of divine impulse and inspiration. So let Carneades stop insisting on asking what Panaetius also used to, whether it was Jupiter who ordered the crow to sing on the left, the raven on the right. These things have been observed over an immense period of time and noticed and recorded in the significance of the outcome. Indeed, there is nothing which, with memory to preserve it and written records to hand it down, great length of time cannot accomplish and achieve.

---

[18] *Brutus* 330, see above, p. 205.

Such an optimistic vision of the power of historical records is rather remarkable, especially given the consistency with which Cicero has played with *memoria* and *monumenta* in his earlier works; but it is not isolated in Quintus' utterances: *quis est autem quem non moveat clarissimis monumentis testata consignata antiquitas?* ('Who is there whom antiquity, witnessed and endorsed by records, does not move?'), he declares, with similar rhetorical exaggeration later on, and his frequent appeals to historical sources reinforce his standpoint.[19] It would be a little extreme to interpret this rhetoric as demanding, by virtue of its credulity regarding the historical record, an immediate sceptical refutation. Quintus' words represent a tenable faith in the power of history, particularly the historical *monumenta*, to grant examples from the past a powerful influence over the present. But what is interesting about this passage is that, in forming a transition to the reproduction of Cicero's own poetry, it essentially allows the topic of divination to be supplanted by a less specific faith in the regularity of all kinds of occurrences, for which the historical parallel is not really appropriate: the quasi-scientific phenomena which characterize the citations from Cicero's translations of Aratus. The passages included talk about the behaviour of various birds, and then of frogs. When Quintus reprises the appeal to a natural force, also foreshadowing the phrasing of that optimistic rhetorical question about history, with the words *quis est qui ranunculos hoc videre suspicari possit? sed inest in ranunculis vis et natura quaedam significans . . .* ('Who would have thought that frogs could see this? But a certain signifying capacity exists in frogs . . .'), I find it hard to imagine that Cicero's tongue is not firmly in his cheek. But at the same time, this is Cicero's own selection of his own poetry that is providing proof of this same argument.

The long citation from *De consulatu suo* plays a similar game, but the stakes are, with the change of subject matter, correspondingly

---

[19] *De div.* 1. 40. 87. Particularly pointed reference to the historical record can be found at 1. 21. 43 (Fabius Pictor);1. 24. 50 (*plena exemplorum est historia* ('history is full of *exempla*')); 1. 26. 55 (Roman history preferred, for some reason (!) to Greek; 1. 44. 100 (a story also told in Livy 5). The (actually only partial) sceptical refutation must wait until 2. 33. 70: *errabat enim multis in rebus antiquitas* ('antiquity has been wrong on many matters'). Krostenko (2000), 374, suggests: 'He protects Roman identity at the expense of Roman history,' a nice formulation, if too neat a polarity: Quintus and Marcus just present different visions of Roman identity.

higher. Quintus deliberately adds the detail that he is reproducing the words of the muse Urania; she addresses herself to Cicero, and the sweep of her long speech is surprisingly (or prophetically) close to the concerns of the present dialogue. It begins with a presentation of general astrological systems, and moves to describe the portents which accompanied the rise of Catiline, and Cicero's response to them. The closing section is a short eulogy of philosophy, naming the Academy and the Lyceum, and casting Cicero as one who would devote himself to it when the political situation permitted.[20] Urania helps to reinforce Quintus' tactic of presenting to Marcus in advance a particular vision of himself, and in that way the presence of this passage reinforces my sense that part of the function of the dialogue as a whole is to bring forward competing images of Cicero: Quintus' words at the end of the quotation strengthen the case that different personae are actually an important part of the overall argument: he ends by justifying the long citation with an obfuscating flourish:

tu igitur animum poteris inducere contra ea, quae a me disputantur de divinatione dicere qui et gesseris ea quae gessisti et ea quae pronuntiavi accuratissume scripsisti?   (*De divinatione* 1. 11. 23)

So can you induce your spirit to speak against those things which I have argued about divination, you who have done what you have done and written with the greatest vividness what I have just pronounced?

animum poteris inducere ... ('can you induce your spirit ... ?') suggests that what Cicero has in mind is precisely the kind of wilful adoption of a position which the production of different personae implies. It is a challenge which the Marcus of book 2, of course, meets without a qualm, adopting with vigour precisely that form of *animus* required to refute both Quintus' arguments and Cicero's own poetic elaboration of them. Urania herself holds up a mirror to Cicero the consul, but Quintus then, as it were, takes hold of that mirror, brings it into the light of a very different world, and by inviting Marcus to see himself there reflected, exposes the vicissitudes not only of Cicero's career, but also of the variety of ways in which he has had to present himself. Whatever optimism that poem of sixteen years

---

[20] *De div.* 1. 11. 17–13. 22. For a thorough assessment of the *De consulatu suo* and its place both in the poetic context of the time and Cicero's own output, see Hose (1995).

ago may have captured about Cicero's view of himself, there is no doubt that the inclusion in the present context demonstrates a much more fragmented sense of identity.[21]

By placing this extract from the poem in a context which, at the very least, can be described as ironic, Cicero may also be taking charge of a process of poetic parody which, in the hands of Clodius and Antony, had in the past, and more recently, put him on the defensive.[22] The pomposity and overblown sense of destiny which the poem conveys are focused in this context upon a divine voice or vision which conjures up Cicero at the pinnacle of his political career as the mediator between the human and the divine. This Cicero is the focal point for the manifestation of divine destiny in the working out of Roman politics. It is not a different vision from the more general manner in which all the other examples of divination are conceived, but it does express clearly the ideological ramifications of divination: a sense of cohesion between Roman public life and the higher powers of the universe, and the potential for Cicero to act as a bearer of that cohesion. This is, ultimately, one among a number of roles for himself which he explores in the dialogue. Without explicitly dis-avowing the portrait of himself that is clearly visible in Urania's words, and, at the same time, validating and preserving his own text by such a lengthy citation, Cicero demonstrates how far he can go in exerting control over his own image, while at the same time casting an ironic light upon the aspirations of his consulship and his earlier attempts to turn it into an event worthy of such epic treat-ment. The strange conclusion, on Cicero's devotion to philosophy and astrology, as a refuge from the toils of the *patria*, captures nicely the theme of philosophy as refuge which I discussed in Chapter 2, and adds weight to my argument there that this contextualization of philosophy is a fundamental aspect of Cicero's literary persona. But the fact that, although totally irrelevant to the theme of divination,

[21] Krostenko (2000), 383–5, argues that Cicero's irony is directed against the human/divine relationship which the poem propagates, the changed circumstances after Caesar's death making clear the dangers of vaunting such a relationship. Hose (1995), 468, comes to a congruent conclusion, that in *De consulatu suo* Cicero was flirting with a Hellenistic ideal of 'Gottmenschentum'.

[22] For the evidence, and problems, see Peck (1897), 71–4; Allen (1956), 133–5; Harrison (1990).

Cicero makes Quintus include it here is at first sight rather puzzling, since it does little to reinforce the positive presentation of divination. What it does do, however, is strengthen the sense that Cicero is being particularly ironic about the neatness of his former attitude to philosophy, the same irony visible in the *putabam* ('I used to think') of the opening to *De divinatione* 2, discussed earlier. If the theme of philosophical compensation was Cicero's principal trope for establishing his presence as a historical figure, a figure worth of literary *monumenta*, then it is rather less puzzling to see it here subjected to the same general suspicion about any kind of guarantee of historical regularity which the dialogue puts forward. But once again, this irony is not a straightforward demolition: there is still a poignancy in the relevance of Urania's portrayal of the statesman-philosopher: after all, this was a persona that had kept Cicero busy for decades; and neither Marcus in his guise as scourge of Stoicism, nor the final paragraph of the work, demonstrate that Cicero wishes to abandon philosophy. Nevertheless, that philosophy will not be able to do service in providing an integrative vision of the universe in which the human and historical can be harmonized with the divine, universal, or theoretic.

The ideological aspects of *De divinatione*, therefore, are bound up in the dialogue's elaborate version of how politics, history, and representation relate to each other; and it is only by laying proper emphasis upon the dialogic quality of the work, and its deliberate failure to provide a clear philosophical position, that the complexity of Cicero's view of ideology emerges. We can relate the two competing views of the relationship of philosophy to social practice as a dramatization of Cicero's own struggle with Roman institutions. Philosophy here becomes the mechanism whereby ambiguities can be extrapolated into long coherent discourses which present essentially incompatible versions of Roman society. As one of Cicero's last philosophical works, *De divinatione* presents, with unusual starkness, two different ways of dealing with Rome which embody a struggle that has its roots much earlier in Cicero's career. The exclusion of Cicero from Roman political life is generally seen as a source of enormous personal disappointment, rather than as a stimulus to greater philosophical awareness. But this exclusion can be given a different emphasis. Cicero's career is one of a struggle for the harmonization of exceptional intellectual gifts with a political system that did not, in practice, depend upon them. Perhaps in *De re publica* Cicero can still be felt to be optimistic about the possibilities of producing a political life that operates in harmony with political theory, and there is a trace of this same optimism in the otherwise rather grim assessment of Rome in the second prologue to *De divinatione*. Central to this optimism is a coherent integration of theory with practice, an integration which depends upon picturing Rome as a place where Romans could bring to bear the fruits of their study on the execution of their public duties. *De officiis*, of course, is the place where that particular nexus is explored in most detail. But in *De divinatione*, Cicero is certainly in a much less positive frame of mind. Neither the resolute rationalism of Marcus, nor the quiescent traditionalism of Quintus, provides a stable position for a peaceful accommodation of learning to the texture of Roman political life.

In *De divinatione* Cicero tackles what, in the light of this theory, looks like a particularly fruitful domain. Divination, even more than the gods, is the place where the potentially arbitrary forces of the universe are linked to the fates of both individuals and states. In its emphasis too upon dreams as manifestations of an order of things, it focuses closely upon the role of the individual psyche as a focus for historical meaning, or the lack of it. The use of Cicero's poetry is another medium for exploring the same theme: Cicero may cite his own celebration of his poetic integration into the cosmic order of Roman history, but that citation does not get Quintus very far in his arguments. The ideological world which Cicero here conveys to us is one in which individuals are effectively left with a choice of two positions, both of which have their appeal, but neither of which can compel assent. The work of Cicero as a philosopher, therefore, is not to perpetuate the same confident assertion of oneness between speaker and political power which we find in his forensic work. The multi-layered, textual Cicero that emerges from this work is a different figure from the one who in his speeches enacted and recorded the convincing unity between the voice of the individual and the sources of power on which he draws that granted Cicero's speeches such longevity. My investigation of Cicero's theoretical explorations of rhetoric has demonstrated that any vision of the orator as the natural expression of Rome's historical development is an idealization. In *De divinatione*, the ideological focus is broader: the arbitrary quality of man's involvement in that development is revealed. And from a wider perspective, one that, by encompassing so much of Cicero's writings, the dialogue invites us to consider, *De divinatione* reinforces the problematic aspects of any attempt to depend upon a written representation, or indeed a stable authorial persona, to capture and perpetuate historical significance. As one of his final encounters with ideology, *De divinatione* reveals Cicero not just as a sceptic with regard to traditional superstitions, but as someone aware simultaneously of the power of tradition and its limitations. He is prepared, in this work, to give this dialectic a rich and thoroughly ironic exploration.

9

Ironic History in the Roman Tradition

The discussion of the role of irony in history which Cicero opens up towards the end of *Brutus* (292) needs to be considered as the start of a process of thinking about history in which the most profound perceptions of Roman history are implicated. Cicero, after all, in his guise as the typical Roman of the classroom, represents a certainty at least about the institutions of the *res publica*, and his speeches were such popular reading precisely because they convey a powerful harmony between a projected notion of civic order and the arguments and personality of the speaker. But all the works examined here produce a rather different picture, in which Cicero effectively casts doubt not so much upon the possibility of ideological coherence with the *res publica*, but upon the possibility of finding that coherence in Rome's historical record: either in his own representations of the political elites of the 120s or 90s or in the more directly historical survey of *Brutus*. And this is the particular relevance of my reading of *De divinatione*, since there, Cicero exposes in a form that is only just metaphorical the possibility of two competing visions of Rome: one based on order and a harmony between the destiny of the state and the lives of individuals, and another, essentially pessimistic and random. I say 'only just metaphorical', since divination can be seen as a metaphor for the proper functioning of the Roman state; it is, more accurately, a synecdoche rather than a metaphor, since divination is a small-scale emblem for predestination more generally and more specifically for harmony between ritual carried out in the name of the state and the success of the state.[1] However, in the working out of his argument, particularly in book 2,

---

[1] In using these terms, I am appealing to White's application of them to the structures of historical narrative: White (1973), 31–42.

where all predestination is dismissed as coincidence, and by his use of both historical anecdote and representation of history in his own poetry, Cicero makes it clear that divination concerns the general ability of any individual to grasp in advance the order of the universe in its particular application to Rome. The consequences of such scepticism are grim, and in both *De divinatione* and *Brutus* there is an almost frenetic quality to their evocation of the negative potential of Rome, as a poor breeding ground for orators, or as the state where nothing fits with expectations of a divine order.

Yet, once again Cicero's Academic methodology must be brought into the picture. These works are not unremitting indictments of the failure of Rome: they raise that possibility along with other possibilities; and likewise, the history of Rome that emerges from *De oratore* and *De re publica* is one of potential, as much as incredulity. Indeed, it would be an exaggeration of the arguments presented in earlier chapters to claim that incredulity was a more prominent force than potential. Even the positive image of monarchy that emerges in *De re publica* is neither one that can be articulated successfully in the present, nor one which can be fitted with any real plausibility to the past. Certainly, Scipio is as good a figure as Cicero could find to embody the qualities of the ideal *princeps*, and if he expressed that in terms of a positive theoretical picture of monarchy, then the readers of his own day might take Scipio as a source of inspiration. But that is far from any kind of historical analysis, as the elaborate play with the form of the dialogue makes clear. History is explored for its potential to inspire, but also for its ability to contain ideas in the past. Scipio works because he does not need to engage with the tyrants of the following century, and Cicero reinforces this point particularly well by making him die so soon after the dramatic date of the dialogue. Cicero is engaging in complex work with historical representation, in which the foundational potential of history is balanced by a scepticism about knowledge of the past, about the theoretical coherence of anything that happens at Rome, and by the sense that, even in the 50s, Rome does not easily demonstrate a happy harmony between the claims of aristocratic historical continuity and the realities of government or public institutions.

This is a highly sophisticated approach to history, and it is inconceivable to me that it was purely as a result of his attempt to write

Heraclidean dialogues to ground philosophy in Rome's past that such complex historical representations emerged. The balance between the positive and negative aspects of this way of dealing with history can be better judged if we read Cicero in the context of other Roman historiography, where Cicero's practice, on the one hand, illuminates the work of the historians, but on the other, loses some of its strangeness when seen as part of a more general phenomenon. So in this chapter I shall argue that we can see in Cicero's work a way of dealing with Roman history which is best characterized as ironic; and that ironic history is something which is also evident in the work of Sallust, Tacitus, and even Livy, in whose work in general the sense of the harmony of Rome's development is much more positive. The basis for comparing Cicero with actual historians depends upon the premiss—one that is, for the ancient world at least, beyond dispute—that the main aim of historiography is to exploit the resource of the past in order to make the most of the edifying and educational potential of history, rather than any idealized need to uncover the facts about that past. As I suggested in Chapter 6, it is the moral and educational aspects of the exemplary tradition at Rome which condition Cicero's use of history. Here I shall argue that Cicero was not alone in being aware of the problematic quality of this tradition; like him, Rome's great historians were able both to sustain a scepticism about traditional ways of dealing with the past and, at the same time, put it to work for their own pedagogical ends. This double-edged attitude to history corresponds to the approach to writing history labelled 'ironic' by White in his analyses of nineteenth-century historiography. White's is a quite specific definition of irony: while producing a historical account, the historian simultaneously draws the readers' attention to the difficulty or impossibility of the processes of production.[2] So the first part of this chapter will be devoted to establishing the framework for this discussion, as well as for drawing out Cicero's own adumbration of the role of rhetoric within history, since, just as White situates irony as part of a rhetorical framework for describing the construction of historical narratives, so it is helpful to recall the rhetorical context of historiography at Rome. The second part will look at other Roman historians, and

[2] White (1973), 37–8, 54–9.

think about the way in which ironic history might actually be a dominant characteristic of Roman historiography, one which has had a vital role in determining the manner in which Rome itself has been perceived. That, of course, brings us again to the central question of how the neglect of ironic aspects of Cicero's works has led to a minimalist perception of the potential of his philosophical writing, a failure to appreciate the richness of his work with history.

RHETORIC AND THE KNOWABILITY OF THE PAST

As a recurrent thread in his representation of the speakers in both *De re publica* and *De oratore*, and as a more general problem in the characterization of the orators of Rome's past in *Brutus*, Cicero raises the problem of historical evidence. The preservation of written speeches, and the linking of knowledge or expertise, in rhetorical or political theory, to particular periods in history, are opportunities for Cicero to dwell upon the difficulties presented by historical sources, and beyond that the difficulties of interpreting the past as something significantly different from the present. The place where this theme is tackled most explicitly is the opening of *De legibus*, where Cicero makes the speakers of that dialogue (which was clearly composed as a supplement to *De re publica*) suspend their judgement concerning the same kind of early history which made up the discussion of Rome's history in *De re publica* 2. Romulus there was pivotal to the entire project of resolving the dialectic between theoretical and practical knowledge, and his historicity was carefully argued. In *De legibus* he is consigned to the fictional world of poetry. But the scepticism of *De legibus* need not be taken as Cicero's own. Just as the speakers of *De re publica* define historical evidence in such a manner as to suit their own purposes, so too the speakers of *De legibus*, even if they are Cicero and his friends, have their own particular role to play within the setting of that dialogue. Perhaps we are safe in interpreting the scepticism about early history as representative of Cicero's own view, but even so we will be under-playing the complexity of Cicero's approach if we forget that, in the contrast between these two dialogues, there is a contrast between different ways of looking at Rome, particularly through her history. In *De legibus* we find ourselves in a world in which a discussion located in the immediate present aims to extract timeless legal principles from laws which are the product of historical circumstance; in *De re publica* the opposite dynamic is at work, anchoring theoretical discussion of constitutional matters to history.[3]

Furthermore, it is suggestive to juxtapose the opening of *De legibus*, one of Cicero's earlier works, in which Cicero's poem *Marius* is referred to, with the use of poetry in *De divinatione*, one of the latest. The poetic function for history which *De legibus* outlines is one that is still relevant in *De divinatione*, in which recent history, rather than ancient, becomes poetic. By undermining the careful discussion of Romulus as a historical figure, *De legibus* also draws attention to the awkwardness which poetic elaboration poses in the realm of ideology. In *De divinatione*, the tension between self-celebration and a sense of futility is further elaborated as a contrast between a poetic and a prosaic sense of Cicero's own historical function, a parallel to the two versions of Romulus which *De legibus* and *De re publica* offer. The poetic is taken as part of an integrative, essentially conservative notion of Rome's history, and the anti-poetic as one which denies any such fantasy of integration.[4] Cicero is certainly aware of the possibilities of a radical historical scepticism, a vision not just of Rome, but of the traditional way of venerating Rome's past, in which nothing can be proved, and in which the attitude to historical knowledge can determine how far the individual will be bound by tradition. Pushing the interpretation of *De divinatione* perhaps a little far, we can glimpse the idea that submission to tradition is a matter purely of personal choice, rather than the result of any compulsion to express the heritage of the past in a particular form of political activity. The philosophically aware individual is, in effect, freed from history by virtue of his argumentative insights. This is, of course, precisely the aim of the more transcendental forms of Greek philosophy that were available; they offered

---

[3] See Girardet (1983), 123–44; Powell (2001).

[4] Cf. White's account of Hegel's somewhat different distinction between poetic and prosaic history: (1973), 85–92. It would be interesting to explore how Hegel's own readings of ancient historiography led to the development of this distinction.

in different ways some kind of universalizing that would go beyond history. As we have seen, however, from *De oratore* to *De officiis*, Cicero was concerned precisely to make philosophy do the opposite, so rendering it useful for the concrete Roman situation. He has not given up in *De divinatione*, but he does demonstrate in quite an extreme form, albeit within a limited scope, the possibility of a freedom from tradition granted by an anti-poetic scepticism.[5]

These arguments remain implicit in the way in which Cicero presents his philosophical activity, in the manner in which the dialogues function and in which historical material is exploited. But if we look in more detail at the philosophical scepticism in which he was trained, then the interpretation in particular of *De divinatione* will be strengthened. Of particular interest is the manner in which the Stoics managed to combine both a highly sceptical approach to philosophical problems generally with a fundamentally integrative view of the individual within society. Essentially, it was the manner in which the Academy responded to Stoicism that defined the rift that occurred between Antiochus of Ascalon and Philo of Larissa, Antiochus wanting to argue that Stoicism simply represented the continuation of the Academic tradition. In his history of the philosophical schools given in *Academica* 1, Cicero gives a potted history of philosophy from its origins with Socrates down to the extreme scepticism of Arcesilaus, at which point the preserved text breaks off. Within this history, the main emphasis is upon the different positions that different philosophers have taken with regard to the possibility that anything at all could be known. Arcesilaus, as it happens, represents the extreme view:

itaque Arcesilas negabat esse quidquam quod sciri posset, ne illud quidem ipsum, quod Socrates sibi reliquisset: sic omnia latere censebat in occulto, neque esse quidquam quod cerni aut intellegi posset. (*Academica* 1. 12. 45)

---

[5] Ankersmit (1994), 6–7, describes, for the development of modern narrative historiography, a move precisely in the opposite direction, away from the minimal form of knowledge of the chronicle to the kind of analysis necessary with fuller narrations. It is tempting to think about *Brutus* in a similar way: the source material provided by Atticus is like a minimal chronicle, but Cicero supplants the intrinsic scepticism (for Ankersmit, Pyrrhonism) of his source with an ironic scepticism about the basis for any more satisfactory narrative elaboration.

In this way Arcesilaus denied that there was anything that could be known, not even that very thing itself, which Socrates reserved for himself [i.e. the idea that nothing could be known]: so far did he think that everything lay hidden in obscurity, and that there was nothing which could be observed or understood.

I include this quotation because it usefully clarifies exactly how far the scepticism with which Cicero was familiar could go, and, more specifically, I want to draw attention to the extent to which the entire discussion of philosophy in this context centres on scepticism, and in particular on the possibility of philosophical knowledge. What is preserved today as *Academica* 2 goes over much of the same ground, but in considerably more detail, and with discussion of the doctrines of individual philosophers and their associated theories. Philosophy, in these works, is construed as being the development of philosophical method in terms of its responses to the idea of a limit to knowledge and understanding. The testing-ground for knowledge is perception: philosophers have held different views of the extent to which the information provided by the senses could be taken as a basis for certainty. Near the start of *Academica* 1, Varro begins his account of Plato's successors by stating that philosophy at this point was accepted as having three distinct branches:

fuit ergo iam accepta a Platone philosophandi ratio triplex, una de vita et moribus, altera de natura et rebus occultis, tertia de disserendo et quid verum, quid falsum, quid rectum oratione pravumve, quid consentiens, quid repugnans esset iudicando. (*Academica* 1. 5. 19)

Therefore already a threefold scheme for doing philosophy had been handed down from Plato: one concerning life and morality; another, nature and hidden forces; a third about discussion itself, and about judging what is true, what false, what is right and wrong in a speech, what agreeing or refuting might be.

If we had to include history within this scheme, it would have to be within the first category, *de vita et moribus*, and given the prominent role of Varro in the dialogue that is not in itself just idle speculation. Indeed, in introducing the character at the start, Cicero makes clear the extent to which Varro's writings have contributed precisely to a knowledge of the identity of Romans, particularly in relation to their city and their literature.[6] But even within this characterization of

---

6 *Acad.* 1.3.9.

Varro's work, there is a sharp distinction between his philosophical work and his other, more prominent writings. Cicero is not, it is safe to say of this text, interested in exploring how knowledge of the world, even if Varro has contributed directly to that, relates to knowledge of the past. He does not exploit the character of Varro as an opportunity to investigate the epistemology of historical knowledge, in other words. Nor are any of the doctrines discussed in the work (nor, indeed, in any other of the works in which the various philosophical schools are weighed against each other) doctrines that could reasonably be said to be concerned with the possibility of knowing the past. Historical knowledge, in other words, is not recognized as falling within the sphere of philosophy.

In itself, such a conclusion is unsurprising, given the evident absence of philosophy of history as a category in ancient thought. But bearing in mind the visible interest that Cicero has in tracing source material, and in matters of historical veracity, it is surely possible that, even though formally excluded from philosophy, history must fall within the methodological scope of scepticism: it is, at a bare minimum, an area in which it is legitimate to explore uncertainty, and in which the accessibility of knowledge is at least brought into question. And although Cicero does not tackle this area head-on, there are related arguments, about the status of different kinds of writing, which shed light on Cicero's historical practice elsewhere. The figure of Varro in *Academica* is appropriate for these purposes, and the first words that he utters reveal Cicero's concerns:

'silent enim diutius Musae Varronis quam solebant, nec tamen istum cessare sed celare quae scribat existimo'. 'minime vero' inquit ille, 'intemperantis enim arbitror esse scribere quod occultari velit; sed habeo opus magnum in manibus ...'   (*Academica* 1. 1. 2)

'for Varro's muses are silent for longer than usual, and I do not think that he has stopped, but that rather is hiding what he has been writing.' 'Not at all,' he replied. 'It is a rash man who writes down what he wishes to keep hidden. But I have a great work on my hands ...'

Both the dedicatory letter to Varro (*Ad fam.* 9. 8) which accompanies this work and the opening section fixate oddly upon the question of Varro's slowness to publish, something explicable in part by the comparison with Cicero's own frantic productivity. The letter makes clear that we should be aware of the comparison that Cicero is making between himself and the polymath, a comparison that is further explored in the subsequent chapters of the dialogue, where Cicero makes the character of Varro explain why he has failed to turn his hand to Latin philosophy (*Acad.* 1. 2. 4–8). While clearly in part Cicero's tribute to Varro, and probably a genuine attempt to put across a view of the difficulty of philosophical writing in Latin which resonated with what Varro himself thought, there is a further effect to this passage: it both celebrates the success of Cicero's own achievements in overcoming the linguistic difficulties to which Varro draws attention, and also adds a lot of detail to a process alluded to much more briefly in other works (e.g. at *De off.* 1. 2–3; *De fin.* 1. 1. 1–2, both later than *Academica*) concerning the degree of difficulty Cicero experienced in doing philosophy in Latin. In that sense, this tribute to Varro is really a tribute to Cicero. By extension, however, we can see that part of Varro's function as a character is to act as the embodiment of the kind of writing which Cicero was *not* himself doing: writing that was, from a linguistic point of view, less difficult than Cicero's. Why, then, does Cicero draw his readers' attention to Varro's lack of productivity? In part, perhaps to celebrate his own superiority, his productivity in a time of political crisis (as Atticus points out right at the start of the dialogue, *Acad.* 1. 1. 2), compared to Varro's silence. But given that paying a tribute to Varro had been on Cicero's mind for a while, it seems far-fetched to press Cicero's vanity so far as to interpret this tribute as an opportunity to boast of his prolixity over Varro's silence.[7] The solution must lie in the wider context of the work, and specifically in the question of writing philosophy within the sceptical tradition.

This tradition centred on a set of key thinkers who themselves left no written legacy: Socrates, Arcesilaus, Carneades; Cicero refers precisely to this genealogy at the start of *De natura deorum* (1. 5. 11).[8] Varro claims that it is because he is an Academic, rather than an Epicurean or a Stoic, that writing philosophy in Latin is so difficult, and why he has chosen not to do it. It is almost impossible, he suggests, to write in a lucid, accessible style concerning what is in

---

[7] He had been urged by Atticus to make him into one of the speakers of *De natura deorum*, and explained to Atticus at length why he had not done this (*Ad Att.* 13. 19).

[8] See above, p. 46.

effect a particularly technical branch of philosophy. Epicureanism, with its clear doctrines, has in fact already had its representatives in Latin (the tantalizing Amafinius and Rabirius); but because so much of the work of the Academy is the refutation of Stoicism, which has hitherto existed only in Greek, the demands placed upon the Latin language for its effective mediation would give it only a limited appeal. Cicero here is far more likely to be expressing his own anxieties about the possible fate of his own writings, than to be criticizing Varro for a lack of nerve; after all, Varro's output was simply enormous, and failure of nerve would be an implausible criticism in the face of it. The *Antiquitates* are referred to in this passage as already completed, and *De lingua Latina* is the work in hand which Varro mentions in the passage just cited. Varro's comment that only a foolish man uses writing to express things which in fact he wants to keep concealed looks, in this context, like another place where Cicero is using Varro as his shadow: the rash man who writes down what he wants to keep hidden is (potentially) Cicero himself: someone who has got drawn into a process of dogmatic philosophical production against the traditions of their training; who, in the process of popularizing philosophy, has had to neglect its more technical aspects in order to reach a wider audience.

Certainly, Cicero is drawing attention to his achievements in being able to bring the Academy to a Roman readership, but at the same time he is making his readers aware of the difficulty of that process. Central to that difficulty must be the idea that, unlike in the historical researches of Varro, it is not so simple for the Academic philosopher to put his faith in writing. The process of writing could in fact be, for Cicero, what it was *not* for Varro: a bad method of communicating something that would in fact be better communicated by other means, by actual conversation. The exaggeration of Varro's lack of literary production can again be interpreted as a rather too pointed way of referring to Cicero's own over-production; both are done ironically, and if that irony has to be pressed to reveal a clearer meaning, that meaning is surely that Cicero is unsure of the success of his philosophical venture, and is turning to give an account of the Academy specifically in order to locate his own work more securely within a sceptical discourse. Although Cicero finds a rather opaque way to do so, the contrast between himself and Varro is the means for evoking his own position as an Academic: one who, for particular reasons, has taken on the task of committing this non-literary philosophy to writing.[9] But at the same time, he is aware of the ironic potential of writing, and, rather than being rash, as Varro suggests, is foolhardy enough to produce a kind of writing that is something different from directly revelatory. Writing in an Academic tradition, unlike historical or 'antiquarian' research, may in fact be a form of writing that occludes more than it conveys; the opening of the *Academica* indicates that Cicero is preoccupied with this possibility. His praise for the *Antiquitates*, indeed, which are said to have imbued their readers with an entirely new view of what it means to be Roman, and to dwell in that city, to appreciate its history and institutions, comes as a clear indication of the positive value of Varro's writings, so as to confirm his faith in the communicative power of writing.[10] The lessons of philosophy are, especially in a work devoted to the Academy, rather less easy to grasp, and the processes of writing it, more deeply embroiled in problems of revelation or occlusion. In comparison with Varro's works, Cicero's philosophy is a great deal less positive about its ability to inculcate in his readers a cosy sense of Roman identity.

So the opening of this late work gives us an indication of the ironic potential of writing and, in particular, of that potential in philosophy as opposed to historical research. Given that the main thrust of Cicero's account of the Academy is to trace the vicissitudes of scepticism as they relate to questions of philosophical knowledge, it is hardly surprising that in the opening section, we can detect the wider implications of this scepticism: a sense of ambiguity about the compromises necessary to bring an essentially non-revelatory form of philosophy to a Latin readership and an awareness that the writing that Cicero has undertaken may be at least in part about concealing meaning. Cicero might be able to do what Varro could not manage: to write Latin philosophy without betraying the non-literary tradition which characterizes Academic thought at its best. The Academy, it

---

    [9] It is not explicitly stated that the Academy is biased against writing, but as a partial analysis Varro suggests that it was largely in order to rebut Stoicism that Academic writing evolved its own technical vocabulary (*Acad.* 1. 2. 7).
    [10] *Acad.* 1. 3. 9.

cannot be sufficiently emphasized, was characterized precisely by disputes on this very topic: I am not subjecting Cicero to a generalizing deconstruction on the relationship between philosophy and writing, in a manner inspired by Derrida's reading of Plato's *Phaedrus*, even though a deconstructive impulse is helpful in accessing the sceptical mentality.[11] On the contrary, Cicero's preoccupations can be firmly placed by apprehending the context which he himself delineates, albeit allusively: the disputes about the possibility of certain knowledge, the problems of translation, the relative merit of writing over silence, the decision to write Academic philosophy rather than the more positive discourses of history, Roman tradition, and even the Latin language. All these aspects, of course, have a direct bearing upon the way in which Cicero treats history; indeed, they can be seen to coalesce in precisely that use of history which I have described in his dialogues: a sense of how fundamental historical material is to a sense of Roman culture, and how, at the same time, the truths of history are not really amenable to a philosophical approach. They have imaginative potential and, as such, can be used to open up ideas: ideas about ethics, politics, and culture. Without elaborating an explicit theory of historical knowledge, Cicero has nevertheless a framework within which history can be used; it is also a framework which has little time for the kinds of certainties about the past which concern modern historians, an area which I will explore in more detail in the next chapter.

Historical questions, then, are different from questions about knowledge, at least the kind of knowledge with which philosophy is concerned. This leaves the question of how history can itself become a component in a philosophical endeavour. Cicero's compliment to the achievements of Varro must be taken as sincere, I think; but it is significant that Cicero moves quickly into the discussion of philosophical method. This establishes a contrast between a form of writing which is concerned with the past and one which is rooted in a more permanent notion of truth—history versus method, in other words. Philosophy, particularly in a tradition that ascribes its origins to Socrates, aims at truths which are beyond time, and which are therefore dislocated from the passage of time. History, on the

---

[11] Derrida (1981), 63–171.

other hand, is about tracing the relationship between a sense of identity in the present and the basis for that identity in the past, and observing the pattern that links the experiences of the present with the experiences of the past represented in the historical record. The distinction corresponds readily to what we have already observed about Cicero's practice: the tension between a form of discussion that has in sight some kind of absolute truth (even if, in an Academic manner, that truth cannot be attained) and one which is rooted in a historical characterization of Rome. This is sometimes understood as a contrast between real and ideal.[12] It is perhaps more accurate to examine it as a problem which arises specifically with the contrast between Greece and Rome, and in addressing the matter of translation, this is where Cicero himself is inviting us to locate it. In thinking, however, about the transfer of Greek philosophy to Rome, the question of Rome's history inevitably arises, and this is why, in so many of his prefaces, Cicero makes reference to his intentions in adapting Greek material to his Latin readers. It is not so much that the history of Greece has a different texture from that of Rome, but that because of the virtual absence of philosophy up to this point, Rome's history becomes significant as part of the process of adopting this discourse from Greece, and, as a result, history plays a more prominent role in Cicero's dealings with philosophy: hence his play with fixing rhetorical or constitutional theory in *De re publica* and *De oratore* within history and, likewise, the extreme ambivalence about rhetorical expertise in *Brutus*.

History, in such a context, is the demonstration of the validity of Cicero's efforts: Rome has to be presented as a society in which philosophical or theoretical insights can be relevant, even though they have never been relevant in the past. As I have suggested, there is a contradiction inherent in this process from which Cicero does not shy away. The encounter with history, therefore, is always ironic: history is used for its ability, as in Varro's work, to connect the present to the past, but used with a simultaneous awareness of the

---

[12] Michel (1965); Müller (1989). Michel discusses this in relation to *De re publica*. His conclusions are vitiated, it seems to me, because in an Academic tradition, the ideal itself is unknowable, and there is little sign of Academicians pursuing an Aristotelian mean between ideal and reality.

difficulty of this process, and in particular the problem of making the past validate the present. At the start of *Academica*, Varro is the figure for whom the encounter with history has none of these problems: he is confident about the clarity of writing, of being able to express what you want to express. Cicero, on the other hand, comes across as the one who, although he is keen to integrate philosophy to Rome, cannot do so without drawing attention to the attendant difficulties, and in part, these difficulties result from his Academic insistence on avoiding doctrine, and in treating philosophy as a method of enquiry, an interest in theoretical questions for their own sake. The integration of such an approach to Rome has, we have already seen, given rise to a highly ambiguous representation of Roman culture. That ambiguity has resulted, in the dialogues I have looked at, from the exploitation of history as anchorage for philosophy, with the simultaneous demonstration that such a reading of history cannot really be justified.

Essentially this leaves us with the sense of history as a form of representation, rather than as a form of enquiry into truth. In such a context, Cicero's other angle on history, that it requires a particular kind of rhetoric, fits organically with the manner in which history connects the past with the present. The neglect of history by Greek rhetoricians, of which Antonius complains in *De oratore* 2, suggests that historiography requires a different kind of rhetoric in Rome from that which it already possesses in Greece, as a result of the tradition of great historical writers.[13] More than that, however, rhetoric is relevant to Cicero precisely because of the representative nature of his historical endeavours: because history can be written, while at the same time, underlining the provisional quality of that representation, it is possible that Cicero perceives a greater potential for rhetoric to be put to work in history than was apparent in the Greek tradition. Greek historiography simply used rhetoric; style was an intrinsic part of it, right from the start. But because Roman historiography evolved in a more minimal form, one that was connected with a different form of social communication, if it is going to be written in a way that conforms to a more elevated kind of discourse, it will need its own theoretical discussion, and arguments

---

[13] See above, pp. 134–41.

about style in history will need to become explicit. The discussion of funeral orations of the aristocracy in *Brutus* is a useful focus. They demonstrate the primitive quality of both historical study and rhetorical skill which is characteristic of Rome; such material would justify Antonius' sense that Rome needed a special discussion of the rhetoric of historiography. However, in *Brutus* Cicero is, as we have seen, keen to evoke some sense of the continuity of discourse with earlier eras, even if the lessons that can be drawn from it for today's orators are limited. The sense that in Greece these matters are dealt with differently, and that oratory and historiography have a closer connection, is another aspect of the more general conception of Rome as a society thus far immune to the incursions of theory. In all the dialogues examined so far, however, Cicero has been careful to locate that immunity exactly within a historical characterization of Rome. In the next generation, Dionysius of Halicarnassus was to provide a theoretical basis for a cultural revival in Greece that depended upon occluding any sense of a historical boundary that would limit the relevance of the language or political ideals of Classical Greece to Greece's present inhabitants.[14] His appeal to Isocrates usefully encapsulates the importance of a view of history as effectively unchanging, and harnessed to rhetorical performance. Cicero's work in this same area is different, and his struggle to find a way of giving a theoretical fillip to Roman rhetoric without obscuring historical specificity is a sign, I think, of the rather different cultural situation at Rome.

In this context, Cicero's most brazen encounter with the nature of historical writing, his letter to the historian Lucceius in which he canvasses for the appropriate representation of his own historical deeds, takes on a particular importance. That letter has been read as a demonstration that Cicero's interest in history lies solely in its ability to cast glory on himself: but in the light of the complexity of Cicero's integration of rhetoric into Roman history, the letter can also be understood as a supplement to his own practice with historical writing, a practice that is essentially ironic: stressing the necessity of historical representation, but aware of its shortcomings, particularly in a Roman context. This is an irony which we can certainly

---

[14] Swain (1996), 65–100.

recognize in Tacitus and, to a lesser extent, in Sallust: both will be
discussed below, after a more detailed presentation of the *Letter to
Lucceius*.

LETTER TO LUCCEIUS

In his letter to the historian Lucceius, composed in 55 BCE, thus at
the time when work on *De oratore*, *De re publica*, and *De legibus* was
at least under way, Cicero presents an unflattering portrait of his own
relationship with history.[15] Although there are complexities to
Cicero's argument, the essence of that letter is Cicero's demand that
the historian enhance his historical significance to the point of
exaggeration, to provide a flattering picture of Cicero not just for
posterity, but for the positive publicity which Lucceius' work will
bring to readers of the day. A central theme of the letter is Cicero's
impatience to see the swift completion of a historical work which
gives a beneficial account of his consulship, exile, and triumphant
return to Rome. The letter presents historical writing as an essential
part of Cicero's political success; the challenging aspects of the letter
concern the struggle between Cicero's desire for a permanent celebration of his glory and his sense that it is inappropriate for historical
figures to attempt to determine the manner of their own representation. The letter demonstrates perfectly Cicero's distance from historical writing: he recognizes the power of history to bestow status
and fame, but at the same time is aware that, as text, history is
susceptible to distortion, and may not provide an accurate record
of events. The letter has been taken as evidence of the general
incapacity of the Romans to make an adequate distinction between
the realm of rhetoric and the realm of historiography.[16] It has also
been analysed for the light it sheds upon the elaborate processes by
which Cicero negotiates the conventions of epistolographic favour-
seeking.[17] My own approach to the letter is focused on the element of

---

[15] *Ad fam.* 5. 12.   [16] Woodman (1998), 70–5; Fantham (2004), 157–9.
[17] Rudd (1992); Hall (1998).

self-presentation and, in particular, the image of Cicero as a man implicated in the historiographical process. The letter is an elegant statement of the same kind of double-edged thinking that I have observed in the dialogues, simultaneously insisting on the advantages of history as a form of commemoration and manifesting scepticism about the notion of an authoritative historical account. The great additional benefit of including the letter here is that it is a remarkably self-aware piece of writing, in which Cicero plays ironically with his own sense of self-importance.[18]

The main drift of the letter is clear from the start: Cicero is concerned with history as the vehicle for the fame of the individual, and this theme is prominent throughout the entire letter. Cicero is approaching Lucceius to write an account both of his consulship and of his subsequent exile and return. This, apparently, is something which Lucceius had already indicated to Cicero that he would do; the letter is written in order to precipitate the execution.[19] Cicero's arguments in forwarding his case are carefully crafted to overlap an evaluation of different kinds of historical narrative, and of the particular value of historical writing. The arguments of the letter are essentially these, in the order in which they appear:[20] the immortality which a written history will bestow on Cicero will be more useful to him if it happens while he is still in a position, as an active politician, to enjoy the authority that it grants; Lucceius' existing commitments then lead Cicero to weigh up whether a discrete monograph on his achievements would be better than inclusion in a longer narrative history; again, these different forms matter in themselves less than the implications for a delay in the realization of Cicero's historical legacy. That legacy, Cicero begs, should be one of enhancement; the history should praise him, perhaps more than at first sight necessary, or indeed strictly accurate. On that basis, Cicero concludes that a separate monograph dedicated to him will have other advantages

---

[18] My argument here, of course, diverges widely from that of Shackleton Bailey (1997), *ad loc.*, who takes Cicero's vision of his own importance at face value.

[19] *quod etsi mihi saepe ostendisti te esse facturum, tamen ignoscas velim huic festinationi meae* ('even if you have often made clear to me that you would do it, nevertheless please excuse this pushiness of mine').

[20] A convenient online translation (from the old Loeb edition) can be found at http://www.bartleby.com/9/3/10.html. See too Woodman (1988), 70–4.

too: the drama of his life is likely to appeal to readers. Cicero flatters Lucceius' literary talent, and suggests that if he writes this history, then both their reputations will be well served. If, for some unimaginable reason, Lucceius fails to grant Cicero's request, he will have to resort to writing his own account, something much less preferable, and unlikely to grant the authority which Cicero is looking for. The letter ends with Cicero reiterating the reason for writing: to remind Lucceius that he has already promised to do this, and that he should get a move on.

The main reason for including a discussion of the letter here is that in it Cicero displays a particularly cynical attitude towards historical fact. Almost the sole purpose of history seems to be the celebration of the individual, the immortalization of heroic deeds. It is a vision of the role of history which deliberately flouts the boundaries between genres. The poetry written by Archias is depicted in very similar hues in Cicero's defence of him: the immortalization which literature grants, the grandeur which clings as much to the author as to his subject matter.[21] Indeed, at one particularly emphatic moment, Cicero refers to one of Lucceius' own historical prefaces, a place, as we know from the practice of Sallust and Livy, where the role of history tended to be discussed:

itaque te plane etiam atque etiam rogo, ut et ornes ea vehementius etiam, quam fortasse sentis, et in eo leges historiae negligas gratiamque illam, de qua suavissime quodam in prooemio scripsisti, a qua te flecti non magis potuisse demonstras quam Herculem Xenophontium illum a Voluptate, eam, si me tibi vehementius commendabit, ne aspernere amorique nostro plusculum etiam, quam concedet veritas, largiare. quod si te adducemus, ut hoc suscipias, erit, ut mihi persuadeo, materies digna facultate et copia tua.

(*Ad familiares* 5. 12. 3)

And so I ask you, quite openly, to embellish these events rather more energetically than perhaps you feel. In so doing, neglect the laws of history and don't resist that expression of personal favour, about which you have written most elegantly in one of your prefaces, where you show that you could no more be swayed by it than Xenophon's Hercules could be by pleasure, if it commends me to you more powerfully; and indulge your affection for me even a little bit more than truth allows. I am convinced that

---

[21] *Pro Archia poeta* 12–24.

if I can persuade you to undertake this, the material will be worthy of your capabilities and stylistic resources.

This exhortation to distort the truth in Cicero's favour is part of the same confusion of genres that then finds the letter ending with a comparison between history and panegyric. There is very little room here for the sense of a historical account determined primarily by the demands of a true record of events. However, if we look more closely, Cicero does in fact give some space to that theme. His exhortation to Lucceius is not to ignore the truth, but to distort it slightly. Similarly, further on, Cicero does refer to the idea of a basic historical record, in rather disparaging terms:

etenim ordo ipse annalium mediocriter nos retinet quasi enumeratione fastorum: at viri saepe excellentis ancipites variique casus habent admirationem exspectationem, laetitiam molestiam, spem timorem; si vero exitu notabili concluduntur, expletur animus iucundissima lectionis voluptate.

(*Ad familiares* 5. 12. 5)

Indeed the list of the annals hardly holds our attention, just like the records on the state calendar. But the perilous and various fortunes of a man, often a great one, hold admiration and suspense, happiness and irritation, hope and fear. If they are finished by a glorious outcome, the soul is filled with the most pleasant enjoyment in reading.

This distinction between fully-fledged literary pleasure and the minimal historical record that lies behind it, the *Annals*, is an important thread in Western thinking about historiography, one that provides an essential continuity between ancient and modern thought. The description explored by White between history and chronicle for the mediaeval period is very similar, and Lucian, in his *On How to Write History*, lays out another version of the same contrast in his much fuller elaboration of the contrast between a plain, unadorned historical narrative and a richer historiographical tradition (of which, largely, he disapproves).[22] The continuity is important, given the apparent scorn for historical truth which Cicero betrays here: the tradition which Caesar represents in his minimal war diaries and the non-rhetorical historiography to which Antonius refers in *De oratore* 2 are ready alternatives to the more highly wrought

---

[22] White (1987), 1–20; on Lucian, Fox (2001).

products of the Greek historiographical tradition; but, as the letter makes clear, by the time Lucceius is writing (as opposed to the impoverished historical tradition in *De oratore*), the dramatic potential of historical writing was not something that required particular justification.[23]

Cicero asks Lucceius to apply his skills as a historian to the task of ensuring a glorious place for him in the historical record, but the request rests on appealing to Lucceius' sense of himself not so much as a man concerned to put down an account of the past as one capable of producing an effective and energetically written piece of historical writing. Taken in the context of Roman historiographical traditions, a striking, but neglected, aspect of this appeal is that Roman leaders normally had no qualms about writing such histories themselves. Cicero's decision to do so in verse was a remarkable break with tradition, and, so far as we know, so was his request to Lucceius. If taken as two complementary aspects of Cicero's ambition for posthumous glory during his lifetime, they act as clear repudiation of any naïve endorsement of the idea that the past can simply be rendered into a memorial in a neutral manner: elaboration of some kind, whether in poetic fantasy or in enhancing prose, will always be necessary to convey the meaning of history, and the significance of individuals. What Cicero repudiates, however, is not just a modern notion of ideal historical writing, something, of course, of which he can have had no notion: it is far more the traditional historical method of the Roman aristocracy, in which prominent statesmen take up the pen in retirement and write an account of their own achievements for posterity, as if they themselves were fit to function as their own narrators. Aemilius Scaurus, Sulla, Rutilius Rufus, and Lutatius Catulus had all written prose accounts of their consulships;[24] and in the annalistic tradition generally, it was the norm rather than the exception for historians to be ex-consuls writing accounts of history which included their own period spent in office. These two established standards for writing history about oneself are alluded to

---

[23] That *De legibus* reduplicates *De oratore*'s picture of Roman historiography as impoverished, in contrast to the image here of a full rhetorical context, confirms my sense that we need to think more carefully about the use of the fictionalized present in that work.

[24] Allen (1956), 140–1; Fantham (2004), 152–60.

in Cicero's presentation to Lucceius as different possibilities for structuring his account. Cicero's decision to request such an account from Lucceius, and simultaneously to dismiss the conventional self-promotion of the consular monograph, are a vital clue to understanding the political context of an approach to historical writing that consolidates the ironic quality found in this letter.

Cicero's exile must be seen as a determining trauma, both for himself and for his readers. The letters of utter demoralization from exile were a significant element in the character assassination of Drumann and Mommsen; yet here, within only a few years of his return, Cicero invites Lucceius to view the reversal of his fortune as the material for the most dramatic kind of narrative. At the same time, those events seem to have given Cicero the impetus to begin his endeavours to apply a theoretical framework to the workings of politics and history at Rome, with the ambiguous results that I have already looked at in *De oratore* and *De re publica*. There is some support in letters to Atticus from this period that those endeavours are at least in part a response to a sense of being out of step with the political processes at Rome: he realizes that the disaster that has befallen him is the result of his own mistakes, and the work not so much of his enemies, as of those who envy him.[25] Without constructing an elaborate psychological profile for Cicero, one plausible explanation of the ironic attitude towards history lies in the readjustment of his position with regard to the mainstream of politics at Rome which the exile and his return had necessitated. Having already written a poetic celebration of the consulship, it is unsurprising that Cicero would want to avoid writing again about his own place in history if he had already had cause to reflect that he had been mistaken in his own judgement of his historical success; and also unsurprising that he should be sceptical about the conventional mechanism for rendering the contribution of Rome's leaders into the historical record. Certainly, the efforts of Lucceius would be most welcome; but there is no need for Cicero to abandon the critical

---

[25] *scio nos nostris multis peccatis in hanc aerumnam incidisse* (*Ad Att.* 3. 14. 1) ('I know that I have fallen into this calamity through my many errors'); *nos non inimici sed invidi perdiderunt* (*Ad Att.* 3. 9. 2) ('it was not enemies but those who envy me who have destroyed me').

distance to the myths of his own historical significance which the exile had given him: this critical distance also applies, given his disdain for the notion of self-penned panegyric, to the conventional outlet for the literary efforts of an ex-consul. Cicero's literary path is a great deal more ambitious; in the same letter in which he writes to Atticus recommending him to read the *Letter to Lucceius*, he also refers to a piece of writing about Hortensius, something which may have mutated into a portion of *De oratore* or, more likely, simply lain dormant until the much later composition of *Brutus*.[26] The problematic relationship between Cicero's own position as an orator and the conventional narratives of Roman history is already evolving when Cicero writes to Lucceius; the letter suggests that Cicero was beginning to develop a consistent position, in which he could recognize the potential power of historical writing, but where his own engagement with it would require a greater degree of flexibility, as well as a healthy dose of irony.

There is little place, in this reading of the letter to Lucceius, for the notion that Cicero was entirely serious about his ambitions to be immortalized as a great historical figure. Such seriousness as there was is balanced by the clarity with which Cicero portrays himself as shameless and importuning, a clarity which, given the ambivalent quality of all Cicero's historical ventures, we can now more easily read as a sign of a healthy self-irony. The praise that Cicero himself gives to this letter when recommending Atticus to get hold of a copy is to be taken not as evidence of Cicero's overwhelming sense of his own importance but, rather, of the degree of wit with which the letter puts down on record his sense of the problematic nature of historical representation.[27] If nothing else, the very opening sentence of the letter is good support for this argument:

coram me tecum eadem haec agere saepe conantem deterruit pudor quidam paene subrusticus, quae nunc expromam absens audacius, epistula enim non erubescit.   (*Ad familiares* 5. 12. 1)

A certain almost primitive sense of shame has prevented me from dealing with these matters in your presence. Away from you I will now express them more boldly, for a letter does not blush.

---

[26] *Ad Att.* 4. 6. 3, with Shackleton Bailey (1965), *ad loc.*
[27] *Ad Att.* 4. 6. 4.

I find it hard to interpret these as the words of a man who lacks a sense of self-irony in respect of his literary memorial. Certainly, Cicero wanted Lucceius to grant him immortality, and the contrast between the effect of Lucceius' work and that of his own poetic accounts supports my sense that Cicero was quite aware of the ironic potential liberated by citing *De consulatu suo* in *De divinatione*. Self-praise is clearly not going to be as effective or convincing as inclusion in the monographs of others, where the problems of self-presentation are avoided; in poetry, Cicero would be expected to exaggerate. But the fact remains that Cicero was happy for this letter to be read, and presumably also had its eventual publication at the back of his mind; as a set-piece on the topic of his own inclusion in the historical record, Cicero does not shy clear of that irony concerning historical representation which characterizes his own engagements with it.

SALLUST (AND LIVY)

One aim of this chapter is to explore the idea that Cicero's ironic attitude towards historiography resonates with what we find in Latin historians, either through possible influence or because of a shared perspective: although detailed analyses of Sallust, Livy, and Tacitus would be inappropriate in this context, it is worth drawing out points of contact, even if some of my interpretations of these authors may, as a result of the necessary specificity of the context, seem to some readers a little unbalanced. In the works of Sallust, and most visibly in *Bellum Jugurthinum* (*The Jugurthine War*) we find a historical method which corresponds in part to Cicero's concerns. Sallust is determined to stress the close involvement of the past as a mechanism for understanding the present, and, like Cicero, he takes relatively recent historical periods to do this. Sallust's relationship to the traditions of aristocratic historiography also shares something with Cicero: at least in the two monographs that survive, Sallust is deliberately taking on the idea of exemplary history, and at least in part writing contrary to the expectations of the genre. Beyond the drama of reversal of fortune with happy ending that Cicero envisages for his own consulship, in *Bellum Jugurthinum* Sallust selects the moment in history when the authority of Rome's nobility is challenged, as he sees it, for the first time, and when, indeed, a train of events is set in motion which leads not to the restoration of some sense of the order of the *res publica* but, rather, the absolute devastation of Italy.[28] It is worth observing that Sallust, in contradiction to the entirely negative teleology he points to when introducing the topic of his monograph, in fact allows competing versions of history to exist side by side, in a manner that again suggests a similarity to Cicero: the corruption of the nobility is a constant theme, Jugurtha's threat to Rome being to a large extent based upon his ability to exert financial pressure on leading senators to overlook his misdeeds, and individual Roman leaders are all, at various points, incapacitated by their own greed or other character failings associated with the aristocracy.[29]

At the same time, Sallust opens his work with a preface on the utility of history which is underpinned by the appeal to the glories of past achievements which characterizes the aristocratic traditions of historiography. Something about his narrative is clearly aimed at producing this kind of inspiring effect. Sallust, however, is rather more explicit in dealing with this contradiction than is Cicero. The corruption of the nobility is a recent phenomenon, one which began when the sack of Carthage removed the discipline necessitated by a foreign enemy.[30] This decisive moment makes it possible for Sallust simultaneously to sustain an ideal vision of Rome's history as one in which individual merit and devotion to the *res publica* unified Senate and people under a common purpose, while at the same time characterizing both the present day and, in *Bellum Jugurthinum*, the climate of that period as ones where those ideals were visible in only momentary examples of individual virtue. Publius Scipio is used rather pointedly as a pivot at the opening of *Bellum Jugurthinum*, since he is both a notable example (along with Quintus Fabius Maximus Cunctator) of the veneration of the ancestral *imagines* and

---

[28] *quia tunc primum superbiae nobilitatis obviam itum est; quae contentio divina et humana cuncta permiscuit eoque vecordiae processit, ut studiis civilibus bellum atque vastitas Italiae finem faceret* (*Bell. Jug.* 1. 5).

[29] M. Aemilius Scaurus is a particular target for Sallust's disdain for the nobility (*Bell. Jug.* 15. 4); but other characters receive similar treatment: L. Calpurnius Bestia (ibid. 28. 5); Metellus (ibid. 64. 1).

[30] *Bell. Jug.* 41; cf. *Cat.* 10.

also the one who consolidates the talented young Jugurtha's position at Rome and in Numidia: Sallust even evokes the secret encounter at which Scipio is supposed to have warned Jugurtha to respect the collective quality of Rome's constitution and not to think of resorting to bribery. The disappointment both of Jugurtha's youthful promise and of Scipio's friendship and aspirations for him are the principal conditions for the dramatic tension which makes so compelling the account of the demise of both Rome and Jugurtha in the events that follow.[31] So Scipio represents an idealized version of aristocratic virtue, but is also the agent for the destruction of that ideal.

A fuller example of the same kind of technique of the embodiment of contradictory historical impulses can be found in Sallust's depiction of Marius: in particular, the decision to leave out of his narrative any direct reference to Marius' terrible final years.[32] Given that Sallust writes directly (in the passage cited above) about the devastation caused by the Social War as being the direct result of the conflict between the orders, and that he is at pains to stress the difficulties that Marius faced from the opposition of the nobility, the omission of any mention of the later Marius, tyrannical, crazed, and murderous, in effect makes the reader imagine this very personage, when reading about the upright honest character who actually appears in the monograph. We might recall the dead Scipio Aemilianus or Crassus who haunt the representations of them in *De re publica* and *De oratore*. The speech in which Marius directly reiterates Sallust's own contrast between the traditional reputation of the *nobiles* and the corruption of their actual incarnation (*Bell. Jug.* 85, esp. 36–44), and offers instead a form of inheritance in which his own upbringing and a respect for more traditional Roman values, particularly military ones, produces what can almost be read as an alternative version of nobility. But Marius' words have an ironic quality, both because of the double-edged veneration of the idea of nobility itself and because of the horror of Marius' later decline.

Sallust's technique in these different aspects revolves around a dialogic principle: the true value of aristocratic inheritance, as opposed to the corrupted, superficial adherence to the name of *nobilis*;

---

[31] *Imagines* (*Bell. Jug.* 1. 4. 5–8; Scipio and Jugurtha (ibid. 1. 5–1. 9).
[32] Levene (1992).

real aristocratic virtue instead of pretended; Rome as a city whose history was made glorious by traditions of ancestral reverence; Rome that has been corrupted by the domination of the aristocracy; Marius as a figure who challenges the authority of the nobility; Marius as one who, in a manner clearly foreshadowed by the entropic characterization of Jugurtha, ultimately cannot live up to the promise of virtue by which he rose to prominence. A less extreme example is Metellus, Marius' superior as the consul and commander of Roman forces in Numidia. Sallust represents him as resisting the trend to corruption that had enveloped his peers and colleagues, but reserves damning judgement of him for the moment when he is confronted with Marius' desire, acting on the basis of a prophecy, to become consul (*Bell. Jug.* 64). It is tempting to imagine that on such a detail as the prophecy, Sallust is exploiting the poetic vision of Marius elaborated in Cicero's poem.

By creating these competing visions of the course of Rome's history, and in particular of the role of individual vice and virtue in determining the evolving character of Rome from the fall of Carthage onwards, Sallust modifies the notion of exemplary historiography: he does not simply suggest that the past, instead of justifying and explaining the present, has, rather, led to inexorable decline; he clings to an ideal of primitive virtue, while simultaneously pointing out the discontinuities between tradition and the present day. The choice of the war with Jugurtha is particularly resonant, since it was a topic which fitted none of the conventional structures of historical narrative: Sallust needs to define a particularly elaborate relationship between past and present in order to explain why he is tackling it, as it is not particularly recent; nor does he have any particular connection with the events; nor does he allow the bounds of his account to extend beyond the narrow chronological focus to link it directly to the more dramatic events that both preceded it (the Gracchi) and followed it (the demise of Marius or the Social War). So it is a good choice for challenging not just conventions about the relationship between past and present, but also conventions about the choice of historical topics. The gains are that readers are invited into a more complex dialogue with the past, one which allows identification with the main moral concerns, while at the same time leaving doubt as to Sallust's purpose in drawing them out: it is by no means clear that any improvement in Rome's moral condition could result as a reading of this monograph. In this manner, Sallust can really be said to be working with an ironic framework that he applies in a number of different areas: historical continuity, exemplarity, the potential of the individual to have an effect. In all of these, the sense of decline and desperation about the present is balanced by an idealization of human potential that is not simply to be reconciled to it. The end result is a kind of scepticism about the clarity of the historian's aims, which, I would argue, has a clear similarity to Cicero's practice.

It would seem likely that Sallust himself was aware in some degree of Cicero's approach to history: his account of the Catilinarian conspiracy, like the *Bellum Jugurthinum*, defies conventional types of historical monograph; but in this case, the obvious generic paradigm is the account of his own consulship written by Cicero, the consular monograph which Cicero in fact avoided. Sallust in effect usurps both Cicero's right to control the narrative of the events of which he was the hero, and also, famously, relegates Cicero himself to the status of a minor character. Similar contentions about different kinds of nobility and different prerogatives for leadership from those found in *Bellum Jugurthinum* shape this work too, and given the enormous fuss which Cicero had made about the literary record of the conspiracy (not just *De consulatu suo*, but also *De temporibus suis* (three books thereof) and a Greek version), it seems probable that Sallust's reshaping was a deliberate attempt to demonstrate the shortcomings of Cicero's version of events, and also his attitude towards Caesar. In a similar manner, it is possible that in focusing the *Bellum Jugurthinum* on Marius, Sallust was reoccupying ground which Cicero had also already laid claim to, in his poem *Marius*, although the loss of more than a few lines makes it impossible to know how much divergence their celebrations of the man might demonstrate. At all events, Sallust's monographs, with their complex reshaping of conventional forms of historiography, their questioning of the relationship between political power and individual virtue, and their ironic form of exemplarity, all mirror concerns expressed in Cicero's writings.

The double-edged response which Sallust makes to the tradition of exemplary history is firmly negated by Livy: his preface is in fact a carefully shaped refutation of Sallust's analysis of decline, arguing that although Rome has without doubt declined, this decline has happened late, and that no other country was for so long so rich in good examples.[33] Livy's early narrative does contain occasional moments of ambiguity, both concerning the problems of historical evidence for early periods (under which I would also place the clearly ironic digression on Livy's conflict with Augustus on the evidence of the corselet of Cossus) and concerning the uniformity of Roman virtue. After all, exemplary history tells us what to avoid as well as what to imitate, and we cannot expect everything in Rome to be simply glorious: as the letter to Lucceius makes clear, reversal is central to the drama of history, and is central to its readability. But these features do not make Livy an ironic historian: his narrative depends upon the acceptance of the historian's omniscience, and upon the exhortation to the reader to learn directly from historical example, not, as in Cicero, Sallust, or Tacitus, constantly to see in history the problematic quality of contemporary institutions and values. He can be seen as the historian who takes on the expectations of Cicero's contemporaries, writing the history *de Romulo et Remo* which Cicero could not.[34]

   In the preface, Livy also expresses the expectation that readers will want to ignore the long improving narrative of the Early and Middle Republic, and will betray their historian's better instincts by turning to the more entertaining narratives of Rome's slide into the moral abyss. It is not clear how Livy's narrative of the Augustan era would have provided a route out of this abyss; but the foundations had clearly already been laid by the earlier narrative of national foundation which is Livy's response to the more narrowly focused traditions of consular historiography. There is certainly an ironic slant to Livy's acknowledgement of the attractions of a narrative of decline, but it is only a tiny moment where the competing possibilities of historiography, improvement or titillation, are allowed to emerge. The occlusion in Livy of most of the processes of historic irony found in Cicero and Sallust is further proof, I think, of the main reason why Cicero did not write that history: the parade of examples lacks the complexity

---

[33] H. Opperman (1967).
[34] *De leg.* 1. 3. 8; see above, pp. 142–3. Rawson (1972), 42–3.

and richness shown in Cicero's more focused meditations on the nature of Roman history and of the role of the individual within it. Livy has, in fundamental contrast to both Cicero and Sallust, a much less ambivalent attitude to the nature of the human contribution to Rome's development. His work shows little sign of the desperation that Cicero reveals concerning the true nature of Rome's statesmen and their ability to shape the course of events or the ultimate good of the *res publica*.

TACITUS: ON NOT BEING ABLE TO WRITE ANNALS

The ambiguity which is evident in Sallust is much more developed in Tacitus, whose highly ironic approach to historical representation has received fuller scholarly treatment. O'Gorman's recent study of Tacitus draws attention to the workings of his ironic dynamic: the reader of Tacitus, she argues, is obliged to confront incompatible representations of the same event or theme while accepting that the incompatibility cannot be resolved. History itself, she argues in her conclusion, depends upon conflict: between appearance and reality, and in Tacitus' case between liberty and the Principate, the institutions of the Republic, including annals as a historical form, and those of the Empire.[35] Such a description of Tacitus' practice immediately demonstrates the resemblance to Cicero. I would argue, indeed, that the evolution that can easily be detected in Tacitus' writings, between the relatively uncomplicated prose style and presentation of *Agricola* and the overtly convoluted *Annals*, actually represents a development of his sense of the ironic potential of historiography, and in particular, is a response to the demands of the different genres which these different works represent.[36] Although it is clear that the highly elaborate style of the *Annals* must have taken a great deal of effort to perfect, it is also true that in undertaking to write annals at all Tacitus locates himself in a place which is more overtly amenable to

---

[35] O'Gorman (2000), *passim,* but especially clear examples: 1–13, 39–49, 106–9, 176–83. Plass (1988) is O'Gorman's clearest precursor.
[36] On the historical vision of *Dialogus* see Heilmann (1989); Levene (2004).

irony than either the smaller monographs (*Agricola, Germania*) or the relatively self-contained *Histories*, and that, if we are looking for explanations of why Tacitus' work seems to acquire greater irony with time, we should look at the traditions of the genres. It is when he decides to take on the task of a comprehensive history of Rome, and in particular, gives it a context and structure taken from the most traditional form of historiography at Rome, that he must also confront the impossibility of that undertaking. The result is a style of writing which in every sentence seems to deny the possibility of clear expression, and a historical text which at points challenges the project of historical writing itself.

As with Sallust, there is only space here for a cursory exploration of these ideas; they become most explicit at two points in the *Annals*: in the opening chapters of the work (as Henderson explains in detail)[37], and in book 4, where Tacitus interrupts his account of the treason trials under Tiberius to compare his history to the glories of republican historiography. Then, returning to the main narrative, he recounts the case of Cremutius Cordus, the historian from the reign of Tiberius whose books were publicly burnt after his condemnation in CE 25 for positive representations of Brutus and Cassius.[38] The second section is more explicitly programmatic, in that it is a clear digression from the narrative frame and a direct moment of self-reflection. Tacitus addresses the reader, and draws a contrast between the glories of the history of early Rome, and those of the early Empire: *ingentia illi bella, expugnationes urbium, fusos captosque reges ... memorabant* ('they would record huge wars, sackings of cities, kings routed and captured'), as opposed to *nobis in arto et inglorius labor* ('my work is inglorious, confined').[39] He then justifies his account as a useful analysis of a constitutional phenomenon, which has the wider effect of educating readers in moral truths. To end the digression, he returns to his earlier theme, the contrast this time between the literary pleasure of the glorious deeds available in battle narrative and the unpleasant catalogue of cruelty and injustice. He then sidesteps into the strangest part of the passage, a defence of the exemplary quality of his own history against those whom it might offend:

---

[37] Henderson (1998), 257–80.   [38] Tacitus, *Annals*, 4. 32–5.
[39] Ibid. 4. 32.

tum quod antiquis scriptoribus rarus obtrectator, neque refert cuiusquam Punicas Romanasne acies laetius extuleris: at multorum qui Tiberio regente poenam vel infamias subiere posteri manent. utque familiae ipsae iam extinctae sint, reperies qui ob similitudinem morum aliena malefacta sibi obiectari putent. etiam gloria ac virtus infensos habet, ut nimis ex propinquo diversa arguens. (Tacitus, *Annals* 4. 33)

It was rare for writers of old to have a critic, and it bothers no one if you exalt the armies of Carthage or Rome. But the descendants remain of many who endured punishment or degradations when Tiberius was on the throne. But even if the families themselves have died out, you will find people who think, because of a similarity in manners, that other people's sins are being cast in their faces. Even glory and virtue have their enemies, by pointing out differences from too close up.

The logic of including this rebuttal of possible criticism is strange. Tacitus reiterates Livy's vision of the traditional exemplarity of history: moral models to imitate and avoid, so conventional as to make one wonder what any reader could possibly object to. But in fact what Tacitus is disputing is that this very exemplary function can possibly have a place in the writing of imperial history: people will be offended if they feel themselves criticized for the vices they share with Tacitus' characters; they will feel the taint of disgraced ancestors as if they themselves are disgraced; and not even the fact that almost the entire drift of Tacitus' account of the reign of Tiberius is that such disgrace is arbitrary and unjust, will enable them to admire their ancestors. Even examples of virtue can have their standard exemplary function inverted, since the wicked will feel that their own vices are being criticized by contrast. The only histories that an audience is likely to approve, in this analysis, are early history which is sufficiently disconnected from any present, or history which reveals a constitutional truth about monarchy. Hereby Tacitus not only curtails the exemplary function traditional to annals; he also casts away any hope that he himself will be admired. Obviously, there must be a heavy irony to this self-deprecation, but the pessimistic tone provides a neat bridge to the account of the trial of Cremutius Cordus.

It is left to readers to draw their own conclusions from the contrast between the defence speech of Cordus and the *apologia* for Tacitus' own historiography which precedes it. The most obvious connection is that both 'speeches' centre on the relationship between political liberty and historiography. Cordus begins his citation of outspoken predecessors tolerated by autocrats with Livy, then moves on to other historians, statesmen (Cicero, Antony, Caesar, Brutus), and poets (Bibaculus and Catullus), whose literary freedom provoked no repression. Cordus pleads as his final defence precisely the same disconnection from the present which Tacitus has just evoked: Cassius and Brutus are not at Philippi; I am not encouraging civil war.[40] But the futility of this defence replicates Tacitus' own failure to find a clear position on the same topic. There is one consolation for the historian, however, and again Cordus and Tacitus share it: authority cannot dampen the work of the imagination; in fact, it will increase its power; memory will persist in spite of tyranny.

quo magis socordiam eorum inridere libet qui praesenti potentia credunt extingui posse etiam sequentis aevi memoriam. nam contra punitis ingeniis gliscit auctoritas, neque aliud externi reges aut qui eadem saevitia usi sunt nisi dedecus sibi atque illis gloriam peperere.   (Tacitus, *Annals* 4. 35)

All the more reason to deride the apathy of those who think that the power of the present is able to extinguish the memory of a later age. On the contrary, the authority of condemned geniuses thrives, and neither foreign kings nor those who rely on the same brutality bring forth anything but disgrace to themselves, and glory to them.

The undertaking to write imperial history in a republican form is justified in this paradox: the suppression of creative work will, like Cremutius' own works, result in a persistence of some vestige of creative freedom. Foreign monarchy represents the norm for this kind of repressive regime, so Tacitus neatly avoids any reference to intolerance as a feature of imperial government as such, just as Cremutius had praised the lack of censorship under Caesar and Augustus. The historian himself is the measure of the fairness of the regime in which he is living, but Tacitus still does not hold out much explicit hope for the pleasure of readers. This must, of course, given the enormous impact of his style, in turn be interpreted as ironic; there must also be pleasure to be gained from irony, of course, as Tacitus is no doubt pointing out in one of his more cynical moments, describing the invisibility of the future emperor Claudius:

---

[40] Tacitus likewise records the punishment meted out by Nero for veneration of an ancestral *imago* of Cassius (*Annals* 16. 7).

mihi quanto plura recentium seu veterum revolvo tanto magis ludibria rerum mortalium cunctis in negotiis obversantur.   (Tacitus, *Annals* 3. 18)

The greater my knowledge of recent or past history, the more ridiculous absurdities are observed in all human affairs.

The investigation of the historian is the uncovering of ever greater degrees of absurdity, and *ludibria* are certainly the kind of thing to evoke a laugh, even if that amusement is rather different from the elevated kind of literary pleasure that Cicero envisages in the *Letter to Lucceius*.[41]

Tacitus' irony may not, after all, share much with Cicero's when examined more fully, and likewise, there is little to be gained from an understanding of Cicero's anxieties about the difficulties of working with Roman historiographical traditions from an author for whom those traditions had a radically different character. However, as is clear from Tacitus' most direct homage to Cicero, his *Dialogue on Orators*, the problems of fixing ideas in history and locating rhetoric at Rome were such that, in spite of finding different solutions, the irony of Cicero's own solutions was not lost on Tacitus.[42] There is potential for more work in this area; but cursory though my treatment of later historians has been, I hope that it has fulfilled its task of making claims for the irony of Cicero's approach to historical representation seem less extravagant. In the following chapter, I shall be looking at how, in the eighteenth-century reception of Cicero, we can observe a less grim view of the potential of the ironic approach to Rome, and in the process discover more about the processes through which the evident ironies in Cicero's practice would come to seem improbable—in the main by virtue of more general changes in the expectations of philosophical and educational writing.

---

[41] Plass (1988) makes Tacitus' wit the centre of his discussion.
[42] Levene (2004), 187–95.

10

Cicero from Enlightenment to Idealism

It is the aim of this chapter to explore in more detail a theme begun in Chapter 3: the rupture in the understanding of Cicero that took place during the eighteenth century. The effect of this rupture was to encourage a mistrust of Cicero's philosophical achievement, to foster the view of him as a mere philosophical compiler, and, on that basis, to produce a tradition of reading which was uninterested in the more sophisticated exploitation of irony which I have been examining. Much of this chapter will be devoted to one particularly interesting text: a little-known treatise on Cicero, written in Latin by the radical philosopher John Toland (1670–1722). Toland's booklet gives a fascinating insight into Cicero's significance at a time when the understanding of the relationship between rhetoric, learning, and politics was much closer to Cicero's own than to ours.

Born in Ireland, Toland achieved considerable notoriety on account of his first two publications. *Christianity not Mysterious* (1696) caused him to be declared a heretic in Ireland and his book to be publicly burnt; his *Life of Milton* (1698) also gave rise to considerable controversy. Clearly something of a maverick, his writings, which are mostly in the form of pamphlets or short books written with varying degrees of radical zeal, were taken seriously by several more canonical philosophers, including Leibniz and Berkeley, although much of his influence was among those who needed to articulate theological defences against his radicalism rather than actually accepting his ideas.[1] Although his

---

[1] On Toland see Champion (2003), and for a succinct synthesis, Daniel (2004); earlier: Heinemann (1945); Gawlick (1963); Sullivan (1982); on his atheism, Berman (1992). This prolific polymath's main interest lay in revealing true religion beneath its trappings, and he wrote a number of angrily contested treatises on various aspects of what became a form of pantheism, culminating in *Pantheisticon* (1720). A diplomat

treatise on Cicero could not be regarded as central to his output, it was nevertheless thought worthy to be included in the posthumous edition of a selection of his writings, and it does reveal a great deal about how Cicero could be taken as a model for a form of educated citizenship at a time when ideas about the state, the citizen, and, in particular, religion were a matter of great contention. Toland found in Cicero a paradigm for the politically engaged philosopher, perceiving a unity between his philosophical approach, his political ideals, and his rhetorical mastery that is barely represented within modern historical analyses. The title of the work, *Cicero Illustratus*, is evocative: Toland will shed new light on Cicero and, in the process, uncover a figure who fits into the wider ambitions of the Enlightenment: education, discursive skill, and the growth of critical understanding over received opinion and superstition. Cicero is both being brought into the light and, in the process, having his own contribution to the Enlightenment drawn out.

The eighteenth century, at the start of which stands Toland, is generally seen as the period in which the continuity with the Classical world which characterized the rediscoveries of the Renaissance was broken, and in which the development began of the specialist disciplines which would put an end to the ideal of the Universal Man. The public figure and the artistic genius rapidly became polar opposites, and although the destiny of the well educated and high-born was still idealized as dedication to public life, in practice, the life of the mind started to acquire a more ambivalent relationship to the realm of public service and political power. This demarcation of artistic and political had a particular significance for an understanding of the role of rhetoric, and essentially led to a situation which is still visible today in some of the scholarship on rhetoric: an insistence on rhetoric as a skill associated above all with the formal qualities of a speech, with the analysis of style as a means to produce a particular effect, and as a source of technique that is in essence politically and ideologically neutral.[2] The most authoritative statement

as well as a man of letters, among his more interesting works for the Classicist are *Adeisidaemon* (1709), in which he finds in Livy support for his own view of religion (modern edition: Sabetti (1984)), and *Hypatia* (1720), a life of the philosopher configured as a martyr to the excesses of the early church, specifically St Cyril. He also wrote a poem in praise of Rhetoric, *Clito* (1700), and published translations of a number of letters of Pliny, as well as a short book on Roman education, containing some of the letters of Theano (repr. in Toland (1726), ii. 1–27).

[2] See e.g. Gadamer (1990), 48–87; White (1987), 58–75; Eagleton (1990), 31–119. Mergenthaler (2000) explores the fascinating idea that fortunes of the Commedia

of such a vision of rhetoric is Vickers's *In Defence of Rhetoric* (1988), a history of anti-rhetorical polemic from Plato onwards which portrays that polemic as based on a misunderstanding of a fundamentally innocent repertoire of techniques that made up the art of rhetoric. Vickers's aim is to minimize what those very critics viewed as the dangerous and destabilizing potential of rhetoric; but, by taking a defensive attitude, he in effect makes the polarity between rhetoric as dangerous and rhetoric as harmless into something historically constant. For most of its history, this polarity was not the norm; but because of his pivotal role in the establishment of stylistic standards and as a model of a rhetorically active statesman, Cicero was certainly a casualty of the polarization once it became more firmly established. The political vacillation seems of a piece with the ability to take up employment as an advocate for contradictory causes; the rhetorical aspects of the philosophy only contribute to a reading of it which neglects Cicero's contribution as one of style rather than substance, and, in the realm of his philosophical works, allows the Hellenistic philosophers on whom he draws to take greater prominence than the ideological dramas that his works articulate. Toland's essay represents in detail how a different view of rhetoric enables a closer adherence to the way in which Cicero represents it. Throughout his treatise, Toland uses Cicero's own words, often literally his own rhetoric in the form of extracts from speeches, to refute claims that Cicero was too much of a lawyer to be a good model for citizenship. Those claims are surprisingly clearly conceived, given the general view that it was not until the nineteenth century that Cicero's reputation really began to suffer under such charges. Toland is able to market Cicero on the basis that he shares with him a sense of rhetoric's purpose and identity.

The polarized attitude to rhetoric, in which it is seen as either a threat to social stability, representing a tricky relativism, or a correspondingly harmless discourse concerned solely with aesthetics, is clearly one that develops in the eighteenth century. A useful figure for gauging this development is Gianbattista Vico, a staunch defender of rhetoric, and a younger contemporary of Toland. Vico understood

dell'Arte paralleled those of Cicero: like him, it was a casualty of the Kantian separation of *ingenium* from *imitatio*.

how much the rise of the natural sciences threatened to undermine rhetoric's position; in one of his earlier publications, *De nostri
temporis studiorum ratione* (1709) he points out the utility of rhetoric
compared to the study of the natural sciences, and promotes the study of
rhetoric as the means to produce a kind of rhetorically accomplished
statesman that would be recognizable to Cicero. Rhetoric is useful public
discourse, in contrast to the abstract transcendence of Descartes' scientific truths. Toland's own defence of rhetoric, written originally as a
poem intended for private circulation only, is a lot more subversive
than Vico's, and I will discuss it briefly below. For both Toland and
Vico, however, there was no doubt that it was in rhetoric that the
reforming energies of the Enlightenment should be channelled, and
that it was still the route to a well-organized community.

Yet, we need to be cautious about treating the eighteenth century as
a monolithic cultural entity, and about concrete periodization and
assumptions of linear progress. Rhetoric is a particularly clear case for
such caution, since there were during that period a range of different
cultural impulses at work. On the one hand, by the end of the
eighteenth century, the reputation of rhetoric was generally low.[3]
Philosophy too had taken a direction which was bound to be inimical
to Cicero.[4] But on the other hand, there were a number of significant
figures whose interest in the continuation of the Classical tradition of
rhetoric was motivated not by a conservative form of neo-scholasti-
cism, but rather by the ambition to harness rhetoric to the humanistic
ideals of the Enlightenment (ideals which were, in more mainstream
thinkers, associated with the progress of the natural sciences and the
demise of Classicism). Vico and Fichte are good examples.[5] And in
spite of the attacks of the great philosophers (principally Kant and
Hegel), rhetoric remained, throughout the eighteenth century at least,
the dominant medium for integrating philosophical ideas and political practice; but of course, in spite of their disavowal of rhetoric,
those philosophers were themselves so immersed in their Classical
training that in their development of anti-rhetorical categories, they
could themselves not be immune to those categories.[6]

---

[3] Fuhrmann (1983).   [4] See above, pp. 57–62.
[5] On Fichte, see Bezzola (1993), 101–13. On Vico, e.g. Mooney (1985); Amodeo
(2005).
[6] For this alternative history of rhetoric in the eighteenth century, see Dyck and
Sandstete (1996), pp. xv–xxiv, and more briefly, J. Dyck (1991); Meyer (1998), 19–22.

The complex relationship between Classical ways of thinking and the idealism that later came to dominate philosophy, and to have such a profound effect upon the development of academic disciplines, is easily overlaid by a linear narrative of intellectual history, in which Classical ways of thinking gradually recede and the development of the modern academic disciplines casts them as a manifestation of an inexorable progress.[7] This in outline, is the story of the reception of Cicero which I presented in Chapter 2, and it is certainly helpful in explaining the changing fortunes of Cicero. The problem of the linear, progressive narrative, however, is that it suggests that we are to a large extent predetermined to take up the position defined for us by the history of our disciplines and the traditions of reading that they generate. The methodological advances in the study of Classics and Ancient History do not bear out this claim. My aim in this chapter, therefore, is to substitute a detailed discussion of this one text for the generalizing history of reception, and by examining Toland's reading of Cicero, show both what has changed in terms of understanding of Cicero since then, and also which of Toland's insights are worth closer consideration or revival. Whether one interprets Toland's enthusiasm for Cicero as a sign of a moribund world-view, or whether he is seen as just one of a number of voices that do not harmonize with a grand narrative of the progress of science over humanism is a point that does not require resolution. What is interesting about Toland's work is the details of his arguments: what he sees as important about Cicero and, in particular, what he saw, at the start of the eighteenth century, as the dangers that had already beset Cicero's reputation. In his reading of Cicero, we are able to observe a more direct approach to Cicero's own aims, which can serve as a model for the attempt to disentangle our own reception of Cicero from subsequent trends that have contained the excitement of his thought and, in particular, the potentially liberating spirit of his scepticism.

Because it is a dangerous temptation to seek a precedent for my own way of reading Cicero in Toland's work, I will rather suggest that, as a moment in the reception of Cicero, Toland can show us the difficulties that our own habits of reading can cause. I shall argue that

---

[7] Against this progressive view of the history of historiography, see Phillips (1996).

Toland's approach represents a way of dealing with Cicero that has closer contact with Cicero's own sense of the purpose of his philosophical writings; further, Toland's negotiation of the relationship between philosophy and history is much closer to Cicero's. But it is not just that Toland's treatise puts across a more faithful version of Cicero; such a conclusion would put too much weight on reading the one text in isolation. Toland cannot necessarily be taken as typical of his age: his other writings were regarded by many at the time as thoroughly scandalous, and he was a controversial figure, to say the least. But with these caveats, Toland can help us to think about reception as a dynamic process: not by providing an interpretation which responds to our own standards of what a critical evaluation should be, but rather, by raising awareness of the impediments to understanding which later traditions of reading put in our way. In part, I am hoping here to provide a way of thinking about reception that moves beyond a model in which 'influence' is perceived as something that operates between two texts. Toland is interesting because he explicitly appreciates an open-ended Cicero, and his aim is to facilitate the encounter between Cicero's readers and his works. Certainly, Toland's ideas about Cicero do emerge in the treatise, but they are nothing like as prominent as the method of approaching Cicero that his arguments imply: *Cicero Illustratus* is about how to represent Cicero so that he can be better read. So reception can certainly tell us about Cicero's place at the start of the eighteenth century.[8] But I would argue that it is more helpful to work against such a fixed idea of 'what Cicero meant' at any particular moment, and concentrate instead upon what the presentation of Cicero and how to read him shows us about our own methods and understanding. Toland captures in useful detail the effect of Cicero at a point in history before the development of professional academic categories made an approach to him more problematic. Surprisingly, however, we can already observe in Toland's rabid polemic against the practices of scholarship and historical research the same ideas which, in more concrete form, damaged Cicero's reputation in the following centuries. A look at this episode in Cicero's *Wirkungsgeschichte* grants a perspective on our own way of approaching

---

[8] Gawlick (1963); on Academic scepticism in this period, Maia Neto (1997).

Cicero, and shows how admiration for Cicero as a historical character can coexist with an appreciation of his Academic philosophical method, and with a particular way of reading his works.[9]

LIGHT ON CICERO

Toland's treatise was first published in 1712. Addressed to Baron von Hohendorf, the field marshal of Eugene of Savoy, it is in fact a prospectus aiming to raise funds for a planned edition of Cicero's complete works, including various aids to reading such as *indices*, introductory essays, and explanatory notes. We should not underestimate the novelty of such an idea: the Dauphin edition of Latin texts had recently appeared in France, and probably inspired Toland's sense of what was possible in terms of high-quality book production and the notion of what a complete edition should include.[10] But the idea of a standard edition of one author was still unusual, and for Cicero did not occur until Johann Caspar von Orelli brought one out in the early nineteenth century. Toland abandoned his project after distributing the prospectus (which is a nicely produced volume) and preparing himself to receive subscriptions to pay for its production: his own maintenance, presumably, as well as the printing costs. The treatise, like Toland himself, is very much a product of the Enlightenment. Toland's main claim to fame was as the coiner of

---

[9] For those unfamiliar with the term, *Wirkungsgeschichte* was the concept elaborated by Gadamer from which the rather more manageable idea of *Rezeption* was derived: Gadamer (1990), 305–12. For the current situation: Martindale and Thomas (2006). Unhelpfully rendered as 'effective history' by Gadamer's English translators, what it actually refers to is the history of the effect/influence (*Wirkung*) of a particular text/author/motif upon later authors. Recent changes in English idiomatic uses of the word *work* make this easier to convey: 'Does this *work* for you?' (e.g. in discussing a painting, piece of music, or clothing) is quite close to the connotations with which Gadamer defines the term. So a history of how authors or texts have *worked* is *Wirkungsgeschichte*. It is a way of thinking about reception that lays greater emphasis upon charting the development in understanding of the original than upon interpreting particular instances of that impact. See too Ankersmit (1994), 22–4.

[10] That edition was itself guided by another avowed sceptic, Huet: Popkin (2003), 277–82.

the term *deist*, and he was internationally known as an enthusiastic promulgator of an anticlerical, philosophical kind of religion, divested of all traces of superstition. His readership was likewise part of an international circle of erudite men (and women) of action, interested in such radical ideas, and the prospectus, printed at Toland's own expense, was conceived for private distribution to friends and connections, rather than to be sold.[11] Much about his work seems quaint and very specific to his time. But he is valuable for the light he sheds upon the place of the Classical world in the intellectual life of that time, and for the presentation of scholarship in a period before the study of the Classical world had developed that distinct branch of criticism that later became Ancient History.[12] Toland's view of Cicero is, to modern eyes, rather uncritical: he uses Cicero's own writings as a good source for evaluating Cicero's achievement, rather than regarding them, as most historians since Drumann have done to some extent, as biased, bad evidence on which to judge Cicero.[13]

However, this method itself requires closer scrutiny, especially as it has a bearing on the vexed question of authorial intention and irony.

---

[11] Full title: J. Toland, *Cicero Illustratus, Dissertatio Philologico-Critica: sive Consilium de toto edendo Cicerone, alia plane methodo quam hactenus unquam factum* (London: John Humfreys, 1712), repr. in Toland (1726), from which, more widely accessible edition, I quote. See Champion (2003), 50, for a brief account of the circumstances of publication, and pp. 236–8 for the visit to London of Eugene and Hohendorf which forms the immediate context for the work, and which Toland himself briefly describes: (1726), ii. 235–6. Champion slightly misleadingly describes the dedication as a joint one; the dedicatee (on the title-page) is the Baron, and he is addressed regularly throughout the dialogue. His boss, Eugene of Savoy, named as such on the title-page, appears in a postscript to the original edition, ostensibly included as a page-filler: *ne sequens vacaret pagella* ('to fill the following page'): Toland (1712), 74. The work was reprinted without the postscript dedication in the posthumous collection of Toland's *miscellanea*, brought out by his friend and biographer P. Desmaizeaux, who also wrote a biography of the encyclopaedist Bayle, as well as publishing his own smaller dictionary of Classical antiquarian and philological material (Desmaizeaux 1740). Desmaizeaux reports that the original text was now scarce, as it had not been intended for a wide public, only for friends and subscribers: Tolland (1726), p. lxvii. In fact, Toland paid for the printing of 300 copies of the pamphlet, and collected as well 500 receipts, presumably for possible subscriptions; see *Letters and Papers of John Toland,* BL Add. MSS 4295, fol. 24.

[12] Momigliano (1987).

[13] Fuhrmann (2000), 104–7, argues that Drumann had a forerunner in Christoph Martin Wieland, who explicitly criticized this methodology, as practised by Middleton in his popular *Life of Cicero* (1741), in his edition of Cicero's letters.

It may be bad historical practice to take as evidence for Cicero's own historical significance the material that he himself gathers together, with his eye fixed firmly on his reputation; but it is, nevertheless, an inevitable part of all readings of Cicero: the condemnatory readings of Drumann and Mommsen just as much as of those who have subsequently rehabilitated him. What distinguishes the work of the nineteenth-century scholars is the insistence upon the ability to resist the appeal of Cicero's own writings, and find a 'critical method' to look beyond or behind them for the true facts of Cicero's political career, and his place in the late Republic. Modern accounts of Cicero are in this respect not very different from those of the pioneers of academic ancient history. The account of Dugan (2005), for example, takes as its central idea to reveal the pervasive rhetorical strategy by which Cicero convinces us of his centrality in the development of oratory at Rome; analyses of Cicero's speeches routinely follow a congruent approach, demonstrating the irresistible quality of Cicero's rhetoric and the great skill with which he occludes any possible contrary interpretations of events.[14] Modern scholarship can, with reasonable accuracy, be characterized by its desire to resist Cicero's rhetoric, and to fix upon the strength of method as a way of uncovering what Cicero was *really* about: attempting with enormous energy to persuade his readers that he was a person of far greater power and significance than he actually was.

By contrast, Toland uses Cicero's own accounts of his rhetorical, philosophical, and political methods to encourage his readers to find inspiration in his life and writings. His principal point of polemic is with the scholars who are sure that they know better what Cicero ought to have done, or what he ought to have written. Attacks on Cicero's biographers and editors make up a large part of the treatise, largely, of course, because in advertising the need for a new edition, Toland has a clear interest in pointing out the failures in the presentation of Cicero that result from the existing scholarship. But aside from its colourful Latin, his polemic is characterized by a drive to allow Cicero to emerge with his own voice from the obstacles of scholarship. It is the failure of the scholars to distinguish between their own agendas and the need for readers to be able to engage with

---

[14] Dugan (2005); speeches: May (1988); Vasaly (1993).

Cicero that inspires Toland's ire. Most interestingly, Toland ends by considering that engagement to be best encapsulated in terms of prose style, and in the process makes a connection between rhetoric and the interpretation of Cicero from which we have much to learn. In the realm of style, questions about Cicero's ideological consistency or political vacillation recede. He presents a reading of Cicero in terms of Cicero's effect, and focused on the kind of discourse which a thorough grounding in Cicero can produce. Toland is not determined to see beyond Cicero's rhetoric; and that is partly because he also focuses upon the sceptical exploitation of that rhetoric in his philosophy. Toland's expectations of both rhetoric and philosophy are rather different from those that developed later. The advantage of giving this one text close examination is therefore to move beyond the all-or-nothing approach to rhetoric and the pervasive tradition of making a moral or historical judgement about Cicero on the back of it.

'THE STYLE IS THE MAN': READING, BIOGRAPHY, AND RHETORIC

Much of *Cicero Illustratus* is taken up with arguments as to why a new edition of Cicero is desirable, and the work is a mixture of energetic criticism of the shortcomings of existing editions, the received opinion about Cicero promulgated in existing scholarship, and the kinds of error into which earlier readers of Cicero, presented in such a light, are likely to fall. As such, of course, the work is at first sight a gift to those interested in Cicero reception, since it deals head-on with that very topic. It is evident that Toland has in mind, as principal financial sponsor of his edition, Eugene of Savoy: as well as Europe's most famous military commander at the time, also one of its richest men, and possessor of an enormous library. The addressee of the pamphlet is Baron Georg Wilhelm von Hohendorf, Eugene's field marshal, and himself a bibliophile; their collections later formed an important part of the Austrian National Library. Toland vividly eulogizes Eugene's love of the arts in the opening section of the work, which is dedicated to the celebration of his potential sponsors.[15] He has already discussed his plans for this edition with Eugene, and the prospectus is aimed at providing Hohendorf with an account of his views on Cicero, as well as on what he calls 'certain notorious Aristarchus' (*quidam maleferiati Aristarchi*); Aristarchus was a byword for excessive critical zeal, presumably because of his radical attitude to the text of Homer.[16] This is the first broaching of a theme which dominates the treatise: the misrepresentation of Cicero by scholarship, a process which Toland explores with some care, and which expresses the radicalism in Toland's approach to Cicero.

First of all, he points out the enormous debt to antiquity of the culture of his times (language, laws, customs, proverbs), partly as a demonstration of the importance of a knowledge of antiquity, but then to point out that this knowledge need not in fact be derived from close study of it. Cicero, of course, is the pinnacle of this Classical survival, surpassing even the Greeks (and indeed the whole of humanity) in his achievements in passing down philosophical history and doctrine, in political thought, and in developing rhetoric.[17] But in spite of the fact that his name is so well known, Cicero is in fact enormously misunderstood. Toland attacks, in colourful language, two classes of people who have had a determining effect on the wider reception of Cicero (Toland uses *acceptus* to describe reception): (1) the would-be grammarians, who, seeing Cicero in their own image, and taking as their ideal the Renaissance scholar Filelfo,[18] shrink from Cicero as if he were nothing but a

---

[15] *Cicero Illustratus*, ch. 2.

[16] See *OED*[2] under Aristarchus, and likewise, *Zedlers Universal Lexicon* (1733), in which the usage is attested from Cicero and Horace; although as Shackleton Bailey (1965), on *Ad Att.* 1. 14. 3, points out, he did not ascribe this connotation of harshness for Cicero himself. In a volume that appeared in the same year as *Cicero Illustratus*, Joshua Barnes, Regius Professor of Greek at Cambridge, published a satirical attack on Bentley's edition of Horace entitled *Aristarchus Ampullans* ('Bombastic Aristarchus'), appealing on its title-page to Ovid, *Ex Ponto* 3. 9. [Barnes] (1712) makes a similar distinction to Toland between the value of true criticism and the self-seeking excesses of this Aristarchus.

[17] *Cicero Illustratus*, ch. 4.

[18] On Filelfo (1398–1481), see Robin (1991). Toland's scorn for Filelfo is hard to explain; Filelfo's attitude to Cicero seems to be the typically respectful one of his age, but as Diana Robin has suggested to me, perhaps for Toland, Filelfo was simply an archetype of the dusty scholar.

trivialem ludimagistrum or *petulantem paedagogum* ('frivolous pri-
mary-school teacher' or 'whingeing schoolmaster' convey something
of Toland's vivid style); (2) the orators: they are worthless and shady
declaimers, who likewise use all their wiles to prove the case that
Cicero is no better than they, with the result that he comes across to
those who have no real experience of him as verbose, immoral,
corrupt, and litigious. The result is that there is no petty public
official who does not fancy himself a new Cicero.[19]

Toland's argument here seems at first sight like an exaggerated
polemic: but in fact the process he describes is an important part of
Cicero's legacy, with significant resonances with our own engagement
with him. Cicero has acted as a figure who allows easy identification,
and this is an identification predicated upon a sense of Cicero's
status, but that does not bring with it any particular degree of precision
in understanding. Indeed, even professional scholars have been too
keen to identify Cicero with themselves, and this has had the effect of
producing a neglect of his actual historical achievements and an over-
familiarity. What the scholastic misappropriation of Cicero as a pedant
and the social appropriation of Cicero as a jumped-up petty magistrate
have in common is that both combine an underestimate of Cicero's
real achievements with a willingness to judge him by their own image.
This is a process which can clearly be seen in later assessments of
Cicero's historical significance, as even the editor of Drumann's Dictionary was to observe, regarding the lack of perspective in that
account.[20] In the nineteenth century, it was the negative judgement
of his political will and ability to adopt different positions and, more
recently, the suggestion that Cicero overstates the case for his own
intellectual excellence. The remedy which Toland proposes is simple:
better access to Cicero's own writings.

After elaborating in more detail Cicero's achievements, Toland
returns again to the reasons why Cicero is so neglected: this time,

---

[19] *Cicero Illustratus*, ch. 5. The model of education which Toland envisages is
essentially the same as the one that evolved in the late Middle Ages: *ludi magister*,
the elementary schooling, *grammaticus*, to acquire a knowledge of Latin grammar
and some literary study; and the final stage based on proper training in rhetoric,
aimed at the ability to improvise public speeches. See Kennedy (1999), 198–24; Witt
(2002), 7–12.

[20] Drumann (1929), pp. x–xi.

the use of Cicero in the schoolroom. The physical abuse of pupils by their teachers is obviously a deterrent, but Toland is more precise in targeting educational practice: his works are used as a linguistic resource, read as a verbal repository, devoid of all meaning and context.[21] Cicero is looked on not for his ideas, but only as a stylistic model. The speeches are treated as though they are comparable to contemporary exercises in declamation, and the letters as though they were occasional pieces written by gentlemen of leisure on themes that have no direct relationship with the political concerns of the time. Those taught in this manner grow up into public figures, most of whom thus, unlike Toland's addressees, have no real acquaintance with Cicero, and Toland then gives an outline of the significance of Cicero's political career. Relying largely on references to the *Pro Sestio*, he outlines the achievements of the consulship and the return from exile; and against those who accuse Cicero of pliability or timidity (*qui nimiam in eo lenitatem aut timiditatem culpabant*) he cites a passage of self-defence from the *Pro Plancio*.[22] After elaborating a little more on this theme, Toland turns directly to the purpose of the new edition: to make Cicero more easily available to those for whom his works were written—men of action, politicians, and judges, who will appreciate the power of literature. A quotation from *Pro Archia*, stressing its relevance to the Baron as a man familiar with the immortalizing power of literature, rounds off this introductory justification of the project, and Toland then begins to lay out the aspects of the edition in detail, from the quality of the paper, to the presentation of the text (punctuation, orthography, textual variants), to the supplementary aids to reading: a reprint of Fabrizio's life of Cicero, Toland's own historico critical dissertation, introductory essays, relevant fragments, and *spuria*.

A constant feature of Toland's method is to deduce Cicero's character from his own writings. This, of course, is not exceptional; it is a fundamental methodological problem when dealing with Cicero, and the one which Mommsen, in his quest to develop a more scientific approach to the Roman world, would overcome by adopting a firm critical standpoint. But what is striking about Toland is that he seems to have in mind a firm distinction between the

---

[21] *Cicero Illustratus*, ch. 7.   [22] Ibid. ch. 8.

prejudices which critics have with regard to Cicero and the power of Cicero's own words to refute them. This looks at first sight like an absence of critical perspective on his part; but it can be seen from another angle, as a particular view of the relationship between the individual and his written record. Toland treats Cicero's works as though they are the record of the man himself; in the same manner, Toland's first biographer, putting together a posthumous rehabilitation of him shortly after his death, opens his account by expressing his own aspiration that he will be able to give 'a faithful Account of the Man from *his own Works*'.[23] Toland was also himself a biographer, having achieved public notoriety in an early publication, his biography of Milton. The ensuing controversy was so intense that it then required a further written defence both of his practice as a biographer and of his characterization of Milton and the Commonwealth.[24] Toland's faith in the relationship between man and text is much more a sign of the centrality of published texts in the political processes of his era than it is of Cicero's, and whatever continuity there may be in terms of Toland's understanding of Cicero's rhetoric needs to be modified by an awareness of the radical difference that the distribution of printed material makes to those assumptions.[25]

Toland tackles the problems of judging Cicero's historical significance again when he gives more detail about his planned historical dissertation in chapter 14. As well as the same accusations of timidity, he discusses Cicero's political vacillation and tendency to self-praise; he will deal with these, and other similar topics, by providing summaries of the views of Cicero's biographers and critics, and examining Cicero's writings for the light that they shed on them. The topic of

---

[23] Curll (1722), 1–2. He then refers to a recent biographer of Bishop Bull for the doctrine that the biographer must be to some extent 'animated ... with a *Portion* of that *Genius* which made the *Person* ... *famous in his Generation*'. But in this case, Toland's qualities emerge so clearly from his writings that such personal grandeur is less necessary. At the end of a seventeen-line posthumous epitaph on Toland, the author instructs his readers: 'If you would know more of him search his writings, and in the Latin version of the same, *Cetera ex scriptis pete*': (BL Add. MS 4295, fols. 76 and 77).

[24] Toland (1699). Toland's biographer mentions a further controversy of some relevance: that in his life of Socrates he was thought (wrongly) to have compared the philosopher to Jesus Christ: Curll (1722), 22. Reproduction of extracts from Toland's published writings and unpublished letters makes up the bulk of the biography.

[25] Raven (1998); O'Brien (2001); Champion (2003), 39–44.

excessive self-praise, which Toland describes as almost a universal feature of the literature on Cicero, is illustrated by him by brief references to the *Letter to Lucceius*, by the desire for the history by Archias, and by the comment that Brutus criticized his constant references to the Nones of December.[26] Toland particularly admires the manner in which Cicero's own writings can repudiate these accusations, drawing attention to the accusations of his opponents and countering them with expressions of his patriotic dedication. He concludes this section with an extract from *De domo sua*, followed by these words:

I have transcribed this whole passage so that at one stroke the triviality of this popular accusation will be clear, and so that the omissions which I have imputed to Fabrizio will not seem worthless. My dissertation will contain more observations of this type; but because I will indicate the passages as briefly as possible, it will be neither too dull nor over-long.

(Cicero Illustratus, ch. 14)

The defence of Cicero involves laying out the accusations of his critics before readers, and then presenting them with the evidence of Cicero's own writings. This is the same biographical technique which Toland had developed in his life of Milton and stoutly defended against its critics only a year later.[27] Toland is careful to outline the context for his understanding of Cicero: he has already expressed his fundamental admiration for Cicero as a politician and a writer, and is not driven to adopt a standpoint which is superior to the self-knowledge that Cicero articulates in these particular passages. He does not attempt himself to argue the accusations against Cicero, but refers to his achievements and his answers to those accusations to refute them, thus setting the historical record straight, as he sees it. It is something of a surprise to see Toland driven so much on to the defensive; we do not normally regard the damage to Cicero's status as a force for cultural authority requiring

---

[26] *Cicero Illustratus*, ch. 14. Allen (1954) is a useful modern parallel to this passage, obviously with more copious sources and discussion. *Ad Brut.* 1. 17. 1 is the letter in which Brutus complains about Cicero's obsession with the Nones, although Toland gives the reference as *Ad fam.* 1. 9.

[27] Toland (1698 and 1699); see Champion (2003), 100–5, for details on the techniques of the Milton biography, as well as the ensuing controversy.

such defence until much later. Crucial to Toland's defence is the close relationship between the speeches and their political context, the notion of Cicero as a man of action rather than an adornment of the schoolroom. His negotiation of this particular way of considering Cicero's public role and its textual record does not, however, lead to him producing an authoritarian version of his hero. As well as allowing room for Cicero's own description of his political vacillations, he also wants his readers to engage with the texts themselves, and the passages which he selects in Cicero's defence are all those where Cicero himself takes on those same criticisms. He is in effect pointing out that charges of vacillation and cowardice were ones which Cicero's own contemporaries had made, and there is therefore no need to look elsewhere than Cicero's own answer to those criticisms in order to silence modern critics making the same accusations.

A further explanation of Toland's desire to avoid taking up a critical standpoint that privileges the critic over the original source may well be found in the historiographical theories current at the time. In particular, I am thinking of the work of the French encyclopaedist and historian Pierre Bayle, with whom Toland was connected, both through correspondence and by virtue of sharing the same biographer, Pierre Desmaizeaux. In his biographical essay on Toland, Desmaizeaux explains the process whereby Toland's life of Milton came to be the source for Bayle's dictionary entry on him and makes a substantial digression into the controversy which then arose.[28] Bayle's notion of criticism, embodied emblematically in the title of his great project, *La Dictionaire critique*, clearly acted as a marker to which Toland's own aspiration to a critical method

---

[28] Toland (1726), pp. xxxvii–xlii. Thomas Birch, whose collection of memorabilia and notes on the literary world of the late seventeenth and early eighteenth centuries describes the same controversy, takes a much dimmer view of Toland's motivation, accusing him of deliberately machinating to insert his outrageous views into what he hoped would be an authoritative reference work: BL Add. MS 4224, fols. 20–32, esp. 26–8. This manuscript appears to be notes, collated in preparation for the dissertation on the controversy which he published as part of an appendix for his Milton biography: Birch (1738). The polemic did not make it into his revisions of the English edition of Bayle, published in the same year: Bayle (1738), 567–88. Toland continued to be cited extensively as a source for Milton's life in the revised French editions of Bayle (Bayle (1820), x. 446–60), while the observations of Wagstaffe (Birch's main source) received minimal acknowledgement (p. 457 n. 45).

alluded.[29] Bayle was certainly a sceptic in the sense that his method was aimed at uncovering the errors of earlier scholars, and in the sense that an ultimately authoritative vision of the past was an illusion, but he was by no means a historical Pyrrhonist, claiming that the past itself could not be known.[30] The aim of the Dictionary was the removal of error, and Toland's portrayal of Cicero works along similar lines.

In the same year that *Cicero Illustratus* was published, Toland brought out a *Letter against Popery* (London, 1712), in which he attacked the church fathers and their tradition of scholarship. His critique is much sharper than that on the philologists who have misinterpreted Cicero, and in that field Toland's religious anti-orthodoxy had a particular polemic zeal. It would perhaps be a little careless to conclude that his distrust of Classical scholarship was motivated by the same reforming passion as his desire to liberate religion from restrictive scholastic influences. Nevertheless, the select readership of this volume was united by its political and intellectual interests, and the idea of liberating an Enlightenment Cicero from the accretions of scholarship may well have appealed to the same instincts for reform to be seen in areas of more obvious political controversy. In the original edition of the work, Toland includes an afterword (omitted in the reprint), in which he asks his readers, as well as sending comments or support, not to draw conclusions about the quality of production for the new edition on the basis of this *tumultuaria Dissertatio*. He was evidently aware of the potentially subversive effect of his presentation.[31] If it was disturbing in its high-flown rhetoric against the scholars, it was presumably also intended to appeal to the same instincts of reform which Toland's readers would share. Hohendorf, Eugene, and Toland's other connections formed an international set of republican thinkers and readers.[32] Toland's ambition was to find a

---

[29] In the subtitle to *Cicero Illustratus* and his *Dissertatio Critico-Historica* one of the supplementary sections of the edition: Toland (1726), i. 255. Presumably he used the hybrid terms *philologico-critica* and *critico-historica* in order to escape the conventional meaning of the term *criticus*, traditional textual criticism.

[30] Borghero (1983), 217–37; Popkin (2003), 288–302. For a survey of recent conceptions of Bayle, Paganini (2004). Rivers (2001*a*) analyses Bayle's role in the genre of biographical dictionaries.

[31] Toland (1712), 73.   [32] Champion (2003).

way of presenting Cicero that freed him from the limitations and obscurity which existing scholarly practices brought with them. His aim was not, however, to impose a particularly coherent view of Cicero. Here the production of the edition expresses perfectly the suspension of judgement which the sceptical historical approach brought with it. Simply to present Cicero clearly would in itself be an expression of the spirit of the age, and Toland's task was to mediate his readers' encounter with their hero without interposing his own interpretations.

THE NEW EDITION

A substantial portion of the treatise is taken up with explaining the rationale for Toland's presentation of the text. This includes sections on the use of punctuation, the methods for including annotations and discussion of textual variants, introductory prefaces and supplementary material such as the historico-critical biography of Cicero and various indices. In explaining his proposed methods, Toland becomes particularly exercised on the theme of textual criticism, and discusses a number of examples where previous editors have made unnecessary changes to the text found in the manuscripts, or where their method of annotation demonstrates an intrusion of inappropriate material which will in Toland's view only occlude the reader's access to Cicero. He is quite clear that often such an intrusive editorial style is motivated not by the production of a faithful or readable text but by the desire of the editors to engage in a controversy with their predecessors that does nothing to improve the state of the text, and which often only demonstrates their obsession with hair-splitting pedantry. *Nihil idcirco hujus farinae in nostra Editione* ('There will be none of this dross in our edition'), he proclaims, and in spite of indulging his polemic against such pedantry, he is careful to point out that he will be distinguishing carefully in his own *apparatus criticus* between the outcome of such *farina* and variant readings where the text in fact requires them. To give a flavour of Toland's Latin at its most colourful, this example, inspired by a variant of the text of *De natura deorum* 1. 7, is worth citing:

hic iterum Cocmannus post Gruterum ex Pithoeano adducit *disparuerunt,* ac *disparaverunt* conjiciti licentius (ut solet) & infelicissime Gulielmius. Nihil idcirco hujus farinae in nostra Editione, nis breviter aliquando indicatum, comparebit: neque tantus mihi ipsi unquam permittam, ut quenquam propter opiparas hasce delicias, vel notatas scrupulosius vel neglectas, stipitem appellem, fungum, bardum, asinum, temerarium, impudentem, aut ineptum; ac multo minus ut nequam, mastigiam, scelestum, ferum & ferreum, sacrilegum, pagiarium, moechum, vel caprarum maritum, talem nominem.   (*Cicero Illustratus*, 272–3)

Here again Cocmannus (following Gruterus from the Pithoeanus) brings in *disparuerunt*, while Gulielmius conjectures *disparaverunt*, with greater freedom (as usual) and with minimal felicity. There will be no dross of this kind in our edition, except occasionally in a brief note. Nor will I ever so much as allow myself, on account of these sumptuous delicacies, be they more carefully noted, or neglected, to call anyone a blockhead, a fungus, witless, an ass, foolish, shameless or stupid; even less would I call any such person worthless, a scoundrel, a crook, a beast, cruel, a blasphemer, plagiarist, fornicator, or a sheep-shagger.

He continues by pointing out what a menial task the sifting of manuscripts actually is, how excessive the prestige to which the critics aspire is compared to the work itself, and how, in this edition, the further depths of scholarly controversy will be avoided, while still giving due account of genuine problems. Similar polemic is doled out to the traditions of adding unnecessary comment to texts; and Toland draws a parallel between his attitude to the critics and the annotators; both are engaged in introspective self-aggrandizement and intellectual empire building, with which this edition will have little to do.[33] After a section outlining his intentions regarding indices for the edition (of which the one for the passages most useful for the defence of Christianity is particularly interesting: Cicero is the *malleus Superstitionis*, the 'hammer of Superstition'), Toland turns directly to address his dedicatee and to explain his use of excessive polemic. He explains that it is not the actual disciplines themselves (*artes*) of the *Grammatici* or the *Critici* that he despises; they are essential for learning correct Latin and understanding the origins of language, and for the production of an authentic text and a good

---

[33] *Cicero Illustratus*, 281–2.

style. It is just that human failings have affected these fields in just the same way that they have produced bad doctors, philosophers, or theologians; it is not the fields of learning themselves that are at fault—indeed, they are essential to all scholarship—and Toland then cites examples of brilliant and disinterested scholars recently deceased, as well as praising without naming them many examples of scholars still living. Here Toland is obviously alluding to Cicero's practice in *Brutus*.[34]

One of Toland's most interesting insights comes in the section in which he promises to introduce Cicero's works with a synopsis of their arguments. Here we become aware of the continuity between Cicero's own brand of sceptical philosophy and the free-thinking approach popular with leading thinkers of the early Enlightenment; Voltaire was especially fond of Cicero in this respect, and Descartes, Spinoza, and Locke appreciated Cicero's widespread repudiation of clear philosophical doctrine.[35] Here there is a consistency with Toland's account of Cicero as a political figure: readers should be able to engage with what Cicero has written, without that being obscured by the scholarly conventions which make Cicero into something that he is not. Toland begins by pointing out that a bare synopsis should not be taken to represent Cicero's own views.

Philosophicos omnes & *Rhetoricos* quosdam Libros ipse argumentis ab integro donabo: siquidem absque hoc, genuina Ciceronis de rebus sententia haudquaquam dignosci queat; quoniam non semper quid vere cogitarit, sed quid causa, tempus, locus, & auditores postularant, dicere consueverit.

(*Cicero Illustratus*, 261)

I shall myself furnish anew all the philosophical and certain rhetorical works with arguments (i.e. synopses); indeed without this, it is hardly possible to

---

[34] *Sed nemo e tam moltis nomini citandus venit, ne vel gratiam foeda adulatione aucupari, vel reliquos ... ipso silentio notare videar* (*Cicero Illustratus*, 289). ('But from so many, none will be mentioned by name, as I do not wish to seem to be aiming at favour by filthy flattery, nor to be marking out the others by not mentioning them').

[35] See Gawlick (1963); MacKendrick (1989), 269–77; Fuhrmann (2000), 103–7. Interest in *Academica* as an inspiration for philosophical scepticism can be traced as far back as the mid-sixteenth century: Popkin (2003), 28–35. It is salutary to remember that Plato was almost unknown in England at this period: Glucker (1987), 152–4. The hermeneutic difficulties which readings of Plato were to bequeath to Cicero are still far in the future.

ascertain Cicero's genuine opinion on any matter, since he would have been accustomed to say not what he really thought, but what the case, the time and place, and the audience demanded.

There follows a detailed discussion of how, in various places within his *œuvre*, Cicero takes up different voices representing incompatible views, particularly concerning divination and the gods, and that at no point should the reader fall into the easy trap of thinking that any one of these voices actually represents Cicero's own thoughts. This is true as much for the oratory as it is for the philosophy. Toland is particularly clear about the extent of Cicero's ability to adopt different voices and positions depending upon the demands of the argument, and alerts his readers to the fallacy of reading Cicero's own thoughts into ideas expressed in his oratory and his theoretical works.[36] He cites a passage from *Pro Cluentio,* and then concludes:

If Readers had noticed this passage, and others like it, we would not find Cicero cited so very absurdly, nor would all those ideas which are so thoroughly foreign to what he did or felt be attributed to him. ... But this should be observed in particular in his Dialogues, since those are popularly read for confirmation of ideas which conflict entirely with his true opinions. As if it were sufficient that this or that idea be found in Cicero, with no thought taken for the manner of the speaker.

(*Cicero Illustratus,* 261–2)

He then points out that although in some places (Crassus in *De oratore* is the clearest example) Cicero uses one character to put across his own view, this is by no means a consistent practice, and between different works, Cicero is contradictory. Cotta, in *De natura deorum,* does represent the views of Cicero, and readers should not be deceived into thinking that this is not the case by the final sentence of the work (which Toland cites; see above, pp. 4–5). This is, he says, the same kind of gesture towards authority which writers make when submitting their works for approval by the Catholic Church. Anyone who doubts that Cicero is indeed radically opposed to superstition

---

[36] He cites *Pro Cluentio* 139, a passage used in almost exactly the same manner three centuries later by Dyck: 'It is well to remember Cicero's remark that his speeches in advocacy need not show his true opinions' (A. R. Dyck (2001) 125).

need only look at the end of *De divinatione*, where Cicero takes off his mask (*larva*) and makes it quite clear that he is himself endorsing the repudiation of superstition.

After quoting from the final paragraph of the *De divinatione*, he sums up his approach as follows:

> eadem regula in *Tusculanis Disputationibus*, et aliis omnibus dialogis perlegendis, est sedulo observanda, ut in Argumentis iis praefixis fusius explicabimus: non quod sollicitus sim quaenam fuerit Ciceronis de ulla re sententia (cum nullius in verba jurandum censeam) sed ut critice tantum & historice lecturis de vera ipsius mente, seu erraverit necne, constaret.   (*Cicero Illustratus*, 264)

The same method is to be rigorously observed in the *Tusculan Disputations* and in reading all the other dialogues, as we shall explain more fully in those synopses: not because I might be concerned about what was Cicero's own opinion on any matter (since I regard that as something which can be judged from no man's words) but so that, by enabling people to read critically and historically, anyone will be able to come to a conclusion about their own true opinion, whether it is mistaken or not.

Given the scepticism expressed in the parenthesis, Toland's hermeneutics can be characterized as a process of reading in which the reader uses the text as a guide to their own opinions. There appears at first sight to be a contradiction between this claim not to be able to detect Cicero's views and the arguments of the previous page, that even in his impersonations we can detect Cicero. But Toland's approach is in fact consistent: the very end of *De divinatione*, where the mask is removed, presents the argument that religion must be preserved, even if superstition is rooted out. Even though the speaker is, technically, still the rabid rationalist Cicero who has occupied the entirety of book 2, Toland singles this out as a moment where the different personae of Cicero can be distinguished. This passage, of course, was of particular importance for Toland, since as a pioneer of atheism he was, like Voltaire, particularly impressed by Cicero's disdain for *superstitio* and his sceptical approach to traditional religion.[37]

---

[37] Among Toland's papers is a sketch for a book on priesthood, consisting of a mock title-page and table of contents. Both convey his reliance on Cicero: *Priesthood without Priestcraft: or Superstition distinguished from Religion, Dominion from Order and Biggotry from Reason.* The title of the last chapter reads: 'The Conclusion, wherein of tradition in sacred matters': British Library Add. MS 4295, fol. 66.

Nevertheless, his sympathy does not lead him to look within the work as a whole, or in Cicero's other treatises, for an authoritative statement of the author's opinions. Cicero's *sententiae* are neither recoverable nor relevant; what matters is the manner in which the philosopher encourages the reader to engage with the issues under discussion. The work, particularly of dialogue, was not supposed to exert a dogmatic influence upon its readers; rather, it stands as a stimulus for the reader to consider and refine his own understanding of the issues.

Interestingly, the final arguments tend back to the point with which Toland began: prose style, that very arena in which Cicero's reputation has worked against careful reading. The most compelling cause for a new edition of Cicero is the improvement of Toland's own style, a style which he will then put to the service of writing a history of Britain in Latin. In the last chapter of the work Toland explains to his patron his particular interest in producing this new edition:

> But to reveal myself with complete freedom to you, nothing has provided me with keener inspiration to produce this edition of Cicero, than that my style, which is the craftsman of expression, may emerge most fully polished and shaped. In my view, the best style is the one that is wisely fitted for what is appropriate, considering a whole variety of subjects. Great matters should be expressed seriously, grand ones ornately, ordinary ones moderately, and more trivial ones succinctly, showily or subtly according to what is needed. You may ask what is the point of this discourse on types of style? So that after I have emerged from this rugged field of Criticism, I may gird myself to produce a History, adorning in writing the most beautiful deeds.   (*Cicero Illustratus*, 291)

He then quotes Cicero, *De oratore* 2. 15, on the laws of history, and continues to explain his plan for the historical work, the subject of which will be the revolution of 1688, its origins and consequences, particularly from a European perspective. Toland will ensure the glorification of heroes such as Eugene of Savoy and the Duke of Marlborough; and he works in more references to Cicero: the description of his *De consulatu suo* from *Ad Atticum* 2. 1. 1 is used to explain the kind of account which Toland will give of Marlborough; William of Orange finds himself compared to Trebonius, as Toland adapts a sentence from *Philippic* 2. 11. 27, substituting *populi Angli-cani* for *populi Romani*.[38] To conclude the entire treatise, Toland provides a passage from *De officiis* in order to demonstrate that the standards he is setting for his history derive not just from his own personal preferences, but from a great sense of public utility.[39] He chooses a pregnant moment to curtail the quotation, however: Plato's idea that competition in government is like two sailors competing to steer the ship. Certainly within this work, Toland remains strictly bound by the reverence for monarchic authority upon which his hopes of patronage for this project (as indeed for his livelihood as a scholar) depended.

RHETORIC AND DISCIPLINE

The idea that the ultimate goal of the enormous scholarly endeavour which Toland outlines should be gains in his own mastery of Latin prose, and the subsequent creation of a Latin account of recent British history, is one that does require some critical adjustment. Perhaps, of course, it would also have struck Toland's readers as a little strange; it rests upon Toland's understanding of the role of rhetoric, and style more generally. His particular interest in *De oratore* is perhaps most revealing. Just as in that work Cicero explores the idea of the forms of Latin required to do justice to the substance of Roman history, so here Toland is appealing to the subject matter of the recent past, and looking to its protagonists to sponsor its rendition into a form that will be suited to the events, and which will glorify them. The argument fits well with the approach to Cicero which Toland adopts because, both in reading Cicero and in writing history, what is important is the effectiveness of the text itself. Literary production, whether in terms of reading oneself or writing for others to read, is about ensuring that the right kinds of inspiration are appropriately conveyed. The harmony that is implied

---

[38] *qui libertatem populi Romani* (populi Anglicani) *unius amicitiae praeposuit depulsorque dominatus quam particeps esse maluit* (*Phil.* 2. 11. 27).

[39] *De off.* 1. 85–7.

between the veneration for Eugene (in the opening sections) and the adulation of Cicero as the ideal public figure is, by the end of the work, made more explicit in the assumption that Cicero provides a means through which the true historical significance of Eugene, and the events of his time, can be conveyed.

Texts are there for their public utility, and Toland's exasperation with the poor representation and teaching of Cicero, the pedantry of the specialists, and the partial understanding of the biographers, is an expression of the same holistic understanding of the relationship between public rhetoric and public life. As I have suggested, Cicero for Toland is the opposite of the mere scribbler who has lurked on the edges of even more positive readings in subsequent periods. As I suggested in Chapter 2, Cicero himself expressed anxiety about the potential power of literature, and that anxiety is also manifested in the difficulties which Cicero has about producing unequivocally positive historical representations. Toland responds rather differently to this anxiety, homing in on Cicero's own defences against political vacillation, and regarding the ambivalence of the philosophy as a sign of enlightened scepticism. He evaluates the historical achievements in terms not of the eclipse of the final years, which he does not mention, but of the consulship and the return from exile. His admiration of the philosophical works at no point takes into account the political marginalization that conditioned their production. At the root of all this is a different approach to reading: one that is less interested in forms of authority within writing, and more responsive to the political and educational resources of texts.

To substantiate this interpretation of Toland's rhetoric more exactly, we can turn to his short poem *Clito,* published in London in 1700 and subtitled *a Poem on the Force of Eloquence.*[40] The poem was, apparently, written only for private circulation, but then, in response to pressure by

---

[40] Toland (1700). For a good assessment of the poem in its context, see N. Smith (1996). Soon after appearing in print the poem was the subject of a critical response from S. F., whose *Mr Toland's Clito Dissected* (1700), a pamphlet written in the form of a 'Letter to a Friend', in which passages from the poem are vehemently criticized for their anti-religious and revolutionary principles. In the following year, the poem found its way into a collection entitled *Poems on affairs of state, from the reign of K. James the First, to this present year 1703. Written by the greatest wits of the age, ... Many of which never before publish'd* (London, 1703), where it took its place alongside a miscellany of subversive poetry including works by Dryden and Rochester.

friends, was published, although not under Toland's own name. Toland
derives much of the authority for his take on rhetoric from Cicero; the
editor/publisher of the poem, William Hewet, used *De oratore* 2. 9 as
the epigraph, a text which Toland himself paraphrased in a passage
of his history of Celtic religion and the Druids where he justifies
rendering historical material concerning the ancients in an accessible
and polished style.[41] The poem is actually more reminiscent of Lucretius in its zeal for enlightenment, but that enlightenment is derived
from eloquence:

> I'll sooth the raging Mob with mildest Words,
> Or sluggish Cowards rouse to use their Swords.
> As furious Winds sweep down whate'er resists,
> So shall my Tongue performe whate'er it lists,
> With large impetuous Floods of Eloquence
> Tickle the Fancy and bewitch the Sense;
> Make what it will the justest Cause appear,
> And what's perplex'd or dark, look bright and clear.
> Not that I would the wrongful side defend;
> He best protects who's ablest to offend:
> As the same Force which serves to curb our Foes,
> Can hurt those Friends who on our Love repose,
> And for whose sake we wou'd our Lives expose.
>   Thus arm'd, thus strong, thus fitted to persuade,
> I'll Truth protect, and Error straight invade,
> Dispel those Clouds that darken human Sight,
> And bless the World with everlasting Light.
> A Noble Fury does possess my Soul,
> Which all may forward, nothing can controul;
> The fate of Beings, and the hopes of Men,
> Shall be what pleases my creating Pen.

The crusading orator will take on natural science, religion, and the
political constitutions, crushing established forms of authority and
superstitions, and setting up truth, rationality, and justice in their
place. This energetic tribute to the powers of rhetoric, and in particular to the power of the written word to effect political and social
change, certainly resonates with the Cicero of *Cicero Illustratus*, and

---

[41] *A Specimen of the Critical History of the Celtic Religion*: Toland (1726), 1. 18–19.

it supplements the positive image of rhetoric central to Toland's rehabilitation of Cicero. What is so interesting about Toland is that he can both appeal to the traditional authority of Cicero as the bedrock of education and the model for all gentlemen, and make him look like a radical. The nobility of Cicero's achievements is something that interests Toland rather less than the immense power of his prose, and again, there is a tension here between different ideas of authority: the quest to write excellent Latin has been, in Toland's account of Cicero reception, the main cause of restrictions to his reading and effect. Nevertheless, in this politicizing agenda, powerfully written Latin prose will become the international medium of communication for a new form of rational excellence in public service. The history which he proposes to produce will, like the edition of Cicero which is its forerunner, clarify the achievements of this new type of leader, as well as giving Toland himself a special role as the great Latin stylist needed to produce this account.

It is not my intention to suggest that we can look to Toland for a definitive hermeneutics for approaching Cicero. Nevertheless, by appreciating the threads that unite his love of Cicero with his desire to glorify the history of the 1688 English Revolution, it is possible to see a reading of Cicero that corresponds more closely to his own idea of what writing could achieve. Fascinatingly, Toland himself tackles the main problem with any such comparison: namely, the enormous difference in the distribution of texts between the Roman and post-Renaissance worlds, in his treatise on the invention of printing.[42] Although he believes that Cicero could envisage type in the form of letters (the source is *De nat. deorum* 2. 93, where the chances of the random emergence of Ennius' *Annals* from the random scattering of metal letters is discussed), he is careful not to go beyond the context of this particular argument.[43] In a sense, his ambitions for new standards in the clarity of production of a text of Cicero, on high-quality paper and minimizing any distracting typographical or orthographical clutter, are aimed precisely at bringing Cicero up to date, removing him from the context of the schoolroom, and unlocking his potential as a resource for government. The light which Toland will shed on Cicero is physical as well as intellectual:

---

[42] Repr. in Toland (1726), i. 297–303.   [43] Toland (1726), i. 297–300.

the expensive paper and the clarity of the typeface are nearly as important to the project as the consistent orthography and rationalized notes and explanatory material. Toland may be the most sympathetic reader that Cicero could have wished for; but if he is, this is not predicated upon a sense that he is simply rehearsing a picture of Cicero's authority which is widely accepted. This is a campaigner, and the image of Cicero that emerges, inspiring his readers, his texts working on their readers, both with their style and their sense of how a great man should serve his community, was defined with a particular context and particular aims in mind. But crucially, Toland's main concern is to let Cicero's writings do their own work, to clear away misconceptions and to facilitate readers' encounters with a clearly presented text. He may admire Cicero's repudiation of superstition, but he does not think about purveying Cicero for a set of messages or doctrines. The fact he ends his treatise on the subject of his own stylistic improvement makes it clear that it is for the generation of new texts and new ideas that a reading of Cicero is so valuable. We are close here to the imitative rhetoric familiar to Greek writers of the first century BCE and beyond, where the educational value of a canonical text resides as much in its stylistic qualities as in its ability to inspire under ideological conditions quite different from those of its inception. Properly stripped of unnecessary scholastic accretions, Cicero can play this role, but he does so not by virtue so much of his own ideas as by the power of his writing, the fact that his works deserve to be read carefully.

Toland's Cicero is thus rather different from the image of Cicero dominant today, the reason being that developments in Cicero reception from the nineteenth century onwards had a determining effect upon the way in which Cicero is used. Toland's uncritical attitude to Cicero's political activities, combined with his greater interest in his philosophy as a non-dogmatic educational resource, is very different from the traditions of reading for 'the source', be it of Hellenistic doctrine or of historical or political judgement, which developed in the century after Toland was writing. Whereas Enlightenment thinkers like Toland found in Cicero a model of intellectual flexibility, the dominant philosophers of the nineteenth century, and in particular those historians who in the development of the modern discipline of history produced the most powerful paradigms for the understanding of Cicero as a historical figure, had little sympathy for what was perceived to be Cicero's ideological and political vacillation. The excessive scorn heaped upon Cicero by the founders of the discipline of Roman History, Drumann and Mommsen, should not be taken as representative, particularly in Britain, of the dominant opinion of Cicero; and even in Germany, scholars seem in little doubt that Cicero's value as an educational resource was left untouched by these two powerful and very negative accounts.[44]

Nevertheless, it seems clear that Drumann and Mommsen were, if not representative, at least drawing together a number of threads which did run deeper: vital here is the concretization of a polarization between literary and political activity, which was clearly detrimental to Cicero's reputation. His role as a stylistic model could no longer, as it did for Toland, act as an inspiration for writing history more effectively: the polarization between rhetoric and truth had become clearly established, affecting not only the judgement of Cicero's morals, but also his status as a politician. The ability to perceive the interplay between literary and political in terms that resembled Cicero's at all closely was lost, and what was perceived as Cicero's failure as a historical figure—the failure, therefore, of his vision of the *res publica*—was regarded as the result of a dialectic that of course deeply exercised Cicero himself: that between the man of action and the man of letters. It was, in effect, because he was a scribbler that Cicero lost his place as a historical protagonist.[45]

There is an oedipal quality to the birth of the discipline of academic historiography: Cicero's writings were of course the main source for all Republican history, but that history was constructed in such a way that he himself had no pivotal role within it. His reputation was the sacrifice made by those most dependent upon his writings, in order to substantiate the methodological purity of their own efforts: history was to be a discipline whose practitioners had no need to reveal their intellectual dependency, since it was the material contained in the sources, not the writing of those sources, that was the object of

---

[44] See Fuhrmann (1989 and 2000).
[45] For a sophisticated analysis of Cicero's vacillation between philosophy and politics, see Görler (1990*b*).

study.[46] The very textuality of Cicero needed to be ignored in sifting his writings for events and institutions, and a decline in the status of rhetoric, from a central tool of communication to an accessory, would facilitate this move. The ambiguous position of Cicero in the schoolroom became even more sharply focused: historians may all have learnt their Latin from Cicero, but that was almost irrelevant to an understanding of the Roman world. And although proficiency in Latin prose continued to be the main training for work in public life, the close connection which Toland perceived between good Latin prose and effective government was unsustainable. The tensions upon which it foundered are easily visible within his treatise: the vision of Eugene as the ideal embodiment of the unity of *literae* and *arma* reinforces the impossibility of an easy relationship between text and power.[47] Even Toland has to allow that in his day these are very diverse areas (*junxit* EUGENIUS, *res hoc tempore diversissimas, Literas & Arma*). Toland may be loudly proclaiming the advantages of such a relationship; but, like Cicero, he was to be proved wrong by circumstance. The Latin history was never written; neither did his edition of Cicero ever see the light of day. Readers of Cicero would have to wait more than a century for a complete edition that would bring together the range of different materials that Toland promised: the complete works edited by J. C. von Orelli, with many of the same biographical, historical, and textual tools which Toland envisaged.[48] Toland devoted himself to more direct forms of campaigning, and to the development of a more overtly sceptical and radical philosophy. The constellation of republican authority, social deference, and regeneration through rhetoric, particularly when applied to history, certainly suits Cicero well; but in the clarity of his depiction, Toland is also pointing to the processes which prevented this veneration of Cicero from withstanding the onslaught of the historical empiricists and the philosophical idealists, and the degradation of rhetoric to a branch of aesthetics.

---

[46] Gadamer (1990), 306, presents a concise account of the disavowal of historical influence inherent in the striving for historical objectivity, and opposes to it the project of *Wirkungsgeschichte*.
[47] Toland (1726), i. 235–6.   [48] Canfora (2000).

11

Conclusions

Toland's admiration for Cicero, when looked at from the perspective of the treatise as a whole, takes much of its flavour from the immediate concerns of patronage within which it is presented: Cicero provides a model of statesmanship which will appeal to Toland's high-ranking addressee; but at a deeper level, the vision of Cicero projects a set of aspirations about society, about the role of the talented individual within it (Toland, his patron, his patron's patron), and thus about defining the role of the citizen. This is a radical group of readers, looking to the past for the potential to animate their quest for a break with traditions, and finding in Cicero a model for an open-minded and rhetorically accomplished statesman. But he is not one who is concerned to paper over the cracks in his self-image or to impress his readers with a dogmatic approach either to himself or to the world of ideas. It is almost a cliché to stress the role of *De officiis* in perpetuating the image of Cicero as a figure of philosophical and cultural authority, of pedagogy and a paradigm of paternal instruction, enshrining Cicero's values in the creation of ideals of citizenship and civic participation from the Renaissance. What Toland shows us particularly vividly is the role that more philosophical works could have within the same discourse, and that those works produce a rather less closed image of how texts work, and of how Cicero's authority functions. As a conclusion to this book, I shall be tying together the studies of the preceding chapters so as to draw out their importance for a vision of what Cicero can contribute to our view of citizenship, and in particular, of the idea of the citizen as the product of a philosophical encounter with history. This is not primarily in order to set up my own reading of Cicero as a parallel to earlier ones from eras where there was no embarrassment about drawing on Classical authors to provide inspiration for political or social reform. It would be disingenuous, however, to claim that the vision of Cicero that I have presented is beyond the range of political interpretation, or that such an interpretation would violate the rules of reading which I have laid down for myself. It will annoy some readers to begin to argue that 'all readings are political'; it will annoy others if I start to weigh up the priorities of the political aspects against the demands of scholarship or historical objectivity. Cicero does have a particularly important role to play in such discussions, however, and it is the purpose of this chapter to show how this importance demands a frame of reference that is wider than the readings of any individual. So, rather than focus upon my own particular sense of method or political orientation, I will explore the ramifications of his philosophy of history for wider questions about Cicero's role within the modern Academy, and about that academy's relationship with concepts of the citizen and education, areas where Cicero is of obvious relevance, but where a change of perspective may generate productive debate.

Existing interpretations of Cicero bring with them their own political implications, whether or not those are openly articulated. The vision of Cicero as a dogmatic thinker has had a tenacious hold upon his evaluation as a historical figure: the famous condemnation of Mommsen had complex political implications, but essentially required Cicero to function as a failure in order that the successes of Caesar and Augustus could be seen to make sense of the Roman political system. This was history written from the perspective of the winners, and Cicero needed to appear as though he simply did not have what was necessary (charisma, military skill, resolve) to handle political power effectively. The vacillation which characterizes Cicero's love of the Academy is indicative of a failure of political will, and for Mommsen and Drumann in particular was an indication of the same failure of political principle which would allow Cicero to change his loyalties and to represent, in his work as an advocate, conflicting interests. Cicero was an unprincipled role-player and, when threatened by those with greater power, was not able to stand up for his principles, because his philosophical and rhetorical training had not equipped him with any. As we can see in Toland, this critique of vacillation was already well established in the historical literature by the end of the seventeenth century. The latest rehabilitations of Cicero, however, are arguably no more than the obverse of that critique: Cicero was so aware of his educational superiority that he was driven in most of his literary output not only to persuade his readers of the power of centrality of the written word to Roman politics, but to do so successfully.[1]

To readjust our interpretation of Cicero's Academic ambitions, and to see in his work with Roman history an acute sense of the problems of that history, will allow us to read Cicero differently. He is not striving, and then failing, to provide a convincing narrative of Roman institutions with himself at the centre; he is not attempting to convince his readers that he himself, the orator-statesman, represents the logical conclusion of the processes of Roman cultural development. He may want his readers to share with him the political desirability of such a vision, but his writings provide plenty of opportunity to observe the weaknesses in his arguments, the exaggerations of his self-representation, the hopeless optimism of regarding literary and philosophical endeavour as a means to the better exercising of political power. These are all questions which in fact relate closely to the identity of the modern academy, and to the values around which those who work in it structure their research; but also mediate notions of truthfulness, or of authoritative thinking, to their students. This process of mediation takes place for the most part, since the evolution of institutionalized academic disciplines, as a collective activity, and there is little visible demand for individual practitioners to confront wide questions of method or authority. Cicero's philosophy of history, however, while not necessarily providing a model for current academic activity, does prompt a reconsideration of the relationship between political power, education (particularly literary and philosophical), and the possibility of an authority that, while still providing a foundation for political action, is nevertheless non-dogmatic, and which promotes self-scrutiny rather than a display of impenetrable rhetoric.

Particularly with regard to this last point, the controversial quality of my interpretation of Cicero is clear: there is no doubt that Cicero's forensic rhetoric is indeed an attempt at political mastery; his rhetorical

---

[1] Butler (2002) is the most explicit example.

theory also takes the next step and provides some kind of theoretical underpinning to this aspiration to mastery, making Cicero's own position as the orator-statesman into something like a measure of success in Rome. But, it is one of the most important claims of this book that the image of Cicero which emerges from the theoretical works is not of one whose rhetorical skill enables him to retain full control of that image. In this respect, my position is different from that of other recent work on similar aspects of Cicero's writing, most notably Dugan (2005), which considers some of the same texts. Dugan's main argument is that Cicero's social origins lead him to explore new avenues for the immortalization of his position rather than those that were conventionally available to the offspring of families more central to Rome's governing elite. By taking on the concept of self-fashioning, Dugan, following on from the work of Gleason (1995), presents Cicero as someone determinedly in control of his image; where this control fails, it is the result of the same overestimation of his talents which characterizes the condemnation of Cicero as a historical failure: so Dugan (2001), 55: 'That Archias does not reciprocate Cicero's artfully crafted speech with a poem in the consular's honor, but instead offers his services to the Luculli and Metelli ... underscores both the collapse of the *Pro Archia*'s self-fashioning strategies and Cicero's misplaced confidence in the power of literary polish to compete on the same level as long-standing political alliances.' Dugan's argument here is sound, but my reading of Cicero's philosophy suggests that, perhaps as a result of such failings, but actually also already at a stage in his career where his prospects looked a great deal brighter, Cicero took a much more sceptical view of the potential of rhetoric than this determinist designation of self-fashioning suggests. Dugan's argument supposes that Cicero could see a way around his intrinsic exclusion from the forms of symbolic representation available to the elite, but that he was in effect mistaken about the efficacy of his new route. In the context of particular speeches, in which an individual case is being argued, this argument has a great deal to recommend it. When extrapolated to a reading of Cicero's theoretical writings, however, it suffers from the same failing to recognize the dialogic qualities in Cicero's philosophy as most other readings. This is, I hope, where the value of my approach lies: Cicero was all too aware of the marginalization of rhetoric within Roman society, and had even at the start of his correspondence accepted the notion of literary achievement as a form of political failure. It seems to me that in his presentation of Roman history, and in particular in those works where he positions rhetoric within Rome's history, Cicero makes full use of the dialogic potential of his philosophical schooling in order to make clear to his readers the shortcomings of too firm a faith in the power of rhetoric.

My focus on Cicero's use of historical representation supports this argument. Precisely because there was a clear convention of using history as a foundation, it is particularly obvious what the ramifications are of those moments where dialogue about the past disrupts its foundational function. If Cicero had wanted to make *Brutus* into a straightforward endorsement of the teleology of Roman rhetoric, it would not have been difficult for him to have done so. But I hope that by now readers will be convinced that the open play of the dialogue form, even in a work so dogmatic for much of its compass, enables both the foundational quality and its pitfalls to be made apparent. Perhaps because as a *novus* he had such admiration for the tradition of *memoria* that he could not properly inhabit, Cicero understood the importance of using history as a foundation, and it is a crucial part of his adaptation of Greek philosophy to Rome that ideas become historical. That includes the desire to use history to provide a basis for theory, a basis that comes from a consideration of real life, as expressed both by anecdote and by the historical record. The attempt to anchor theory within history was not one with a strong tradition in Greek thought. In the climate in which Cicero was writing, both the dominant philosophical schools, Stoicism and Epicureanism, were unequivocal in their quest to provide individuals with a route to escape from history into transcendent truths, even though Stoicism did this by reinforcing the relationship between terrestrial and universal achievement. By contrast, Cicero's political pragmatism expressed itself in his wish to combine philosophy with political reality, and in that attempt to use the record of that reality which was Roman history.

It is possible here that I have even underestimated the originality of Cicero's contribution to the development of philosophy. As I suggested in Chapter 3, that history has generally been concerned not with the manner in which abstractions have been anchored in reality, but rather, the quality of the abstract arguments themselves, so that as a theme in the history of philosophy, the role of anecdote is not prominent. The use of historical anecdote depends upon a particularly acute perception of the potential of the Roman political scene: *exempla* and appeals to *memoria* were useful tools in political and forensic rhetoric, and clearly audiences and juries would respond to the authority of such appeals. By inflecting philosophy so as to enable it to work within that context, Cicero comes up against the problem of extracting the universal from the particular, but he is actually remarkably sensitive in using historical representation to keep both of these before his readers' eyes. At no point, I would argue, does he obscure the shortcomings of a foundational way of using the past in order to demonstrate his own centrality to Rome's historical development. Perhaps that was the original function of his poem on his consulship, a wholly non-ironic integration of Cicero into Rome's history and destiny; but his treatment of that poem in *De divinatione* can be interpreted more effectively not as a last-ditch attempt to get the poem to do the same work again, to revive the image of himself as the embodiment of Rome's destiny in the vacuum left by Caesar's death; not even Cicero's most ardent admirers could have imagined this role for him at that stage and, despite the moments of optimism that the assassination allowed him, there is little doubt that the threats of the new order could not have responded to Cicero's intervention.[2]

Cicero resurrects his former self-image precisely in order to demonstrate its absurd optimism, and to contrast it with the militant rationalism of his current incarnation. The fact that, at the end of the dialogue, he retreats slightly from this position of ideological desperation is some form of redemption; but we are still a long way from any idea of Cicero defining himself as the answer to Rome's problems. Even in *De oratore* and *De re publica*, Cicero uses history in such a way that readers remain aware of the cautions necessary if central features of Rome's identity are going to have substantial universal claims made for them. Readers of *De re publica* would be repelled by an unequivocal endorsement of monarchy, and particularly shocked to receive it from Cicero. So history plays a role in containing the universality of those arguments, as well as in granting

---

[2] Steel's interpretation of *Philippics* is particularly relevant here: Steel (2005), ch. 4.

them a foothold at Rome. Their appeal can be demonstrated, but also their limitations. Readers of Plato's *Republic*, or at least those who recognized it as a thought-experiment in the potential of the *polis* rather than as an attempt to codify a real state, would have had no problem reading Cicero's *Republic* in the same manner, and it must have been a particular cause of pride to Cicero to be able to spell out with such clarity that he could conduct his thought-experiment within a historical narrative. This was certainly an advance on Plato: to historicize theoretical concepts in this manner, to accept the provisionality of universal truths, was not just an expression of a different cultural milieu; it was also a progressive step in terms of philosophy, one which was determined to integrate philosophical insight into the concrete processes of government. History, of course, is the record of those processes. So those who want to read the constitutional debates of *De re publica* as Cicero's considered opinion of what is best for Rome are missing out on a central part of his technique and of the hermeneutic expectations of his readers.

So, rather than using history simply to validate and ground his own views of rhetoric and the order of the state, in order to bolster his own position, Cicero uses Rome's history to act in a different direction: not aimed to demonstrate the success of his own integration into a teleology of Roman power, but rather to present and simultaneously interrogate the process of any such integration. The paradigm presented in *De divinatione* is the one that most pointedly captures the pluralistic quality of Cicero's presentation of himself in relation to Roman institutions: readers are presented with a dialectic which does not necessarily include its own resolution. Debate and self-knowledge constitute a continuous process, in which one may move from one point of stability to another: from the voice of Quintus, to the voice of Marcus; but there is something to be learned from both.

SCEPTICISM AND THE PROCESS OF READING

It has not been possible to reinforce at every turn of my argument the context of Cicero's Academic training, and the difference in interpretation made possible by the expectations of a well-conceived scepticism. That is largely because Cicero's writings are so unique: one must not always look for lost Greek writings as the clue to understanding this. Looking over Cicero's work with historical material between *De oratore* and *De divinatione*, however, the difference is clear, as are the political and pedagogical implications of that difference. Cicero approaches historical material with the outlook shared by his contemporaries and exploited repeatedly in his speeches: the past is the foundation of the moral and political system of the present day, and references to *mos maiorum* are a mechanism for both appealing to and reinscribing a consensus. However, in writings that aim to put forward a theoretical structure for improving upon or consolidating particular features of Roman culture (rhetoric, the constitution, religion, public duty), or even bringing them within the remit of philosophy, he comes up against an immediate difficulty: how to harmonize theory with practice.[3] His answer is the one which corresponds closely to his philosophical training: he allows theory and practice to struggle before his readers' eyes, making them aware of the difficulties, suggesting provisional solutions, but not providing any final version.

Within this technique, history plays a particularly important role. Because of the deeply engrained structure of exemplary historical reference, history can naturally provide one of the means for testing the reliability of any hypothesis. It should be stressed that in many of the works not discussed in this book, it is philosophical dialectic that plays that role, and the role of history is minimized. In *De officiis* the pedagogical clarity of the adopted structure, a 'letter' from father to son, likewise entails a more direct approach to the question of historical examples, and the historical material in that work is mostly conventionally exemplary. So the potential use of history to animate dialectic is not a constant practice. Nevertheless, in the works discussed here, history is the place where the ambiguities of Cicero's quest to show Rome as a republic founded upon ideas and principles is most clearly expressed. As I pointed out in Chapter 2, this is a

---

[3] Gigon (1973), 254–7, provides an elegant synthesis, looking at Cicero's rejection of dogmatism and his appeals to Roman history to incorporate philosophy into Rome. See too R. Müller (1989).

tension which cannot easily be separated from ambiguities expressed in relation to the present about the possible role of a philosopher in Roman politics. Cicero has aspirations for a political role for philosophy, but he is not naïve about them and, at the same time, is aware that for most of his colleagues, philosophical activity constitutes some kind of repudiation of the norms of Roman public life. If one is going to repudiate those norms, then Stoic idealism is a lot more beneficial to the state than Epicureanism, but both dogmatic schools are unable to accommodate themselves effectively to the realities of the political situation, which demands greater flexibility. In terms of Cicero's development between *De oratore* and *De divinatione*, I would argue *not* that Cicero begins his attempts at a theoretical definition of Rome with some confidence, but that even in the earlier works there is a diffidence about making claims for theory that are too grand, as well as a caution about casting himself too clearly as the symbol of how well theory can work in the Roman context. Certainly, he allows himself that privilege in the prologue to *De re publica*, although almost at the expense of banishing philosophy itself from the Roman political scene. But in the main body of the work, he remains largely out of sight, letting the characters explore the same ambiguities that the prologue raises.

If, in reading the works of the 50s, one starts with a close examination of Cicero's self-presentation (or lack of it), and approaches the text with non-dogmatic expectations, then it is easier to avoid having to reconstruct an attitude for Cicero in the 50s brimming with confidence and keen to show how well his career can function for his colleagues in the Senate as a case study in the universal applicability of a philosophical and rhetorical education. This is obviously risible as a historical analysis, but something like this is necessary to sustain the idea that these texts do not need to be read with an eye to their *aporia* and their dialogic quality. For the late works, of course, that confidence is further shaken by Caesar's dictatorship. The militant rationalism of *De divinatione* 2 expresses an impatience for that idealizing Stoicism which had received a better press in *De natura deorum*, and although that position is clearly not, of itself, a sufficient description of how to find some kind of spiritual basis for working within the political system, the dialogue as a whole makes a strong case for an Academic manner of thinking about Roman ideology, and not getting seduced by the false hope offered by an idealized notion of providence.

Rhetoric is the way in which government achieves verbal expression, and there is no doubt that whatever else Cicero thinks about power at Rome, his one unequivocal ambition is to raise awareness of the potential of a well-trained form of communication to produce a better kind of political culture. But he does not do this in a manner that is historically implausible. So in *De oratore* we can already see Cicero on the defensive about the place of rhetoric at Rome. Taking *De oratore*, *De re publica*, and *De legibus* together, it seems clear that Cicero was aiming at a wide-ranging theoretical assault on Rome: the state must be defined, and given a coherent theoretical identity. The constitution and its central values—justice, law, leadership, and expertise in political discourse—could all be tackled as theoretical concerns, and be shown to have an identity which enabled Rome to look like a well-ordered and rationally organized society.

I will now indulge briefly in hypothesis about how Cicero's own experience, and his sense of the place of philosophy at Rome, could have determined the kind of historical representation that those dialogues produce. Certainly, as Cicero's friend Sallustius pointed out, there would be many at Rome who would take such a confident intellectual endeavour from so splendid an ex-consul, and would be open to an authoritarian kind of discourse that presented Cicero's views on the state in his own voice. But I suspect that it was not his own supporters that Cicero had in his sights as his main audience; that would be preaching to the converted. What he wanted was to articulate the systems of Rome in such a way that a rational and educated debate could take place, and such that he could find a readership that transcended the immediate context of the political struggle. In order to do that, his theoretical insights would need to be grounded in an acceptable version of Roman culture. However great his own confidence about his actions as consul, he was under no illusions about the negative effect that this confidence had upon his enemies, and he judged rightly, I think, that to promulgate his own views on the constitution and on rhetoric would be unlikely to persuade readers of the necessary integration of a philosophical approach to Rome's problems.

His solution was to adopt a more inspirational form of philosophy, and one which left unresolved questions about how far Cicero himself should be identified as the central authority for this undertaking; simply to have written these works would be enough authority.[4] For the arguments to work, an imaginative encounter with Rome's history would be infinitely more effective, especially if, during that encounter, readers could be made aware of the difficulties, and allurements, of historical idealization. Cicero's most sophisticated critics, if they read carefully, would not be able to accuse him of exploiting Crassus to put forward an unopposed vision of rhetoric as an integral part of Rome's history, even if, when it came to matters of style, they had followed Quintilian and read Crassus as a cipher for Cicero.[5] To a far greater extent, the dialogic games and careful distancing of Scipio's vision of monarchy would have been a particularly provocative way of getting the most powerful men at Rome to reflect upon their own position. Cicero's authority came from the production of the dialogue, not from attempting to push his own valorization of leadership down his readers' throats. The reminders of Plato, the setting of the dialogue, the clear nostalgia, and the inapplicability of much of the constitutional debate to the readers of the 50s, make it difficult to find a Ciceronian source of authority within the work. And that is precisely the point: history, both in terms of the speakers and in terms of their representation of Rome's past, can embody ambiguities much more effectively than if the arguments need to be spelt out directly.

I hope that the texts I have examined, and the arguments I have brought forward on that basis, will have by now persuaded even sceptical readers that the desire to read into *De re publica* an account of Cicero's constitutional views is the result of a failure to respond

---

[4] In *De legibus* it is plausible to argue that the adoption of the authoritarian position fitted the subject matter, and that the debates about law reflected directly the kinds of controversies which Cicero and his colleagues would discuss. The fact that Cicero never completed or published this work makes it difficult to come to firm conclusions, but I would suggest that, in contrast to *De oratore* and *De re publica*, there was both less need for, and less to be gained from, a more artificial dialogue form, and closer working with historical representations. See Powell (2001) and Schmidt (2001).

[5] Quintilian, *Inst.* 10. 3. 1. Unlike Quintilian, they would not have been themselves dependent upon Cicero's rhetorical achievements for most of their understanding of rhetoric, so had, in all probability, a greater chance at critical distance than he.

naturally to the Academic philosophical method. The representational quality of the arguments and the strategy of leaving readers to examine their own preconceptions would both have been normal for Toland. The wish to struggle against such a broadly Platonic approach to the text is one that has emerged in the wake of an anxiety about rhetoric (a fear that representational argument must be dangerous and that we need to have things spelt out literally) and a preference for dogmatic readings, even of Plato, in the expectation of philosophical method; and in the general sense, from Cicero's dominance of the schoolroom, that he was, as a typical Roman, engaged in an authoritarian form of writing. Once we have grasped the effect that these adverse conditions have had upon our expectations of Cicero's philosophy, we can develop a better understanding of this grand philosophical project. The attempt to imprint theory on Rome was undertaken with an awareness of the dangers of appearing to do so too confidently. Cicero did not want to construct Rome in his own image, since he was aware, as his experience of exile had clearly shown him, what a frail thing that self-image was when compared to the manner in which power functioned at Rome. In part this can be seen as a problem about being a *novus homo*; but we should be wary of overestimating how unique a position Cicero held in this respect, and how unfamiliar this situation would be to his readers. There may not have been many consular *novi*, but historians have been aware for many decades of the permeability of the elite in this period. The problems of the relationship between skill, money, and birth were by no means ones with which only Cicero had to grapple, and the struggle, as far as it is perceptible in his philosophy, which Cicero articulates would have had wide echoes for many of his readers.[6]

In this context, Cicero's focus on the historical context of rhetoric takes on a particular importance. Self-image is of course central here, since it was by virtue of rhetorical skill that a public career could be produced without the status normally granted by genealogy—that is, family history. But the relationship between rhetoric and history is

---

[6] On *Brutus* Henderson (2006), 174, captures this well: 'Through his revolutionary ancestor L. Brutus, this twinning of (like-minded) "friends" makes of Cicero a "we" that takes in the entire founding establishment of Rome as the free Republic normed to an aristocratic ethos that by definition included the parsimonious incorporation of meritorious recruits.'

more than simply one of the substitution of a faculty that could be acquired by study for a condition that only historical circumstance could grant. In *De oratore*, particularly in book 3, Cicero does suggest that rhetoric is the key to achieving a particular kind of leadership: one based on wisdom and a mastery of a range of different discourses. That is the view that Crassus puts across, and even a sceptical approach to the methods of the dialogue would be hard pressed to find much daylight between that view and the one that Cicero himself holds. But in *De oratore* 1, he questions the historical basis of that view, so that once again we are caught between an idealization and the difficulties of locating it within a particular historical moment. History prevents rhetoric from becoming a timeless faculty, a transcendent method that enables an escape from real historical conditions (as in a way, it was for Isocrates). It is, therefore, essential to the dialogic structure that it is Crassus, not Cicero, who articulates that view. When applied to Cicero, such an appeal to method might be seen to work, but this would limit the appeal of his arguments, and once again the nostalgia for this kind of aristocratic discourse is itself a product of history.

Nevertheless, within these two earlier works, history does have a didactic function: in *De re publica* connected with philosophy and political theory, and in *De oratore*, with rhetoric. That function is to provide an authoritative foundation for a way of talking: a theoretical language and a model of civilized, educated debate. The different *coteries* of the two works may be unrealistic historical idealizations; but nevertheless, their main effect is to make Crassus, Scipio, Laelius, and Antonius into speaking models, figures for imitation by Cicero's readers. Any change that Cicero may hope to exert through his writings will only be possible if triumvirs or ex-consuls can start to talk like these models. This is not a fanciful overestimation of Cicero's ambitions. It is a commonplace of all the scholarship on these works that Cicero is forging a new theoretical language for Rome, and that among his highest linguistic achievements, and those with the most pervasive influence down the ages, has been provision of a stylistic model for theoretical debate. Cicero has in effect perceived that the exemplary quality is what gives Roman history its unique character, and has transferred that quality to political discourse. These are speaking characters from history, who provide models for admiration and imitation, who frame a discourse, in the same way that Sallust's Marius or any number of Tacitus' characters will do in the future.[7] This is one way of reading Antonius' digression on the style of history: to outline the aspiration that history will be able to find a style which will enable it to carry out its function properly, in the manner that Greek historiography has already achieved.

That function would be the proper stylistic animation which would enable effective imitation of the great figures of the past, not just the facts about how they lived, but how they expressed themselves. Cicero then tackles this head-on in *Brutus*: the genealogy of orators turns out not to be that, but rather, an examination of how the great men of Rome's past spoke in public, how they expressed themselves, and a quest for those among them who can act as adequate models for the kind of educated discourse that Cicero thinks will benefit Rome. At the start of *De oratore* 3, Crassus gives a foretaste of this, praising a selection of recent and living figures who have made discernible contributions to the expansion of expressive possibilities. We know that Greek teachers of rhetoric at Rome could already look to Greek historiography for examples of oratory: Dionysius of Halicarnassus (a generation later) is our best evidence, but we can be sure that he was working within a well-established tradition. Cicero is approaching Rome with the same agenda, broadly speaking one built on Isocrates, in which political power overlaps the insights granted by education, where philosophy and rhetoric are the keys to effective statecraft. But although this agenda is clear, Cicero does not suppress the fact that history will act as an obstacle to its implementation. This is true in the works of the 50s, and it is doubly true in the later texts: *Brutus* presents us with no illusions about how few and far between such inspirational models were in Rome.

The citizen, therefore, is a being within history; and Cicero seems fundamentally opposed to any attempt to use theory to wrest that citizen free from captivity. Nevertheless, that history is telling two stories at once. And because Cicero is determined to keep his philosophy relevant, to prevent it from becoming too abstract, or too foreign to the Roman context, any notion of a philosophical solution to Rome's problems will not be a dogmatic one with a single, foundational,

---

[7] Rancière (1994), 24–30.

historical narrative behind it. It is here that Cicero's work with history provides us with a different model of pedagogy, and a different notion of textual authority, one which is well adapted to the ambiguous ideological climate of Rome, and the equally ambiguous needs of our own academies. The increased marginalization of the humanities during the twentieth century can be seen in part as a response to the ever increasing success of scientific models of investigation and truth; but it is not the natural sciences, so much as the social sciences and those branches of historical study which aspired to their methods, that have left an education based on reading and interpreting struggling to redefine its educational value. In so far as modern Western education implies a model of productive citizenship, that model centres on practical, vocational skills, and in spite of the increasing complexity of the social and economic realities, dominance of a way of thinking about problems that demands some kind of unequivocal 'right answer' shows few signs of losing power. There is little authority within the Academy for a form of enquiry that stresses the need for an ongoing dialectic, and I am not aware of a positive paradigm for rhetoric which lays an emphasis upon the generative power of texts to produce better discourses in the future. Particularly in a complex world, where the dangers of cultural, religious, and social miscommunication are apparent, such a model might in fact have a lot to recommend it. In the prehistory of our own disciplines, it is still visible. Toland's vision of a future for his own style that will emerge from having himself worked over Cicero seems to represent a foreign way of thinking about intellectual endeavour, and likewise, what Toland most values about Cicero is the very existence of his writings. He does not need his philosophy to provide answers. Neither does he require Cicero to constrain his own reading in order for him to vindicate his own role as a reader, student, or expert. Indeed, the appeal of Cicero as a weapon of Enlightenment lies principally in Toland's faith in the inspirational and generative quality of reading itself, and in removing scholastic excrescence which stands in the way of that encounter.

   Cicero's own quest to bring philosophy into history never entirely sheds its scepticism about the entire undertaking, and the vision of Rome as a society of poor communicators unable to apply rational insights to public discourse never entirely disappears. That vision is a great deal more concrete than some vague anxiety about how Cicero himself fits in to Rome; perhaps in the works of the 50s such an analysis is plausible, but it strikes me as more likely that Cicero is responding to the unpredictability which his own experience of power witnessed, and attempting to formulate ways in which power and authority within an established framework can be exercised with greater self-awareness. Certainly there are aspects of *De oratore* such that the solution to this looks like some kind of ahistorical ideal of political wisdom based, as in Isocrates, on a benign consensus between articulate and well-educated statesmen; or, in other parts of the work, the solution is theory itself, a possibility that Cicero never abandoned. As his work develops, however, Cicero's solution is to encourage his readers to continue thinking, and to continue thinking in particular about the relationship between the resources offered both by Roman historical traditions and by theoretical insights. The pessimism that is more latent in *De oratore* becomes more visible even in *De re publica*, and by the time of *Brutus*, it is explicit.

The picture of citizenship which emerges from this engagement with history is, therefore, rather more complex than the one which has characterized the image of Cicero that has been influential for much of his more recent afterlife. Toland's work suggests that this may be due not so much to an increased sophistication in our understanding of Cicero, as to the elaborate structures of the Academy, and the preoccupations of scholars with their own reputations. Fantham has recently lamented the turn which Cicero scholarship has taken in rupturing the tradition of humanistic education with an insistence on power politics.[8] This dichotomy of approaches, it will by now be clear, rests upon a misconstruction of Cicero's rhetoric, and upon the difficulty of responding to the generative impulse of theoretical works that were written to situate that rhetoric in its particular context. Likewise, the whole assumption of the work of our academies as aiming at authority, and of reading as a form of obedience to instruction, is the product of post-Enlightenment disciplinary developments of which Cicero has certainly been more a victim than a founder. The eighteenth-century turn away from scepticism towards idealism in philosophy, and the wane of any interest in an integrative

---

[8] Fantham (2004), 327.

rhetoric in which reading and textual production could work towards a sense of common values, has made it almost impossible to accept the play of irony and refusal of synthesis that characterize Cicero's theoretical encapsulation of Rome, simply because we expect more of our theory than Cicero did, and also of our history.

I will end by considering in more general terms how, to the mediators of Cicero in today's Academy, this image of Cicero can help negotiate the notions of identity which ultimately lie behind the controversies about how to read. Recent studies of Cicero with their focus on performance, self-fashioning, rhetorical coercion, and the putative attempt by Cicero to identify himself as master of the Roman discourse of power are actually continuations of the same traditions which Toland isolated as inimical to Cicero's reputation: an interest in rhetoric as mere verbal display, a quest for philosophical authority, and an over-identification of the reader with the text. This last problem is closely related to the other two, since it is the loss of contact with the idea of texts as inspirational and generative that enables the reader to imagine that Cicero is going through the same processes of self-projection that characterize the identity politics of the postmodern era. Those politics themselves insist upon the centrality of self-fashioning and performance, and upon the freedom of the individuals to liberate themselves from history, to attempt to control, rather than be controlled by, discursive practices. The repertoire of concepts can be bought to bear on Cicero in much the same way that, in the nineteenth century, the concept of political will could be, or, indeed, in a more pervasive form, the notion of Cicero as a gentleman. In every case we are dealing with a too-close identification based upon a fundamental inability to grasp instinctively the ambiguous quality of ancient rhetoric. That rhetoric, I have suggested, could at the same time present sources of authority and provide the means for questioning that authority; in the process, its inspirational quality would not be damaged.

The dynamics of Cicero's work with historical representation suggest that we need to look at a different relationship between discourse and history if we want to find a Cicero who is not foreclosing on questions of authority. But it is not difficult either to find the roots of that discourse in Cicero's own practice, in his frequent appeals to the Academy, or to appreciate its educational advantages today. In a world in which conflicts of identity, and a fragmentation of any idea of social consensus, are far more extreme than Cicero could ever have imagined, there is an obvious relevance in the application of scepticism to the attempt to ground identity in history, and to use history to modify philosophical transcendence. Cicero exposes the provisionality of such position taking, and in the process encourages his readers to continue to read and to continue to think. This is a form of discourse that, in my mind, will grant a securer future for the humanities in today's Academy than one that seeks to politicize them by identifying rhetorical power with political power in a long-dead society, in which the reality of those power structures can only ever be a matter of wild conjecture. This, it seems to me, is the real product of Cicero's aspirations to immortality, at least as far as his theoretical works are concerned: not that his personality or his political reputation should act as models for future citizens, but rather that the process of reading and learning should continue to work, partly through imitation, partly through the encounter with a wide range of differing viewpoints, conflicting histories and voices in dialogue. Perhaps it was marginalization and over-compensation, or grief, that propelled Cicero's theoretical work; but when reading that work, I prefer an approach that sustains the ambiguities inherent in his project to one which closely identifies the image of Rome which emerges in them as an attempt to superimpose some kind of personal authority. That approach is encouraged, I believe, by the dialogic picture of Rome's history that Cicero's encounter with it produces.

Bibliography

All of the original material for John Toland published after 1700 is available online in *Eighteenth Century Collections Online*. *Gale Group*. (http://galenet. galegroup.com/servlet/ECCO)

Adamietz, J. (ed.) (1989), *Marcus Tullius Cicero: Pro Murena*, Darmstadt.

Algra, K. A., P. W. v. d. Horst, and D. T. Runia (eds.) (1996), *Polyhistor: Studies in the History and Historiography of Ancient Philosophy Presented to Jaap Mansfeld on his Fiftieth Birthday*, Leiden.

Allen, W. (1954), 'Cicero's Conceit', *TAPhA* 85, 21–144.

—— (1956), ' "O Fortunatam Natam ..." ', *TAPhA* 87, 130–46.

Amodeo, I. (2005), 'Giambattista Vicos *Neue Wissenschaft* und die antike Rhetorik', in W. Kofler and K. Töchterle (eds.), *Pontes III: Die antike Rhetorik in der europäischen Geistesgeschichte*, Innsbruck, 292–303.

Ankersmit, F. R. (1994), *History and Tropology: The Rise and Fall of Metaphor*, Berkeley.

Annas, J. (1992), 'Plato the Sceptic', in Klagge and Smith (1992), 43–72.

—— and C. Rowe (eds.) (2002), *New Perspectives on Plato, Modern and Ancient* (Center for Hellenic Studies Colloquia 6), Cambridge, Mass.

Astin, A. E. (1967), *Scipio Aemilianus*, Oxford.

Attridge, D. (2004), *The Singularity of Literature*, London.

[Barnes, J.] (1712) Philargyrius Cantab., *Aristarchus Ampullans in Curis Horatianis*, London.

Barnes, J. (1989), 'Antiochus of Ascalon', in M. Griffin and J. Barnes (eds.), *Philosophia Togata*, i, Oxford, 51–69.

Batstone, W. M. (1994), 'Cicero's Construction of Consular Ethos in the First Catilinarian', *TAPhA* 124, 211–66.

Bauman, R. A. (1996), *Crime and Punishment in Ancient Rome*, London.

Bayle, P. (1738), *A General Dictionary Historical and Critical*, vii, London.

—— (1820), *Dictionnaire historique et critique de Pierre Bayle: Nouvelle Edition*, ed. Beuchot, Paris.

Beard, M. (1986), 'Cicero and Divination', *JRS* 76, 33–56.

—— (1987), 'A Complex of Times', *PCPS* 33, 1–15.

—— (1998), 'Vita Inscripta', in W.-W. Ehlers (ed.), *La Biographie Antique* (Entretiens Hardt, 44), Geneva, 83–114.

Bell, D. A. (1994), *Lawyers and Citizens: The Making of a Political Elite in Old Regime France*, Oxford.

Berlioz, J., and J.-M. David (1980), 'Introduction Bibliographique', *Méfra*, 92, 15–23.

Berman, D. (1992), 'Disclaimers in Blount and Toland', in M. Hunter and D. Wootton (eds.), *Atheism from the Reformation to the Enlightenment*, Oxford, 225–72.

Bezzola, T. (1993), *Die Rhetorik bei Kant, Fichte und Hegel*, Tübingen.

Bigalli, D., and G. Canziani (eds.) (1990), *Il dialogo filosofico nel '500 europeo: Atti del convegno internazionale di studi, Milano, 28–30 maggio 1987*, Milan.

Birch, T. (1738), *A Complete Collection of the Historical, Political, and Miscellaneous Works of John Milton ... with an account of the life and writings of the Author (by T. Birch)*, London.

Blondell, R. (2002), *The Play of Character in Plato's Dialogues*, Cambridge.

Blößner, N. (2001), 'Cicero gegen die Philosophie: Eine Analyse von *De re publica* 1,1–3', *N. A. d. W. Gött. Phil-Hist. Kl.*, no. 3, 201–71.

Borghero, C. (1983), *La Certezza e la Storia: Cartesianesimo, pironismo e conoscenza storica*, Milan.

Brinton, A. (1988), 'Cicero's Use of Historical Examples in Moral Argument', *Philosophy and Rhetoric*, 21, 169–84.

Brittain, C. (2001), *Philo of Larissa: The Last of the Academic Sceptics*, Oxford.

Brunt, P. A. (1997), 'Cicero and Historiography', in *Studies in Greek History and Thought*, Oxford, 181–209.

Buck, A., *et al.* (eds.) (1983), *Die Antike-Rezeption in den Wissenschaften während der Renaissance*, Weinheim.

Büchner, K. (1980), *Römische Literaturgeschichte*, 5th edn., Stuttgart.

—— (1984), *M. Tullius Cicero: De Republica: Kommentar*, Heidelberg.

Burke, S. (ed.) (1995), *Authorship: From Plato to the Postmodern*, Edinburgh.

Butler, S. (2002), *The Hand of Cicero*, London.

Candau Morón, J. M. (2000), 'Plutarch's Lysander and Sulla: Integrated Characters in Roman Historical Perspective', *AJPh* 121, 453–67.

Canfora, L. (2000), 'L'edizione ciceroniana di Johann Caspar von Orelli', in Ferrari (2000), 119–29.

Cavaillé, J-P. (1998), 'Le retour des sceptiques', *Revue Philosophique*, 123/2, 197–222.

Champion, J. (2003), *Republican Learning: John Toland and the Crisis of Christian Culture, 1696–1722*, Manchester.

Charrier, S. (2003), 'Les années 90–80 dans le *Brutus* de Cicéron, (§§304–312): La formation d'un Orateur au temps des guerres civiles', *R.É.L.* 81, 79–96.

Chassignet, M. (1996), *L'Annalistique Romaine*, i: *Les Annales des Pontifes et l'Annalistique Ancienne (Fragments)*, Paris.

324 *Bibliography*

Chassignet, M. (1999), *L'Annalistique Romaine II: L'annalistique moyenne*, Paris.

Chevalier, R. (ed.) (1984), *Présence de Cicéron: Homage au R. P. M. Testard* (Collection Caesarodunum 19 bis), Paris.

Christes, J. (1989), 'Bemerkung zu Cicero, De re publica 1,60; 2,21–2; 2.30; 3,33', *Gymnasium* 96, 38–48.

Clark, G., and T. Rajak (eds.) (2001), *Philosophy and Power in the Graeco-Roman World*, Oxford.

Classen, C. J. (1989), 'Die Peripatetiker in Cicero's *Tuskulanen*', in Fortenbaugh and Steinmetz (1989), 186–200.

—— (2003), *Antike Rhetorik im Zeitalter des Humanismus* (Beiträge zum Alterstumkunde 182), Munich.

Coleman, K. M. (1990), 'Fatal Charades: Roman Executions Staged as Mythological Enactments', *JRS* 80, 47–73.

Cornell, T. J. (2001), 'Cicero on the Origins of Rome', in Powell and North (2001), 41–56.

Cotton, H. M., and A. Yakobson (2001), '*Arcanum Imperii*: The Powers of Augustus', in Clark and Rajak (2001), 193–209.

Croll, M. W. (1969), *Attic and Baroque Prose Style: Essays by Morris W. Croll*, ed. J. M. Patrick *et al.*, Princeton.

Curll, E. (1722), *An Historical Account of the Life and Writings of the Late Eminently Famous Mr. John Toland. ... By one of his most intimate friends*, London.

Daniel, S. H. (2004), 'John Toland', in *Oxford Dictionary of National Biography*, Oxford, liv. 894–8.

David, J-M. (1980), 'Maiorum exempla sequi: l'exemplum historique dans les discours judiciaries de Cicéron', *Méfra*, 92, 67–86.

Demandt, A. (1972), *Geschichte als Argument*, Konstanz.

Derrida, J. (1981), *Dissemination*, trans. B. Johnson, Chicago.

Desmaizeaux, P. (1740), *Scaligerana, Thuana, Perroniana, Pithoeana, et Colomesiana*, Amsterdam.

Desmouliez, A. (1982), 'A propos du jugement de Cicéron sur Caton l'Ancien', *Philologus*, 126, 70–89.

Döpp, S. (ed.) (1999), *Antike Rhetorik und ihre Rezeption*, Stuttgart.

Douay, F., and J.-P. Sermain (2002), 'Présentation', *Studies in Voltaire and the Eighteenth Century* 2002/02, 1–16.

Douglas, A. (1964), 'Cicero the philosopher', in T. A. Dorey (ed.), *Cicero*, London, 135–70.

—— (ed.) (1966), *Cicero: Brutus*, Oxford.

Drumann, W. K. A. (1929), *Geschichte Roms in seinem Übergange von der republikanischen zur monarchischen Verfassung*, vi: *M. Tullius Cicero*, ed. P. Groebe, 2nd edn., Leipzig.

Dugan, J. (2001*a*), 'How to Make (and Break) a Cicero: Epideixis, Textuality, and Self-Fashioning in the Pro Archia and In Pisonem', *Classical Antiquity*, 20, 35–77.

—— (2001*b*), 'Preventing Ciceronianism: C. Licinius Calvus' Regimens for Sexual and Oratorical Self-Mastery', *C.Ph.* 96, 400–28.

—— (2005), *Making a New Man: Ciceronian Self-Fashioning in the Rhetorical Works*, Oxford.

Dyck, A. R. (1998), 'Cicero the Dramaturge', in G. L. Schmeling and J. D. Mikalson (eds.), *Qui Miscuit Utile Dulci: Festschrift Essays for Paul Lachlan MacKendrick*, Wauconda, Ill., 151–64.

—— (2001), 'Dressing to Kill: Attire as a Proof and Means of Characterization in Cicero's Speeches', *Arethusa*, 34, 119–30.

—— (2002), 'Text and Commentary: The Example of Cicero's *Philosophica*', in R. S. Gibson and C. S. Kraus (eds.), *The Classical Commentary: Histories, Practices, Theory*, Leiden, 319–29.

Dyck, J. (1991), 'Überlegungen zur Rhetorik des 18. Jahrhunderts', in Ueding (1991), 99–101.

—— and J. Sandstede (1996), *Quellenbibliographie zur Rhetorik, Homiletik und Epistolographie des 18. Jahrhunderts im deutschsprachigen Raum*, Stuttgart-Bad Cannstatt.

Eagleton, T. (1990), *The Ideology of the Aesthetic*, Oxford.

Eck, W. (1997), 'Rome and the Outside World: Senatorial Families and the World They Lived In', in B. Rawson and P. Weaver (eds.), *The Roman Family in Italy*, Canberra and Oxford, 73–99.

Edwards, C. (1993), *The Politics of Immorality in Ancient Rome*, Cambridge.

F., S. (1700), *Mr. Toland's Clito Dissected*, London.

Fantham, E. (2004), *The Roman World of Cicero's De Oratore*, Oxford.

Feeney, D. (1998), *Literature and Religion at Rome*, Cambridge.

Ferrari, M. C. (ed.) (2000), *Gegen Unwissenheit und Finsternis: Johann Caspar von Orelli (1787–1849) und die Kultur seiner Zeit*, Zurich.

Fleck, M. (1993), *Cicero als Historiker*, Stuttgart.

Flower, H. (1996), *Ancestor Masks and Aristocratic Power in Roman Culture*, Oxford.

Flower, M. A. (1994), *Theopompus of Chios: History and Rhetoric in the Fourth Century BC*, Oxford.

Forsythe, G. (1991), 'A Philological Note on the Scipionic Circle', *AJPh* 112, 363–4.

—— (2005), *Critical History of Early Rome: From Prehistory to the First Punic War*, Berkeley.

Fortenbaugh, W. W. (2005), 'Cicero as a Reporter of Aristotelian and Theophrastean Rhetorical Doctrine', *Rhetorica* 23, 37–64.

Fortenbaugh, W. W. and P. Steinmetz (eds.) (1989), *Cicero's Knowledge of the Peripatos*, New Brunswick, NJ.

Fox, M. (1996), *Roman Historical Myths*, Oxford.

—— (2000), 'Dialogue and Irony in Cicero: Reading *de Republica*', in A. Sharrock and H. Morales (eds.), *Intratextuality*, Oxford, 263–86.

—— (2001), 'Dionysius, Lucian, and the Prejudice against Rhetoric in Historiography', *JRS* 91, 76–93.

—— (forthcoming), 'Heraclides of Pontus and the Dialogue Form', in W. W. Fortenbaugh and E. Schütrumpf (eds.), *Heraclides of Pontus*, New Brunswick, NJ.

Franke, W. (2000),'Metaphor and the Making of Sense: The Contemporary Metaphor Renaissance', *Philosophy and Rhetoric*, 33/2, 137–53.

Frede, D. (1989), 'Constitution and Citizenship: Peripatetic Influence on Cicero's Political Conceptions in the *De republica*', in Fortenbaugh and Steinmetz (1989), 77–100.

Freedman, J. S. (1986), 'Cicero in Sixteenth- and Seventeenth-Century Rhetoric Instruction', *Rhetorica*, 4, 227–54.

Frier, B. W. (1999), *Libri Annales Pontificum Maximorum: The Origins of the Annalistic Tradition*, 2nd edn., Ann Arbor.

Fuchs, H. (1959), 'Ciceros Hingabe an die Philosophie', *MH* 16, 1–28.

Fuhrmann, M. (1973), 'Das Exemplum in der antiken Rhetorik', in Koselleck (1973), 449–52.

—— (1983), *Rhetorik und öffentliche Rede: über die Ursachen des Verfalls der Rhetoric im ausgehenden 18. Jahrhundert*, Konstanz.

—— (1987), 'Erneuerung als Wiederherstellung des Alten', in R. Herzog (ed.), *Epochenschwelle und Epochenbewußtsein* (Poetik und Hermeneutik 12), Munich, 131–51.

—— (1989), 'Die Tradition der Rhetorik-Verachtung und das deutsche Bild vom "Advokaten" Cicero', *Rhetorik* 8, 43–55, also *Ciceroniana*, 6 (1988), 19–30.

—— (2000), 'Cicero im 19. Jahrhundert', in Ferrari (2000), 101–17.

Gadamer, H-G. (1934), *Plato und die Dichter*, Frankfurt.

—— (1990), *Wahrheit und Methode*, 6th edn., Munich.

Gaines, R. N. (2002), 'Cicero's *Partitiones Oratoriae* and *Topica*: Rhetorical Philosophy and Philosophical Rhetoric', in May (2002), 445–80.

Gawlick, G. (1963), 'Cicero and the Enlightenment', *Studies in Voltaire and the Eighteenth Century*, 25, 657–82.

Gigon, O. (1973), 'Cicero und die Griechische Philosophie', *A.N.R.W.* 1/4, 226–61.

Gill, C. (1996), 'Afterword: Dialectic and the Dialogue Form in Late Plato', in Gill and McCabe (1996), 283–311.

Gill, C. and M. M. McCabe (eds.) (1996), *Form and Argument in Late Plato*, Oxford.

Giovannini, A. (ed.) (2000), *La Révolution romaine après Ronald Syme* (Entretiens Hardt 46), Geneva.

Girardet, K. M. (1983), *Die Ordnung der Welt: Ein Beitrag zur philosophischen und politischen Interpretation von Ciceros Schrift De Legibus* (Historia Einzelschriften 42), Wiesbaden.

Gleason, M. W. (1995), *Making Men*, Princeton.

Glucker, J. (1978), *Antiochus and the Late Academy*, Göttingen.

—— (1987), 'Plato in England, the Nineteenth Century and After', in H. Funke (ed.), *Utopie und Tradition, Platons Lehre vom Staat in der Moderne*, Würzburg, 149–210.

—— (1996), 'The Two Platos of Victorian Britain', in Algra *et al.* (1996), 385–406.

Goar, R. J. (1968), 'The Purpose of De divinatione', *TAPhA* 99, 241–8.

Görler, W. (1974), *Untersuchungen zu Ciceros Philosophie*, Heidelberg.

—— (1990*a*), 'Antiochus von Askalon über die "Alten" und über die Stoa: Beobachtung zu Cicero, Academic posteriores 1,23–43', in Steinmetz (1990), 123–39.

—— (1990*b*), 'Cicero zwischen Politik und Philosophie', *Ciceroniana*, 7, 61–73.

—— (1995), 'Silencing the Troublemaker: *De Legibus* I.39', in Powell (1995), 85–113.

Gottschalk, H. B. (1980), *Heraclides of Pontus*, Oxford.

Gowing, A. (2000), 'Memory and Silence in Cicero's *Brutus*', *Eranos*, 98, 39–64.

—— (2005), *Empire and Memory: The Representation of the Roman Republic in Imperial Culture*, Cambridge.

Granatelli, R. (1990), '*L'in utramque partem disserendi exercitatio* nell'evoluzione del pensiero retorico e filosofico dell'antichità', *Vichiana: rassegna di studi filologici e storici*, 3rd ser., 1–2, 165–81.

Grenler, D. F. (2002), *The Universities of the Italian Renaissance*, Baltimore.

Griffin, M. (1997), 'The Composition of the *Academica*: Motives and Versions', in *Assent and Argument: Studies in Cicero's Academic Books*, ed. B. Inwood and J. Mansfeld, Leiden, 1–35.

—— and Atkins, E. M. (eds.) (1991), *Cicero: On Duties*, Cambridge.

Habinek, T. N. (1998), *The Politics of Latin Literature: Writing, Identity & Empire in Ancient Rome*, Ewing, NJ.

Hall, J. (1996), 'Social Evasion and Aristocratic Manners in Cicero's *De Oratore*', *AJPh* 117, 95–120.

—— (1998), 'Cicero to Lucceius (Fam. 5.12) in its Social Context: Valde Bella?', *CP* 93, 308–21.

Hankinson, R. J. (1995), *The Sceptics*, London.

Harris, W. V. (2003), 'Roman Opinions about the Truthfulness of Dreams', *JRS* 93, 18–34.

Harrison, S. J. (1990), 'Cicero's "De temporibus suis"': The Evidence Reconsidered', *Hermes*, 118, 455–63.

Häussler, R. (1965), *Tacitus und das historische Bewusstsein*, Heidelberg.

Heberden, W. (1825), *The Letters of Marcus Tullius Cicero*, London.

Hegel, G. F. W. (1969–1971), *Werke in 20 Bänden: auf der Grundlage der Werke von 1832–1845*, ed. E. Moldenhauer and K. M. Michel, Frankfurt.

Heilmann, W. (1989), ' "Goldene Zeit" und geschichtliche Zeit im Dialogus de oratoribus', *Gymnasium*, 96, 385–405.

Heinemann, F. H. (1945), 'Toland and Leibniz', *Philosophical Review*, 64, 437–57.

Henderson, J. (1998), *Fighting for Rome*, Cambridge.

—— (2006), 'From ΦΙΛΟΣΟΦΙΑ into *PHILOSOPHIA*', in J. I. Porter (ed.), *Classical Pasts: The Classical Traditions of Greece and Rome*, Princeton, 173–203.

Hendrickson, G. L. (ed.) (1962), *Cicero: Brutus* (Loeb edn., rev.), London.

Hose, M. (1995), 'Cicero als hellenistischer Epiker', *Hermes*, 123, 455–69.

Hunt, J. M. (1981), 'Review Article: On Editing the Letters of Cicero', *Cl. Phil.* 76, 215–24.

Innes, D. C. (1978), 'Phidias and Cicero', *CQ* 28, 470–1.

Jahn, O., and W. Kroll (eds.) (1962), *Cicero: Brutus*, rev. B. Kytzler, Berlin.

Jocelyn, H. D. (1973), 'Greek Poetry in Cicero', *YCS* 23, 61–111.

Johansen, K. F. (1991), *A History of Ancient Philosophy from the Beginnings to Augustine*, London.

Jones-Davies, M. T. (ed.) (1984), *Le Dialogue au temps de la Renaissance* (Centre de Recherches sur la Renaissance, Université de Paris-Sorbonne 9), Paris.

Kahn, C. H. (1998), *Plato and the Socratic Dialogue*, Cambridge.

Kany-Turpin, J., and P. Pellegrin (1989), 'Cicero and the Aristotelian theory of Divination by Dreams', in Fortenbaugh and Steinmetz (1989), 220–45.

Kant, I. (1910–), *Gesammelte Schriften*, ed. königliche preussische Akademie der Wissenschaften, Berlin.

Kennedy, G. A. (ed.) (1989), *The Cambridge History of Literary Criticism, i: Classical Criticism*, Cambridge.

—— (1999), *Classical Rhetoric & its Christian and Secular Tradition*, 2nd edn., Chapel Hill, NC.

—— (2002), 'Cicero's Oratorical and Rhetorical Legacy', in May (2002), 481–501.

Kessler, E. E. (1983), 'Die Ausbildung der Theorie der Geschichtsschreibung im Humanismus und in der Renaissance', in A. Buck and K. Heitmann (eds.), *Die Antike-Rezeption in den Wissenschaften während der Renaissance*, Weinheim, 29–49.

Kierdorf, W. (2003), *Römische Geschichtsschreibung der republikanischen Zeit*, Heidelberg.

Klagge, J. C., and N. D. Smith, (eds.) (1992), *Methods of Interpreting Plato and his Dialogues* (Oxford Studies in Ancient Philosophy, suppl. vol., 1992), Oxford.

Koortbojian, M. (1996), '*In commemorationem mortuorum*: Text and Image along the Street of Tombs', in J. Elsner (ed.), *Art and Text in Roman Culture*, Cambridge, 210–33.

Koselleck, R. (ed.) (1973), *Geschichte, Ereignis und Erzählung* (Poetik und Hermeneutik 5), Munich.

Kraus, C. S. (ed.) (1994), *Livy, Ab Urbe Condita Book VI*, Cambridge.

—— (2005), 'Hair, Hegemony, and Historiography: Caesar's Style and its Earliest Critics', *Proceedings of the British Academy*, 129, 97–115.

Krostenko, B. A. (2000), 'Beyond (Dis)belief: Rhetorical Form and Religious Symbol in Cicero's de Divinatione', *TAPhA* 130, 353–91.

—— (2001), *Cicero, Catullus, and the Language of Social Performance*, Chicago.

Leeman, A. D., and H. Pinkster (eds.) (1981, 1985, 1996), *M. T. Cicero: De oratore libri III*, 3 vols., Heidelberg.

Lefèvre, E. (2001), *Panaitios' und Ciceros Pflichtenlehre: vom philosophischen Traktat zum politischen Lehrbuch*, Stuttgart.

Leigh, M. (1995), 'Wounding and Popular Rhetoric at Rome', *BICS* 40, 195–212.

—— (2004), 'The *Pro Caelio* and Comedy', *Class. Phil.* 99, 300–35.

Leonhardt, J. (1999), *Ciceros Kritik der Philosophenschulen* (Zetemata 103), Munich.

Levene, D. S. (1992), 'Sallust's Jugurtha: An "Historical Fragment"', *JRS* 82, 53–70.

—— (2004), 'Tacitus' *Dialogus* as Literary History', *TAPhA* 134, 157–200.

Lévy, C. (1992), *Cicero Academicus: Recherches sur les* Académiques *et sur la philosophie cicéronienne* (Collection de l'Ecole française de Rome 162), Rome.

—— (2003), 'Cicero and the *Timaeus*', in G. J. Reydams-Schils (ed.), *Plato's Timaeus as Cultural Icon*, Notre Dame, Ind., 95–110.

Long, A. A. (1995), 'Cicero's Plato and Aristotle', in Powell (1995), 37–61.

—— (2003), 'Roman Philosophy', in D. Sedley (ed.), *The Cambridge Companion to Greek and Roman Philosophy*, Cambridge, 184–210.

Luce, T. J. (1989), 'Ancient Views on the Causes of Bias in Historical Writing', *CP* 84, 16–31.

Mack, P. (1984), 'The Dialogue in English Education of the Sixteenth Century', in Jones-Davies (1984), 189–209.

MacKendrick, P. (1989), *The Philosophical Books of Cicero*, London.

Maia Neto, J. R. (1997), 'Academic Skepticism in Early Modern Philosophy', *JHI* 58, 199–220.

Margolin, J-C. (1990), 'Le Dialogue philosophique comme manifeste socio-culturel: le "Ciceronianus" d'Erasme (Mars 1528)', in Bigalli and Canziani (1990), 83–112.

—— (1991), 'Le Moment historique d'Erasme', in Ueding (1991), 109–18.

Marincola, J. (1997), *Authority and Tradition in Ancient Historiography*, Cambridge.

Martindale, C., and R. F. Thomas (eds.) (2006), *Classics and the Uses of Reception*, Oxford.

May, J. M. (1988), *Trials of Character: The Eloquence of Ciceronian Ethos*, Chapel Hill, NC.

—— (1990), 'The Monologistic Dialogue as a Method of Literary Criticism: Cicero, *Brutus* 285–289 and Horace, *Epistle* 2.1.34–39', *Athenaeum*, 78, 177–80.

—— (ed.) (2002), *Brill's Companion to Cicero: Oratory and Rhetoric*, Leiden.

Mellor, R. (1999), *Roman Historians*, London.

Mergenthaler, V. (2000), 'Imitatio und Ingenium in der Commedia dell'arte: Spuren des Ciceronianismusstreits im Stegreiftheater', in H. Laufhütte (ed.), *Künste und Natur in Diskursen der Frühen Neuzeit*, Wiesbaden, 591–602.

Meyer, U. (1998), *Politische Rhetorik: Theorie, Analyse und Geschichte der Redekunst am Beispiel des Spätaufklärers Johann Gottfried Seume*, Paderborn.

Michel, A. (1960), *Rhetorique et Philosophie chez Cicéron*, Paris.

—— (1965), 'A propos de l'art du dialogue dans le *De Republica*: l'idéal et la réalité chez Cicéron', *REL* 43, 237–61.

—— (1977), 'Dialogue philosophique et vie intérieure: Cicéron, Sénèque, Saint Augustin', *Helmantica*, 28, 353–76.

—— (1984), 'L'Influence du dialogue Cicéronien sur la tradition philosophique et litteraire', in Jones-Davies (1984), 9–24.

Mooney, M. (1985), *Vico in the Tradition of Rhetoric*, Princeton.

Momigliano, A. (1987), 'The Introduction of History as an Academic Subject and its Implications', in *Ottavo Contributo alla Storia degli Studi Classici*, Rome, 161–78.

Morford, M. (2002), *The Roman Philosophers*, London.

Morgan, K. (1998), 'Designer History: Plato's Atlantis Story and Fourth-Century Ideology', *JHS* 118, 101–18.

Morgan, L. (2000), 'The Autopsy of C. Asinius Pollio', *JRS* 90, 51–69.

Mortstein-Marx, R. (2004), *Mass Oratory and Political Power in the Late Roman Republic*, Cambridge.

Mouritsen, H. (2001), *Plebs and Politics in the Late Roman Republic*, London.

Müller, R. (1989), 'Das Problem Theorie-Praxis in der Peripatos-Rezeption von Ciceros Staatsschrift', in Fortenbaugh and Steinmetz (1989), 101–13.

Murphy, J. J. (1974), *Rhetoric in the Middle Ages*, Berkeley.

—— (2005), *Latin Rhetoric and Education in the Middle Ages and Renaissance*, Aldershot.

Narducci, E. (1997), *Cicerone e l'eloquenza romana*, Bari.

—— (2002), '*Brutus*: The History of Roman Eloquence', in May (2002), 401–25.

Nickau, K. (1999), 'Peripateticorum consuetudo', in Döpp (1999), 15–28.

Oakley, S. P. (1997), *A Commentary on Livy Books VI–X*, i: *Introduction and Book VI*, Oxford.

O'Brien, K. (2001), 'The History Market in Eighteenth Century England', in Rivers (2001), 105–13.

Ockel, E. (1991), 'Zur rhetorischen Bildung als Indiz gesellschaftlicher Strömungen', in Ueding (1991), 362–70.

Ogilvie, R. M. (1965), *A Commentary on Livy Books 1–5*, Oxford.

O'Gorman, E. (2000), *Irony and Misreading in the* Annals *of Tacitus*, Cambridge.

Oliensis, E. (2002), review of A. Sharrock and H. Morales (eds.), *Intratextuality* (Oxford, 2000), *BMCR*, 21 June 2002.

Oppermann, H. (1967), 'Die Einleitung zum Geschichtswerk des Livius', repr. in E. Burck (ed.), *Wege zu Livius*, Darmstadt, 169–80.

Oppermann, J. (2000), *Zur Funktion historischer Beispiele in Ciceros Briefen* (Beitrage zur Altertumskunde 138), Munich and Leipzig.

Ordine, N. (1990), 'Teoria e "situazione" del dialogo nel Cinquecento italiano', in Bigalli and Canziani (1990), 13–33.

Osborne, C. (1996), 'Creative Discourse in the *Timaeus*', in Gill and McCabe (1996), 179–211.

Paganini, G. (2004), 'Towards a "Critical" Bayle: Three Recent Studies', *Eighteenth-Century Studies*, 37, 510–20.

Peck, T. (1897), 'Cicero's Hexameters', *TAPhA* 28, 60–74.

Petzold, K-E. (1972), 'Cicero und Historie', *Chiron*, 2, 253–76; repr. in Petzold (1999), 86–109.

—— (1999), *Geschichtsdenken und Geschichtsschreibung* (Historia Einzelschriften 126), Stuttgart.

Phillips, M. S. (1996), 'Reconsiderations on History and Antiquarianism: Arnaldo Momigliano and the Historiography of Eighteenth-Century Britain', *JHI* 57, 297–316.

Pina Polo, F. (2004), 'Die nütlzliche Erinnerung: Geschichtsschreibung, *Mos Maiorum* und die Römische Indetität', *Historia*, 53, 147–72.

Plass, P. (1988), *Wit and the Writing of History*, Madison.

Pohlenz, M. (1931), 'Cicero De Republica als Kunstwerk', in A. Fraenkel and H. Fränkel (eds.), *Festschrift Richard Reitzenstein*, Leipzig, 70–105.

Poncelet, R. (1957), *Cicéron traducteur de Platon: l'expression de la pensée complexe en latin classique*, Paris.

Popkin, R. H. (2003), *The History of Scepticism: From Savonarola to Bayle*, Oxford.

Popper, K. R. (1945), *The Open Society and Its Enemies*, i: *The Spell of Plato*, London.

Powell, J. G. F. (ed.) (1995), *Cicero the Philosopher*, Oxford.

—— (1998), 'The Manuscripts and Text of Cicero's *Laelius de Amicitia*', *CQ* 48, 506–18.

—— (2001), 'Were Cicero's *Laws* the Laws of Cicero's *Republic*?', in Powell and North (2001), 17–39.

—— and J. A. North (eds.) (2001), *Cicero's Republic* (BICS Supplements 76), London.

Puelma, M. (1980), 'Cicero als Platon Uebersetzer', *Mus. Helv.* 37, 136–78.

Rahe, P. A. (1994), 'Cicero and Republicanism in America', *Ciceroniana*, 8, 63–78.

Rancière, J. (1994), *The Names of History*, Minneapolis.

Rathofer, C. (1986), *Ciceros 'Brutus' als literarisches Paradigma eines Auctoritas-Verhältnisses* (Beiträge zur Klassischen Philologie 174), Frankfurt.

Raven, J. (1998), 'New Reading Histories, Print Culture and the Identification of Change: The Case of Eighteenth-Century England', *Social History*, 23, 268–87.

Rawson, E. (1972), 'Cicero the Historian and Cicero the Antiquarian', *JRS* 62, 33–45.

—— (1973), 'The Interpretation of Cicero's "De Legibus" ', *A.N.R.W.* i/4, 334–56.

Reinhardt, T. (2000), 'Rhetoric in the Fourth Academy', *CQ* 50, 531–47.

Reynolds, L. D. (ed.) (1986), *Texts and Transmissions* (repr. with corrections), Oxford.

Rich, J. (1988), 'Augustus' Parthian Honours, the Temple of Mars Ultor and the Arch in the Forum Romanum', *PBSR* 56, 71–128.

Rivers, I. (2001*a*), 'Biographical Dictionaries', in Rivers (2001*b*), 135–69.

Rivers, I. (ed.) (2001*b*), *Books and their Readers in Eighteenth-Century England: New Essays*, London.

Robin, D. (1991), *Filelfo in Milan*, Princeton.

Rösch-Binde, C. (1998), *Vom 'deinos anêr' zum 'diligentissimus investigator antiquitatis': zur komplexen Beziehung zwischen M. Tullius Cicero und M. Terentius Varro*, Munich.

Rubinelli, S. (2002), 'The Invention of the Young Cicero', *CQ* 52, 612–15.

Rudd, N. (1992), 'Stratagems of Vanity: Cicero, *Ad Familiares* 5.12 and Pliny's Letter', in T. Woodman and J. Powell (eds.), *Author and Audience in Latin Literature*, Cambridge, 18–32.

Runia, D. T. (1989), 'Aristotle and Theophrastus Conjoined in the Writings of Cicero', in Fortenbaugh and Steinmetz (1989), 23–38.

Rutherford, R. B. (1995), *The Art of Plato*, Oxford.

Ryan, F. X. (1999), 'The Chronological Arrangement of Cicero, "Brutus" 239–242', *Latomus*, 58, 525–33.

Sabetti, A. (1984), *John Toland: Adeisidaemon e origines Judaicae*, Naples,

Schäublin, C. (1985), 'Cicero, "De divinatione" und Posidonius', *Mus. Helv.* 42, 157–67.

Schmidt, P. L. (2001), 'The Original Version of *de republica* and *de legibus*', in Powell and North (2001), 7–16.

Schmitt, C. (1983), 'Zur Rezeption antiken Sprachdenkens in der Renaissancephilologie', in Buck *et al.* (1983), 75–101.

Schmitt, C. B. (1972), *Cicero scepticus: A Study of the Influence of the 'Academica' in the Renaissance*, The Hague.

Schneider, W. C. (1998), *Vom Handeln der Römer* (Supdasmata 66), Hildesheim.

Schofield, M. (1986), 'Cicero for and against Divination', *JRS* 76, 47–65.

Schütrumpf, E. (1988), 'Platonic Elements in the Structure of Cicero "De oratore" Book 1', *Rhetorica*, 6, 237–58.

Shackleton Bailey, D. R. (ed.) (1965–71), *Cicero's Letters to Atticus*, Cambridge.

—— (ed.) (1977), *Cicero: Epistulae ad Familiares*, i, Cambridge.

Skinner, Q. (2002), 'Classical Liberty and the Coming of the English Civil War', in M. van Gelderen (ed.), *Republicanism: A Shared European Heritage*, Cambridge, 9–28.

Smith, N. (1996), 'The English Revolution and the End of Rhetoric: John Toland's *Clito* (1700) and the Republican Daemon', *Essays and Studies*, 49, 1–18.

Smith, P. R. (1995), 'How not to Write Philosophy: Did Cicero get it Right?', in Powell (1995), 301–23.

Smith, S. H. (2002), Tacitus *Agricola*: Representing Imperial Rome (unpublished Ph.D. thesis, Birmingham).

Spannagel, M. (1999), *Exemplaria Principis: Untersuchungen zu Entstehung und Ausstattung des Augustusforums*, Heidelberg.

Stalkever, P. (1992), Review of Klagge and Smith (1992), *BMCR*, 3.5.9.

Steel, C. E. W. (2001), *Cicero, Rhetoric, and Empire*, Oxford.

—— (2002–3), 'Cicero's *Brutus*', *BICS*, 46, 195–211.

—— (2005), *Reading Cicero: Genre and Performance in Late Republican Rome*, London.

Steinmetz, P. (1989), 'Beobachtung zu Ciceros philosophischem Standpunkt', in Fortenbaugh and Steinmetz (1989), 1–22.

—— (ed.) (1990*a*), *Beiträge zur hellenistischen Literatur und ihrer Rezeption in Rom* (Palingenesia 28), Stuttgart.

—— (1990*b*), 'Planung und Planänderung der philosophischen Schriften Ciceros', in Steinmetz (1990*a*), 141–53.

Stierle, K. (1973), 'Geschichte als Exemplum-Exemplum als Geschichte', in Koselleck (1973), 347–75.

Stokes, M. (1986), *Plato's Socratic Conversations*, Baltimore.

Strasburger, H. (1990), *Ciceros philosophisches Spätwerk als Aufruf gegen die Herrschaft Caesars* (Spudasmata 45), Hildesheim.

Straume-Zimmermann, L. (1976), *Ciceros Hortensius*, Frankfurt.

Streckenbach, G. (1979), *Stiltheorie und Rhetorik der Römer im Spiegel der humanistischen Schülergespräche*, Göttingen.

Suerbaum, W. (1996–7), 'Vorliterarische römische Redner (bis zum Beginn des 2. Jhs. v. Chr.) in Ciceros "Brutus" und in der historischen Überlieferung', *WJA* 21, 169–98.

Sullivan, R. E. (1982), *John Toland and the Deist Controversy: A Study in Adaptations*, Cambridge, Mass.

Swain, S. (1996), *Hellenism and Empire*, Oxford.

Sweeney, R. D. (2002), 'Art and Temporality', *Analecta Husserliana*, 77, 375–84.

—— (2004), 'Narrative Self and World', *Analecta Husserliana*, 79, 327–37.

Taylor, C. (2002), 'The Origins of our Present Paradigms', in Annas and Rowe (2002), 85–92.

Töchterle, K. (1978), *Ciceros Staatsschrift im Unterricht*, Innsbruck.

Toland, J. (1698), *The Life of John Milton*, Amsterdam.

—— (1699), *Amyntor: or a Defence of Milton's Life*, London.

—— (1700), *Clito: A Poem on the Force of Eloquence*, London.

—— (1712), *Cicero Illustratus*, London.

—— (1726), *A Collection of Several Pieces of Mr John Toland*, 2 vols. London.

Ueding, G. (ed.) (1991), *Rhetorik zwischen den Wissenschaften* (Rhetorik-Forschungen 1), Tübingen.

Van der Zande, J. (1995), 'In the Image of Cicero: German Philosophy between Wolff and Kant', *JHI* 56, 419–42.

Varwig, F. R. (1991), 'Über die dialektischen Orte des Rhetorikbegriffs bei Cicero', in Ueding (1991), 63–83.

Vasaly, A. (1993), *Representations: Images of the World in Ciceronian Oratory*, Berkeley.

Vickers, B. (1988), *In Defence of Rhetoric*, Oxford.

Vogt, J. (1935), *Ciceros Glaube an Rom*, Darmstadt (repr. 1963).

Waddell, C. (1988), 'The Fusion of Horizons', *Philosophy and Rhetoric*, 21, 103–15.

Wallace-Hadrill, A. (1987), 'Time for Augustus', in M. Whitby *et al.* (eds.), *Homo Viator: Classical Essays for John Bramble*, Bristol, 119–29.

Wassmann, H. (1996), *Ciceros Widerstand gegen Caesars Tyrannis: Untersuchungen zur politischen Bedeutung der philosophischen Spätschriften*, Bonn.

Watson, J. S. (trans.) (1889), *Cicero: Oratory and Orators*, London.

Weische, A. (1961), *Cicero und die neue Akademie*, Münster.

White, H. (1973), *Metahistory*, Baltimore.

—— (1987), *The Content of the Form*, Baltimore.

Whitmarsh, T. (2005), *The Second Sophistic* (Greece & Rome: New Surveys 35), Oxford.

Wilkerson, K. E. (1988), 'Carneades at Rome: A Problem of Sceptical Rhetoric', *Philosophy and Rhetoric*, 21/2, 131–44.

Wilson, J. P. (1994), 'Grex Scipionis in *De amicitia*: A Reply to Gary Forsythe', *AJPh* 115, 269–71.

Wiseman, T. P. (1979*a*), 'Cicero, *De Divinatione* 1.55', *CQ* 29, 142–4.

—— (1979*b*), *Clio's Cosmetics*, Leicester.

—— (1994), *History and Imagination*, Exeter.

—— (1998), *Roman Drama and Roman History*, Exeter.

—— (2002), 'History, Poetry, and *Annales*', in D. Levene (ed.), *Clio and the Poets: Augustan Poetry and the Traditions of Ancient Historiography*, Leiden, 331–62.

Wisse, J. (1995), 'Greeks, Romans, and the Rise of Atticism', in J. G. J. Abbenes, S. R. Slings, and I. Sluiter (eds.), *Greek Literary Theory after Aristotle: A Collection of Papers in Honour of D. M. Schenkeveld*, Amsterdam, 65–82.

Witt, R. G. (2002), *In the Footsteps of the Ancients: The Origins of Humanism from Lovato to Bruni*, Leiden.

Woodman, A. J. (1988), *Rhetoric in Classical Historiography: Four Studies*, London.

Yavetz, Z. (2001), 'Cicero: A Man of Letters in Politics', in Clark and Rajak (2001), 173–80.

Zetzel, J. E. G. (1972), 'Cicero and the Scipionic Circle', *H.S.C.Ph.* 76, 173–9.

Zetzel, J. E. G. (2003), 'Plato with Pillows', in D. Braund and C. Gill (eds.), *Myth, History and Culture in Republican Rome: Studies in Honour of T. P. Wiseman*, Exeter, 119–38.

Zielinski, T. (1912), *Cicero im Wandel der Jahrhunderte*, 3rd edn. (4th edn. 1919, repr. 1973), Leipzig.

Zoll, G. (1962), *Cicero Platonis Aemulus*, Zurich.

General Index

I have not included the names of historical figures where they occur only as topics of discussion or characters in Cicero's writing: references for particular works can be found below under 'Cicero', and in the *index locorum* for particular passages. Latin names are given in their familiar anglicized form where one exists (e.g. Cato the Younger, not Porcius Cato, M. Uticensis; Sallust, not Sallustius Crispus).

Index Locorum

Except for a few exceptions where important passages are discussed but not cited in full, this index relates only to passages where the text is presented. The general index includes references to all discussion of individual works.

Lightning Source UK Ltd.
Milton Keynes UK
UKHW040902190223
417171UK00001B/32